The Most Learned Woman in America

The Most Learned Woman in America

A LIFE OF ELIZABETH GRAEME FERGUSSON

Anne M. Ousterhout

THE PENNSYLVANIA STATE UNIVERSITY PRESS
UNIVERSITY PARK, PENNSYLVANIA

Library of Congress Cataloging-in-Publication Data

Ousterhout, Anne M.
    The most learned woman in America : a life of Elizabeth Graeme Fergusson /
Anne M. Ousterhout.
        p.   cm.
Includes bibliographical references (p.   ) and index.
ISBN 0-271-02311-2 (acid-free paper)
1. Fergusson, Elizabeth Graeme, 1737–1801.
2. Philadelphia Region (Pa.)—Biography.
3. Women—Pennsylvania—Philadelphia Region—Biography.
4. Women scholars—Pennsylvania—Philadelphia Region—Biography.
5. Women poets—Pennsylvania—Philadelphia Region—Biography.
6. Philadelphia Region (Pa.)—Intellectual life—18th century.
7. Philadelphia Region (Pa.)—Social life and customs—18th century.
8. Philadelphia Region (Pa.)—Politics and government—18th century.
I. Title.

F158.4 .F47O96   2003
811'.1—dc22
2003022419

Frontispiece: "Francis Hopkinson in Conversation with
Elizabeth Graeme," by Benjamin West. The Historical
Society of Pennsylvania.

Contents

Foreword

I knew Anne Ousterhout as colleague and then friend for more than thirty years. Our careers in the Department of American Thought and Language at Michigan State University developed side by side. Both of us were mothers; both of us had four children; both of us shared a deep interest in the history of colonial and revolutionary America. I had come to the United States as a graduate student after receiving my degree in history from the University of Bristol where I specialized in the "Political Programs of the American Revolution" at a time when the vast majority of my classmates found study of the British Commonwealth or Europe more to their liking. Anne came to graduate study in American history after receiving a baccalaureate degree in chemistry from Barnard College and working for the Allied Chemical and Dye Corporation for four years. The tragic death of Anne's husband, which left her with four young sons to bring up and educate, necessitated her move to East Lansing where she had close relatives. It was also home to a large and growing university with a fine history department. Anne entered the university in 1963 and received her master's degree in history in 1965, her Ph.D. in 1972. After a couple of years as an instructor at Central Michigan University, Anne was appointed as an instructor in the Department of American Thought and Language at Michigan State University and then promoted to assistant, associate, and full professor.

Let me say a few words about the unique character of the department in which Anne and I taught for over thirty happy and fulfilling years because its mission influenced Anne's scholarly trajectory. As part of the unusually fine general education that Michigan State provided for its undergraduate students for over thirty years, the Department of American

Thought and Language was responsible for the teaching and improvement of expository writing using a reading curriculum of historical and imaginative American literature. The first term was devoted to works from, or about, the seventeenth and eighteenth centuries, the second to the nineteenth, and the third to the twentieth century. In short, the students became acquainted with the intellectual history of the United States. They read documents, sermons, poetry, plays, and novels; and writing about these works refined our students' skills as essayists as well as increasing their knowledge of American culture. For the instructor, this American Studies curriculum was a treasure. Those of us, like Anne and I, who were used to historical literature, entered into a closer association with the less familiar but enlivening company of poets, novelists, and playwrights. With the Mayflower Compact and Winthrop's "City of God" sermon only a few pages back we moved to the poetry of Anne Bradstreet and Phyllis Wheatley. Alongside Jefferson's "Declaration of Independence" we could read Howard Fact's *Citizen Tom Paine*. Thus, the courses Anne taught had a profound effect upon her intellectual development as a scholar, and her books reflect her interest in both the history of American society in the eighteenth century and the life of the literary artist in that society.

But before I comment further upon Anne's scholarship, I should like to refer to her reputation as a teacher of undergraduate students. Under different circumstances, she might have chosen a more conventional career route, seeking an appointment in a traditional history department where she would have been a teacher not only of undergraduate students, but presided over graduate seminars and the direction of dissertations. Anne, however, did not feel it wise to disrupt her sons' education and sense of well-being by moving from East Lansing. Moreover, she had married Bill Johnston, a member of the medical faculty at Michigan State, a congenial companion with whom she enjoyed a lively cultural and social life that was rich in friendships as well as travels abroad. So, Anne built a reputation as an excellent and dedicated instructor of mainly freshman students. She became a notably conscientious, engaged, and dedicated teacher who steadfastly adhered to a rigorous curriculum of reading and writing. She earned thereby the great respect of her students as well as their affection and admiration. Her classes were always full, her choice of materials for reading and study innovative but appropriate, her writing assignments thoughtful and stimulating. Nor did she fail to regularly revise and review her reading assignments to include the contributions of women and minorities as their work became more accessible. During the years in which I served as chairperson of the department, Anne was a person upon whom the department could always depend for her wealth of common sense and good judgment. She was a woman who never, never demanded favors or special privilege; a woman of fine principles. She taught over 250 students every academic year, reading and critiquing the hundreds of essays they produced and consulting with them individually. In spite of this close attention to the faithful fulfillment of her teaching duties, Anne was supremely successful in carrying out a significant research project.

Anne's first book, *A State Divided: Opposition in Pennsylvania to the American Revolution,* was published in 1987. It was the culmination of two decades of painstaking research in which she investigated the role played by the loyalists in that state during the critical era that led up to and followed the Declaration of Independence and the conclusion of the Revolutionary War. The book was preceded by the publication of several well-regarded articles that examined the origins and treatment of those who dissented against the movement towards separation from the British Empire. Anne's meticulous investigation of the loyalists in Pennsylvania took her to innumerable dusty boxes in town and city archives, in church basements, in libraries and athenaeums large and small to examine property records, genealogical registries, collections of letters, and newspapers. The book that resulted from this painstaking and often uncomfortable inquiry received universal praise from other professional historians and constituted a significant contribution to our knowledge and understanding of this critical period in American history.

Having completed this work on the opponents of the American Revolution, Anne's interest turned to a different kind of project. Her research had brought her into contact with important figures in Philadelphia's eighteenth century history and she became intrigued with the story of a woman who lived in this city from 1737 to 1801, herself deeply affected by the crisis and its aftermath. Moreover, Anne was, I think, interested in the burgeoning field of Women's Studies and wanted to contribute to its scholarship. She also felt like writing a different kind of book, one that would have appeal not only to academics, but to the lay reader of history and the lover of biography. Elizabeth Graeme Fergusson, the daughter of a prominent Philadelphia physician, granddaughter of a governor of Pennsylvania, was acquainted with most of the leaders and opponents of the American Revolution. Informally engaged at the age of seventeen to Benjamin Franklin's son, William, she later married a young Scotsman, Henry Hugh Fergusson, who served with General Howe and retreated to England after the defeat of the British armies. Elizabeth Graeme Fergusson never saw her husband again and lived for the rest of her life as an impoverished single woman, a citizen of Pennsylvania and the new republic.

Full-length biographies of colonial and revolutionary American women are rare with the notable exception of Abigail Adams and one or two others who, like her, were the spouses of distinguished men. Women were excluded from formal education and from public life; most were also burdened by familial and parental duties that took up most of their time. Elizabeth Graeme Fergusson was an exception. Choosing separation from her loyalist husband rather than exile and having no children, she developed an active literary and social life holding weekly salons for the reading of poetry and literary discussion. These were attended by the leading literary, intellectual, and political persons in the city and, Anne believes, may have been the first such gatherings held on this continent. In spite of the loss of a significant portion of Fergusson's papers (two cartloads are recorded as having been burned by space-saving relatives), her remaining works are plentiful. In five common-place books or journals that Fergusson kept, she wrote regularly on literature, politics, contemporary events and personalities, on family affairs, and her own life. Hundreds of poems, some published, and hundreds of letters have also survived. Her family home, Graeme Park, confiscated as her husband's legal property but later restored to her ownership after she vigorously petitioned the new government of Pennsylvania, still stands on the outskirts of Philadelphia. From this heritage and surprisingly rich paper trail, Anne has succeeded in painting a full biographical portrait of a remarkably creative and productive woman. In doing so, Anne has thrown further light upon the politics of the Revolution, upon the position of women in society, and on the intellectual life of the new nation. Moreover, as Anne herself rejoiced, Elizabeth Graeme Fergusson's life constitutes a lively and captivating story.

Anne's sudden passing in 1997, as she was anticipating the challenges of full retirement and already enjoying its prelude, was a grievous and totally unexpected loss to her many friends and colleagues who, like me, had looked forward to seeing much more of her for many years to come. She is sorely missed in the community of Michigan State University and East Lansing as well as among those who are devotees of eighteenth-century America. The publication of this book is a long awaited and eagerly anticipated event. We are sure that readers will be as fascinated by Elizabeth Graeme Fergusson as Anne.

Joseleyne A. Slade
Professor Emeritus
Michigan State University

Preface and Acknowledgments

During the era of the American Revolution and long after, the name Elizabeth Graeme Fergusson was well known in Philadelphia, recognized as belonging to an exceptional and much admired woman. She knew everyone who was important in the city and many who were not important. People she did not know nevertheless knew of her. Her step-grandfather had been a lieutenant governor of the province of Pennsylvania. Her father was one of its earliest physicians, holding several posts of honor, and her popular mother was noted for her intelligence and piety. Although women were denied higher education, Elizabeth read widely, educating herself in literature, history, and languages, even reading classical literature in the original tongues, an unusual ability for a colonial woman. She wrote prolifically, often until midnight or later, spending but a few hours sleeping, and published her poetry. Her journals of a trip to England and Scotland circulated widely among admiring Philadelphians. When she returned, she began holding open house every Saturday night at her home and gathered Philadelphia's intellectuals to discuss books and other subjects that interested her. These meetings have been called the first literary salons in this country. One admirer later dubbed her "the most learned woman in America."[1] To another, Elizabeth Graeme Fergusson was "the most gifted and accomplished woman of Philadelphia during provincial times and for some time after the revolution. . . . She was long remembered with an interest that was bestowed equally upon no other woman in the whole country."[2]

Because she was recognized as significant in her own right, hundreds of her letters, poems, and prose pieces were preserved, despite her lack of attachment to a famous man, the usual criterion in those days for keeping a woman's papers. As a result, many of her documents remain, scattered across the United States, some of them in unlikely depositories. In addition, there are manuscripts in private collections, unknown or unavailable to researchers.[3] This plentitude exists in spite of the destruction in the mid-nineteenth century of "three cartloads" of her papers by descendants. It took them three days to burn all the manuscripts. The historian who heard this news several years after the event commented bitterly, lamenting the loss, that "Mrs. Fergusson, in all respects, was undoubtedly the most distinguished literary woman this country produced in the last century or any time previous."[4]

Among the writings by Elizabeth Fergusson that do remain are several commonplace books, or intellectual journals, collections of her poetry and her reflections on the writings of other people, including copies of their poetry and prose, transcriptions of letters she had written and received, and anything else that interested her. She wrote most of her commonplace books to give to other people, usually by request. Several of those known to have been written have disappeared. These books were highly valued by the women who received them; they discussed the contents, copied excerpts into their own journals, and passed Elizabeth Fergusson's writing from hand to hand among their connections, both male and female. Thus, although not printed, they were circulated and read by a numerous audience, spreading word of her learning. As a result, people who had never met Elizabeth Fergusson felt they knew her.

Throughout the past, several people have begun her biography, although her full life story has never reached publication. The first, very short, biography was published eight years after her death, written by the famous physician and Revolutionary leader Dr. Benjamin Rush, a close friend, and lifelong correspondent.[5] Although Rush's work contains some factual errors and is effusive in her favor, its general descriptions of her character and achievements are accurate. In the 1850s, Henry C. Whitmore of Fishkill Landing, New York, and Pennsylvania historian William Buck began the first full-length biography of Elizabeth Fergusson. At that time, there were still people living who remembered her, and Buck was able to interview them. Whitmore's records have disappeared, but Buck's papers were saved by Albert Cooke Myers and are kept in the Chester County Historical Society. Among these is a ledger entitled "Graeme Park Ms. Notes on," which contains records of Buck's interviews, copies or extracts of family letters, many of which are no longer available, and transcriptions of some of her poems. Whitmore and Buck negotiated a contract with publisher J. B. Lippincott, but for some unknown reason, the book was never published. The manuscript has disappeared, perhaps lost when Lippincott's publishing plant burned in the early 1900s.[6]

Thirty years after Buck and Whitmore began their research, some of the material they had collected was used by Buck in writing the section on the Graemes' estate in Horsham Township for Theodore Bean's *History of Montgomery County*. Longer and more accurate than that of Benjamin Rush, Bean's history tells the story of Graeme Park, its purchase by Elizabeth's step-grandfather, its development by her father, and its sale by Elizabeth. It also includes stories of the various early inhabitants of the property, concentrating on Elizabeth and transcribing some of her poems.[7]

Throughout the nineteenth century, Elizabeth Fergusson's name and poetry appeared periodically in anthologies and other books about colonial women. Joshua Francis Fisher, in his account of Pennsylvania poets and poetry to 1831, mentioned Elizabeth on several pages but called her poetry not "polished or harmonious" and did not include any examples. Her lines, Fisher wrote, "are not perfumed with that 'fragrant nectar,' which those divinities are said to sprinkle over the verses of their friends." Rufus W. Griswold in 1848, obviously differed since he included excerpts from her translation of *Télémaque* in his *Female Poets of America*. Evert and George Duyckinck also printed several of her poems, as well as anecdotes from Elizabeth's life, in their *Cyclopedia of American Literature*. Later in the century, Anne Wharton discussed the significance of Elizabeth's Saturday night salons in her *Salons Colonial and Republican*. In 1896, Dr. S. Weir Mitchell published a novel called *Hugh Wynne* about a free Quaker who fought with the American army during the Revolution.[8] A woman named Elizabeth Fergusson plays a minor part in Mitchell's book, but his portrayal has little resemblance to Fergusson herself. Distorting her character in the extreme, he portrays her as a silly, giddy, shrewish woman with little intellectual prowess, quite the contrary of her true character.

In the twentieth century, although recognition of her name has decreased, Elizabeth Graeme Fergusson has been mentioned in many works. Early in the new century, Katherine Jackson judged her important enough to include in *Outlines of the Literary History of Colonial Pennsylvania*.[9] In 1915, collector-historian Simon Gratz published, in *The Pennsylvania Magazine of History and Biography*, "Some Material for a Biography of Mrs. Elizabeth Fergusson, *née* Graeme." In his two articles, Gratz transcribed many letters to and from Elizabeth, hoping to pique the interest of a prospective biographer.[10] The late Edwin Wolf of the Library Company of Philadelphia also suggested Elizabeth Fergusson as a subject for a biography and summarized her story in the Library's *Annual Report* for 1962. Two persons have written unpublished master theses that describe Elizabeth Fergusson's life and poetry, many writers have mentioned her, and several anthologies have included her poems, accompanied by short biographies.[11]

Elizabeth Graeme was born into a society that preached certain fixed ideas about women and their place. She was taught that men and women had separate spheres of responsibility. Since women had been designed by God to be wives and mothers, those were the roles they should seek. Because they were physically weaker than men, their husbands would care for and protect them. They were also less mentally competent and, therefore, should not expect to pursue professions or to be concerned with politics. It was agreed that they should receive some education, enough to manage a household, to nurture their children, and to initiate their learning, but not higher education, which was unnecessary to prepare women for their lives and perhaps dangerous to their fragile constitutions. How much education was provided for females probably varied in the individual colonies. In Philadelphia, Quakers had encouraged the education of girls, and learning was respected, even in women. There was a fine line, however, between an admirable amount of erudition and too much. Women must not be too outspoken or forward in their opinions if they would avoid encroaching upon the world of men and if they expected to attract someone of the opposite sex to secure them a place in the world of women.

When a couple married, it was believed that they became one unit. God had created women to be the helpmates of men, whose minds and muscles were superior; therefore, it was appropriate for husbands to make decisions and act in the best interests of the whole family, and for their wives to concur. Under the doctrine of coverture, a husband became the owner of his wife's personal property and the manager of her realty, although he could not sell it without her permission. Judicial decisions largely enforced coverture and denied married women the freedom to manage their own property or to take financial or legal actions without their husbands' consent.

These were the views with which Elizabeth Graeme was imbued from childhood and that she espoused quite readily. She and her women friends acknowledged their own intellectual inferiority in formulaic concessions and ridiculed the "female savante." Yet it is not clear that women really had internalized this self-characterization, no matter what they indicated in the company of men and no matter how it was reinforced by the law. For example, poet Annis Stockton, wife of Richard, a signer of the Declaration of Independence from New Jersey, wrote to her daughter about feminist Mary Wollstonecraft's *Vindication of the Rights of Woman* that "the Empire of reason is not monopolized by men. . . . I do not think any of the Slavish obedience [to men] exists, that She talks so much of."[12] Stockton indicated that an expression of personal inferiority was only a surface convention, used as a courtesy to men to smooth relations between the sexes.

How widespread women's acceptance and practice of this philosophy actually was remains to be studied. It only could have been reality for upper- or middle-class women, whose fathers and husbands earned enough money so that their daughters and wives could be sheltered. Lower-class women, whether single or married, had to work outside the home, and many of them acted very independently. Single women immigrants, for example, some with children, left their homes and indentured themselves to pay their passages across the ocean. Many became the servants who made possible the comfortable lives of upper-class wives. Other women owned self-supporting businesses in Philadelphia, some of which competed with men: tavern- and innkeepers, storekeepers, silver smiths, brewers, and tanners, some thirty different trades, according to historian Joan Hoff Wilson.[13] These women undoubtedly conflicted with men whose rhetoric deemed them inferior but who may have discovered otherwise. Laws incorporated the prevailing philosophy and denied married women the economic independence that their single sisters were permitted to exercise. But how many women, no matter their marital condition, accepted their own inferiority and how many women's lives conformed to it—these are unanswered questions.

Elizabeth Fergusson's life did not always correspond to this philosophy. In reality, she received a fine classical education, in many areas as good as or better than that received by the young men at the College of Philadelphia. She was encouraged to think critically and allowed to state her opinions. After she married, she persuaded her husband to give her a power of attorney, permitting her to manage her own estate in his absence. With the approach of the Revolution, Elizabeth disagreed with her husband's politics. He was a British supporter while she maintained her loyalty to Pennsylvania. After the war, he insisted on spending the rest of his life in England, but she refused to follow him. When her property was confiscated by Pennsylvania due to her husband's wartime defection, she peppered the state legislature with petitions of her own formulation until its members relented and passed a special act revesting Graeme Park in herself. After the war, she published twenty-five or more of her poems, nagging the publishers when her pieces did not appear promptly. Childless, she lived alone with a woman companion for almost twenty years. All of these activities were contrary to the accepted model for women's lives.

Yet Elizabeth was not unaffected by her anomalous behavior and tried unsuccessfully to reconcile her own actions with those demanded by society. The conflict between society's view of what she should do and her own inner voice caused Elizabeth much anguish. It may explain why such an intelligent woman showed such poor judgment in selecting the two men who received her affections. Society said she must marry, but she was not overwhelmed with choices. So she accepted the two men who presented themselves, in spite of her own misgivings in each case. It may also explain why in her later years, when she lived as a "deserted woman," she could not adjust to her position as single, while married. She did not live comfortably with her refusal to join her husband in England. Society, judging her to be the deserter, expected her to set aside her own justification and conform to her husband's wishes. Refusing to comply with society's interpretation of her marriage responsibility, she still sought to justify her actions, endlessly explaining, alienating friends, and making the last fifteen years of her life miserable.

Elizabeth used several names during her lifetime. While she was growing up, her intimates called her by the nickname Betsy. After her marriage, she was addressed as Mrs. Ferguson or Madam. For the last twenty-five years of her life, her companion was Betsy Stedman. To distinguish between the two Betsys, I have elected to use Fergusson's complete name, Elizabeth. Also, for some reason that I cannot explain, the name Elizabeth seems to fit her character better than her nickname. Regarding the spelling of her married name, her husband, Henry Hugh Fergusson, always signed his name with two *ss* rather than with one, and Elizabeth followed suit. Their contemporaries, not as careful about spelling as we are today, left out one *s* in writing the name. I have used the spelling that Elizabeth and Henry preferred, except in quotations, which conform to the original. Elizabeth and her friends, both men and women, also used pen names to sign their writing and to address each other in playful social occasions. This was not unusual. Eighteenth-century writers in newspapers and magazines usually adopted pen names; rarely did they sign their real names. Although Elizabeth used other pseudonyms on occasion, such as Fawnia, Delia, Arachne, and Salmon Gundy, her favorite was "Laura," probably derived from Petrarch's *Canzoniere*.

The quotations in this book have been copied from the originals exactly as they were written; at least they are my best reading of the originals. Elizabeth's lack of formal schooling was reflected in her orthography, which was sometimes faulty by our standards, and in her handwriting, which was abominable by any period's standards. In some places, it is impossible to decipher words even when the sentence meaning is clear.

❧

Before ending this preface and opening Elizabeth Fergusson's life, I want to thank those who have been essential in the production of this book. One of the many pleasures of working on Elizabeth Fergusson has been the opportunity to know Mrs. Welsh Strawbridge. She and her late husband donated to the State of Pennsylvania the mansion and grounds called Graeme Park, and she continues to live on the property in a house of more recent construction. I was able to spend a day with her, microfilming the Fergusson commonplace book and letters she owns and enjoying her hospitality. She also has two ledgers of Dr. Thomas Graeme. These have been microfilmed, and John Shelly of the Pennsylvania Historical and Museum Commission in Harrisburg provided copies. Also helpful have been the past and present state administrators at Graeme Park, Marion Ann Montgomery and Douglas Miller.

Several people contributed to the manuscript. Professor Sheila L. Skemp took time out from completing her book on Judith Sargent Murray, another colonial woman, to read the entire manuscript and give it her insightful, informed comments. Professors Catherine Blecki and Gary Hoppenstand read parts of the manuscript. Professor Karin Wulf shared advance quotations from the book she has co-edited with Professor Blecki, an edition of a commonplace book of Milcah Martha Moore.[14] Moore was a friend of Elizabeth, and her commonplace book contains extracts from the missing journals Elizabeth Graeme kept on her trip to England and Scotland. Professor Wulf's thoughtfulness is reflected in the text of Chapter 3.

Others helped track down the material remains of Elizabeth's life. Susan Kleckner, at Christie's, located information about a recent auction of a portrait of Elizabeth as a young child and sent me a picture. Mrs. Meg Stevens and her sister, Mrs. Richard Krementz, provided pictures of and information about a Fergusson chair now owned by Mrs. Krementz. Susan Ishler Newton, Winterthur Museum, unsuccessfully searched the museum's holdings for other similar chairs, but instead located a Graeme tea table of which she, too, provided a picture and description.

The following archivists located pertinent documents: Wendy V. Good, Rosenbach Museum and Library; Wanda Gunning, Princeton Historical Society; Dr. Edward T. Morman, Institute of the History of Medicine, Johns Hopkins University; Rosemary B. Philips and Pamela C. Powell, Chester County Historical Society; Diana Franzusoff Peterson, Haverford College Library; Theresa Snyder, University Archives and Record Center, University of Pennsylvania; Edward Skipworth, Rutgers University Library; Lorett Treese, Mariam Coffin Canaday Library, Bryn Mawr College; and Jean Zajac, New Jersey Historical Society. Special thanks are due to Linda Stanley of the Historical Society of Pennsylvania, whose ability to produce documents quickly and whose wide knowledge of Pennsylvania history and its personalities have facilitated scholarship and provided a link between scholars working in the same field.

Michigan State University and the American Philosophical Society both provided grants that enabled me to take time away from the classroom to research and write. They also made possible the hiring of Christopher Muntiu, who transcribed several documents in the Boston Public Library, and of Tanya Carson, a graduate student in the English department at Michigan State University, who saved months of work by transcribing several of Elizabeth's commonplace books and other documents.

And last but always first, my husband, William Johnston, has sat through recitations of parts of the life of Elizabeth Fergusson as I worked through problems, patiently listening to the same stories over and over again for far too many years, without reminding me that he already had heard that story. Many thanks to you all.

Introduction

ELIZABETH FERGUSSON AND BRITISH–AMERICAN LITERARY HISTORY

SUSAN M. STABILE

Until recently, Elizabeth Graeme's famed travel journal remained an apoc-ryphal text for over two centuries.[1] "Her modesty alone prevented it from being made public," remarked Benjamin Rush in 1809, "thereby affording a specimen to the world and to posterity, of her happy talents for observa-tion, reflection and composition."[2] The stuff of oral legend, the journal was rumored to contain a catalogue of her adventures: socializing at the fashionable Scarborough spa and hot-wells at Bristol; rubbing elbows at the York races with "the celebrated Lawrence Sterne. Author of Tristram Shandy";[3] attending Sterne's literary salon at Shandy Hall; visiting Benja-min Franklin at his Craven Street address in London; walking through the illustrious grottos and caverns at Clifton Hill and Wanstead; and witnessing "so many Huzzas as one might expect from the publick Appearance" of King George III. Framed between the epic moments of departure and re-turn—"On the Passage from Phila:a to Liverpool" in June 1764 and "Upon Leaving England" in September 1765—the journal presents her transatlantic voyage as a heroic odyssey. Fashioning herself as a female Odysseus who leaves her native home for unforeseen adventures abroad, she watches Philadelphia fade into the horizon, as the fragmented journal begins: "I could not help observing, that whatever way the Ship moved she appeared to be in the Centre of a Circle. The Sea seems to be a perfect Circle, surrounded by Clouds, that look as if they bent down at the Edges to join it, so that our own Eyes form the Horizon, & like Self-Love, we are always placing ourselves in the Middle, where all Things move round us."

Unlike Penelope, who stays dutifully at home awaiting Odysseus's return, Elizabeth Graeme situates herself at the center rather than in gendered margins of her narrative. Rather than rehearsing the imperial exploits of great men, "whose Hearts must glow & Head must toil for his Country," her female epic traces the evolution of polite society from England to America. Though she resists the lure of fame that propels Odysseus's narrative, conceding that "a Woman's glory is to shine unknown," Elizabeth Graeme nevertheless made an indelible mark on British-American literary history. She returns to what she called "the Athens of North America," completing the heliotropic journey of progress—from classical Greece to neoclassical England to Philadelphia. Poised to establish one of the first literary salons in North America, she fulfilled George Berkeley's prospect of planting arts and learning in America.

Twenty years later in 1789, Elizabeth Graeme Fergusson recorded the realization of this prospect in a set of companion poems, "Ode to the Litchfield Willow" and "Ode the Second, A Tribute to American Genius and Friendship," which carefully map the westward progress of cultural refinement promised by her earlier English voyage.[4] Marked by the aesthetic principles of neoclassicism, or the veneration and imitation of the classical social order and literary customs of ancient Greece and Rome, the odes chronicle the emergence of an early national literature. In the first poem, Fergusson condenses British literary history to highlight the particular contributions of Dr. Samuel Johnson and his famous Litchfield group: essayist Joseph Addison, actor David Garrick, painter and caricaturist William Hogarth, epistoler Hester Thrale, and poet Anna Seward. Given the Litchfield group's influence over Philadelphia's burgeoning republic of letters, Fergusson composes a poetic sequel to her willow ode. Returning from England in 1765 with Richard Peters (whom she mythologizes as the Greek "Mentor who parent like distill'd / Maxims with pure Religion fill'd"), she superintended her literary salon at Graeme Park through the next decade. The poem begins with habitué Thomas Godfrey, "Whose Verse and Hours beguild / . . . the tunefull Nine." Joining Godfrey at the famous Graeme Park salon was poet Nathaniel Evans. Though he died young, Evans was not forgotten as "*Laura* did *Evans* Merits Breath[e] / Full twenty years now gone." Thoughts of Evans provoked EG's memories of Thomas Coombe, whose "Mellifluous ardent Mild" elocution and "whose

Accents Melt the Soul." Coombe's poems, in turn, remind Fergusson of Jacob Duche's "Strains in their own Subject grand." Like Evans, Duche lived immortally through his verse as "A Triple Garland placd upon / Thrice favord of the Nine!" Fergusson then rounds out her biography of male habitués with Philadelphia College President William Smith and musician James Bremnar. While she compares Smith to her favorite British poet Edward Young ("To whom pathetic Powers are lent/ Strong as the Bards who Sung"), she applauds Bremnar's music for its "Magic Powers," which was like "quivering Mounting Fire / Ere quite to Heaven it towers."[5]

With the men properly acknowledged, Elizabeth Fergusson goes on to enumerate the women in her artistic circle. Not surprisingly, first mention goes to Annis Boudinot Stockton, her life-long friend and correspondent, whose "illumind Pen" in "Brilliant Rays Reflected back" the salon's ethos of friendship and politeness. Fergusson mentions sculptor Patience Wright for her "Sculptor's Skill displayd . . . innate Genius." Regretting Wright's departure for a career in England, she moves on to artist Betsy Pyle. Pyle drew with "Elegance and Ease," creating pleasing landscapes that "Our Fields she Skims; Our Woods she Roves." Pyle's landscapes, finally, remind Fergusson of her beloved niece, poet Anna Young Smith. A "soon Cropt Rose Bud of the Muse," Smith was among "the smoothest of Parnassian Maids!"

Read concurrently, the two odes trace the progress of arts and literature from England to America through the persistent metaphor of the willow tree. Cultivated on "<u>Albions</u> Coast; / On <u>Litchfields</u> favord plain," the willow was "Transplanted thence" to Philadelphia, where it "flourish'd Fair." "If we the Metaphor pursue / Symbolic of the wise," Fergusson predicts, Philadelphia "may to Perfection rise." In a long annotation to the poem's third stanza, she explains the metaphor's literal origins:

> About thirty years past a Basket made of Willow came from England and lay a Winter in a damp Cellar belonging to Dr. Franklin. . . . Dr. Franklin gave it to Miss Deborah Norris, a lady who had a particular taste for Gardening. She had it planted in her Garden near the State House in Philadelphia. . . . the great part of the Willows which are now so plentifully planted over the State of Pennsylvania took Rise from this Emigration.

Some say the original willow was planted by Samuel Johnson's father; others suggest the tree came to England "in a basket from the Euphrates by Mr. Vernon," which was sent by bluestocking Lady Mary Wortley Montague to Alexander Pope, "who planted it with his own hand."[6] But brought to Philadelphia by Benjamin Franklin and cultivated by Deborah Norris, the willow tree continued the heterosocial refinement of Samuel Johnson's Litchfield group and Alexander Pope's Scriblerian circle.

Preserved in their respective commonplace books, Elizabeth Graeme Fergusson's travel journal and companion odes together represent women's aesthetic preference for manuscripts at a time when printed texts were proliferating during the eighteenth century.[7] Written by hand, read aloud in company, and circulated among intimates, women's commonplace books mediated between the lively oral and print cultures in early Philadelphia. They continued the improvisational, conversational style of salons and belles lettres, on the one hand, while mimicking the publication of literary miscellanies and collections, on the other.[8] More important, the female commonplace book negotiated the rhetorical nuances between the "private" and "public" spheres. Though the private sphere has long been imagined as the feminine domain of home and family, with the public sphere encompassing everything beyond it, recent scholars of early American literature and history have reconfigured—and correctly merged—these supposedly separate spheres. Drawing on Jürgen Habermas's influential work on civic culture, historiographers recognize the public sphere as a complex network of private discursive institutions, including salons, taverns, coffeehouses, tea-tables, and clubs. Diverging from the Habermasian notion that shared reason and disinterested political critique cemented these exclusive societies, however, literary historian David Shields offers an innovative reconstruction of a British-American public sphere dictated by manners. Self-selected and voluntary, Shields argues, these institutions cohered because of common taste, sociability, and politeness.[9] Unlike the masculine prerogative of reason, politeness not only guaranteed one's ease and pleasure, but also promoted a relatively ungendered participation in public conversation, allowing women as well as men to participate.

Shield's formulation of a heterosocial public sphere as an aesthetic culture of civility has important implications for interpreting Elizabeth Graeme Fergusson's biography, especially in placing her in British-American literary history. While the rhetorical discourse of the private (i.e., domestic, material, feminine) and the public (i.e., civic, cerebral, and masculine) spheres ostensibly excluded women from the institutions of politeness, Fergusson collapsed these boundaries by channeling politeness into her literary salon and its textual analogue, the commonplace book. Unlike the rigid rules and classical learning promoted by scholasticism, politeness provided a model of learning based on an accumulation of universal and generally applicable knowledge, which was cleverly expressed to elicit pleasure from one's company. Because politeness "branched into a thousand little channels and flow[ed] through all the minutiae of human life," moreover, it reified women's relegation to the home, while at the same time accommodating their inherent affinity for pleasing in company.[10] In other words, it transformed domesticity into sociability.[11] Though admonished to "Let your knowledge be feminine as well as your person," letting it "glow within you rather than sparkle on others about you,"[12] women could dazzle their company with polite learning without being censured as pedantic. "If the theme is treated quite in a domestic Manner," remarked Elizabeth Fergusson about her literary ambitions, "I hope the author will not be accused of S[tray]ing into Subjects improper for her Sex; For a female pedant is a most disagreeable character."[13] On the contrary, a woman could superintend a literary salon without leaving the privacy—or feminine decorum—of her best parlor.

As the handwritten analogue to the salon, the commonplace book similarly made polite learning more readily available to women. Just as the rise of female academies after the American Revolution increased literacy and improved education for young women, so the commonplace book served as an informal mode of education for elite women of the previous generation. Begun by classical oratory and punctuated by the eighteenth century's gradual transformation of rhetoric into belles lettres, the commonplace book was sociable rather than scholastic in its accumulation of usable knowledge from oral and printed sources alike. Women supplemented their dame-school education or home schooling by transcribing information from classical and modern texts. Then circulating these compilations with female friends, they instituted a pedagogy based on politeness as well as friendship. Similarly conflating a woman's knowledge with her house, moreover, the commonplace book continued the salon's domestication of knowledge. Based on a rhetorical tradition that considered *topoi*, or places in the mind, as domestic spaces where one gathered, arranged, and displayed ideas, the commonplace book recuperates the house—and the female mind—as sites of knowledge. Typically, a female space associated with the material (rather than intellectual) world and the feminine body (rather than the masculine mind), the house, it follows, was a potent, epistemological metaphor for Elizabeth Graeme Fergusson's neoclassic literary aesthetic.

THE GRAEME PARK SALON: AN AMERICAN PARNASSUS

Returning to Graeme Park in 1765, Elizabeth Graeme recounted the pleasures of her homecoming in a long commemorative poem, "Some Lines upon my first being at Graeme Park; after my return from England." Though she fondly remembers her adventures in England, "yet like Ulysses with his darling spot, / the much-lov'd Ithaca was not forgot."[14] More than suggesting her nostalgia for home, however, her allusion to Ithaca underscores the conventional literary predilection for the pastoral over the urban world. "The sweet Domestic Joys" of Graeme Park were far from the "Bustle & noisy Strife" of London. Unlike the empty and external forms of what she called England's "mechanical Politeness," the pastoral scene in Horsham, Pennsylvania, promised a world of retirement and ease, which encouraged Elizabeth Graeme and the other inhabitants to "associate the ideas of peace, of leisure, and of innocence . . . and banish from her thoughts the cares of the world."[15] Seemingly reinforcing the domestic ideology that binds women to the house, pastoralism imagined domestic life as an aesthetic privilege. Privacy, leisure, and contemplation comprised the country-house ethos. As long as women fulfilled their family obligations, the argument went, they could spend their leisure hours in more pleasing intellectual pursuits. Leisure, Graeme asserts, is best suited to women as "our Sex have a greater Chance of obtaining it as the Publick has no Demands on us."[16]

Based on a nostalgia for the classical golden age and the neoclassical tradition of the country house, the pastoral not only guaranteed leisure but also advanced civility and manners.[17] Leisure and politeness went hand in hand. As Thomas Parnell explains in his popular poem, *The Hermit:* "The contemplation of the objects of Nature, displayed in rural scenes, produce the cheerfulness and diffuse calmness and serenity over the minds . . . that is a natural inducement to check the rise of passion and gradually meliorates & refines the hearts of man."[18] Women could check their own passions, refine those of their male companions, and in the process, find time for contemplation and writing. Upholding domestic order and social propriety, Fergusson thus sees her home as a place to do intellectual work: "I wish to lead a calm & tranquil Life," resolves Graeme, "The Book, the Work, the Pen can all employ / The vacant Moment to some peaceful Joy."[19] Transforming the alienating effects of domesticity into the welcome aesthetic of solitude, Fergusson sees the house as an inspiration for contemplation and creativity. It is at home that "the mind reviews and arranges, with the happiest effect, all the ideas and impressions it has gained in its observations in the world."[20] A familiar *topoi,* the house both afforded and represented the accumulation of common knowledge.

Underscoring the topographical importance of the country house to the female intellect, Elizabeth Fergusson imagines her mind as a pastoral landscape. In her poem, "Laura's Effusions on Friendship and Fancy," for instance, she presents Graeme Park's garden retreats as mental *topoi:*

> For Similes of mental Sweets
> Are Shewn in Flowers and Shell Retreats,
> Love, Light, and Harmony are found,
> Painted in Nature's Scenes around;
> As Correspondent to the Mind.

The garden's symmetrically organized flowers and contemplative grottoes expressed the harmonic virtues of sociability, while also reflecting a woman's thoughts. The mind's "correspondence" to the material world accordingly understands knowledge as studied perception.

As Fergusson explains in a related poem, "On the Mind's being engross'd by one leading pursuit":

> When one fond Object occupys the mind
> In <u>Natures</u> Scenes we still that Object find
> The <u>Trees</u> and <u>Brooks</u> but <u>Trees</u> and <u>Brooksunderstand are still</u>
> <u>We make them Mirrors</u> by Ingenious Skill,
> They all reflect the object of our thought
> Strong with that Image is each substance frought.

Nature, she asserts, embodied the viewer's imagination. To prove her empirical argument, the poem then goes on to catalogue practical examples of how humans project their feelings, desires, and ideas onto the material world.

The Peasant observes cultured soil. The Alchemist sees gold. The Lover beholds his lost Delia. The poet witnesses divinity in nature. The scene, she concludes, perpetually changes with the landscape of the viewer's mind. Following such theorists as David Hume and George Berkeley, Fergusson suggests that the phenomenal world was wholly the product of the subject's observation. Knowledge rested in perception and imagination.

Given the pastoral's association with domesticity and female knowledge, and given the corresponding aesthetic theories of perception that link knowledge with taste, or "the power of receiving pleasures from the beauties of nature and of art," women extended their predilection for politeness and perception to the realm of taste.[21] Though aestheticians believed the foundation of taste "is the same in all human minds," they agreed that taste evolves and eventually exists in different degrees. Women may have been "marked by the difference that displays the function to which they are called and the passive state to which nature destines her," according to one critic. But it was precisely the "different frame of their natures [and] nicer organs and finer internal powers" that made them the natural arbiters of taste.[22] As British moralist and litterateur Hannah More explains, "that Sex have lively imaginations, and those exquisite perceptions of the beautiful and defective, which come under the denomination of taste."[23] Like politeness, taste suggested the universal and pastoral pleasures of neoclassicism, for as rhetorician Hugh Blair insisted, "what interests the imagination, and touches the heart, pleases all ages and all nations."[24] The pastoral setting of Graeme Park, coupled with Elizabeth Graeme's powers of taste, thus set the classical scene for her "attic" gatherings. As her nephew John Young predicted: "I am sure Graeme Park may vie with Arcadia; for poetry may easily convert Neshaminy into Helicon, the meadows into Tempe, and the park into Parnassus."[25]

Benjamin Rush's often quoted description of Elizabeth Graeme's impressive salon performances not only presents her gatherings as the epitome of taste, but also illustrates the influence of neoclassical taste over rhetoric's transformation into belles lettres during the eighteenth century. As Rush fondly remembers Graeme:

> she instructed by the stores of knowledge contained in the historians, philosophers, and poets of ancient and modern nations, which she called forth at her pleasure; and again she charmed by a profusion of original ideas, collected by her vivid and widely expanded

imagination, and combined with <u>exquisite taste</u> and <u>judgment</u> into an endless <u>variety of elegant and delightful forms</u>.[26]

At first glance, Rush seems to reiterate Aristotle's tripartite definition of rhetoric: invention (finding proofs or arguments); disposition (arrangement of materials); and style (display). Elizabeth Graeme compiled "stores of knowledge" (invention), which she "called forth at her pleasure" (disposition) through "an endless variety of elegant and delightful forms" (style). But read again through the lens of neoclassicism, her "stores of knowledge" and "profusion of original ideas" exemplify the notion of "imitation," or copying and improving correct models. The collection of ancient and modern materials suggests neoclassicism's partiality toward universal and applicable knowledge, while the elegant and delightful forms illustrate both politeness and "wit" (or, as Alexander Pope defined it, "what oft was thought, but ne'er so well expressed"). Politeness, finally, demonstrates the ease and pleasure with which she called forth this knowledge; wit points to the pleasure elicited by her stylistic innovations.

Interested in balancing wit with politeness in her salon performances and later writings, Elizabeth Fergusson copies her niece Anna Young Smith's poem, "The Distinction between good naturd and Ill Naturd wit attempted," into her 1789 Commonplace Book. A type of universalized knowledge displayed in cleverly turned rhetoric, a refined wit complemented polite conversation. While ill-natured wit provides "poisons men tho men Refined; / And festers in their Heart," good-natured wit offers a morally correct antidote. Wit, Smith's poem suggests, has a "pleasing Influence" that "Enlightens Charms, and Warms in One." Sociable in intent and pleasing in nature, wit flourishes in the Graeme Park salon:

> While gathering oft in Circles gay
> Around the Social Fire
> That Wit shall Charm our Cares away
> And Mirth and Joy Inspire.

Wit inspires pleasure and sociability; like retirement, it replaces worldly care with mirth and joy. And it contributes to hospitality, for when properly displayed, "Sweet smiling Peace shall keep the Door; / And Friendship Reign within." Initiating heterosocial friendship, wit brings men and women together through their shared taste in polite discourse.

The tension between good- and ill-natured wit in Anna Smith's poem points to the partially gendered understanding of wit during the eighteenth century. Though Elizabeth Fergusson wrote in the belletristic genres associated with verbal play, her first responsibility as a woman and salonierre was to ensure her company's continued pleasure. Since wit could degenerate into bawdy repartee unsuitable for mixed company, she carefully imitated the models provided by Alexander Pope and the British Bluestockings. Describing Pope's work in her poem, "A Farewell to the Muses," she remarks, "How do we relish taste so here, / So Elegant his turns, / Harmonious numbers known by few."[27] Then "turning from the Door / Of Philosophic Men" to the Bluestockings, Fergusson illustrates the salonierres' antithetical responsibilities between politeness and wit. Known for their didacticism rather than banter, the Bluestockings offered a meliorating dose of piety. Lauding psalmist Elizabeth Rowe, for instance, Fergusson writes: "How like a <u>Seraphim</u> refind, / Does <u>Rowe</u> our Hearts inspire; / <u>Warm</u>, <u>tender</u>, <u>Pious</u> and <u>Resigned</u>." Like Rowe, her sister Bluestockings exemplified Anna Smith's sociable definition of wit, as Fergusson explains:

> <u>Carters</u>, <u>Mores</u>, <u>Sewards</u>, and <u>Smiths</u> we view
> In verse mean vice oppose;
> <u>Genlis</u> and <u>Burney</u> nobly show
> Their talents great in Prose.

In verse and prose, the Bluestockings supplied appropriate neoclassical examples that would delight, but more importantly, instruct their audience. Following their lead, Fergusson fashions her salon accordingly, as she explains to Benjamin Rush: "tho alliteration was not study its my wish for this Country <u>Peace, Plenty, Piety, and Politeness</u>."[28]

Balancing wit and politeness, Fergusson's contributions to belles lettres included such quintessential genres of wit as the rebus, anagram, and the acrostic. Traditionally a phonetic puzzle pieced together through pictures, a rebus was also a poem that posed a question, working toward an answer by its conclusion. In "A Rebus upon the Name of a City the Sollution of which is for Mystical Reasons most humbly referd to the Fraternity of Free Masons" (1754), for instance, Elizabeth Fergusson mimics the reciprocal repartee of salon conversation. Carefully structured into three parts (the introduction, the rebus, and the answer), the poem begins by address-

ing the fraternal order of Freemasons, a model society (despite its homoso-
cial exclusiveness) for Fergusson's literary salon. An example of a private
institution in the public sphere, Freemasons epitomized what moral philosophers called a *sensus communis*. Masonic symbols and gilded rituals established order and unity among the members, "the Cement which does most
your Society bind," according to Fergusson. Though intensely enigmatic
in their coded symbolism and gestures, Freemasons also projected themselves into the public sphere: on one hand, private society connoted innocence and charitability; on the other hand, it bespoke the frivolity and
triviality of insular clubs.[29] Seeing Freemasons as the ideal readers for her
rebus, Fergusson accordingly gives them the appropriate clues:

THE REBUS

Take the <u>Cardinal Virtue</u> most tincturd with Art;
And what High the <u>left Breast</u>'s the most delicate part
With the qualification so fam'd among <u>Bees;</u>
And what <u>Orpheus</u> playd sweet on to animate Trees.
What contain all the <u>living</u> within a small space;
And the <u>Fate</u> thats [entaild] upon Man and his Race.
The <u>Bird</u> which the <u>Romans</u> displayd in their Arms;
With What moves the Swiftest; and as it moves warms.
The Name which for <u>Doctors of Physick</u> agree;
And the rising which still next to a <u>Valley</u> you see,
The word thats most common for <u>Water congeald;</u>
And that <u>Letter</u> which first is to Children reveald.

Similar to an acrostic, whereby the initial letters of each line have meaning
when read downward, the rebus requires answers to successive images,
which are accumulated line by line. Then taking "all the <u>Initials</u> of these
Mentiond Things," the poem's reader solves the rebus. Answered in verti-
cal sequence, the solutions are as follows: the cardinal virtue most tinctured
with art is <u>Prudence</u>; the most delicate part of the left breast is the <u>Heart</u>;
the bee's qualification is <u>Industry</u>; Orpheus played the <u>Lute</u>; the small life-
containing space is the <u>Atom</u>; humanity's common fate is <u>Death</u>; the
Roman coat of arms displays an <u>Eagle</u>; <u>Light</u> moves quickly as it warms;
<u>Physicians</u> are Doctors of Physick; A <u>Hill</u> rises next to the valley; <u>Ice</u> is
congealed water; and children first learn the alphabetic character, <u>A</u>. Read-

ing down the column and collecting the initial letters of each row's answer, the solution, she hints, is the name "Of a neat decent City; of no small renown":

Philadelphia.
Prudence
Heart
Industry
Lute
Area
Death
Eagle
Light
Physicians
Hill
Ice
A

Connecting the rebus's "Introduction" to the Freemasons with the civic culture of ancient Greece, Fergusson gives one final clue: "A Town once so famous in the Lists of <u>Greece</u> / A Name Expressive of <u>Fraternal Peace</u> / Of <u>Seven</u> great <u>Churches</u> that alone was found." While she explains in a footnote that "The meaning of the word Philadelphia is Brotherly Love," her allusion to the classical world underscores her ambitions to create a refined culture of belles lettres at Graeme Park.

The gender distinctions between the male-centered Freemason society and heterosocial salon not only accentuates the potential rift between wit and politeness for women, but also highlights the related tension between "sense" and "sensibility," or as Benjamin Rush put it, between judgment and taste. Possessed by men and women alike, sense was an inherent awareness of propriety, which legislated both moral and aesthetic judgment. Closely associated with reason, sense guaranteed the platonic friendships forged through heterosocial conversation. Linked to taste, sensibility was the neurological and psychological susceptibility to "feeling"— both physical and emotional. Like taste, sensibility was associated with the delicacy and suggestibility of the female sex. Threatening to the salon's Platonism in its explicit corporeality and potentially excessive passions, sensibility became the exclusive discourse of women. British Americans made the cultivation of sense an overriding concern of conversation in mixed company after 1760, while establishing sensibility as the dominant ethic of sororal communication.[30] Elizabeth Fergusson thus illustrates the markedly gendered distinction in describing her salon as "A Society of Friends whose Actions are guarded by Affection, Chearfulness, Probity, and Good Sense."[31] Platonic friendship and correct judgment ensured the emotional restraint demanded by neoclassical (and sexual) decorum.

Just as the Freemasons forged a communal masculine identity through secret mysteries, so Elizabeth Fergusson and her circle established a shared feminine identity through uncensored expressions of sensibility.[32] Sending copies of her poems at Annis Stockton's request, Fergusson explains in an accompanying letter that sensibility—exemplified by female friendship—justifies the scribal publication of her manuscript commonplace books:

> Remember <u>my dear Friend</u>, that you often ask'd me for my little pieces. And I Have comply'd with your Request. It is time you Said, that if I Survivd you would wish to have them. But I know that you have a <u>Sensibility of Friendship</u> which would make you Sigh at Reading them when this writer is no More, But alas when I copy them I find it makes past ideas very feverishly in my mind . . . tears obtrude itself But I show Patience more than my Genius in these Works of your <u>Obligd Friend</u>. Laura[33]

The affections of friendship, she confesses, are reciprocal: just as Stockton would sigh at reading Fergusson's work posthumously, so she faced a torrent of nostalgic tears in copying the poems. Effusive and uncensored, sensibility disregarded the emotional restraint and rigid formality required of neoclassicism. As such, it served as the prelude to the emergent Romantic movement marked by William Wordsworth's *Lyrical Ballads* in 1798.

Though markedly gendered, "sense" and "sensibility" merged in the ethical discourse of "sympathy." Positioning oneself in relationship to another, sympathy (much like modern empathy) is an act of the imagination. According to the Scottish Common Sense School of Philosophy (popularized by David Hume, Frances Hutchinson, Adam Smith, and Thomas Reid, among others), sympathy marks a *sensus communis* of like feeling and collaborated taste. As Elizabeth Fergusson notes in her 1789 poem, "On the Preference of Friendship to Love," sympathy is like a steadily burning star that outshines even the sun:[34]

> Let Girlish Nymphs and Boyish Swains,
> Their amorous Ditties Chant!
> Make vocal Echoing Hills and Plains;
> And Loves frail Passion Paint.
> But Friendships steady flame as far;
> Out shines that transient Blaze;
> As Mid Day suns a glimmering Star
> Which faintest Beams displays.

The constellation metaphor recalls philosopher David Hume's electrical description of sympathy between female friends. As women carefully watched, diligently imitated, and theatrically mirrored one another's manners, they not only reflected "one another's emotions," according Hume, "but also those rays of passions, sentiments and opinions may be often reverberated."[35] Such rays, beams, flames, and blazes of feeling suggest a distinctively physical and natural energy between friends. Such a reverberation, comments salonierre Annis Stockton, is like a collective pulse animating the group. As she suggests to Elizabeth Fergusson in 1769: "How often when I am reading Mr. Pope's Letters, do I envy that day when the knot of friends that seem'd to have but one heart by which they were united and their greatest pleasure was giving each other pleasure."[36] Reverberating passions, like a communal heartbeat, kindled private society.

Long after the pleasures of her salon had subsided by the century's end, Elizabeth Fergusson fondly remembers the intimacy afforded by sororal conversation. Revising Stockton's respiratory metaphor for a magnetic one, Fergusson subsequently describes sympathy in physical terms:

> For we are all of us such Domestic fire-side beings that a certain degree of nearness seems absolutely necessary to make us meet. Characters of such a Cast may well be compared to the Magnet and the Loadstone. They must be placed at a certain point Before the attraction operates and then when that prevails the two Objects adhere with the utmost force.[37]

While her metaphor suggests that the *sensus communis* can only be sustained by emotional intimacy ("a degree of nearness"), her aesthetic of proximity also intimates geographical closeness. Separated from one another in their respective country retreats, women needed another means of sustaining their sympathetic bond. They turned toward the handwritten word, acknowledging its indebtedness to the uniquely oral culture of the domestic sphere. Transferring the heterosocial conversation of salons into a markedly sororal circulation of their commonplace books, women substituted the literal space of their parlors with the figurative space of commonplace *topoi*. As Elizabeth Fergusson explains to Ann Ridgely in 1797:

> I declare when by peculiar Circumstances I am as it were a Link Cut off from the Chain of Society both by Birth and Education which I was once taught to expect, and devote my Hours to Retirement and my Pen, I feel a Latent Wish that those whose tasks are congenial to my own, might with the Eye of not <u>Candor</u> But <u>Partiality</u> see my turn of thought and mode of Life.[38]

Through the domestic or scribal publication of her commonplace books, Elizabeth Fergusson—and her female friends—upheld the *sensus communis* of the public sphere based on congeniality and partiality. Handwriting made absence presence, revising solitude into sociability.

THE TOPOGRAPHY OF KNOWLEDGE: THE FEMALE COMMONPLACE BOOK

Privately circulating her commonplace books among her female coterie throughout the last half of the eighteenth century, Elizabeth Fergusson domesticated the ancient art of commonplacing by comparing universal *topoi* to the intimate spaces in her house in Horsham, Pennsylvania.[39] Like the pastoral retreat from the beau monde into the unfettered world of the imagination, commonplaces are universal ideas that transcend historical time and space. As cumulative passages selected from printed texts (or "*copia*"), commonplaces were copied into a notebook and organized into general topics (or "heads") for later retrieval. As essayist James Beattie suggests, "A methodical composition, rightly divided into its several heads or members, which do all naturally illustrate each other, and whereof none can be misplaced or wanting, without injury to the whole, is readily understood, and quickly remembered."[40] Memory, rhetoricians further insisted, depended on familiarity. Most familiar with their homes, women consequently adapted the classical architectural metaphors for commonplaces (i.e., "sedes," "dwelling places," or "local habitation") to their individual circumstances. As Elizabeth Fergusson explains:

> If one has been long accustomd to a certain <u>Sett of Objects</u>, which have made a <u>strong Impressien</u> on a man's Mind, <u>such as a House</u>, where he has passd many agreeable years, . . . <u>they seem endowd with Life</u>, They become objects of his affection . . . I have also in my Life felt the Force of those <u>Local attachments</u>.

A "local habitation," the Georgian country house was figuratively divided into rooms (or "heads") filled with useable figures, quotations, or images (i.e., "moveables," as women's dowered objects were called). Like furniture, knowledge could be arranged, rearranged, practically utilized, and decorously displayed.

Until its confiscation in the political aftermath of the American Revolution and Elizabeth Fergusson's consequent removal to Seneca Luken's farm, the ephemera of Graeme Park's household provided familiar *topoi* for organizing her commonplace books. Witnessing the inventory of her domestic possessions and later buying back what she could afford, Fergusson may have reiterated rhetorician Hugh Blair's question, "How then shall these <u>vacant spaces</u>, these unemployed intervals, which more or less, occur in the life of everyone, be filled up?" The answer was simple: through commonplacing, or "the study of arranging and expressing our thoughts with propriety," which "teaches us to think as well as to speak accurately."[41] As her companion Betsy Stedman describes Fergusson in her unfortunate circumstances: "Calculated to impart and receive pleasure in society her confined income, not her inclination, caused her for years to live a retir'd life. Her active mind must have employment. Writing became her constant pursuit; her unremitted application to this mode of filling up her hours often astonished me."[42] House poor, but verbally rich, Elizabeth Fergusson accumulated stores of knowledge in her commonplace books that could never be taken away. Since domesticity provided ample rhetorical figures, since rhetoric moved the emotions and evoked a moral response, since a moral response was recognized through sympathy, since sympathy deferred to the imagination, and since women were credited with a superior imagination, commonplacing well suited Elizabeth Fergusson and her circle.

As literary critic Susan Miller contends, commonplacing was an invaluable method of reading and storing information in the early United States: "the copying and imitation that licensed commonplace acquisitions under republican rationalism also invested them with a transformative dynamism."[43] More important, this dynamism (typically subsumed by the rhetoric of "Republican Motherhood") made learning more readily available to women.[44] More than valued for their reproductive capacity in perpetuating the Republican citizenry, women were also esteemed for their domestic contributions to education. As useful knowledge was requisite for all Republican citizens, commonplace books could be used by men and women, boys and girls, at school and at home. Unlike the original Latin commonplace books for schoolboys, the early modern variant did not stress classical learning as much as the universality of ideas and the correctness of taste. As the Age of Enlightenment, the eighteenth century ushered in a new mode of learning based on accumulation, order, and classification. It was a time when the collection—including dictionaries, encyclopedias, miscellanies, "repositories," "cabinets," and anthologies—promoted useful knowledge. Sound bites of memorizable and applicable ideas accordingly became the hallmarks of polite learning. Taken from a variety of printed sources and copied into manuscript commonplaces, this new pedagogy of transcription enabled girls and women alike to practice their handwriting, catalogue their reading, order their thoughts, and inspire their own compositions—despite the exclusionary gender codes in colleges. Commonplace books thus inaugurated a feminine genealogy of learning, where mothers and daughters taught successive generations of women.

Learning the value of a commonplace book at a young age, Elizabeth Fergusson warmly remembers her mother's home instruction:

> When the dear Anna led my Infant mind
> Up those Ascents which God and Truth designd
> Should be displayd to opening tender Age,
> Nicely adapted to each rising Stage.

Monitoring her daughter's reading and penmanship, Ann Graeme carefully planned the curriculum, progressively adapting the lessons "to each rising Stage." On December 3, 1762, for instance, Ann Graeme wrote a letter to her daughter Elizabeth, explaining the pedagogical and moral value of transcribing the Bible. As part of the commonplace tradition of praising virtue and correcting vice, paraphrases and translations of the Scripture provided women with textual exempla to model in their life and writing:

> I was extreamly surprised and shocked when my Child told me she did not believe a directing hands towards individuals in their trifling events, how such a thought could take place in a mind so well acquainted with the Scripture and believes them as they are so very full and clear to the contrary, I wonder at.

Having discussed the textual validity of transcription, she then explains its usefulness for women's moral understanding. Interpolating biblical passages into her letter, Graeme provides her skeptical daughter with a model to emulate in her own commonplace book:

> I shall quote but two, one out of the Old and the other out of the New Testament, because I might as well attempt to transcribe the whole Bible as to enumerate texts to this purpose, but if there were none but these, they are so clear and full that they alone are sufficient to beat down all contradiction, King David in the 55 Psalm ves. 23, O, cast thy burden upon the Lord, and he shall nourish thee, and shall not suffer the righteous to fall for ever, endeed most part of that Psalm, as well as many others is extremely applicable to your Case.

Then quoting the Beatitudes, she reads one text against the other: "Come unto me all ye that are weary and heavy Laden and I will give you rest."[45] Paraphrases are not only acts of spiritual devotion and meditation, but also aesthetic endeavors that replicate the balanced order of the natural world in balanced meter, careful diction.[46]

Following her mother's pedagogical model, Elizabeth Fergusson similarly took charge of her niece Anna Young's education after Jane Graeme Young's death:

> Since Providence has placed it in my Lot I shal[l] try to educate Anny . . . as Well as I can . . . Her length of time at Graeme Park in the Sumr is a very great Draw Back on her writing, and Sewing. Her reading and A Proper Choice of Books with Explanations on them is my Branch, and I keep her close to it. . . . I have no

ambition to Make her a Distinguished Character was it in My
Power, But I could Wish to see her Afectionate a tolerable Show of
Understanding, and passable Agreeable. Moderate as this Character
appears to be it takes some attention to form it.[47]

Fergusson not only compiles the reading list and guides her student's interpretation, but she also undoubtedly monitored Young's commonplace
book transcriptions. Seemingly sharing the educational duties with Young's
father (making reading and writing "my Branch"), Fergusson's pedagogy
is notably premised on politeness. Keeping Young close to her studies
through habit and discipline, she initiates her niece into the world of manners. With appropriately polite learning, Anna might become an affectionate, bright, and agreeable character. Though Young dies before she has a
chance to fully participate in the Graeme Park salon, evidence of her successful education and literary ambition are found in a small collection of her
poems, which Fergusson scatters through several of her own commonplace
books.

Given the original pedagogical purpose of the commonplace book,
one might trace the progress of Elizabeth Fergusson's polite learning
through the six commonplace books she compiled over the course of her
life. From roughly 1750 to her death in 1801, she carefully organized transcriptions from and neoclassical imitations of her favorite authors; she copied poems by members of her literary circle; and she interpolated draft and
fair copies of own verse. Given her introduction to English literary society
by Lawrence Sterne in the 1760s, Fergusson applied the discourse of politeness to the process of transcription. A form of copying, transcription was
inherently neoclassical. Rereading and copying her favorite authors not
only gave her pleasure, but also ensured the pleasing performances in company. Copying, moreover, meant directly reflecting poetic forms; these
forms, in turn, mirrored human nature. Much like the reverberating sympathy between women, poetry mirrored and perpetuated the *sensus communis*. Personifying her books as intimate companions, then, Elizabeth
Fergusson explains the transcribing art:

> I cannot help classing my Books like my Friends, they all have
> their respective Merits, but I am not equally acquainted with
> them.—Doctor Young is a Friend in Affliction, that I could open
> my Heart to, Mrs. Rowe flatters my Imagination, & takes walks

with me in a summer evening,—Mr. Addison suits me in all Humours, Mr. Pope I am a little afraid of, I think he knows so well the turnings of the human Heart, that he always sets me into Examination.—Harvey says the same Thing over & over so prettily, & I am persuaded has so much Goodness of Soul, that I revere him, amid all his Prolixity, as for Mr. Richardson,[48] he is a perfect Proteus, ever assuming a new Form, but in all sensible.—

Since polite learning, I have shown, was predicated on proximity, Fergusson negotiates the alienating effects of the printed medium (which erases a writer's handwritten marks and hushes the salonierre's voice) by reading literary texts as direct emanations of authorial character. Friendship, goodness, and sense opened her heart, excited her imagination, and prompted her examination.

While her commonplace books contain prose excerpts and experiments, the lion's share of material are examples of neoclassical poetry. As Fergusson explains her generic preference: "Poetry is my weak Side, and I never can pass over a Beautiful passage But I wish to transcribe it."[49] For instance, speaking of her admiration for graveyard poet Edward Young (and his "strict Orders [that] all his Manuscripts & Papers should be burnt" at his death), she remarks in her travel journal: "For my own Part I acknowledge myself, to be among the Number, that have been deeply touched with his Writings, & extracted many useful Sentiments from them, which if not sufficiently remembered, is owning to myself, not to the Writer who is admirable."[50] Sometimes she responds directly to printed texts by writing her poetic response in the book itself. She composes a poetic reply in the blank leaf of her copy of *Night Thoughts,* for instance, and similarly writes an impromptu rejoinder to a question posed by Adam Smith in his *Theory of Moral Sentiments.* Writing in the margins of Smith's text, Fergusson engages in a written form of dialogue. Much like salon conversation and the intimacy forged through personifying her favorite texts, transcription enacts another mode of sociability. The translator takes an impersonal imprint and humanizes it through script, leaving her own marks on the newly handwritten text. With additional marginalia and annotations, the commonplace book's intertextual format resembles the reciprocity of actual conversation.

Arranging transcriptions, imitations, and original compositions in her commonplace books, Elizabeth Fergusson loosely organizes her entries.

Unlike published models for organizing a commonplace book, such as John Locke's dizzyingly complex *New Method of Commonplacing,* Fergusson typically begins with a detailed table of contents listing a description or title as well as a page number for each entry. Sometimes preceded by a short quotation, the table of contents is then followed by some version of her dedicatory poem to her readers, titled "Laura's Effusions on Friendship and Fancy," which emphasizes scribal publication's continuance of the salon's *sensus communis*. The successive poems, diligently numbered, also have detailed annotations and footnotes, indicating the instructive component of neoclassical entertainment. In addition, she often includes helpful head notes (i.e., "On Needlework," "On Benevolence," etc.) as a supplemental index for her readers. As essayist James Beattie describes the process:

> It is easy, and far more advantageous, to write correctly and legibly, with durable ink, and in note-books provided for the purpose, and carefully preserved. And when a volume is finished, it will be an amusement, and a profitable one too, to read it over; to make an index to it; and to write upon the cover such a title, or summary of contents, as may serve for a direction, when afterwards you want to revise any particular passage.[51]

These textual features not only point to Elizabeth Fergusson's integrity as an author, but also to her skills as a "compiler." Unlike an editor, who fixes and corrects texts, a compiler collects and arranges them according to her particular literary aesthetic. In other words, Elizabeth Fergusson's coterie promoted sociability and pleasure by projecting their domestic authority as collectors of household *topoi* to their stockpile of literary miscellany. Through commonplace books, women transformed the rhetorical art of artificial memory into works of the imagination, for "by Memory, we acquire knowledge. By Imagination, we <u>invent</u>; that is, produce arrangements of ideas and objects that were never so arranged before."[52]

While Elizabeth Fergusson follows Beattie's general rules for compiling commonplace books, she rarely categorizes *topoi* under general heads, "under which may be arranged the manifold treasures of human Memory." "Under each of these heads," Beattie explains, "what an infinity of individual things are comprehended!" Given the intermittent nature of her organizational "heads," I would suggest another approach to interpreting Fergusson's modern adaptation of rhetorical commonplacing. Setting her six commonplace books side by side, one notices that each book essentially comprises a single, comprehensive theme.

Her first book, *Poemata Juvenilia* (1752–72), traces her developing sense of civility inspired by her trip to England. Including some of the same poems transcribed in her travel journal, *Poemata Juvenilia* illustrates the young woman's introduction to polite society in such poems as "The Invitation a Song," "A Parody on the Life of a Belle," "To Miss Betsy Stedman in Philadelphia: giving her an Account of the Movements of one Day as spent by people of Fashion in the full Season at Scarborough," and "Upon the Pleasure convey'd to us by writing; wrote on receiving Letters when in England from my Friends." After recounting her trip in verse, she then composes a long, retrospective poem, "On Being at Graeme Park after my return from Britain."

The next book, compiled for Annis Stockton in 1787, testifies to the burgeoning salon culture after returning to Graeme Park in 1765, with roughly thirty of her own poems, fifteen by Anna Young Smith, and several by habitué Francis Hopkinson and Major Andre. Assembled in 1789 for the five Willing sisters, the subsequent commonplace book continues the theme of British-American literary history, supplementing the previous books' depiction of polite literary society with her two Willow Odes to British and American Genius. Using various trees as metaphors for universal knowledge throughout the book, she also includes "An Extract Relative to Chaucers Oak"; Extracts from Tomsons <u>Seasons</u> on Groves, Woods, and Shade; "An Extract from Milton on Groves," Pliny's Epistle on Woods"; and an "Extract from Milton on the Tree of Knowledge." With a ready store of established authors on neoclassical nature writing, Fergusson's Willow Odes boasted an impressive historical resonance.

In her 1796 commonplace book kept for either Elias Boudinot or Benjamin Rush, moreover, Fergusson shows the intellectual maturity reached in her later life when cut off from the civil society she once enjoyed at Graeme Park. While this volume includes poems copied in the other commonplace books (i.e., "Country Mouse," "The Dream of a Patriotic, Philosophical Farmer," and "Hymn on the Beauties of Nature," to name a few), the majority of poems explore the related themes of solitude, aging, and death. She includes a transcription of Thomas Parnell's poem, *The Hermit;* Annis Stockton's poem, "On the Advances of Old Age," along with her verse, "Youth and Old Age Contrasted"; and finally, a collection of elegies for such life-long friends and habitués as Richard Peters, Francis

Hopkinson, Rebecca Moore Smith, and Ann Willing. The last two commonplace books, compiled around 1800, contain the metrical versions of the Psalms as well as poems exclusively on the homely art of spinning. Seemingly unrelated at first glance, these books suggest Fergusson's seasoned morality and continued contemplation. Spinning was more than a material craft employing the fingers; it fully engaged the mind. Just as the former paraphrases the Bible for her continued ruminations, so the latter contemplates ethical questions about socioeconomic class, marriage, education, and motherhood.

Elizabeth Fergusson thus uses the commonplace book—like the pastoral salon—as an imaginative escape from the particularities of her life. Read sequentially, these books collectively form a kind of poetic autobiography. As much as the impressive documentary evidence presented in Anne Ousterhout's ensuing biography, these manuscripts richly chronicle Elizabeth Graeme Fergusson's intellectual life in verse.

FROM *TOPOI* TO TYPES: WOMEN'S POETRY IN THE PUBLIC SPHERE

Though Elizabeth Fergusson publishes some thirty poems in local newspapers and literary magazines in the latter part of the eighteenth century, the majority of her poems are preserved through sororal publication. Kept in commonplace books, enclosed in personal letters, and signed with her characteristic pseudonym, "Laura," Fergusson's poetry was "private" in its exclusive circulation, but decidedly "public" in nature. Unlike our contemporary relish for confessional lyrics, Elizabeth Fergusson and her literary world preferred neoclassical decorum, which demanded order and correctness, symmetry and balance, proportion and taste. Poetry, aestheticians contended, was a social rather than private activity with the simple aim of delighting and instructing its audience. Elizabeth Fergusson consequently begins each of her commonplace books with a standardized invocation to her critics to read her poetry according to the rules of politeness:

> Let not the Critics Rigid Eye,
> Poor Laura's Odes and Sonnets spy!
> Good Nature should the Opticks be,
> Through which her Verses they should See.
> Beauties if there, will then be viewd,
> And Errors not too close pursued.

Calling for an expressly sociable demeanor in her critics' shared good nature, she abandons the notion of "criticism" popularized by Dr. Samuel Johnson. "Censure is willingly indulged, because it always implies some superiority," he claims, "men please themselves with imagining that they have made a deeper search, or wider survey than others, and detected faults and follies which escape vulgar observation."[53] Ending the introductory poem with vernal twigs instead of traditionally heroic laurel bays, Fergusson provides a standard apologia for her writing. At the same time she downplays her intellectual accomplishments, however, Fergusson emphasizes the domestic epistemology of politeness begun in her literary salon. Since authors and critics share the common taste of the salon's benevolent *sensus communis,* and since the rules for taste emphasize beauty over imperfection, then writers of polite learning, Fergusson suggests, can expect a generous reception from their critics.

Explaining her tendency toward poetry, Elizabeth Fergusson echoes the poetic ambitions set forth in her travel journal and willow odes:

> There is a certain Elevation of Soul, a noble turn of virtue that raises a hero of the plain honest man, to which Verse can only raise us, His Bold Metaphors and Sounding members peculiar To the Poets, Rouse up all our Sleeping faculties And alarm all the powers of the Soul like Vergils Exelent Trumpet.[54]

Poetry, she argues, awakens the sleeping faculties through the practice of imitation. Her allusion to Virgil recalls her earlier Homeric identification with Odysseus. It also reiterates neoclassical aesthetic theories. While rhetorician Hugh Blair defined poetry as the "language of passion, or of enlivened imagination," essayist James Beattie agreed, for poetry is deadening when "our passions are not occasionally awakened by some event that concerns our fellow-men."[55] But because her primary aim—as a poet and as a woman—was not only to emotionally move, but also to please her audience, Elizabeth Fergusson justified her epic ambitions by mimicking polite, neoclassical forms.

Given its general aim to delight and instruct, neoclassical poetry shared more than universal *topoi* with classical rhetoric. Like commonplace *topoi,* neoclassical poetry was classified into specific genres or "types": for example, the ode, elegy, verse epistle, satire, pastoral, allegory, occasional verse, Biblical paraphrase, and hymn were among the most practiced forms. Typically written in heroic couplets (i.e., aabb rhyme) or quatrains (i.e., abab rhyme), each genre was rhetorically structured to elicit a specific response from its audience. While the ode and elegy might eulogize a person or venerated ideal, the verse epistle or satire might ridicule social folly. As such, neoclassical poetry had a universal quality, much like rhetorical *topoi,* which appealed to and personified abstract qualities in order to express the general, the typical, the ideal. Poetry, in other words, was highly allusive and derivative; it imitated and improved idealized models. As Joseph Addison argued in the *Spectator* (20 December 1711): "Wit and fine writing doth not consist so much in advancing things that are new, as in giving things that are known an agreeable turn. . . . We have little else left, but to represent the common sense of mankind in more strong, more beautiful, or more uncommon lights." No knowledge is original, he contends; good art is good imitation. Addison describes good-natured wit and common sense. One can only appreciate poetry according to the standards established by the *sensus communis.* The neoclassical emphasis on wit and sympathy extends the conventional wisdom about the nature of knowledge and beauty from salons and commonplace books to poetry itself. Though the terms may change—public versus private, universal versus local, masculine versus feminine—the aesthetic debate remained the same.

Though Elizabeth Fergusson wrote prolifically in each of these genres, I haven't the time nor space in this introductory essay to elucidate them in any detail. Instead I will end with a brief discussion of her 1760 verse translation of Abbé Francois Fenelon's *The Adventures of Telemachus.* Translating Fenelon's popular philosophical romance on the proper education of the young into English heroic verse, Fergusson beautifully embodies the tenets of sociability, commonplacing, and domestic publication so important to her life and work. Working on the multi-volume poem for almost thirty years, she not only transcribed and translated the story of Odysseus's son, but also imitated his exploits as he awaited his father's return to Ithaca. While she claims "she is sensible the translation has little merit," but that "it is sufficient for her that it amused her in a period that would have been pensive and solitary without a pursuit," Fergusson also adds footnotes and other explanatory aids in 1786 and 1787. The completed text, she explained, was meant "for a particular Friend But if I live I intend to give it a more correct Version And perhaps if I meet with encouragement have it printed." Though she tried unsuccessfully to publish the epic poem in1793, the impressive manuscript remains in the annals of the Historical Society of Pennsylvania.

The poem, I would suggest, exemplifies the importance of commonplace books to female education and epistemology in eighteenth-century British America. In her prefatory poem, "Ode to Wisdom," where Wisdom was the "guardian of the modest youth/soul of knowledge and source of truth," Elizabeth Fergusson traces the domestic genealogy of Wisdom, which she previously outlines in "Contemplation and Cunning: An Allegory."[56] Commonly associated with erudite knowledge by midcentury, wisdom was also understood as moral judgment and proper conduct. Marrying "Wisdom" (descended from "Experience") and "Truth" (descended from "Jove") in her poem, Fergusson uncovers the intellectual bloodline of their daughter, "Contemplation":

> She had a clear Head, and Warm Breast, with a Retentive Memory: yet before she admitted any thing to fix on her mind as a Rule of Life and Manners, She weigh'd it in her Fathers <u>Scales</u> which were priz'd with the utmost Escatings; or viewd it through the <u>Mirror</u> of her mother, a <u>Glass,</u> which for Just Representations had no equal.

With superior sensibility (i.e., "Warm Breast") and a natural proclivity toward commonplacing (i.e., "Retentive Memory"), "Contemplation" dwelled with her parents in "The Placid Grove, their Habitation." A privileged heir of pastoral leisure, she is served by her handmaidens, "Sincerity" and "Content." While Honesty principally serves Wisdom, Ingenuity is his pupil. Taken together, Contemplation's family preserves the ethic of polite learning that informs Elizabeth Fergusson's literary career.

A staple of education in early America, then, Fenelon's book—and Elizabeth Fergusson's verse translation of it—provided moral guidance through example, fable, tale, and parable. Such literary commonplaces, she suggests, would "catch the fluttering mind and fix the sense" of its readers. Although originally written for a prince's courtly education, Fergusson's version of *Telemachus* served female pedagogy as well: "Then struggling Passion might its portrait view, / And learn from thence its tumults to subdue." Following Telemachus from one earthly temptation to another, the reader would imitate his good choices and avoid his bad ones:

"Through his Telemachus he points to view / What youth should fly from and what youth pursue." By translating and circulating the text in manuscript, moreover, Fergusson continued the commonplace practice of praising virtue and vilifying vice. As Erasmus once explained the process, organizational headings or themes should be gleaned "partly from the main types and subdivisions of the vices and virtues. . . . These should be arranged (digerere) by similars and opposites; for things which are related naturally suggests what comes next and the memory is prompted in a similar way by opposites."[57]

Though Fenelon's *Telemachus* shows that "Passion and Wisdom hold perpetual strife / Through the strange mazes of man's chequered life," Fergusson's translation combines wisdom and passion as the complementary requisites for women's experiential knowledge. No longer at odds, passion and wisdom, feeling and knowledge, body and mind come together in her feminized epistemology. She defies the critics' warnings that "a passion for poetry is dangerous to a woman." And she disproves their gendered logic that this poetic passion "heightens her natural sensibility to an extravagant degree," making writing "utterly inconsistent with the solid duties and properties of life."[58] Transforming Graeme Park's parlor into a vibrant literary salon and preserving her poetry in manuscript commonplace books, Elizabeth Graeme Fergusson domesticated the otherwise public world of letters, writing herself into literary history. Like Odysseus, who embellishes his extraordinary adventures with each retelling; or like Telemachus, who repeats his father's journey with his guardian, Mentor, Elizabeth Fergusson envisions herself as part of a British American epic. Becoming a mentor for the next generation of female writers in her coterie, however, Elizabeth Fergusson resists the lure of Odysseus's hubris, assuring her friend and confidant Ann Steadman in 1762: "I hope I never shall be tempted to strain a sentiment of Truth for the sake of a jingling Rhyme; which would be converting an innocent amusement into a Criminal pursuit."

1

Sweet Period of Vernal Youth

The slight gray-haired woman stood in front of the stone house at midday on Christmas Eve 1793 and asked herself how she had come to this situation. Tears misted her spectacles, as she bid farewell to the home where she had passed fifty summers and twenty-one winters but where she would live no more. How had she become "a Link Cut of from the Chain of that Society" she had been led by birth and education to expect as her place, Elizabeth Fergusson wondered.[1] How had the brilliant granddaughter of a Lieutenant Governor of Pennsylvania, the daughter of a wealthy, distinguished physician, become an unhappy, impoverished boarder in someone else's home?

Certainly, there had been no forebodings in her childhood, which had been passed "in the lap of parental affection," as Benjamin Rush put it. Both parents were well educated and prominent in Philadelphia society. Her father, Thomas Graeme, was a very successful physician and informal adviser to Thomas Penn, a proprietor of Pennsylvania. Her mother, the popular Ann Diggs Graeme, was a pious and intelligent woman. Born in St. Albans, England, in 1700, she had been brought to this country by her mother, Ann Newberry Diggs Keith, and Sir William Keith, Ann Keith's second husband. Dr. Thomas Graeme had been born at Balgowan, the ancestral seat of the Graemes in Perthshire, Scotland, October 20, 1688, and may have been the son of Sir William's half-brother.[2] Educated at Leyden University and possibly Edinburgh, Graeme came to Pennsylvania in 1717 with the party of Sir William and Lady Ann, their four sons, one born during the trip, and her daughter by the deceased Robert Diggs. Two years after they arrived, Thomas Graeme and Ann Diggs were married on November 12, 1719. Elizabeth was their last child, born February 3, 1737.[3]

Sir William came to the province of Pennsylvania to serve as its deputy governor, which position he held until the Penn family replaced him in 1726. The colony of Pennsylvania comprised land that had been given by the king of England to William Penn. Thereafter Penn and his heirs owned all the land to sell, give, or keep at their pleasure. Either one of the proprietors, as they were called, served as governor of the province or they appointed someone to be deputy governor and provided that person with very explicit instructions as to how the colony should be run in their absence. Bills passed by the popularly elected unicameral legislature, called the General Assembly or simply the Assembly or the House, went to the governor for his approval or rejection, just as they do today in the states. But the governor's judgment was not final unless he rejected a bill. If he approved, it had to be sent to England to be accepted by the King. The governor's instructions told him which measures he should sign and which he should disapprove, and he was required to post a bond with the proprietors promising to obey their orders.

Whether Sir William was or was not thought to be a successful governor would have depended upon whose opinion was consulted. At first, the Penns ignored him, expecting him to follow their instructions and manage their colony as they wished, but soon they found him too independent for their liking. He challenged the concept of the proprietary being able to give its governors instructions that had the force of law in the colony. He saw the governor's role as more than just an enforcer of the proprietary's commands. He believed that he should judge what was good for the colony and act accordingly. Because of these beliefs, Keith was a very popular governor with the ordinary people of Pennsylvania. Citizens who were attached to the proprietary, however, disliked Keith's governorship.

Even Benjamin Franklin, who was treated shabbily by the governor, had a favorable view of Sir William's administration. In his autobiography, Franklin related that Keith had befriended the eighteen-year-old Benjamin and sent him to England to purchase equipment for a print shop, promising to provide him with letters of introduction and the credit necessary to make the purchases possible. When Franklin landed in England, he discovered that Keith had made no provision for him at all and, in fact,

Portrait of Elizabeth Graeme, School of John Smibert (1688–1751). As a member of a prominent Philadelphia family, Elizabeth Graeme and her family would have both sought and had
ample opportunity to have her likeness painted in the prevailing fashionable grand manner
style of the English Court. While many wealthy colonials at this time traveled to England
for this purpose, the number of accomplished academically trained portrait artists such as
John Smibert and Robert Feke made this voyage unnecessary; Elizabeth Graeme did not
travel to England until she was an adult. © Christie's Images Inc. 2003.

could make no such provision because of the governor's own insolvency. Keith had had to borrow from men in England for transportation to Pennsylvania and for the necessary outfit to take up his job as governor. That money had yet to be repaid. In addition, he had borrowed extensively in Pennsylvania to support the high style he craved. The governor's irresponsibility had left the young, friendless Franklin stranded in England with little money and no patrons to help him. Other young men might have been unable to cope, but Franklin used the next two years in England to polish his printing skills and make friends. In the long run, Keith did him a favor.

Franklin, writing many years later about the "pitiful tricks" Keith had played on him, was able in his maturity to view Keith's administration in Pennsylvania objectively. He wrote that Sir William was "an ingenious, sensible man, a pretty good writer, and a good governor for the people, tho' not for his constituents, the Proprietaries, whose instructions he sometimes disregarded. Several of [Pennsylvania's] best laws were of his planning and passed during his administration,"[4] Franklin conceded.

The particular debate that brought down Keith's administration concerned the province's paper money. A small amount had been struck in 1723, but it was about to be sunk. The wealthy people in the province opposed the creation of more paper money, believing that it would depreciate and devalue debts. But many people argued, as did Franklin, that the first sum had increased "trade, employment, and the number of inhabitants in the province."[5] Keith agreed. When the Assembly passed a law creating new paper currency, he signed it, contrary to his instruction from the proprietary. The Assemblymen, fearing that the Penn family would change governors because of Keith's action, wrote to the proprietors in December 1725 defending Keith's regime, but to no avail. Keith lost his job the next year. When Patrick Gordon replaced Sir William in June 1726, the voters immediately elected the popular ex-governor to the Assembly.

Keith's unpaid bills continued to mount, however, and finally in 1727 he resigned his Assembly seat and left Pennsylvania. In England he had some temporary success, winning election to Parliament. But he was unable to live within his income or increase his income enough to cover his extravagant tastes. Indebtedness finally brought him to jail, and he died imprisoned for debt in the Old Bailey in November 1749. Keith never returned to Pennsylvania and never saw his wife again, although their relations continued very amicably by letters in which they expressed their regard for one another. Elizabeth, born ten years after Keith left Pennsylvania, never met her step-grandfather.

Most of the Graemes' other relatives lived abroad or had died by the time Elizabeth was old enough to nourish family relationships. She never knew any of her grandparents, except for her mother's mother, and she could not have known her very well. Lady Keith died in 1740 when Elizabeth was only three. Thomas Graeme had at least two brothers. One, Patrick, lived in Philadelphia, was married, and had children. He was still alive when Elizabeth was born, but neither he nor his children are mentioned in any of Elizabeth's extant writings. Throughout Thomas Graeme's lifetime, the family maintained contact with the Graemes of Balgowan, Scotland, and Elizabeth would visit her cousin there in 1765.

On the other side of her family, Sir William and Lady Ann had had four sons and one daughter, in addition to Lady Keith's daughter, Ann Diggs, Elizabeth's mother. Two of the sons had died, without children, by the time Elizabeth was four, while the other two had joined their father in Europe and made their homes there. The third son, Robert, became the fifth baronet, but the line ended when neither of Robert's sons had children, and when the fourth son died childless. The Keiths' daughter, Jane, had married and lived in Jamaica. Her daughter Deborah, married to a man named William Senior, also of Jamaica, became a correspondent of Elizabeth. This is the only Keith relative with whom we have any record of her maintaining regular contact. Her mother did hear from Robert Keith, but there is no record of Elizabeth corresponding with him or his children.[6]

When Thomas Graeme arrived in the colony, there were only a few trained doctors. His medical knowledge combined with his connection to Keith and his own pleasing, gentle personality soon made him a leading citizen of Pennsylvania. His medical practice grew, and there is nothing in the records to indicate that his medical skills, primitive at best, were anything but satisfactory to his contemporaries, who knew no better.

Dr. Graeme's income from his practice was increased by his appointment to several political jobs. During Keith's tenure, Graeme was appointed to the office of Naval Officer of Philadelphia and then to membership in the Governor's Council. Apparently, he was able to establish good relations with the incoming deputy governor despite his connections with Keith. In 1731 Gordon appointed Graeme one of the three justices of the Supreme Court and the next year a "Justice of Oyer and terminer and

Dr. Thomas Graeme. From Thomas Allen Glenn, ed., *Some Colonial Mansions and Those Who Lived in Them: With Genealogies of the Various Families Mentioned*, vol. 1 (Philadelphia: H. T. Coates, 1898), 388.

General Goal Delivery for Philadelphia, Bucks and Chester." Later, he was appointed physician of the port and physician and surgeon to the Pennsylvania Hospital. He also helped found the St. Andrews Society in 1749, dedicated to helping indigent Scotsmen, and served as its president until his death. Thus, Elizabeth's father was a prominent member of the medical community, recognized by the proprietary colonial administration with appointments. He also had learned from his father-in-law's unfortunate experiences that debt was to be avoided, and he managed his affairs well until the last years of his life.

By the time Elizabeth was born, the Graeme household included three older children. Thomas, the first child, born in 1721, was between fifteen and sixteen years old at the time. Before Elizabeth had an opportunity to know him well, he left home to become Collector of the Port of New Castle in Delaware and died young and unmarried in 1747. Ann, aged eleven, had been born in 1726, and Mary Jane, called by her second name, in 1727. Elizabeth became very close to her two sisters, even though they were considerably older than she.

Specifically how many other children Ann and Thomas Graeme had is not clear. Baptismal records of Christ Church in Philadelphia, engravings on the Graeme family tombstone in the churchyard, and transcriptions of family records agree that at least nine children were born to Ann Graeme. In addition to Thomas, there was: William, who lived to age ten and died in 1733; Ann, who died at age forty in 1766; Jane, who died in 1759 at age thirty-two; Rebecca and Rachel, born in 1728, and Patrick and Elizabeth, born in 1731, two sets of twins, all of whom died as infants or very young children; Elizabeth, born in 1737; and perhaps a twin of hers named Sarah, who died in infancy. These are the only children for whom records remain. Elizabeth, however, in her writings referred in various places to her parents having anywhere from ten to twelve children.[7] There is a gap of almost six years between the twins Patrick and Elizabeth and Elizabeth, during which Ann Graeme could have borne two more children. The number twelve could also include the two infant children of Jane Graeme Young, who are buried in the Graeme family grave in Christ Church churchyard and named on the tombstone.

After Elizabeth was born, her mother, by then thirty-seven years old, underwent no more recorded pregnancies, so that the daughter did not witness the personal distress her parents suffered to conceive infants only to have them die soon after their births. When Ann Graeme "first

Buryd an infant of 3 months old She at that time thought she could not feel more sorrow" but as she buried successive children she learned "that each one was harder than the last."[8] The litany of births and subsequent deaths in the Graeme family is a sad reminder of the parental and sibling grief that was typical of the times. In old age, Elizabeth wrote a prose meditation on a clock that had been in the Graeme family for many years. Reminiscing about scenes timed by the clock, she reflected upon the children lost by her parents:

> What a Series of tedious, weary nights must these Parents and their Children have waked and Watched in tedious illness or acute Through the Long Gallery of Pain to Death! . . . How many Times ye dear Departed, venerable Authors of my Being have heard that Clock . . . while Breath drew trembling in Bodies dearer to you than your own; your Children a part of your Selves! And again what have you who have survivd felt to be a party in all the Funereal Ceremonials of Sorrow, when the Solemn undertaker begd 'The Hour is Struck! may not the Coffin be Closed?' Then came the Last Last Look but not Last Last Sigh.[9]

The Graemes, by Elizabeth's time, maintained two homes, one rented in Philadelphia and one owned in Horsham township, Philadelphia (now Montgomery) County. At first, Thomas and Ann Graeme lived with the Keiths in a house built by Edward Shippen, the first mayor of Philadelphia, on the west side of Second Street between Walnut and Spruce, called "the governor's house."[10] Their son Thomas was born in that house and probably William, as well.[11] By the time Ann was born in 1726, Sir William had lost the governorship, and his debts had forced him to give up a Philadelphia residence for one on his property at Horsham. Since Governor Gordon moved into the Shippen house, the Graemes also had to make other arrangements. The family was reported to have lived in a house on the north side of Chestnut Street between Sixth and Seventh Streets, built by Joshua Carpenter.[12] By 1737 when Elizabeth was born and in January 1749 when her sister Ann married Charles Stedman, family records show that the family was living in a house "in Second Street." Possibly this was the Edward Shippen mansion, although records do not identify it any more specifically.[13] From then until 1772, the family occupied various mansions in Philadelphia in the winter.[14] Dr. Graeme, who loved flowers, cultivated the gardens, planting tulips and other landscaping. The Shippen and Carpenter places were noted for their beautiful gardens, especially the Carpenter house where visitors flocked in the spring to see the flowering fruit trees.[15]

Meanwhile, the family was developing a country estate in the northern part of Horsham township, Philadelphia County, near the Bucks County line, where they spent the summers. The land that became known as Graeme Park had been acquired by Sir William, who began construction on the property in late 1721.[16] At first, Keith had intended to use the property for commercial purposes. Planning to make beer for the Philadelphia market, he had had a large three story stone malt house built, a so-called "long house" or farmhouse to shelter workers, and a large stone barn. In 1725, however, Keith, heavily indebted, had to move his family onto the property. The next year, he lost his office and in April 1727, he left for England ostensibly to attend to business but probably to escape his debts in Pennsylvania. Before his departure, to save his household goods from his creditors, he mortgaged them to Graeme and another man for £500. The list of mortgaged personal items indicates that the Keiths lived in very high style.[17] Silver plate, including a punch bowl and ladle, chinaware, fifty tablecloths, much furniture, four coach horses, seven saddle horses, a large glass coach, and two chaises are only part of the long list of possessions that helped account for Keith's heavy indebtedness. In addition he had fourteen slaves, including five or six children.

Keith had the opportunity to work on the Horsham estate only from 1718 to the sale of his personal property May 21, 1726, and probably did not begin until 1721. Yet he managed to accomplish a surprising development of the property, all virgin woodland. The list tells us that by 1726 he possessed, besides the coach and saddle horses, "6 working horses, 2 mares and I colt, 4 oxen, 15 cows, 4 bulls, 6 calves, 31 sheep, and 20 hogs."[18] Seventy-five acres had been cleared for grazing stock and planting crops and an extensive garden planted to provide vegetables for the family, slaves, and servants.[19]

In 1731, Keith deeded the Horsham estate to his wife. She found the responsibility more than she wished to manage and put it up for sale after unsuccessfully attempting to persuade one of her children to live there. Horsham was purchased in 1737 by Philadelphia merchant Joseph Turner for £750, who, the next year, conveyed the tract, consisting of 848 acres, to Thomas Graeme for £760.[20]

It is uncertain whether Keith or Graeme was responsible for beginning to make the malt-house into the elegant residence it became, but Charles Harper Smith, a descendant of Graeme, speculated that Keith was too strapped for cash just before he left for England to have begun the expensive renovations. Sir William wrote later that he had spent £2,000 on the Horsham estate, although much of this must have gone into the acquiring of stock and the clearing of land. It is not known in which building Keith and his family lived. The farmhouse was a more logical choice than the malt house, since it had been designed to house people. Smith speculated that probably it was Graeme who divided the malt house into rooms and put in the elaborate paneling after he obtained ownership in 1738.[21] The Graemes lived at the Park during the summers until 1772, after which time Elizabeth lived there year round, visiting friends and relatives when she wished to go to the city.

Under Dr. Graeme's creative management, the Keith property, renamed Graeme Park, became a beautiful estate. He was very interested in the latest horticultural methods and landscape architecture and stocked his library with many books on these subjects. In addition he was committed professionally to the medicinal value of country air for the treatment of illness. He concentrated first on further developing the land before he worked on the house and garden. He had purchased a functioning farm, but he also wanted a gentleman's country estate. To do this, he needed to make it beautiful as well as practical. He enclosed 300 acres which he "double Ditched and double Hedged." Walls erected around this area with dirt thrown on the outside made it possible for deer to climb to the top of the wall and jump into the park but impossible for them to leave. At one point, Graeme decided to enclose the whole estate this way, but his neighbor informed him that "he did not believe there was stone enough in Horsham township to do it."[22] In 1755, when Elizabeth was eighteen, Graeme was clearing the enclosed acres and had removed all undergrowth from about 150 acres, leaving nothing but the tall trees and saplings. This land he had harrowed, seeded in grass, and rolled. He expected it to be "one of the finest Parks for Deer that could be imagined."[23] By 1765, a visitor described the scene as "gay and blooming . . . each field and grove dressed in rich attire." She wrote of birds, sheep, and cattle roaming the park.[24] Elizabeth loved to walk through the woods, to watch the changing seasons, and to observe the wild animals who shared the grounds. She wrote often of the beauty and quiet of nature at Graeme Park.

When Dr. Graeme died in 1772, the inventory filed with his will for probate listed eleven horses, a pair of oxen, four steers, one bull, twenty cows, two heifers, one yearling, six calves, fifty-seven hogs and shoats, twenty-three sheep and lambs. When compared with Keith's list, Graeme had not added substantially to the park's holdings in stock except in the number of pigs, but the clearing of 75 more acres and the enclosing of 300 were substantial feats. In addition to raising animals, Graeme's estate also produced marketable crops. The inventory listed 360 dozen bushels of wheat, 103 of rye, 90 of barley, 250 of oats, 60 loads of hay, and a pound of flax and seed.[25] He had built an extensive agricultural enterprise. Unfortunately, he had not prepared his daughter and only heir to manage it after he was gone. It was assumed that she would marry a man capable of carrying on the business. It did not take many years of war and neglect, however, to destroy all that Graeme had built except for the three-story mansion house, which is still standing, although not occupied.[26]

Sixty feet long by twenty-five feet wide, the house has stone walls over two feet thick and was divided into three rooms on each floor. Although no longer standing, a separate stone kitchen near the mansion, a stone barn, the farm house, and other out buildings were also on the estate during Elizabeth's lifetime.[27] When the house was converted from a malt house to an elegant mansion is not known precisely. Graeme wrote Thomas Penn in July 1755 describing the deer park and his other refinements to the estate, acknowledging that he had not done much about the house. In 1762, Ann Graeme wrote Elizabeth, then in Philadelphia, that since carpenters and masons were working in the kitchen, it would not be a good time for a friend to visit. Perhaps this was when the house refurbishings were taking place.[28]

Each room in the mansion held memories for Elizabeth. The drawing room on the first floor in the east end, with its walls wainscoted and paneled and its fireplace of imported marble,[29] echoed with the voices of Philadelphia's most prominent people, sometimes raised in song as they clustered around the harpsicord that had been purchased in England for her by family friend Francis Hopkinson. And sometimes the words they sang had been written by Elizabeth to Scottish tunes that she loved.[30] She could still see Jacob Duché sitting there playing and hear his wife, Hopkinson's sister, singing, while others joined in.

The second-floor room over the parlor, the east bedroom, had been her parents' room and then her father's after her mother had died.

She and Henry had moved into this room after their marriage and her father's death. She had been sitting in the window seat in the room above and had seen him stricken by a heart attack near the two sycamore trees out front that had been there since she was a child. He had died in this bedroom, the same room where two of her sisters previously had died.[31]

Each item in the house reminded her of dear-ones or of significant events in her life. On the second-floor landing had stood the wonderful tall clock, made in England in 1722, that had marked time for the Graeme family.[32] It was in the wagon waiting to go with her to Hatborough, a neighboring town, where it would continue to toll the hours of her life. In her bedroom had stood the tall writing desk that was too big for Mrs. Todd's farm house where she was going to be boarding. Not willing to part with it permanently, even though it was obvious that she would never be able to have it with her again, she had lent it to a neighboring parson named Irwin.[33] In the east bedroom, she had spent many hours in later years bent over the loom on which she had made fringe for herself and her friends. That, too, could not fit in her new accommodations. Hanging on the wall in that same room had been the needlework representation of a crocodile executed by her mother. Elizabeth would not part with it no matter how crowded her new quarters would be.

It reminded her of that dear lady and the skills, such as spinning, weaving, and embroidering, that she had patiently taught her daughters, skills that Elizabeth practiced all her life. When an old woman, she would write "Lines in Praise of Needlework," in which she commented that

> Oft when the Weary languid hour, I knew,
> And <u>Time</u> with Leaden Foot Slow Crept nor flew
> When <u>Books</u> and <u>writing</u> tasteless seemed around
> No varying Pleasures marked Lifes narrow bound.
> Then has the Needle Stole away the time.[34]

Her mother was noted for her fine embroidery, a talent so admired in women that one of the subjects taught to girls in their schools was needlework. When Elizabeth was twelve, she embroidered a picture of a dog, which she gave later in life to a neighbor's daughter. The dog-sampler was passed down through the daughter's family. Its present location is unknown, but the Bucks County Historical Society has a picture of it.

Ann Graeme had been responsible for teaching Elizabeth not only

Ann Graeme. From *The Pennsylvania Magazine of History and Biography* 39.3 (1915): 269. Courtesy of Rare Books and Manuscripts, Special Collections Library, The Pennsylvania State University Libraries, University Park, Pennsylvania.

needle work but also reading and writing. Before the Revolution, there was no system of public primary or secondary education provided by the colony for all children. Education was handled by religious denominations, by private schools or tutors, or by parents. The Quakers, who comprised at first the majority of the Pennsylvania population and by mid-eighteenth century a large minority, stressed education, and they were joined later by other denominations, such as the Presbyterians, Lutherans, the German Reformed, the Moravians, and the Baptists, all of whom opened schools. The Friends pioneered in the education of women, and their "Publick School" admitted girls. Quaker Anthony Benezet taught "reading, writing, arithmetic and English grammar to about forty girls" and later added Latin and Greek to the curriculum.[35] Private schools for girls' education also developed under teachers such as David James Dove and William Dawson. Thus, by Elizabeth's childhood, schooling, except for college, was available for "girls of all classes" in Philadelphia. There is no indication, however, that Elizabeth attended any of these schools. It has been suggested that she may have attended Benezet's school, but this is highly unlikely.[36] She did not mention schooling in any of her manuscripts, and her epitaph to Benezet does not call him teacher. At first, she was taught by her mother. Later, her father added instruction in classical languages, and the family hired specialized tutors, who had instructed the young of well-to-do Philadelphians from at least the 1720s.

Mrs. Graeme used a Horn-Book to teach her daughter the basics of reading and writing and then gradually increased the difficulty of the assignments. "Dear *Anna* led my Infant mind" Elizabeth poetically reminisced in one of her commonplace books,

> Up those Ascents which <u>God</u> and <u>Truth</u> designd
> Should be displayd to opening tender Age,
> Nicely adapted to each rising Stage;
> From Letterd <u>Horn-Book</u> up to Thomsons Theme
> Where God and Nature in his Pages beam.[37]

Instruction was rooted firmly in the Bible. As soon as Elizabeth could read, she was encouraged to memorize and recite parts of the Psalms.[38] Eventually she was taught the best in English literature and learned how to read the classical texts in the original languages. Her father's extensive library contained books written in Latin and Greek,[39] and the young girl learned to read both. Whether this comprehensive an education was usual for Philadelphia girls, even for daughters of the élite, is not known. It was available in schools and by private tutors, however, even if parents were not able themselves to teach their children as the Graemes did.

Elizabeth's education also included the study of contemporary European languages, and she became very fluent in French. As early as 1746, a Monsieur Peter Papin de Préfontaine was teaching French to young women in Philadelphia.[40] During Elizabeth's winters in the city, she could have been tutored by him or his successors. In January 1764, at age twenty-seven, she had a French lesson every day for an hour in preparation for a European trip she was about to undertake.[41] In 1770, she began the study of Italian, which occasioned Abigail Streate Coxe to comment that she did not doubt that

> Miss Graeme will make a swift Progress in ye Italian, she is a Lady who claims my great Regard & Esteem, tho I never yet had ye Pleasure of seeing her but have gather'd my Sentiments of her Understanding & ye goodness of her Heart entirely from Her Journals & Letters, which alone are sufficient for me.[42]

Graeme family life often centered around reading. On a cold winter's evening when they were without guests, the Graeme women gathered around a small round walnut table pulled close to a crackling hickory fire and took turns "reading some moral story or dramatic piece." On the other side of the fireplace, Dr. Graeme sat in his comfortable chair "with his own small mahogany stand reading the paper of the day or some treatise on his own profession." From the walls, sixteen life size famly portraits observed the scene, and four oil paintings of the Park reminded the family of the landscape at various seasons. "Twelve small medal plaister of Paris . . . Heads of the Poets"[43] graced other parts of the walls, showing the cultural interests of the family. Bedtime for the youngest member of the group was promptly at eight except on those rare occasions when she could beg successfully for an extra fifteen minutes, but never any more. "Perhaps the Clock struck in the middle of that Excellent Comedy, the journey to London, where Humor and Sentiment are so happily Blended," Elizabeth late in life reminisced. "'Oh Mama do let me stay and hear whether Lady Townly repents and makes a good Wife?' 'No no my Child you shall hear tomorrow; Mama says Betsy must go to Bed.' Shut was the Book and shut the Scene."[44]

Upper-class young women in eighteenth-century Philadelphia were also expected to develop gracious social skills. These, too, were the province of their mothers, and older women helped one another polish the manners and graces of their children. Girls were often sent to stay with family friends, sometimes for extended periods. This was a logical action to take with youngsters in their teens who might pay more attention to non-family members than to their own parents. Women visited one another frequently, and since transportation was slow and uncomfortable, they tended once arrived to stay for several days or weeks. And they took their female children with them. The girls relished these visits and looked forward to them as entertainment. Through these visits, women built friend-ships and support groups that lasted all their lives and that sustained them during the many tragedies that marked their existences.

In 1752, Elizabeth Graeme made her first visit without her mother. No specific invitation from her hostess was considered necessary. The young woman simply arrived at the home of Mrs. Mary Campbell, wife of the minister of St. Mary's Church in Burlington, New Jersey, bearing a letter from her mother. "With this," wrote Ann Graeme, "you will receive My Betsy who has a great desire to spend a day or two with you; as it is the first time she has been abroad by her self I should not chuse to lett her go but to such a Friend as you, who I am sensible will put a good natured construction on innocence and inexperience."[45] The previous year some-thing untoward had happened that is not revealed in the letter. Mrs. Graeme guaranteed that her daughter "will make no such uneasy com-plaints as you was troubled with this time last year" in a "perplexing affair [that] is now quite at an end and ended more to my satisfaction by far than I could have hoped."

In a poem, written that same year, Elizabeth may have left a hint as to this "perplexing affair." In this poem, called "A Dream," she de-scribed in fantasy a young woman's awakening to the opposite sex. While Elizabeth slept, a nymph, "Friendship," came and led her to a bower where

> A lovely Youth scarce reaching Manhoods prime,
> Sat with a <u>Flute</u> to pass the loitering Time,
> The well known Features struck my pleasing View;
> My Favorite <u>Strephon</u> in his Form I knew.

When the nymph left her alone with Strephon, however, she knew mixed emotions.

> Confused I felt nor knew what Course to take,
> Yet found it hard my Strephon to forsake;
> I feard some Danger if I made delay,
> Tho my Heart pleaded for a longer Stay.[46]

The coming of dawn saved her further confusion; Strephon left "with the Shades of Night." To whom "Strephon" referred or the identity of the intermediary is not known. Perhaps this poem, with its obvious sexual tensions, refers in some way to the incident Mrs. Graeme mentioned in her letter to Mrs. Campbell the same year.

In Burlington, the young woman roamed the Campbells' gardens and orchard and admired their beautiful roses. Her hostess's friends invited her to tea at their homes, and she developed the same intimacy with Mrs. Campbell that Mrs. Graeme and Elizabeth's sisters already had. By June 14, Elizabeth was home, and her mother wrote her thanks to Mrs. Campbell: "Betsy is so delighted with your manner that she can talk of nothing else (but this is paying a complement to her Judgment). I am likewise much obliged to all the Ladies of Burlington and Bristol for the kind notice they were pleased to take of her."[47] Elizabeth, at fifteen, was learning in a pleasant non-didactic way how to entertain and be entertained. Later in life, she would return this and other visits by receiving Mrs. Campbell's granddaughter at Graeme Park, for this family friendship was broken only by Elizabeth's death.

When the Graemes were in Philadelphia, Mrs. Graeme, a charming, intelligent woman, often gathered her many friends around her. Benjamin Rush described his hostess as possessing "a masculine mind, with all those female charms and accomplishments which render a woman alike agreeable to both sexes."[48] Her daughters were present at these social occasions, and as they grew older they often presided at the carved mahogany tea table.[49]

Over the years, Elizabeth met other young people and established important friendships that lasted most of her life. Among these friends was Rebecca Moore, whom she met when she was twelve and her friend fourteen. Although Becky and Betsy were specially close, Elizabeth also made life-long friends of Rebecca's many sisters. The Moores and their large family owned a country estate in Chester County, called Moore-Hall, on a hill overlooking the Schuylkill River, and the girls exchanged visits frequently. They "both had a little Romantic turn as to the Objects of nature" and loved to stroll together at Graeme Park or Moore-Hall or to pass "dear delightful hours . . . in reading" together or exchanging their poetry.[50]

Elizabeth wrote Rebecca about their friendship in 1755 in a verse ostensibly about the Indian War.[51] The poem begins:

> To you my dear let me my thoughts impart
> And share the secret dictates of my Heart.

The two women would share their inner thoughts all their lives, until Elizabeth's insistent repetition of her marital problems became too burdensome for Rebecca Moore to bear, and she rejected her life-long friend. The poem is actually about the two women's friendship and only mentions the Indian wars in passing in the first of the three verses. It ends:

> Heaven grant no jarring Passions may divide
> My dearest <u>Sylvia</u> from her <u>Laura's</u> Side;
> So when we go the World may Join each name
> Nor Mention my <u>Miss Moore</u> without her <u>Graeme</u>.[52]

But Elizabeth's "jarring Passions" would divide these friends after the Revolution.

Elizabeth also formed a close friendship with Francis Hopkinson, who would become a signer of the Declaration of Independence, and with his siblings. He was the son of lawyer Thomas Hopkinson, a friend of Dr. Graeme. Hopkinson Sr. had arrived in Philadelphia around 1731 and very quickly had become active in the life of the city and province. Among the many offices he held were delegate to the Common Council of Philadelphia, judge of the vice-admiralty for the province, and member of the provincial council. He was also concerned about education and participated in the Library Company of Philadelphia, the American Philosophical Society, and the Academy of Philadelphia, which became the University of Pennsylvania. All of these learned organizations were interests of Dr. Graeme as well, and the two men interacted frequently at meetings. Thomas Hopkinson died in 1751, leaving a widow, four daughters, and two sons. His children, especially the son Francis, were close friends of

Elizabeth. One Hopkinson daughter, Elizabeth, married Rev. Jacob Duché and another, Mary, became the wife of Dr. John Morgan. Francis Hopkinson and his two brothers-in-law were graduates of the first class of the College of Philadelphia in 1757. Elizabeth's friendship with these young college students meant that she heard about their education and read the books they were studying. Eventually, she became as learned in literature as they, if not more so.

One place where the Graeme girls met other young people was at the dancing assembly of Philadelphia, which Dr. Graeme had joined by 1748. As his daughters grew older they, too, attended the functions, where they did the minuet, Virginia reels, and jigs, among other dances. The members included many men whose children would be close to the Graeme girls: Thomas Lawrence, Phineas Bond, Charles Willing, William Bingham, William Allen, Thomas Hopkinson, Andrew Elliot, David Franks, and many others. Charles Stedman, a member, would marry Elizabeth's sister Ann in 1749, having met him perhaps at one of these affairs. Richard Peters, Thomas Graeme's very close friend, was a member, and Elizabeth would go to Europe with him in the mid-1760s. The membership also included William Franklin, son of Benjamin, who would court her in the 1750s.[53]

Spinning frolics were often held in the country by the young people, who enjoyed any excuse for a party, and Elizabeth wrote the lyrics for several songs to be enjoyed on such occasions. The owner of flax would distribute portions of it to the young women of the neighborhood. They would spin and reel the flax at their own homes and then take the product to the flax owner's home on a designated evening. The owner, in thanks for their labor, would provide a dinner, and the young lads of the neighborhood, bringing a fiddler, would join them for a dance.[54] "Perhaps our Brisk partners may lead us thro' Life / And The Dance of the Night end in Husband and Wife," Elizabeth wrote in a rolicking song to be sung at such a frolic. Each verse ends with the two lines:

> The <u>Wheels</u> and the <u>Reels</u> go <u>Merrily Round</u>
> While <u>Health</u>, <u>Peace</u>, and <u>Virtue</u> among us are found.[55]

Parties were also held after the harvest, celebrating a bounteous growing season, and sometimes after sleighing excursions or fox hunts.

Men, young and old, enjoyed fox hunting as recreation, as well as a practical pursuit. During the summers, gentlemen rode out from Philadelphia to hunt at Graeme Park. Foxes were plentiful in the eighteenth century and often destroyed farmers' lambs and poultry. The General Assembly even passed a law offering a bounty of two shillings each for a full grown fox or one shilling for a whelp. There is no indication that women participated in these hunts, but they were hostesses at parties afterward. Hounds were not kept at Graeme Park during the ownership of Sir William, Dr. Graeme, or Elizabeth, but a neighbor and close friend, Dr. Archibald Mc-Clean, kept hounds and was said to have been "addicted to this sport."[56] Although not herself a participant, Elizabeth experienced this hunting culture all her life.

The biggest problem Elizabeth had during her "Sweet Period of vernal innocence and youth" was her poor health.[57] Although she avoided smallpox and the other severe illnesses that took colonial lives, early in life she started having trouble with gall or kidney stones. In her twenties, her parents sent her to England with family friend Richard Peters, who suffered from the same ailment, so that she could be treated by Dr. John Fothergill, a famous Quaker doctor, but he was unable to effect a permanent cure. In addition, she was often upset by fevers, headaches, and various intestinal discomforts. Spring was an especially troubling time for her, bringing on recurrent incapacitating fevers.

Elizabeth's physical problems were not unique; eighteenth-century Philadelphia women's letters frequently reported illnesses, their own or family members', almost as a matter of course to be expected. It was not surprising that Ann Graeme, her daughter, and their friends suffered from various ailments; Philadelphia was not a healthy place to live. There were many swampy areas where mosquitoes bred heavily, and houses, not equipped with screens, swarmed with insects of all kinds. Pests also bred in garbage thrown out on the streets to be eaten by pigs or to decompose. Although laws forbade this practice, they were not effectively enforced. Furthermore, the people knew little about public health measures that are commonplace today. The water table washed underneath the city, which was situated between two rivers. Houses were not equipped with safe sewerage disposal. Instead people used outhouses or necessaries, as they aptly called them. To avoid having to clean them, people dug them deep enough so that the ground water would wash away the filth. Unfortunately, wells also tapped into this ground water. It is no wonder that people suffered various fevers, chills, and upset stomachs after drinking such water.

In spite of her chronic ill health, however, Elizabeth Graeme's childhood and early adolescence were for the most part happy periods, the happiest in her lifetime. With a good mind, she learned quickly and enjoyed the intellectual challenges that the adults in her life gave her. Doting parents provided all the advantages that were available: an uncommonly large private library, access to stimulating social occasions, and a gracious, even elegant, home. Up until the time she was twenty, Elizabeth's life was free of major worries. It would be her relationships with men that would cause her unhappiness in the future.

2

Love, Politics, and Rejection

Elizabeth Graeme and William Franklin, the son of Benjamin Franklin, probably had known or known of each other almost all their lives. Philadelphia, although called a city, was not much bigger than a twenty-first-century small town. When Elizabeth was born, between 15,000 and 20,000 inhabitants lived there. Anyone who accomplished anything noteworthy, or was related to anyone who did, was known to everyone else. One man reminisced that in the 1750s "he not only knew every gentleman in town, but every gentleman's" servant and dog.[1] By Elizabeth's birth in 1737, Benjamin Franklin had become noteworthy, and by the time Elizabeth and William were beginning to think about spending their futures together, Franklin Sr. was wealthy, prominent, and controversial. Since William became his father's right-hand man, he, too, became well known and controversial, as well as a very eligible bachelor.

Benjamin had returned to Philadelphia in 1726 from the trip to England that Governor Keith had encouraged him to take, and within a few short years had established a family and a reputation for successful undertakings, public as well as private. Within three years, he had become the sole proprietor of his own print shop and publisher of the newspaper the *Pennsylvania Gazette*. William was born in either 1730 or 1731, of an unknown mother, possibly a servant girl who never has been identified. He lived with Benjamin and his wife, Deborah; Benjamin raised his son to be a gentleman.[2] Within about a year of William's birth, Benjamin became clerk to the General Assembly and began publishing the soon-to-be-famous *Poor Richard's Almanack*. In the year of Elizabeth's birth, Franklin was appointed deputy postmaster for the colonies. By 1750, he had created a number of worthwhile public services, such as a volunteer fire company, the first circulating library, and the American Philosophical Society and had invented useful items such as bifocal spectacles, the lightning rod, and the "Franklin stove."

In 1748, Benjamin Franklin was wealthy enough to retire from business. Retirement, he said, would give him the "leisure to read, study, make experiments, and converse at large with such ingenious and worthy men, as are pleased to honour me with their friendship or acquaintance." His future, however, did not develop as he had anticipated. Although he also said upon retirement that he "refused engaging further in public affairs,"[3] he became even more involved in politics and eventually extended his local reputation nationally and internationally. On each step up the ladder, William accompanied his father.

Even though Benjamin's public activities had served Philadelphia well, Thomas Graeme was not pleased with his political activities and looked with disfavor upon Elizabeth's liaison with his son. The problem was Benjamin's relationship with the proprietors. It was unfriendly and critical, even antagonistic. In fact, they had come to dislike each other intensely!

William Penn had died in 1718, and his title to Pennsylvania had passed to his three sons, John, Thomas, and Richard, by his second wife. John Penn died in 1746, leaving his share to his brother Thomas, who became the chief of the two remaining proprietors of Pennsylvania. William Penn had been a Quaker, and the colony had been settled originally as a religious refuge for Quakers, who were persecuted in England. But Thomas Penn had become an Anglican and had little patience for the Quakers in Pennsylvania.

By 1750, there was a running battle between Thomas Penn and the Quakers in the Assembly. The major political party in Pennsylvania was called the Quaker Party, although its members were not all of that religious persuasion. Benjamin Franklin had become one of its leaders, opposing the proprietors' party consisting of the governor and his supporters in Pennsylvania, including Thomas Graeme. The two biggest divisions of opinion between the proprietors and the Assembly concerned the governor's in-

structions and the colony's taxes. Thomas Penn was adamant that his instructions had the force of law in the colony, whereas the legislature still
argued that the people's elected representatives must approve the laws, especially those concerning money. Ever since Governor Keith had lost his
job because he had not followed his instructions, each side had become
more fixed in its opinion. The argument over taxes concerned the proprietors' estates in Pennsylvania. The Assembly believed that these lands should
be taxed to provide defense just as were the lands of the colonists. The
proprietors, however, refused to allow their governors to approve any tax
law that did not specifically exempt the Penns' estates.

A third dispute cut across party lines. The Quakers were ostensibly
opposed to violence in any form, not only in offensive warfare but also in
any defensive measures that involved the use of weapons of war. Thus, the
Quaker members of the Assembly were reluctant to approve any measures
to prepare the colony to resist invasion by either the French or their allies
among the Indians. Although Franklin and other non-Quakers joined
Quaker opposition to the proprietary, they saw the need to arm the
province in time of danger and, therefore, proposed various schemes to
circumvent this Quaker "peace testimony" without upsetting Quaker con-
sciences.

Because Benjamin Franklin led the party opposed to the proprietaries, Thomas Graeme, a friend of the Penns, disliked him. When Thomas
Penn lived in Philadelphia from 1732 to 1741, he and Dr. Graeme had
developed a close personal relationship. After Penn returned to England,
the two men corresponded frequently, and Graeme became one of Penn's
advisors about provincial matters. Penn's brother John, his sister, Margaret,
and her husband, Thomas Freame, were also in Pennsylvania for a time
during this period, and Dr. Graeme cared for Margaret when she was ill.[4]
The youngster Elizabeth associated with the Penn family when they visited
her parents' homes either in Philadelphia or at Graeme Park. Later, when
John Penn, the son of Richard Penn, was in Pennsylvania, he, too, became
friendly with the Graemes, and Elizabeth became one of his favorites. In
September 1755, when Elizabeth was visiting the Campbells in Burlington,
John Penn made a special point to stop by and see her. Ann Graeme, in
pique, wrote to her daughter, "Mr Pen did you a greater Favour than he
did us, for he was never near this House."[5] Franklin, meanwhile, had become the pen of the Assembly, as he put it, no pun intended, and by the

late 1740s, an anathema to the proprietors. Thomas Penn described him to Richard Peters as "of a very uneasy spirit," one whom he would "be very glad if he inhabited any other Country."[6]

Franklin's son, however, was a handsome, amusing, intelligent, well-educated young man, a good catch for any young woman. The first extant records of his and Elizabeth's friendship date from 1752, when he was twenty-one and she only fifteen, although he must have been acquainted with the Graeme children for many years. Late that year, they were in partnership to buy lottery tickets. He teasingly begged her not to notify him that their tickets were worthless. She replied in verse that Fortune was fittingly portrayed as blind and that their tickets were

> . . . like the new fell Snow,
> Or as the Paper Clear;
> Before the Pen that Scribbling Foe;
> Makes Characters appear.[7]

The older man became a friend to whom the young woman could relate confidences and exchange ideas. "With Freedom," she wrote, they their

> Thoughts exprest,
> And talkd of Powers above,
> Of what was Right, and just, and true.[8]

Her conversation must have been very precocious to have interested such an attractive and eligible young man so much her senior. Or perhaps he was interested in her family's wealth and social position to counterbalance his own humble beginnings.[9]

At the same time as Elizabeth was flirting with William, she was also strengthening her bonds to her young women friends. They visited each other's homes, attended frolics together, read books to one another, and wrote each other poetry. She enjoyed folk music, especially the Scottish tunes popular then, and throughout her life occasionally wrote lyrics to accompany them. To Sally Denormandie, Elizabeth at sixteen wrote lyrics to be sung to the tune of "Yo Gentle Gales." In this poem, she wrote of long walks with Sally through "shady Bowers" with a small dog the girls called "Cupid" to protect them. Already she had developed a love of nature that would persist all her life.

The Town in all its sprightly Charms
Was not ordained for Me
More lasting Happiness is found, Beneath a spreading Tree.

She saw nature as teacher, too.

Instruction glides in every Brook
To Sentimental Minds;
Each Shrub conveys some virtuous Truth
And earthly Bliss refines.[10]

At fifteen, Elizabeth stated the ideal life that she wished to live, one of study and contemplation, tempered with companionship, "industry," and, if her income permitted, good works.

Grant me some little Calm Retreat
My Friends all Seated near; . . .
My Book and Pen each peaceful Day
The Moments should employ
And bright Industry intervene
Lest constant Study Cloy.[11]

The poem includes no mention of any romantic attachment in her future; perhaps it was written to please admiring adults rather than to express her inner thoughts because we know from other poems that she had developed the usual teenager's interest in the opposite sex. Her joking, flirtatious relationship with Franklin was evidence of this. Although this poem is certainly pretentious and imitative of her readings, nevertheless, it declares goals she would seek all her life. She read and wrote constantly and always tried to surround herself with friends who would provide intellectual stimulation. These are also goals she learned from her mother, except that her mother would have delegated a large role to religion, as Elizabeth herself would do in adulthood.

Poetry occupied a very important place in eighteenth-century Philadelphia culture. It was written by both men and women, who studied the published poets, memorized their lines, quoted them to each other, wrote imitations of or parodies on them, and used the best of them as the bases of metaphors. A favorite line from a popular poet communicated

whole concepts and negated the need for further explanations. It was believed that poetry encouraged the development of virtue and alleviated
despair. "There is a certain Elevation of Soul," Elizabeth believed,

> . . . a noble turn of virtue that raises the hero from the plain honest
> man, to which Verse can only raise us, His Bold *Metaphors* And
> Sounding members peculiar To the Poets, Rouse up all our Sleep-
> ing faculties And alarm all the powers of the Soul like Vergils Exe-
> lent Trumpet.[12]

Elizabeth and her friends of both sexes exchanged and read their
poetry out loud to one another This was not only recreational but informa-
tive as well, a form of self-improvement. They exchanged ideas and corrected one another's errors. They flirted, they joked, and they amused one
another in rhyme. In the summer of 1753, while Elizabeth was having a
house party for some of her women friends at Graeme Park, William wrote
a poem about how much the young men in the city missed the young
women. He addressed his thoughts to "Ye Ladies! who are now retired /
To Groves, and purling Springs" and related how bored their swains were
in the city. They tried their hand at piquet, a two-handed card game, but
they did not know how to bet and lost money, all the fault, he wrote, of
the absent maids. He toasted winter above all other seasons because

> it brings our Loves;
> 'tis to thy chilling Frosts and Snow
> That we our happiest Moments know.[13]

By the end of October 1753, the men also had been invited to visit
Graeme Park in a group that included William Franklin and Rebecca
Moore. One evening they had a debate, which was recapitulated in a poem
by Elizabeth. The subject matter of this poem, if not the poetry itself, is
remarkable. It is difficult to imagine teenagers today seriously debating and
writing poetry about whether it is better to sorrow for other people's troubles or to pass through life unmoved. The question was argued in a dialogue between Damon (William Franklin) and Alexis (identity unknown),
in which Alexis expressed his distress that his own economic status had left
him unable to help the impoverished family of an old man who recently

had died. Damon asked why Alexis sustained "The weight Severe of others Pain?" and said that

> The truly Wise and happy Man
> Thats he who is not discomposed;
> By others Pleasurs or their woes.

Alexis responded that such a man is "degenerate."

> His Life at best a waking Dream
> In short at Most a mere Machine. . . .
> Cooly they speak they never feel,
> Their Souls are harden'd o'er with Steel!

But, Damon answered, all of life has more pain than joy, and the only way to survive is to adopt "Indifference." As an example, Damon pointed to Alexis's feelings for Sylvia (Rebecca Moore). If she should scorn his suit, Alexis would deplore his wretched fate "And Seek some foreign distant Shore." In contrast, their friend Strephon, when rejected by a fair one, is not distressed but simply finds another. Strephon never had known the pleasures of true love, Alexis responded.

> When Sylvia comes with pleasing Smiles,
> And every Anxious Care beguiles;
> No Sorrow prays upon my mind;
> But flys like Chaff dispent by wind.

Damon was convinced by this argument, and the two friends declared mutual allegiance.[14] The subtitle of this poem is "whether the feeling or insensible Minds were happiest thro' Life." The words "feeling" and "sensibility" appear often in Elizabeth's writing. She used the word "sensibility" as it was used throughout the eighteenth century to mean readiness to respond "to emotional stimuli, particularly to the appeal of pathos."[15] It was believed to be a very desirable attribute for both sexes but especially for women.

During this period, William was studying law, serving as clerk to the Assembly, and helping his father's rise. In 1750, his father had been appointed justice of the peace but finding that he did not have the requisite knowledge to serve properly, he had resigned. Determined that his son would not be so limited, he had arranged for a prominent attorney, Joseph Galloway, to teach William the law and had had a friend in England enroll William at one of the Inns of Court.[16] Meanwhile, William had become his father's closest friend and companion. In 1751, the son helped his father with the famous kite experiment, in 1754, he accompanied Benjamin to the Albany conference, and in 1755, he helped his father procure provisions for the ill-fated expedition led by General Braddock.

After Braddock's disastrous defeat by the Indians, Pennsylvanians were frightened by the colony's inadequate defenses. Although war did not break out officially between England and France until 1756, the French in Canada had close alliances with many of the Indians whom they encouraged to go on the warpath against the English frontier people. Pennsylvanians in the western part of the colony were panic stricken. Yet a standstill existed in Philadelphia. The Assembly refused to appropriate defense money to be raised by taxes unless those taxes were paid by all land owners with no exception, while the proprietors would not permit their estates to be taxed. The Assembly proposed a bill to raise £50,000 by taxing all lands and estates, including the proprietaries'. Governor Robert Morris, however, obeyed his instructions not to sign such a law. The impasse was broken by a ploy suggested by Thomas Graeme. He wrote to Richard Peters, member of the governor's council and close friend of both the Graemes and the Penns, suggesting that Peters advise the governor to give the colony "in behalf of the proprietor a sum by way of free gift perhaps double to what such a Tax would amount to, for the Kings service." "It would, I think," continued Graeme, "take the Thorn out of your foot and place it where I should with pleasure see it. In theirs. It would look well at home [in England] and leave their friends there without an excuse."[17] The Penns adopted this suggestion and gave £5,000 toward the colony's defense. The Assembly, in return, revised the appropriations bill, upping the amount to £60,000 and including the required exemption of the proprietors' estates from taxation. At the same time, Benjamin Franklin proposed and carried through the Assembly a bill establishing a volunteer militia with provisions allowing pacifist Quakers to avoid participation.

That September, Pennsylvanians finally had something to celebrate when Sir William Johnson and a mixed army of colonials and Indians defeated a French and Indian army at the Battle of Lake George on September 8. To mark the occasion, Philadelphians lit the city with bonfires and illuminations for two evenings on September 17 and 18. The following week, the British army officers in Philadelphia held "a grand Entertainment and a Ball for the Ladies and Gentlemen of the City, at the State House; where everything was conducted with the greatest decorum and elegance," according to the *Pennsylvania Gazette*.[18] Ann Graeme described it to Eliza-beth, who had been sent off to the Campbells at Burlington to make room for Sir John St. Clair, Quarter Master General of the British forces, and his party who were visiting Philadelphia and lodged at Graeme Park. The ball "was a sumptuous one," wrote Mrs. Graeme, "the supper dressed by the general's French cook, and his [silver]plate set out on the sideboard, besides a great deal of plate borrowed from the governor, Mr. Allen, and others. Notwithstanding all these preparations," she reported that the officers were not very popular with the ladies, and a "great number," including the Graemes, declined the invitation.[19] As it turned out, the celebration was premature; the victory at Lake George did not stop the Indian depredations in Pennsylvania.

At the end of the year, William joined two friends in a published attack on the proprietors, which did nothing to improve his position with the Graemes. He helped write an answer to a pamphlet by the Rev. Wil-liam Smith, provost of the Academy, proprietary supporter, and close friend of Dr. Graeme, in which Smith had criticized Franklin's militia bill. Smith and Benjamin Franklin originally had been friends, with Franklin helping Smith secure his position. The Academy had been founded in 1749 by a number of colonists at the suggestion of Benjamin Franklin, who had be-come president of the trustees; it had opened in January 1751. Smith had come to New York from Scotland that year and remained there as a tutor until 1753, when he had published a guide for the establishment of a col-lege. He had sent copies to Richard Peters and Benjamin Franklin, who promptly had invited Smith to Philadelphia where he talked with the trust-ees of the Academy about a prospective job. It is likely that Peters, at that time, had introduced Smith to Thomas Graeme and possibly the whole Graeme family. Smith had returned to England late that fall where he se-cured ordination in the Anglican Church and developed the ambition to become the first American Bishop. The next spring he returned to Phila-delphia and became Provost of the College and Academy of Philadelphia and Professor of Natural Philosophy. Smith was only twenty-seven, but people with education and creative ideas were especially valued in colonial society. Franklin had envisaged the Academy as being non-sectarian, but

Smith aimed to emphasize its connection to the Anglican Church, and the two men grew apart. By 1755, William Smith had switched his loyalty from Franklin to the proprietors. That year, he wrote a pamphlet attacking the Quaker management of Pennsylvania government in which he ridiculed Franklin's militia bill. William and his friends Joseph Galloway and George Bryan wrote a response, attacking the proprietors viciously, calling them traitors for trying to deprive the colonists of their legislative rights. Although the pamphlet was signed with a pseudonym, the identity of the authors was well known.[20] This must have been discussed in detail in the Graeme family circle. Richard Peters was a frequent visitor at the Graemes' home. He and William Smith dined at the Graemes' every Sunday that the doctor and his family were in Philadelphia. Both men would have spoken harshly of Wiiliam for his position. Elizabeth, hearing these diatribes against her suitor and his father coming from her own father and the family's closet friends, must have been torn emotionally.

Throughout the political jockeying, the Indians continued their attacks on outlying homesteads, killing the settlers and destroying their property. Refugees were streaming into the neighboring towns and demanding that the government provide them with protection. Even Philadelphians were becoming concerned because the frontier in the 1750s was not far away. In November, an Indian party ravaged a Moravian mission at Gnadenhuetten, only seventy-five miles from Philadelphia.

Governor Robert Morris, forced to act, sent the two Franklins with two other men to lead an expedition whose charge was to build a line of forts and enlist troops to protect the frontier. They left December 18 with fifty provincial cavalrymen and returned February 4. This was a very dangerous mission. Franklin, in his autobiography, described seeing evidence that Indians had watched them build a stockade at Gnadenhuetten, and he speculated that they were saved from attack only by their numbers.

Back in Philadelphia, Elizabeth waited for news of the expedition. There is no record that William wrote to her during his journey, although it is possible that he did since his father found opportunities to communicate with Deborah. In any case, the Indian attacks on individual homesteads were described in the *Pennsylvania Gazette* in gruesome detail.[21] The progress of the Franklin party must have been reported back to Philadelphia and known to the Graemes. Delays in communications, however, would have left periods when the expedition's welfare was not known, periods of great concern for loved ones in the city. First the young man to whom Elizabeth was beginning to give her affections had helped write a scurrilous pamphlet against the Penns, close friends of her parents, and then he had undertaken with his father a very dangerous expedition into Indian territory where he might be killed at any moment.

By May of 1756, Mrs. Graeme was writing to Mary Campbell that she was concerned about Elizabeth. "I think the publick distress of this Winter has given her too thoughtfull a turn." Mrs. Graeme had urged her daughter to spend a few weeks with the Campbells because their conversation always had a salutary effect upon Elizabeth. But she had resisted the suggestion, perhaps wanting to remain in Philadelphia for news, and Mrs. Graeme asked Mrs. Campbell to urge an invitation upon the young woman, relying upon their friendship to persuade her.[22] Mrs. Graeme also may have wanted her daughter out of town and away from William when he returned.

Parental opposition to the contrary, by 1757, William was pressing his suit with ardor. In a February letter, he complained that a visiting clergyman at her home was keeping them apart. "The clergy have in all Ages done more Mischief than Service in the World," he wrote. There was only one service he wished from a clergyman, and he asked her to "Guess what that <u>one Thing</u> is."[23]

The clergyman whose presence was keeping them apart may have been the Rev. William Smith, which would have made the enforced separation even more difficult for William to bear. Smith had written a poem for Elizabeth's birthday on February 14[24] and would have delivered it in person. The clergyman was more acceptable to Thomas Graeme as a suitor for his daughter's hand than was the son of Benjamin Franklin, enemy of the Penns, although it is more likely that Smith was just a family friend. His interests lay elsewhere. The next year, he married Rebecca Moore.

William's letter sent Elizabeth the words to a song, in which he related that although he had been attracted earlier to other pretty faces, he had always been able to keep his heart his own. But then he had met Elizabeth, and now his heart was no longer his.

> But now O *Love* ! I own thy Reign
> I find Thee in my Heart;
> I know yet bear the pleasing Pain
> For *Laura* threw the Dart
> *Laura's* too powerful Charms have shown,
> My Heart is now no more my own.[25]

But William was leaving soon with his father for England to try to reach an accommodation with Thomas Penn. In October 1756, Benjamin, immensely popular after his courageous frontier expedition, easily won reelection to the Assembly.[26] British General Sir John Loudoun, Commander in Chief of the British forces, was pressing the Pennsylvania government for a donation to the defense of the empire. The House agreed to contribute but still called for the taxation of all landowners, including the Penns. Pennsylvania's new governor, William Denny, who had replaced Morris in August, faithful to his instructions, rejected the bill. The legislators decided to send Benjamin Franklin and Isaac Norris to England to argue with the proprietor personally. Norris begged off, citing his advanced age, but Benjamin Franklin accepted the commission and planned to take William with him as his private secretary and aide. He also wanted to enter William in the Middle Temple at the Inns of Court. This meant that the two lovers were to be separated for a long time. Apparently no one suggested that they marry and Elizabeth go with William and Benjamin.

Elizabeth answered William's declaration in a song of her own, indicating some misgivings about the affair, which was being threatened by their differences in politics. In her song, she followed William's form, first declaring that she, too, had appreciated but rejected the charms of the opposite sex.

> I laugh'd at <u>Strephon's</u> lively air;
> Was pleased with <u>Colin's</u> Wit, . . .
> Nor of them thought a single Hour
> But made a jest of <u>Cupid's</u> Power.

Young Damon [William] had come first in friendship and spoken not of love, so that they could freely express their thoughts to one another. When people warned her where the relationship might go, she had scorned their fears and denied that "Love was at th' End." She concluded the poem with rejection of his suit.

> There's various Reasons to be seen,
> Which make it wrong to join
> Tho' Warm Affecion Steps between
> I will the Youth Resign;
> Oh may he ever happy be!
> In loving, or forgetting me.

She left William a ray of hope when she wished that he not "long in distant Climes remain / But meet with <u>Laura</u> once again."[27]

William, nevertheless, pressed his suit and wanted to marry Elizabeth before he left, but the Graemes persuaded the young couple to wait until he returned, obviously hoping the affair would blow over during his absence. He feared the same possibility as much as they welcomed it and urged marriage without delay believing that "once united" nothing would be able to separate them. He wanted them to marry "privately" before he left, but the Graemes refused this option as "improper." The strongest opponent of the match was Thomas Graeme. Apparently Ann Graeme was at least partially won over by her daughter's suitor because William referred later to "repeated Acts of Civility" to him from Mrs. Graeme, "that best of women." William was very persuasive and overcame Elizabeth's reservations to his suit. The main difference between them was the political one, but William assured her that he would be working for the reconciliation with the proprietaries that would smooth relations between their parents and thus eliminate her concerns. Finally, she told him that he need not fear any change in her feelings; her regard for him "could by neither Time or Absence be set aside or diminished."[28]

Benjamin and William left Philadelphia on April 4, 1757, for New York thinking that they would embark for England shortly. War between England and France had spread to Canada, however, and Lord Loudoun, who was preparing to attack the French at Louisbourg, controlled all the packets for England. Known for his indecision, Loudoun ordered the Franklins' packet to wait for dispatches he was going to write but which never materialized, although he kept promising them from day to day. Benjamin and William fretted in the interval and tried to keep amused, but they would not reach London until July 26.

William wrote letters to Elizabeth, although none of them was satisfactory. None showed the depth of feeling he had disclosed when courting her; none would satify the yearnings of the sensitive romantic young woman back in Philadelphia who, expecting from every post a letter from her intended, was often disappointed. Nine of William's letters written while he waited to leave and two from England survive, and there is no indication that any more were written. Unfortunately none of her letters to him exists. We have to reconstruct the contents of her letters from the responses in his.

In his first letter, written from Elizabethtown, en route to New

York, William described the weather when they left as threatening but clearing by noon allowing the sun to shine. He compared this to their love, which

> has likewise been and is still overcast, threat'ning a wrecking storm; who knows but kind Heav'n may graciously permit a charming Sun to scatter these Clouds of Difficulties which hang over us, and afford a Noon and Evening of Life calm and serene. I trust our Conduct will be such as to deserve this mark of Divine Goodness.[29]

His next letter was from New York, in ill humor because Loudoun probably would not let the packet sail for eight to ten days. As it turned out, this was a greatly understated prediction, for the interval would be closer to two months. He had received one letter from her and begged her to write by every post. He, however, had delayed writing to her until it was almost too late for the post because he had been the previous evening "in a large mix'd Company of both Sexes." He hoped his guilty pangs would cure him of "the Crime of Procrastination; and . . . prove a Warning to my Betsy."[30] Certainly this was not a consoling thought for the young woman back in Philadelphia, that her suitor had gone to a party of "mix'd Company of both Sexes," rather than write her a letter. And, furthermore, she might expect more of the same in the future, although he begged her to write to him by every post.

If he thought that Elizabeth was going to continue to write to someone who did not write her, he was wrong. Two weeks later, he wrote her a short letter complaining that she had not written him by two posts and three gentlemen, even though he had missed only one opportunity of writing. Nevertheless, once again he had waited until the last moment to jot a hurried note, confessing that the post stood at his elbow impatiently awaiting his letter. There was no real news in his short note.[31]

The romance was in trouble already, even though he was only three weeks away from Philadelphia on a trip that would take months, if not years. Elizabeth did not feel his attentions were dedicated enough for someone who wanted to marry her. She sent him a present of a silk watch chain woven by herself, but her letter accused an "evil Genius" of guiding his pen to distress her. His response teasingly commented that "having bound [his] Soul to [her] with indissolveable Ties" she now wanted to bind all of his "Moveables." Again this was a very short letter. No news of his activities. Very little of the romantic prose that a person in love would expect from an intended. An acquaintance was waiting to take him out, he excused himself, so he could not write further.[32] Even this brief note reached its destination later than expected. William's servant forgot to take it to the post rider, and it had to be forwarded three days later. Meanwhile he had received another letter from Elizabeth containing a declaration William called "candid and ingenuous." His next letter did not explain; he only says that he cannot find words to acknowledge it. "Actions alone can evince the Reality of my Sentiments," he wrote, "and they shall not be wanting." This was a somewhat longer letter, reporting two social occasions he had attended with friends of Elizabeth, including Margaret Abercrombie, a close acquaintance of the Graemes, and Mrs. Campbell, but he included no loving remarks.[33] It could have been written to any friend.

Elizabeth's next communication from William was a four sentence note acknowledging the receipt of two letters from her and saying that he had just returned from an excursion. The post was about to leave, he had to close, she could "imagine the rest."[34] The excursion was explained by the next post, a few days later. Benjamin had organized a trip into the Jerseys to Newark, to Passayak Falls, and to some copper mines. William's mother and sister and the Willing sisters had joined them from Philadelphia, but Elizabeth had declined to accompany them. William chided her and wrote that he could "scarce forgive [her] not coming." He was only two days journey from her, and yet he could not leave for fear the packet would depart without him. She should have come to see him "when so convenient Opportunity offer'd," William scolded. Of course, he did not admit that he could have gone to Philadelphia rather than taking the trip. Elizabeth had complained in her letter about the infrequency and brevity of his communications and asked him if his feelings for her had changed. William begged her to consider the number of letters he had to write and his responsibilities. She should not be hurt when she had to write twice as many letters as he; she had "more than a double Portion of Leisure."[35]

Two more of his letters from New York remain, each announcing his almost immediate departure for England, which actually did not occur until June 5.[36] Not one of the nine letters William wrote after he left Philadelphia before he sailed for England could be classed as a love letter; none had the warmth of expression that a fiancé would expect. Whether his feelings were cooling, as Betsy accused, or whether his father's demands really left him no time, as he claimed, or whether he feared the opening and publication of his letters is not known and is immaterial. The effect on Elizabeth and their romance was the same.

He was at sea twenty-seven days, during which he had plenty of opportunity to write letters that could have been posted to his anxious friend upon his arrival. Instead he waited until they had landed and were about to leave for London and then jotted a hasty note, pleading that he had "not Leisure to give [her] any of the Particulars of [the] Voyages," and asking her to let "his great Hurry" be his excuse for brevity.[37]

It would be another five months before William would write Elizabeth, and this letter would be the final blow. He had not written sooner because of the distraction of "the infinite Variety of new Objects," the "most curious" things to see, "frequent Engagements amongst Politicians, Philosophers, and Men of Business," and "publick Diversions and Entertainments of this bewitching Country." He was writing at 2:00 A.M. since there was no other time available. He then described briefly some of the places he had visited, each time wishing she had been there to enjoy the sights with him. If he had stopped then, he might have made amends for his long silence.

Instead he continued with a discussion of politics after first saying he would not discuss them because he knew she had "no great Relish" for the subject. He spoke of "the Obstinacy and Wickedness of the Proprietors" making his father's job difficult and reported the proprietors "repeatedly publishing scandalous and malicious Falshoods against the Assembly and People of Pennsylvania." The proprietors had assumed that Benjamin could not respond because he "was obliged to a friendly Negotiation with them." This, however, had not silenced William because he was not involved in any way in the negotiations. He told her what she already knew, that he had published a letter in a London newspaper, *The Citizen or General Advertiser*, blaming the proprietors for problems between them and the Assembly. Since this letter had been reprinted in the *Pennsylvania Gazette* in Philadelphia on December 8, 1757, the day before he wrote, Elizabeth already had read it by the time William's letter reached her. Showing his disregard not only for her often-expressed disinclination to discuss the political controversy but also for her loyalty to her father's opinions and for her family's friendship with the Penns, he asked her to let him know "a few of the Pros and Cons" that she might hear of Philadelphia's reaction to his publication. He concluded by sending her a present of "one of the newest fashion'd Muffs and Tippets worn by the gayest Ladies of Quality at this End of the Town."[38]

When this letter reached Elizabeth, she was furious. On May 7, 1758, she answered, strongly venting her frustrations and hurt feelings. William would not receive her letter until October 24, after his return from a long jaunt through the English countryside with his father. During this period, he had not written her at all, a ten-month gap, and even then he did not answer Elizabeth directly. Instead he wrote to Mrs. Abercrombie, apparently expecting her to relay his message to Elizabeth.

Her letter does not remain, but we can partially reconstruct it from quotations in his.[39] After berating him for writing so infrequently, she accused him of "Want of Generosity in not having frankly told her that [his] own Levity of Temper, or [his] father's Schemes, or [his] Attachment to a Party, prevented [his] perservering in the tender Passion that [he] had professed." Her injured pride showed in her declaration that she was "not of that humble nay abject Temper which she must be, could she look upon [him] as the Person that was to share her Pains and Pleasures during her future Life." She called him "'in every Point' a Strong Party-Man," a very adverse accusation in those days. Because "Neither the Judgment or Morals of a Person can be pure when he is that in full Extent of the Word," she had concluded that "it would be Folly, nay Madness, to think of running all Risques with [him]." As to his presents of the muff and tippet, they were mere "gawdy GeeGaw."

William's responses to these accusations assumed that Elizabeth had meant in her letter to call off their engagement, and he asked why she could not have done it civilly, without rancor. He completely overlooked the frustrations of a proud woman who believed herself to have been treated with indifference, if not with contempt. He acknowledged his neglect of writing but said he "was ever a bad Correspondent" and wrote that in his letter of December 9, he had explained this fault. The whole tenor of that letter, he claimed, demonstrated that his "Affection was in no wise abated." Her affection for him must be lessened, or she would not have written him in such a fashion. Although they were not formally engaged to each other, he had considered himself engaged and "no Consideration on Earth should have induc'd [him] to think of marrying another."

As to her accusations of his political party affiliation, it had been his constant wish to reconcile public differences. He "look'd upon them as the Bane of his future Happiness as well as that of [his] country" and even his article in the *Citizen,* "which seems to have given her so much Displeasure, was partly wrote with that View." He had hoped that when the "little, dirty Aspersions" of the proprietors were "answered and exposed" they would be more inclined to "listen to Proposals for a friendly Adjustment of the Matters in Dispute." Elizabeth may have asked herself whether it was a good idea to insult an adversary in order to persuade him to negotiate differences. William had decided in recent months, however, that there was not "the least Prospect" that the difficulties between the proprietors and the Assembly could be resolved. Because of this, before he had received Miss Graeme's letter, William had planned to write her "of this disagreeable Situation of Affairs" and to "persuade her to forget the Man who in all Probability could never have it in his Power to be so happy as to contribute to her Happiness." Such a declaration was no longer necessary; he, now, had "to learn Forgetfulness." He concluded by explaining his gift of the muff and tippet. Since she had sent him the watch chain, he wanted to make her a present in return. He had chosen those particular items because she often had likened him to Tom Jones and expressed her delight "with the Story of Sophia's Muff mentioned in that Novel." He had hoped that in the same manner his gift would "tend to raise or keep alive some soft Emotions in [his] Favour."

Although what remains of this letter is quite clear, Elizabeth did not believe their relationship was ended. His letter said that he believed she had called off their engagement and that he agreed with her decision. Yet, apparently she did not believe the commitment was ended until she received word in 1762 that he had married in England Elizabeth Downes, the daughter of a wealthy Barbados planter.[40] In several places in her commonplace books, Elizabeth Graeme mentioned that 1762 was the year her engagement to William ended.

William's letter reached Margaret Abercrombie on April 4, 1759, and she immediately alerted Ann Graeme. Margaret was unable to leave her house but urged Mrs. Graeme to come to her. Meanwhile, she wrote that she would keep the contents of the letter secret.[41] We know Elizabeth received the letter because written on it in her handwriting is a comment about its contents,[42] but we do not know when she read it. What happened in the affair of Elizabeth and William for the next two and a half years is not known. The next communications about it date from December 1762.

Benjamin Franklin left London three weeks before his son's marriage, arriving in Philadelphia November 1, 1762. If William had not alerted his friends in America to his approaching marriage, his father did so when he arrived. At that point, Philadelphia learned that William Franklin had married Elizabeth Downes, rather than Elizabeth Graeme.

Reading between the lines of two existing letters written to Elizabeth at this time, one by her mother and one by her father, it appears that when Elizabeth heard of William's nuptials she wrote a long letter, now lost, stating her grievances and delivered it to the Franklin home, probably to be transmitted to William. In it, Ann Graeme reported that her daughter had pictured her "Scituation in a most Lively, just, and proper manner."[43] Deborah Franklin was very fond of Elizabeth, referring to her as "my Miss Grayham," and Benjamin, too, had expressed fondness for her.[44] The Franklins, therefore, attempted to avoid any unpleasantness and tried to smooth matters over. He played his famous glass harmonica for her as she in great "perturbation of mind"[45] tried to listen and exchange social amenities. Elizabeth left town shortly after this encounter and paid a long visit to the Campbells in Burlington.

Mrs. Graeme wrote to her daughter on December 3 reporting that she, too, had made a short call on the Franklins, prompted by Benjamin's recent return from England. She had been firmly determined not to be led into any discussion of their children's broken relationship, and the Franklins apparently had felt the same way.[46] While Benjamin had played a tune on the glass harmonica, Ann Graeme had thought of her daughter's distress during the similar performance.

Elizabeth had given her parents a copy of the letter she had written, and her father read it "with tears running down his Cheeks in streams" and then thanked God that his daughter had "escaped" William. In early January, he wrote Elizabeth, still at the Campbells', trying to console her. When her reason returned, he assured her, she would recognize "the Insidious paths of a Deceiver in every Step taken since that person left this place," and she would "be thankfull to that good Providence, that would not admit so much truth and Innocence, to be allayd [allied] to so deep deceit & light Vanity."[47]

In his communication, Dr. Graeme referred to letters sent Elizabeth from Philadelphia, particularly one sent her "from an extraordinary Quarter," from "a Master in the knowledge of human Nature," which "breath[ed] all the integrity that should accompany Sincerity and truth, and with all a . . . Veneration for [her] which [could] not be well feigned,"

Graeme judged. It is possible that this was a letter from Benjamin Franklin. Many years later Elizabeth remembered that he had written her "some of the kindest and fondest letters" when he had wanted her to become "a member of his family."[48] Benjamin must have been very cordial in his communications because Elizabeth continued that "had vanity taken place, and [she] had had a mind to have Shewn [the letters]; [they] would have been circulated thro all the anecdote writers in Europe and america under the article traits of Dr. Fns Domestic Character." This is all we know about Franklin's letters to her; they could have been sent before, during, or after the Franklins' English visit. Certainly, one could have been drafted to try to soothe Elizabeth's hurt after William's marriage to someone else.[49]

It is difficult to understand the bitterness of Elizabeth's and her parents' reaction to William's marriage. How can one explain Elizabeth's non-acceptance of the obvious? This was three and a half years after Mrs. Abercrombie had received the letter from William that very clearly broke his engagement to Elizabeth. No existing document helps us untangle this strange situation. There is something missing, however, from what remains of William's letter; it does not have a concluding page or signature, and no further communications between the couple still exist. Did William conclude his letter with some hope that their relationship could be reconstituted, and did Elizabeth write him agreeing? Or did she apologize for her stinging letter? Or did Mrs. Abercrombie refrain from showing William's letter to her until 1762 but just summarize it, softening the message and misleading her as to its true tenor? Surely Mrs. Abercrombie must have shown it to Mrs. Graeme, who must have discussed its contents with her daughter, even if the actual letter was not shown to her.

Although we cannot understand why Elizabeth did not know that her engagement to William was ended, perhaps we can understand her anger. For whatever reason, Elizabeth had spent five of her most eligible years waiting for a man who had been the persistent pursuer, who had won her affections in spite of her own misgivings. Now he had found someone else. She was twenty-five years old, and there were no other prospects in the wings. Yet society told her she must marry and have children if her life was to have meaning. There were no other options offered young women.

While she had waited for William, her childhood friends had been pairing off and beginning families. During the summer of 1758, Rebecca Moore had put her girlhood behind her and married William Smith. Although her friendship with Elizabeth continued for many years, never again was it the same as it had been when they were both teenagers. Very soon, Rebecca was tied down with motherhood, an experience her friend would never have. Her first child, a son, was born the following summer. A second followed in November 1760 and a third, a daughter this time, in July 1762. At this child's christening, Elizabeth was a sponsor, and the child received the name Williamina Elizabeth after her grandmother and her mother's dearest friend. Before the second child was born, Jacob Duché and Francis Hopkinson's sister Elizabeth had married, and John Morgan was courting Mary Hopkinson whom he would marry in 1765. One by one Elizabeth's friends were finding life companions while she remained single in a culture that defined a woman's role in terms of marriage and maternity. She recovered quickly from her perceived rejection this time, but later in her life when separated from her husband, she could not recognize the finality of her broken marriage. For the fifteen years before her death, she prolonged her own unhappiness and alienated friends who tired of hearing about the subject.

Back in Philadelphia from the Campbells' by mid-January 1763, Elizabeth must have been recovered somewhat from her shock because she attended many social functions, something one would not expect of a woman who was brokenhearted or embarrassed over her rejection. She reported that she had been "a good deal Engag'd in the Customary invitations of the Season."[50]

Although there is no indication in remaining documents that Elizabeth Graeme and William Franklin ever saw each other again, it is likely that they did. Before William left England to return to America, he acquired not only a bride but also an appointment as royal governor of New Jersey. William and his wife arrived in Philadelphia in mid-February 1763, remained a few days, and then set out for Perth Amboy for his inauguration. Ultimately Burlington, only twenty miles from Philadelphia, became his capital. Visits back and forth to parents and friends were frequent and must have thrown the ex-lovers into contact, since they knew the same people.

Perhaps to avoid an embarrassing encounter with William and his new wife, Elizabeth went to Graeme Park, but she had not forgotten William. She wrote to Margaret Abercrombie, castigating William, whom she called Margaret's "friend." Margaret responded saying she had "little to offer either in vindication of his actions or his arguments." She wished, if possible, for Elizabeth to "erase from [her] mind a person who has been the cause of giving you and the rest of your worthy family so much uneasiness."[51] Margaret's reference to William's "arguments" suggests that Elizabeth by then had been shown his letter to Margaret, if not earlier.

The preceding five years had been very difficult for the Graeme family. On January 28, 1759, Jane Graeme Young, Elizabeth's sister, had died in childbirth, aged thirty-two, at Graeme Park. She had married Captain James Young in 1754, and in the less than five years of her life remaining, she had borne four children, only two of whom survived. Within the next year and a half, Thomas Graeme's brother had also died. His nephew, who had been living in Philadelphia, had "suffered a melancholy in which he did not speak but seemed to understand," and had had to be sent back to England. Graeme wrote Thomas Penn that "these two distresses happening at the same time when [he] lost [his] Daughter Young made it a Scene of melancholy and afliction in [his] family, such as [he] had never felt before."[52] Jane Young left two young children, whom it would have been impossible for James Young to raise alone. The Graemes welcomed the youngsters into their home, and Ann Graeme took on the job of raising and educating John, aged two, and Ann, about three. The children lived with Elizabeth and her parents until 1772. First Ann Graeme and then Elizabeth tenderly cared for their education.

Among Elizabeth's other concerns was the family's continuing ill health. In July 1760, Mrs. Campbell went to Graeme Park for a visit only to discover that the Graemes had not yet left Philadelphia. As much as Ann and Elizabeth Graeme loved her and wished to be with her, neither one was well enough to travel the nineteen miles to their summer home. Ann Graeme, who had become quite melancholy, had hoped that Mrs. Campbell's company would make her first visit to Graeme Park after Jane's death there less painful, but she would have to miss that consolation. "What shall we say," she wrote her friend, "there is nothing to be expected from this Life but to be replete with disapointments." Although she had formed very few "Schemes for pleasure" in the previous years, she "never formed one but [she] was disapointed in it."[53] Again in the summer of 1762, Mrs. Graeme was indisposed, causing Elizabeth "uneasiness."

Grief and illness had convinced Ann Graeme that her death was imminent, even welcome, and she had begun to prepare for it. She had woven her own burial cloth "to Save [her] family trouble" and had planned her funeral. She wanted no sermon preached over her, but she did request the full Anglican service for the dead as specified in the prayer book, with no abridgments. The minister who buried her was to receive £5,[54] she specified. She even wrote letters in 1762 to several of her friends and the members of her family to be delivered to them after her death. The one she wrote to Mary Redman, wife of Dr. John Redman, remains. In it she took leave of her friend, assuring her that she had "been waiting with a pleasing expectation of [her] dissolution a great while." The "same portion of grace" which she had hitherto received, she felt sure would continue to her in death. "My trust is in my heavenly Father's mercies," she wrote.[55] Death would be a release from the unhappiness of life; her earthly existence would be replaced by a much more favorable one in God's kingdom.

Thomas Graeme's health also had begun to fail as early as 1746. That fall he had developed a "lingering intermitting fever," a problem that afflicted many Philadelphians at the end of the summer. Even when the fever was abated, he was left with an "unsupportable fatiguing Cough," which he would have suspected was caused by tuberculosis except for the absence of a fever. The cough forced him to retire to Graeme Park the next spring for a change of air and a diet of "Whey and Buttermilk." He even feared he might not be able to continue his medical practice.[56] Although this speculation did not materialize, and he continued his practice for many years, the cough never went away completely. In June 1760, Graeme commented to Penn that among his "many growing infirmities" the worst was his cough, and he thanked Penn for a gift of Tar Water to relieve it.[57]

Easing the pain of the death of Jane Young was the inclusion of a new member into the Graeme's extended family, who in many ways replaced the lost sister. Elizabeth or Eliza Stedman, called Betsy, was the orphaned niece of Charles Stedman. He had been born in Scotland, supported the Stuart cause, fought at Culloden, and escaped to Pennsylvania with his older brother Alexander about 1746. On January 1, 1748/49, he had married Ann Graeme, Elizabeth's other surviving sister. When Betsy Stedman's parents had died in Denmark, Charles Stedman had brought her to Philadelphia some time in the 1750s. Not much is known about her, other than that she was a few years younger than Elizabeth. Her surviving letters are well written and show that she had had an education.

Betsy Stedman became a favorite of both Ann and Elizabeth Graeme. By 1759, Mrs. Graeme had grown so fond of her that she had given the young woman her commonplace book, which consisted chiefly of sermons of the Rev. Jacob Duché, "her god-son and a great favorite with her" and Elizabeth. When transmitting the commonplace book to

Betsy Stedman, Mrs. Graeme wrote that in it were "many excellent rules, good instructions, and sublime reflections," and she hoped that Betsy would accept it "as a kind token of the affection [she] always bore" her. She also advised the young woman that if she depended "only on the Almighty grace," she would "feel a calm within more valuable than what any of the world's good things can ever give."[58] This is the same advice that Mrs. Graeme also frequently gave her daughter. Betsy kept Ann Graeme company at Graeme Park when Elizabeth was away, although Ann Graeme's fondness for playing cards every night was not shared by the young woman. In August 1761, Betsy complained that she would be glad when Dr. Graeme arrived to take her place at the card table.[59]

During the summer months when most wealthy Philadelphians were at their country estates, there was frequent partying back and forth. Although the men spent more time in the city than the women, still their country homes were close enough for them to visit often. A New York woman, the daughter of James Alexander, visited Philadelphia in June 1762 and reported various social occasions she attended. One of these at the home of Lt. Governor James Hamilton included Elizabeth Graeme and her sister Ann Graeme Stedman. At Philadelphia homes Miss Alexander was served green peas, turtle, trout, pineapple, and an "elegant desert" at one place. Cherries and strawberries were plentiful, she noted.[60]

By August 1762, Elizabeth was again confined to their Philadelphia home because of illness and had missed another visit from her beloved Mrs. Campbell. Betsy Stedman at Graeme Park with Mrs. Graeme warned Elizabeth not "to ramble in the Garden [in the evenings] too much for the delicacy of [her] Constitution."[61] Many commentators have stated that Elizabeth Graeme was so devastated by being "jilted" by William that her health was impaired. It is clear, however, that she had health problems throughout her life, especially in the summer months when she would be bothered by fevers and headaches. William's indifference did not cause them.

Summer and fall 1762 was unhealthy in general for Philadelphians. There was an outbreak among residents of Market Street of a "malignant fever . . . called a Spotted fever from the mortification that appears on the breast and Side at first but Spreads over the whole body."[62] Philadelphia also suffered that fall an epidemic of yellow fever that killed hundreds, foreshadowing the terrible scourge of 1793 that would kill 5,000.

By the end of August 1762, Elizabeth was well enough to accompany her sister and brother-in-law on an excursion around the countryside. The group consisted of Charles and Ann Stedman, Alexander Stedman and his wife, Francis Hopkinson, Betsy Stedman, Elizabeth, and James Bremmer, a composer, musician, and music teacher. They proceeded from Graeme Park to Lancaster, the Elizabeth furnace at Manheim, Ephrata, Reading, Bethelem, and then home, quite a substantial trip of a month or more, probably by horseback. The preceding year, the Stedman brothers had bought the land upon which the town of Manheim had been laid out. By the time of their visit, the town already contained from seventy to eighty buildings. At Manheim, Elizabeth became so ill that she had to recover at the home of Susanna Wright on the Susquehanna, establishing a link with another woman poet. Despite her discomfort, which she blamed on "limestone water," Elizabeth later reminisced about this jaunt, "It seems a fairy dream, like some of Susquehanna's islands, when the magic wand of memory, wakes up those days. We tasted the feast of reason and the flow of soul."[63]

In a letter to a friend about the trip, Elizabeth stressed that the diversity of Pennsylvania's population and religious affiliations did not prevent the people from living in harmony despite the different nations and languages represented. Her visits to Bethlehem, founded by Moravians or United Brethren, and Ephrata, home of the Dunkers, were especially interesting. In Bethlehem, she visited two Moravian sisters, Rebecca and Ann Langly, whom she may have met before on an earlier visit to Bethlehem. Later, in a commonplace book she was preparing for a friend, she related the history of the Dunkers:

> a german Weary of the world, retird to a very solitary place, about 50 miles from Philadelphia In order to give up his whole time to Contemplation[.] Several of his Country men came to Visit him in his pious retreat, and by his Simple pious and peacable manners, many were inducd to Settle near him, and in a short time, adoptng his modes, they formd a little Coloney which they namd *Euphrata* in alusion to that river upon whose Borders the Hebrews were acustomd to Sing Psalms.

She continued with a description of the town, the practices of the people, their religious tenets, their homes and dress, and their vegetarian eating habits. She concluded that she had never seen "anything so Solemn and abstracted as the people[,] their House Habits[,] and Silence In all [her] days" To her the Dunkers resembled "a Sect among the Jews that Josephus gives a full Disscription of Called Essenes Contemporary with Jesus Christ."[64] Elizabeth's writing constantly astonishes the reader with the breadth of her reading and interests.

Nineteenth-century writers sometimes claimed that she started writing poetry to recover from a broken heart after William Franklin jilted her. This is no more than romantic fantasy. She started writing poetry when she was twelve, if not before, although Elizabeth later characterized these verses as "trifling performances." When Ann Stedman asked her for copies of her early poetry, she responded that most of the poems she had written when she was between twelve and fifteen either were so "Childish," that she had not "the patience" to transcribe them or they were not available because she had not kept copies of them. Therefore, she could not fulfill her sister's request.[65] During the period before she learned of William's marriage she wrote several substantial poems. She wrote one celebrating the marriage of Jacob Duché and Elizabeth Hopkinson, another explaining the character of Louis XIV of France, a third informing Dr. William Smith in England of the birth of a daughter, a fourth sympathizing with Betsy Stedman on the death of a pet canary, and a sixth memorializing the death of her sister, Jane. These are only the poems that remain; it is safe to assume that she wrote others. She sometimes tucked a short couplet or quatrain in the prose of a letter. Even when she was supposed to be in a deep melancholy six weeks after she had heard of William's marriage, she wrote a poem describing King George's coach.[66] Little did she know when she wrote this poem that soon she would actually see the carriage she had described from reading about it.

When Elizabeth was visiting the Campbells in December and January 1763, they had frequently discussed the possibility of her going to England as they sat by the fireside in the evenings, speculating what such a trip would be like and what she would see and whom she would meet. This was a fairly common journey for young men from well-to-do families, to further their education both formally and informally. Aspiring lawyers went to London to take instruction at the Inns of Court, as did William Franklin. Doctors went to London or Edinburgh to hear lectures by the famous physicians of the time. Both Benjamin Rush and John Morgan improved their colonial medical education by such a journey. Anyone interested in a career in the Anglican Church, such as William Smith, had to go to London to be ordained because there was no bishop in the colonies. It was not usual, however, for young females to be sent abroad, but Elizabeth Graeme was an unusual woman. Furthermore, an appropriate opportunity presented itself.

Richard Peters, an old friend of the Graemes and of the Penn family, was going to England to seek medical advice, and when Elizabeth returned from Burlington, he invited her to go along as his traveling companion. She reported that he had explained the advantages of such a trip to her and "was Polite Enough to add that My Company Would be Vastly aggreable to Him." After two or three conversations about it and after her friends had urged her to go, she agreed, although there is no indication that she really had to be talked into it. At first, they planned to leave in August, but John Penn, the son of Richard, was coming over to Pennsylvania in October to be deputy governor, and Thomas Penn asked Peters not to leave Philadelphia until he had helped John Penn get "Settled in the Government." The trip was then postponed until the spring of 1764.[67]

Modern parents probably would hesitate before sending their daughter on a trip lasting a year or more with a single man, even if he was sixty years old to her twenty-seven and a man of the cloth as well. But Peters was a very close family friend, and the Graemes felt themselves lucky to have such an opportunity for their daughter. Peters had been born in England. While still in his teens and attending Westminster College, he had fallen in love with and married clandestinely a servant girl, much to his parents' distress. Divorce was impossible in England, so they sent him off to Leyden to attend lectures for several years. Upon his return, he first began the study of law, but then switched to preparation for the ministry. By 1731, he had been made a priest in the Church of England. Several years later, he heard that his first wife had died, and he re-married. Unfortunately, the report was premature, and the first wife appeared. Peters, a curate in the Church of England, had committed bigamy, and his second wife was pregnant. His promising career in the Church of England was ended. Leaving both wives behind, the pregnancy having aborted, Peters immigrated to Philadelphia about 1735 to begin a new life.[68]

In Philadelphia, Peters was destined to become a highly respected citizen, although not without controversy. He first became an assistant to the minister at Christ Church, but a quarrel with the rector forced him to resign. He had earned the regard of the people who counted, however, and had come to the notice of Thomas Penn, who compensated him for the loss of position by appointing him in 1737 secretary of the provincial land office, which job he held until 1760. He was admitted to the Philadelphia bar, and in 1743 he became provincial secretary, private secretary for the proprietaries, and clerk of the Council. In 1749, he became a provincial councillor. By 1762, he had built enough support in the colony so that he could return to his first love, the church. He gave up his government jobs for an appointment as rector of the combined parishes of Christ Church and St. Peters. While in England, in addition to seeking medical help about his health problems and visiting his family whom he had not seen in nearly thirty years, Peters also wanted to formalize his appointment as rector in the Anglican Church.[69]

In discussions with the Graemes and with Elizabeth, it was agreed that Peters would look after Elizabeth, take her on several side trips, and introduce her to the prominent people whom he had met through his family connections before leaving England and with whom he had maintained contacts. Highly educated and widely read, made sexually safe by his age, religious inclinations, and close friendship with Dr. Graeme, although this subject probably was never discussed, Peters seemed a perfect companion for Elizabeth. He could show her the sights and introduce her to interesting people.

The summer dragged with unsatisfied anticipation. Peters waited to help John Penn, and Elizabeth, at Graeme Park, was ill again. By June, she had developed one of her excrutiating headaches and was in "excessive" pain.[70] July brought an improvement in her health, and visits by her brother-in-law James Young and her childhood friend Francis Hopkinson raised her spirits.[71] The weather was lovely and the countryside lush with the prospects of a plentiful harvest. Unfortunately, by the end of July, Elizabeth's headache had returned. The pain in her head was so extreme for three weeks that she was unable to have any visitors. Better by mid-August, she asked Mrs. Campbell to buy her a lottery ticket in New Jersey.[72] Her father, in Philadelphia, was delighted to hear that her health was improved, although he was concerned about the effects of damp weather and prescribed "a glass twice a day of bark and bitters." He was confident enough about her recovery to order his workers at Graeme Park to put a cider-mill into working order for her and to ready a shed for storage of apples.[73]

Although Elizabeth and Richard Peters would not leave Pennsylvania until June 1764, she was anticipating the trip all winter. Plans had to be finalized, money made available, people in England alerted that they were coming, and an itinerary formed. This was a major journey, not to be undertaken lightly or without adequate preparation.

3

This Bewitching Country

As the popular rector of the combined congregations of Christ Church and St. Peters, Richard Peters received more than the usual send-off. The preceding week, the ministers, church wardens, and vestrymen had delivered an address to Peters, thanking him for past services and wishing him a safe voyage and a return of good health, and he had responded with an address of his own thanking them for their good wishes. On Sunday he bid his parishioners goodbye at Christ Church, with Elizabeth and her family probably in the Graeme family pew. After the service, people would have greeted her, too, and wished her a safe voyage and return. An ocean trip was a perilous undertaking in those days, with no guarantee of a return. Monday morning, June 18, 1764, Elizabeth and Peters went by chaise to New Castle, to embark for England.[1]

While on the trip, Elizabeth kept a journal of at least two, possibly three, parts which she sent back to Philadelphia. Her family and friends at home eagerly awaited the arrival of each one, and they passed from hand to hand, giving "great delight to all." In April 1765, Ann Graeme wrote her that the first part had arrived and that they all longed to read the second. She was pleased that her daughter had "seen so many things and places."[2] Benjamin Rush reported that her journal contrasted the "manners and characters in an old and highly civilized country, . . . with those to which she had been accustomed in [her] own," and included "many curious facts and anecdotes." "Her modesty alone prevented its being made public," wrote Rush, "and thereby affording a specimen to the world, and to posterity, of her happy talents for observation, reflection and composition."[3] We, too, wish she had agreed to the publication of her journals because, unfortunately, they and all but one of the letters she wrote during the period have disappeared, even though many people have searched for them ever since the 1850s. All we have left are parts of Elizabeth's journals copied by her friend Milcah Martha Moore into her own commonplace book.[4]

When Elizabeth bid her parents goodbye, conflicting emotions ruled her thoughts and theirs. Anticipation about the trip and the adventures she would enjoy in England and Scotland submerged any fears the daughter had about the voyage ahead or any concerns about the aging parents she was leaving behind. Ann Graeme, however, could not set aside her fears. Sixty-four years old and suffering from recurring illness, she watched with great foreboding as Elizabeth crossed the courtyard at Graeme Park and stepped into the chaise. As the young woman waved goodbye, an internal voice whispered to her mother that she would never see her daughter again. Twice before she had had a similar feeling, and each time it had come true. In those cases, her predictions concerned the other person; this time Mrs. Graeme's premonition concerned not her daughter's safety but her own mortality.[5]

Elizabeth and Peters's ship was probably as well equipped as that taken by Francis Hopkinson two years later. Francis wrote his mother from shipboard just before leaving the continent. "Everything on Board is perfectly agreeable, we have plenty of what is wholesome & elegant . . . our Cow affords us as fine Milk & Cream as ever was used, & we are all in good Spirits. . . . We breakfast at Eight, Dine at One, Sup at Nine & go to Bed when we please." He knew this pleasant schedule might not last, however, and commented realistically, "we cannot expect for a Constancy." He told her not to worry, but at the same time he bid her goodbye just in case something went awry.[6]

To add to the usual discomfort of a long sea voyage, neither Elizabeth nor Peters was in very good health. Governor John Penn wrote his uncle Thomas the next day that Peters was in such bad shape that Penn did not believe he could "have got through the summer, here."[7] He commented that Elizabeth had gone with Peters likewise to recover her health and also to visit her relatives in Scotland. With Peters suffering from severe chest pains and Elizabeth from her usual headaches and intermittent fevers and both discomforted by either kidney or gall stones, it must have been a difficult crossing for them tossing around on the Atlantic in a small vessel.

Ill health, nevertheless, did not dull Elizabeth's awareness of the beauty of the sea and sky nor silence her poetic muse. "Whatever way the Ship moved," she wrote,

> she appeared to be in the Centre of a Circle, for the Sea seems to be a perfect Circle, surrounded by the Clouds, that looks as if they bent down at the Edges to join it, so that our own Eyes form the Horizon, & like Self= Love, we are always placing ourselves in the Middle, where all Things move round us.—I saw the Sun set clear for the first Time, I was reading Priam's Petition to Achilles for the Body of Hector, I think my Eyes were engaged in one of the finest Sights in the Universe, & my Passions, interested in one of the most pathetic that History or Poetry can paint.[8]

The travelers arrived in Liverpool in July. There they visited with Peters's ailing sister Hannah and his nieces and nephews. They also communicated with Dr. John Fothergill, the eminent Quaker physician of London, whom they planned to consult about their health problems. Fothergill had received his medical education at Edinburgh, the best medical school in the British isles, and completed his training by working in the wards at St. Thomas Hospital in London for four years. In 1740, he had begun private practice. By 1764, with an international reputation, he was recognized as one of the foremost doctors in London. Ahead of his time, Dr. Fothergill, as early as 1748, had opposed bleeding and purging as treatments for the sick, advocating less strenuous therapies. In contrast, both were still being practiced and hotly defended by Pennsylvania's famed Dr. Benjamin Rush over forty years later. In 1762, Fothergill had purchased an estate at Upton in Essex northeast of London, where he was developing an extensive botanical garden, collecting specimens from all over the world. He also collected books and had a large library of medical texts as well as others. Fothergill, in his fifties in 1764, was a lifelong bachelor. His unmarried sister Ann had been living with him since 1749. Although Fothergill never had visited Pennsylvania, his father had done so three times, the last in 1736, and his brother, Samuel, had been there once in 1754.[9] During their time in Philadelphia, it is likely that these men had become acquainted with Thomas and Ann Graeme. There is no indication, however, that a correspondence was ever maintained before Elizabeth's consultations with John Fothergill.

Before going to London, the travelers journeyed northeast to Scarborough to take the waters there and recover from their trip, a step undoubtedly recommended by Fothergill. The journey took a week or more and gave the travelers a chance to view the beautiful countryside. By the end of August, they were in Scarborough, a resort in Yorkshire, on the North Sea, about two hundred miles from London. It was noted for its mineral spring water, and the two invalids went there to drink the water and bathe in the sea. Originally known as a health resort, by 1760 it had become a fashionable spa where the noted sported. Dr. Fothergill himself had visited Scarborough at least four times in his life, as recently as the previous year, and since he prescribed tours there to other patients, it is reasonable to assume that he suggested the trip to Elizabeth and Peters to help them recover from their ailments.[10]

Both Fothergill and Elizabeth wrote humorously of the visitors at Scarborough and their activities. Fothergill pointed out that ninety percent of the people at Scarborough were "in perfect health." He derided the practice of supposedly sick people going every night to an assembly room where, crowded into a moderate sized room with 550 people, they stewed until midnight and then came out of that "Stove upon a high sea Cliff" exposing themselves to cold or fog. The next morning they plunged into the sea. "All this," wrote Fothergill, "after they have travelled about 200 miles for the recovery of their health, with many a wise prescription in their pockets."[11] Still he believed that the experience, if handled properly, could be curative. His own practice when at Scarborough was to go to the spa very early in the morning, before most others, ride horseback during the day, and skip the evening activities.

Elizabeth sent Betsy Stedman a mocking poem entitled "an Account of the movements of one Day as spent by people of Fashion in the fall Season at Scarborough." At eight o'clock in the morning, people rose and prepared themselves for the bath. A horse-drawn "house" with glass sides for viewing the beauties of the morning took them to the beach where both men and women put on flannel outfits and bathed in the water. They then had breakfast in the Assembly Room and strolled up and down talking to people and looking at the toys in a "very great Toy shop kept in the Assembly Room." After dinner, the coach arrived at four to take them to the racetrack.

> Now Crys and Oaths are heard around
> Applause or Murmurs quick rebound
> The Victor Gay the loser Sad;
> Some Sullen seem; while others Mad
> Fly from the Turf dejected Home
> With empty Pockets pensive roam.

After the races, they dressed for tea, followed by dancing and card playing and later supper.[12] As Fothergill observed, this was hardly an appropriate routine for sick people.

At the races, Elizabeth had an encounter with a famous British author. She "was in the Balcony, with a Paper, the List of the Horses, in my Hand," Elizabeth wrote,

> a Gent: that stood by & had been chatting to another Lady, ask'd which Side I would bet, I told him that, that every one else was against, For the Race was not to the Swift nor the Battle to the Strong,-we presently fell into a very free Conversation, on his Part a very sensible one, & [he] told me he wished to lengthen the Time, but was under an Engagement to return to his Hermitage the next Morning, but desired I would meet him, at the Assembly Room in the Ev'ning, I told him I would be there, but questioned in such a Groupe whether I would be found—He said he had some interest in Apollo, who would lend him his Torch on such an Occasion. This was no other than Yorick, the celebrated Lawrence Sterne. Author of Tristam Shandy.[13]

Sterne was so intrigued with her comment that he used it as the theme for his sermon "Time and Chance."[14] Despite Yorick's claimed influence with Apollo, a later meeting between the two did not take place.

The visitors stayed at Scarborough possibly a month, possibly less. The waters did not agree with Peters, and he stopped drinking them. There were chilly breezes that made bathing in the sea impossible and walks in the fresh air on the beach uncomfortable.[15] The experience did not do much to improve their health. In late September or early October, they traveled to London where Peters began a six-week visit with Thomas Penn at both of Penn's residences.[16]

Thomas Penn and his wife, Lady Juliana, were very kind to Elizabeth, inviting her to visit their estate at Stoke Poges in Bucks and to dine at their London home at Spring Gardens, near Charing Cross. There she renewed a friendship with Philadelphia Hannah Freame, the daughter of Thomas Penn's sister Margaret and her husband, Thomas Freame, who had lived in Philadelphia for some time beginning in 1734. Philadelphia Hannah, nine years younger than Elizabeth, had been born in Pennsylvania and had known the Graemes in her childhood. When Elizabeth was in London, Hannah Freame was staying with the Thomas Penns and helping Juliana Penn, who was pregnant, take care of her other offspring. Hannah loved to draw and made sketches that she presented to her friends. In 1770, she married an Irishman named Thomas Dawson, Baron Dartney, who became Viscount Cremorne. Hannah and Elizabeth became life-long correspondents.

Elizabeth also developed a deep friendship with Lady Juliana, whom she found to be

> among the few good Things that come up to the Character that is told of them. She has strong good Sense, above Affectation, a most pleasing Manner that takes off the Distance of her Station, & at the same Time a conscious Dignity, that seems to arise more from the Goodness of her own Heart, than from any external Advantages, she has a great flow of Spirits, talks freely, & seems perfectly Mistress of all Subjects, yet with an Air of Humility, as if she was receiving instead of giving Information.[17]

The admiration was reciprocated. Thomas Penn wrote to Peters that Elizabeth was "a very great favorite with Lady Juliana who ranks her among her most valuable acquaintance."[18]

The Penns were unable to accommodate Elizabeth at their London house because every bedroom was filled. Therefore, separate lodgings, now unknown, had to be found for her in the city. In mid-November, Peters left Elizabeth alone in London and journeyed to Liverpool to visit his relatives. From there, he wrote her asking how she fared in her "new manner of Life," what sort of food she was eating, how she cooked it, what visitors she had, and what she did on "those tedious Evenings," when she did not "chance to go to the Play."[19] This was indeed a new existence for a woman who had been surrounded by family, friends, and servants all her life. It was the first time she had to manage independently without her parents to solve problems and recommend, if not dictate, activity.

She was not, however, entirely without support in the city. Old friends from her childhood in Pennsylvania, people such as Sir John St. Clair and his wife, called upon her, as did new friends she had met through the Penns or Peters. Relatives of Betsy Stedman who lived in the city and Betsy's aunt in the suburbs were available in case of emergency. She also had made a new friend in Dr. Fothergill who visited her three times a week. Her health, in a very bad state through November, was "somewhat better" by December, and she could enjoy these new companions.

Nevertheless, despite her visitors, her health problems and concern for her family made her homesick and lonely for loved ones. While Peters was in Liverpool, Thomas Penn kept an eye on his old friend's daughter and reported on her condition to Peters. She had been worried about her family, he wrote, but letters arrived that month reporting that everyone was well. She would discover later that everyone had not told the whole truth; Ann Graeme was terminally ill. Elizabeth was also anxious to reassure her family about herself and wrote them of her improving condition. Yet in a poem she described herself as

> Alone & Pensive & opprest with Pain
> The starting Tear sometimes could scarce refrain.
> Tho' England's Pleasures open to me lay
> Pain barr'd my Entrance & forbad my Way.[20]

Peters did not return to London for another month because his nephew, who would accompany him, could not leave until January 27. This meant that Elizabeth spent Christmas day alone. Peters, in Liverpool with his family, wrote that this gave him great pleasure, because it encouraged her to think of the religious significance of the holiday.[21] Elizabeth's reaction to this comment is unknown.

Peters's letters to Elizabeth during this period leave the modern reader feeling somewhat uncomfortable about his emotions toward his charge. Even though eighteenth-century written conventions included a level of effusiveness not used today, still Peters's letters seem more attentive and affectionate than usual for a surrogate father. By December 4, he had heard nothing from her since his departure. He wrote that if she knew "what pain" he had "sufferd at not hearing any thing" from her, she would "not be so cruel as to do so again." He admonished her to write him at least once a week and "not hide any thing . . . that is material & proper for me to know." "I want much to give you all the Comfort I can," he wrote in his next letter,

> . . . I cannot but be very uneasy at being absent from you. . . . I want to show you your father & Mothers Letters & to say a thousand things to you. . . . Don't you think too much about home? I am apprehensive such thoughts are too much indulged and hurt you. This is one reason why I want to be with you. we can talk about them & that will relieve better than thinking.

In his January letter, he wrote that their shared experiences had "endeard" her to him, and he hoped that "this happiness" would increase "in that variety of Scenes which we shall go through with the same mutual Satisfaction." He begged her to accept all his endeavors to give her "Comfort" "I joy much in your friendship," he wrote "I expect much from it."[22]

For her part, Elizabeth felt only a daughterly affection toward Peters. Her only remaining letter to him, and her only existing letter of the trip, had a very different tone than his did. It was a newsy letter commenting on his activities and relating hers, sharing the reports she had received from Pennsylvania, and describing her health. She wrote that she saw "More Company at Home, than abroad," but when he returned, she hoped to "Go out Something More," as there were many sights "in and About London" that she needed his companionship to see.[23] In 1767, she would write a poem in answer to Hannah Freame's request for a description of the clergyman. In this poem, Elizabeth emphasized Peters's piety and his concern for others, and she spent several stanzas telling Hannah that Peters was awaiting death with resignation.[24]

As for social occasions, she had more of those than she really wanted. In her letter to Peters, she listed about a dozen people who frequently called on her. Since they had equipage and footmen, and she did not, it was easier for them to come to her than she to them. She had spent the previous day at Dr. Fothergill's home and the day before at Colonel Gram's. His wife had regretted that Elizabeth had not yet been introduced at court so that she might have gone with Mrs. Gram to celebrate the king's birthnight. She had also visited with the Penns. Her sparkling conversation and wit apparently enthralled this circle of Londoners, for she received six calls for every one she paid.

Mrs. Gram's wish for Elizabeth to be presented at court was fulfilled sometime later. Although no documentary evidence for this exists, it was repeated by enough others to be true. For example, Elizabeth's neighbor told William Buck that Horsham acquaintances called her "Lady Fergusson" because she had "been so called by George III" and because she was the granddaughter of Lady Keith.[25] In a journal entry, copied by her friend, Elizabeth described King George's reception by the public at an appearance, and this may have been the time when she was presented to him. Exhibiting her sense of humor and ability to analyze character, she wrote that there were

> not so many Huzzas as one might expect from the public Appearance of so good a King, for by the unprejudiced Accounts of the Most Sensible People & those who know most of him, he is a most amicable young Man.—It seems an Offence to some that he enjoys the sweets of Domestic Life, they say he is too fond of his Wife & Children, & leads too regular a Life, I suppose they want a Charles the 2nd on the Throne, to make Mistresses of their Wives & Daughters, & furnish the Nation with a Race of royal illegitimate Children.—Because he turns all his Sense to good Purposes, many endeavour to represent him as a weak Man, but by the best Accounts he is steady, sensible, pious & calm.[26]

She became especially acquainted or reacquainted with Juliana Ritchie who visited Elizabeth often. Mrs. Ritchie had lived with her husband in Philadelphia, but they were separated by 1764, and she lived in London on a small pension. In January, Elizabeth presented her new friend with a fan, on the back of which she had written a poem:

> Accept this Triffle from a Female Friend,
> Selfish the Motive for to gain an End;
> When <u>Western</u> Seas divides us far apart;
> Regard this Bauble of Esteem a Mark!
> When cooling Breezes are denyd by Heaven;

Nor gentle Gales by fanning Zephers given:
This small <u>Machine</u> shall make amends by Art
And guard your Face from wounding many a Heart;
No light coquetish airs Shall flirt it round;
Nor shall it flutter with an angry sound:
Serene and Graceful shall its motives prove,
And tho' attractive, yet forbidding Love!
All Love that rises not From Friendships Flame
Must <u>Juliana</u> from her Breast disclaim.

Mrs. Ritchie responded with a poem of her own, thanking the giver.[27]

Another visitor in London was Benjamin Franklin. The Pennsylvania Asembly, frustrated by its ongoing struggle with the proprietary, had sent him back to London, this time to persuade the king to take Pennsylvania away from the Penns and make it a royal colony. Elizabeth's lodgings were not far from where he stayed with his landlady, Margaret Stevenson, and her daughter Polly. He called on her and reported to Deborah that Elizabeth was "pretty well."[28] Considering her deep friendship with the Penns and her strained encounter with the Franklins after William's marriage had been announced in Pennsylvania, it is questionable whether she was pleased by these visits. It was kind of Franklin, however, to call on the young woman and report back to Philadelphia. Ann Graeme and Deborah Franklin saw each other occasionally, and Franklin knew his wife would reassure Elizabeth's mother.

One day in March, Dr. Fothergill called on Elizabeth and told her, "Betsy . . . you were yesterday made a Slave of." Thinking he was joking about a possible suitor, she replied, "Me Sir I am slave to no man I assure you Doctor my Heart and Hand are free."[29] But her physician was not referring to any potential match for Elizabeth but to the Stamp Act. In it, Parliament had enacted the first direct tax ever levied on the colonies. It placed a tax on all legal documents, which had to be printed on special paper, and on newspapers, broadsides, dice, playing cards, and other items.

A long time friend of the colonies, Fothergill understood the colonial mind very well. Later, in 1765, Fothergill published "Considerations Relative to the North American Colonies," a sympathetic treatise on Great Britain's relations with her colonies, urging repeal of the Stamp Act. The colonies should be treated "with particular indulgence," he recommended. If they should feel mistreated, they will do without the products of the

mother country, causing trade to languish. The English merchants will suffer first, followed by the manufacturers and then the landed interest. Un-
employment was already high in England, he pointed out. Parliament has
"*power* to do many things, which they have no *right* to do." To help England cement her ties with her colonies, Fothergill suggested that scholar-
ships be established for American students in British universities and that
they be given free passage on British ships. Fothergill's analysis of the situation was very accurate. Things came to pass exactly as he predicted. His
information about the colonies may have come from Elizabeth and especially from Richard Peters when they visited him, the doctor asking his
friends about the colonial economy and political beliefs. He argued that
taxes should be levied only by the people who were going to pay them,
yet the distance of America from Great Britain made it impossible for the
colonies to be represented in Parliament.[30] These were precisely the claims
being made by the colonists.

Elizabeth grew very fond of her doctor, who had "that Knowledge
of the World & sweet Humility, that makes the Company of a Man of
Sense, with a good Heart, so very pleasing."[31] So pleasing was he that she
wrote a long poem to him, about the importance of health for personal
happiness, "Its but vain boasting, then, to talk of Bliss, / While this fine
Frame feels-there is aught amiss," the need for good medical treatment
when the body suffered, the skill of English doctors, and particularly his.
She concluded with the wish that he have "ev'ry Pleasure." They developed an informal, non-professional, even joking relationship. One day she
told him that she feared Betsy Stedman would urge her "to use more Exercise & go more abroad" than she wished, and she hoped "he would not
join in." He responded by telling her to write down what she "liked best,"
and he would, if possible, prescribe it.[32]

Even under the tender ministrations of Dr. Fothergill, Elizabeth's
ill health persisted, improving for a short while and then relapsing. She
visited the Penns briefly at their country house but refused their invitation
for a longer stay in order to return to London for Fothergill's attention.[33] If
one of Elizabeth's problems was migraine headache, then within the limits
of eighteenth-century medical knowledge, no place or person was going
to help her. And indeed her headaches continued all her life.

While in London, Elizabeth found time for a "quantity of writing," which she sent off to Betsy Stedman,[34] probably stealing night time
hours when she should have been sleeping, as Betsy guessed. The poem

about Scarborough, one or two parts of her journal, and letters flowed from London to Philadelphia to friends and family who enjoyed and circulated them. Unfortunately, only the Scarborough poem, four others, and the one letter remain in the original. Elizabeth missed her "tender Connextions" in Philadelphia, whose communications she anticipated eagerly. One of the poems she wrote was entitled "Upon the Pleasure conveyed to us by writing; wrote on receiving Letters when in England from my Friends." She concluded the poem,

> <u>Painting</u> and <u>Music</u> with their choicest Arts
> Cant work a passage to our feeling Hearts
> With such a force; such a resistless sway!
> As charming Letters can with Bliss convey.[35]

Still, in spite of her homesickness, she must have written glowing letters about London because Betsy Stedman speculated that if it were not for family and friends, London, for Elizabeth, "would have the preference before Philadelphia was there a necesety for a choice."[36] Elizabeth also found time to shop: a length of silk for Richard Peters's niece in Wales, a dress, stomacher, and bows for Betsy Stedman, and a writing desk for her nephew, John Young.

She also found time to read and comment in her journal. One day she spent

> reading a very beautiful Eastern tale— Almoran & Hamet, where the steady Perseverance of Virtue in spite of the most alarming Appearances leads to Happiness— The eastern Stile when not filled too much with Bombast & Rhapsody I ever admired [.] Truth at last flashes on the Soul, like the purest Rays of Light & by the Splendor & Brightness of its Illuminations drives & discovers Vice, in all its lurking Places & Obscurities & points out the Clue that unwinds the perplexing Labyrinth.

Another day she wrote of her favorite authors:

> Doctor Young is a Friend in Affliction, that I could open my Heart to, Mr. Rowe flatters my Imagination, & takes walks with me in a summer evening,— Mr. Addison suits me well in all Humours.

Mr. Pope I am a little afraid of, I think he knows so well the turnings of the human Heart, that he always sets me into an Examination.— Harvey says the same Thing over & over so prettily, & I am persuaded had so much Goodness of Soul, that I revere him, amid all his Prolixity, as for Mr. Richardson, he is a perfect Proteus, ever assuming a new form, but in all sensible.

While in England, she shed a few tears over the death of Edward Young, a writer she greatly admired and often quoted. She predicted that he would become "a glorified Saint in Heaven, for sure by his Works, . . . for him is laid up a Crown of Glory."[37]

Among the excursions Elizabeth took while in England was one to Stowe Gardens, near the town of Buckingham, in the vale of Aylesbury, one of England's most prosperous agricultural regions. The Stowe Gardens, laid out in the eighteenth century on an estate owned by the Dukes of Buckingham and Chandos, were beautifully landscaped with classical temples and pavillions.[38] "Seeing fine Gardens in the Spring & Summer," she confided to her journal, "ever was ranked among my capitol Pleasures."[39] Remembering Stowe Gardens in a poem written a year later, Elizabeth wrote:

> When *Stow's* vast Gardens pourd their Sweets around
> When In those wallks my wandering Steps I found
> Lost in a wilderness of Bliss I strayd
> And Sunk beneath the lovely rural Shade![40]

She could have visited this place as a detour on the way either to Bristol or to Lea Hall, near Liverpool, a summer home rented by Fothergill in 1765. Or the Penns could have taken her there on one of her visits to them at Stoke Poges.

The Penns' home is located four miles from Windsor Castle, where Elizabeth might have had her first encounter with great visual art. In the poem quoted above, she mentions Van Dyck and Rubens, both of whom are liberally represented at Windsor. She would have seen Ruben's "St George and the Dragon" and Van Dyck's "St. Martin Dividing His Cloak," both painted in the seventeenth century. She wrote:

> When the Soft Canvas glowd wih *Raphaels* Hand
> And Life arose almost from his Command;

Here <u>Vandyks</u> coloring makes you doubt your Sense,
Pure(?) <u>Reubens</u> touch the finishd Strokes dispense:
Where Vaulted Ceilings burnt with Vano's[Verrio's] skill
The wondring Eye with shining Beautys fill.[41]

Probably her exposure to art was from visits to castles or homes of private collectors. In London, the British Museum, although founded in 1753, had not built its biggest collections yet, and the National Gallery, the Victoria and Albert, and the Tate did not come into existence until the nineteenth century. Her only comment about the British Museum, which she did visit, was that its shell collection was less beautiful than that of Dr. Fothergill.[42] The young woman from Philadelphia wandered the picture galleries, experiencing in all her senses the glowing canvases, her knowledge and taste growing, her intellect expanding and maturing. Later, Elizabeth remembered her first reaction to London: "All England Joys rushd full upon my view; / And Pleasurs trod On Pleasures ever new."[43] Did she remember William Franklin's excuse for not writing to her more frequently and have a twinge of guilty conscience for her sharp rebuke to him? He had written that the "infinite variety of new Objects; . . . the Viewing such Things as were esteem'd most curious, engross'd all [his] attention." She, too, now experienced the "publick Diversions and Entertainments of this bewitching Country," although possibly different diversions from those that had distracted William.

She strolled through Westminister Abbey "With Shakespeare, Milton, or with Thomson" as her companions. She remembered and perhaps recited out loud "some favorite Passage of their Works [that] occurd; Some striking Sentence or expressive Word." She thought about Vitruvius, the Roman architect, who wrote the oldest surviving book on architecture, and about the Earl of Burlington, who was called "this Modern Vetruvias," because he had designed so many buildings.[44] At Stoke Poges, she learned that Thomas Gray's famous "Elegy Written in a Country Churchyard" had been composed in a churchyard there. Gray died in 1771 and was buried in that churchyard. Elizabeth's niece, Ann Young, at eighteen, wrote her own version of Gray's poem "Lines Occasioned by Walking One summers Evening in the Churchyard at Wiccoe Church," perhaps inspired by Elizabeth's related experiences at Stoke Poges churchyard. Re-reading Ann Young's poem in 1787 inspired Elizabeth to write an answer. Both poems were published in 1791.[45]

Another jaunt taken some time that winter or the previous fall was to Fothergill's home at Upton in Essex. She admired the old house with its large rooms and "genteel" furnishings, especially a very pretty tapestry. She found pleasure in the five acres of gardens, although it was "not perhaps, what would be called here a fine Garden," she wrote. It was "so full of flowering Shrubs, Variety of Hedges, & so agreeably diversified" that she found it "a pleasing Spot," nevertheless.[46] Apparently, she did not appreciate that Fothergill's intention was to assemble a collection of as many plants as would grow in England, a museum of plants, rather than to create a perfectly designed formal garden. In addition, he had owned the property less than three years, not nearly enough time to create a perfect garden.

In March, Elizabeth went to Bristol, where she stayed with a Miss Frances Finch, a friend of the Penn women. Peters arrived sometime before April 13 and lodged with a Mr. Speed.[47] Fothergill had recommended the hot well at Bristol for drinking and bathing rather than the more popular facility at Bath with its strenuous social life. She remained there for about two months, although the Bristol waters were no more efficacious for Elizabeth's headaches and intermittent fevers than those at Scarborough. Fothergill had advised her that "the Bristol Water loses something every Moment after it is Exposed to the air," and that she should drink it on the spot. But the Penn women discovered, perhaps from correspondence with Miss Finch, that Elizabeth did not like to go to the hot wells and sent for the water instead. Knowledge of her disobeying his orders might have changed Dr. Fothergill's belief that Bristol had "aggravated" her complaint and that he had been "a Bad Physician."[48]

While in Bristol, Lady Juliana and her friend Lady Charlotte Finch took Elizabeth to breakfast with Thomas Goldney, a Quaker friend of Thomas Penn, whose home was reputed to have "one of the finest Views in England" and whose garden was a mecca for many visitors. Elizabeth's fancy was particularly taken by a large grotto, an artificial cave-like structure, built in his garden. Such constructions were very popular at the time in England. Elizabeth had seen another beautiful grotto at the home of "Lord Tilney at Wanstead," but she judged that Mr. Goldney's "far exceeded Lord Tilney's." It was twenty feet wide by sixty feet long, the

> Roof supported by 4 Pillars which are covered with bristol Stones, bits of shining Rocks & petrified Spars, the Floor is a kind of Mosaic which appears to be finely veined & polished, but is only Sev-

eral Kinds of Clay mixed together & baked, . . . At one end is a Neptune in a reclining Posture who holds a large Pipe, thro' which the Water tumbles into a deep Cistern, made of Shells, & on each Side is a Shell of a monstrous Size brought from the East-Indies, that is scolloped . . . There is a Cavern that holds a Lion large as the Life, that faces the Door & guards the Place.

After leaving the grotto, the party climbed to an octagon building on a hill top, which gave a view of the whole countryside. Elizabeth found it "a most agreeable Morning."[49]

The travelers left Bristol about May 20 to return to London,[50] where Peters learned that his sister's condition was much worse. Before he hurried back to Liverpool to see his family once again, he and Elizabeth decided that she would travel with Dr. Fothergill to Chesire, near Liverpool,[51] where he had leased a summer home called Lea Hall. Peters would join her there for a journey to Scotland to visit Elizabeth's cousin Thomas Graeme at Balgowan. After spending August in Scotland, either they would return to Philadelphia together or possibly she would go to Holstein in Denmark to visit her uncle, Sir Robert Keith, while Peters returned to Pennsylvania. By July, however, Peters was writing to Elizabeth that Hannah was declining and that his relatives did not want him to leave. They knew that Peters probably would never return to England and, understandably, did not want to share him with a friend who would have his company in Philadelphia for the rest of his life. Peters wrote that his family was not willing to part with him as soon as Elizabeth proposed to be at Dr. Fothergill's. Peters suggested instead that he send the post chaise for her at Lea Hall and that his servant accompany her to Scotland, while he remained in Liverpool. When she was close to the time she selected for leaving Scotland, he would join her there and ride back to London with her.[52]

This suggestion did not please Elizabeth. Now in good health and eager to tour Scotland, she wrote him a sharp reply, accusing him of insincerity in originally agreeing to go with her to Scotland and implying that his relatives' desires interfered with his promises to her. Peters, torn between his family's importunities, Thomas Penn's need to see him before he left, and Elizabeth's demands, could not see how he could spend a month in Scotland. He explained the tightness of his schedule by the length of their Bristol stay, "tedious" time that had "thrown all into Confusion and spoild the whole." Peters wrote that he could come to her in Balgowan about August 20, stay with her friends, and return with her to London. With this schedule, he could accomplish all he wanted to do before he left England, which he must do "as soon as the Equinoctial Gale" was over, in all probability before September 20 or 30.[53]

In his letter, Peters referred to a packet of letters that had just arrived from Pennsylvania and to the pleasure she must have received from hearing from home. The packet, however, brought Elizabeth the very unhappy news that her mother had died May 29. Since she had left Philadelphia, letters from her family had hinted that her mother was failing, but none had directly prepared Elizabeth for this blow. Her brother-in-law James Young had written in January that Ann Graeme's "delicate and tender constitution" often made him "uneasy as she is very subject to a disorder of the bowel," although he had qualified this by saying that at her age, one could not expect her to be free of "all the disorders that afflict the human form." He had concluded that for these reasons he earnestly wished to see Elizabeth home in the fall. In April, again he had written, this time urging her not to make the trip to Holstein. Her parents were counting on her being home by October. But then he had added that she must not think there had been any change in her parents' health.[54] It had been difficult for her to read between the lines, and, of course, she had not wanted to perceive any reason for cutting short her travels. Therefore, she had skipped over the worrisome parts of her brother-in-law's letters and had focused instead on his reassurances.

In the packet came several letters, written at different dates, that had collected awaiting a departing ship. From them, Elizabeth learned that soon after she had left Pennsylvania, Ann Graeme had become ill with a very severe, incurable intestinal disorder. She had directed her family not to write Elizabeth of her condition, even though it had become increasingly obvious that she would not recover. By her last letters to her daughter, "she was so weak that she could not write above four lines at a time, yet she wrote as cheerful as though nothing had been the matter," reported Ann Stedman's letter. Fourteen days before her death, Mrs. Graeme finally had written Elizabeth in one of the packet letters that her illness would be fatal and bid her "adieu" until they should meet "in endless bliss," which she had "no doubt of."[55] As she lay dying, Ann Graeme had begged Ann Stedman not to mourn, for "she was going to be happy." Her death was "what She most earnestly prayed for," and she willingly was giving up "everything in this Life for a Better."[56]

Emotionally exhausted and physically weakened from the relentless pregnancies and deaths and her own illnesses, Ann Graeme had long anticipated and been preparing for death. As early as 1752, she had planned her funeral.[57] She had woven her own burial linen, to save her family "trouble," and upon it she had written, "The Lord hath mercifully guided me by his Council, and I humbly hope through the merits of my Dear Redeemer will Raise me up to Glory. This is the Hour the joyful Hour I have waited for and long very long wished for to be disolved and to be with Christ which is best of all" and she hoped not to "be Disapointed of my Humble Hopes."[58] Her family and acquaintances firmly believed that God would grant her wish.

Ann Graeme had sent Elizabeth off to England without a word to detain her, despite a premonition of her own approaching death, because this was the way she wanted it. She knew that if Elizabeth had been there praying for her recovery, it would have been difficult for her to let go of life and die. Her daughter's love would have held her,[59] but she believed that she was going to a better life and did not wish to be detained.

On Monday, July 15, Elizabeth received the news from Philadelphia. She had planned that afternoon to go on a little excursion with Juliana Ritchie and several others to Chiswick by barge. Instead the two women spent the day "in a dark Room," as Mrs. Ritchie tried to console Elizabeth in her grief. Later she wrote that she would never forget the kindness Mrs. Ritchie had shown that day to the woman who was "a stranger in a Common lodging" away from her home.[60] Peters might have been able to help her through these difficult hours, but he was not there to give her spiritual solace. When he heard the news or whether he went to Scotland with her are not known.

Probably Peters did not go to Scotland. His biographer reports that Peters went to London from Liverpool in mid-August and then to the Penns at Stoke. On September 16, Peters was in London receiving two certificates from Bishop Richard Terrick. One committed Peters to "conform to the Liturgy of the Church of England" and the other licensed him to "perform the office of priest in the United Churches of Christ and St. Peters."[61] While in London, he stayed at the residence of Thomas Penn in Spring Gardens, where he received a letter addressed to him there and dated September 23.[62] There hardly seems time in this schedule to have squeezed in a trip to Scotland, since it would have taken about a week to get there. Certainly he did meet her at Lea Hall as promised, where he gave her religious consolation on her mother's death. He would have pointed out that although the death was a great loss for family and friends, Ann Graeme was far happier after death than she had been before.

Despite her grief, Elizabeth did go north to visit her cousin, Thomas Graeme, at Balgowan in Perthshire. Peters would not be ready to leave England before the end of September, and she did not want to travel back to Pennsylvania alone. Nothing was to be accomplished by her sitting in her London lodging grieving. She adhered to her planned schedule and was in Scotland by the end of July or early August. On September 5, she wrote a poem about "being at the Hermitage belonging to the Duke of Athol at Dunkeld in the Highland of Scotland" where she spent two days. No details remain of her stay with her cousin other than the report that he "received her very kindly." When she left, her cousin gave her several books, "containing his book-plate and the Graeme coat-of-arms."[63]

Before she left England, Elizabeth made time in London to have the Graeme coat-of-arms engraved with her name underneath. Later in Philadelphia, she had book plates made from the engraving, and several of her existing books bear that plate. She also worked out the coat-of-arms in a silk embroidery about two-feet square, which became a treasured heirloom in the Smith family. She was the only woman in colonial times to use a heraldic plate.[64]

Among the books that her cousin gave Elizabeth during her stay was a "large and very elegant edition of Ossian's Poems and the 'Song of Selma'" as a present for her father. Her host told her that they had been translated into English "by his son's tutor—a man of fine taste, and a good scholar," named James Macpherson, who had lived in their household for three or four years in the late 1750s. After he left the Graemes' employment, Macpherson published several volumes of what he claimed were English translations of poems written by an old Gaelic bard named Ossian. Lady Christian, Graeme's wife, told Elizabeth that Macpherson "after his stay with them . . . made frequent excursions into the Highlands, and always returned with fresh ballads which he had learned, and many written fragments."[65] These melancholy romances became very popular all over Europe, with Ossian being called by some people a great epic poet comparable to Homer. Close analysis of the poems, however, raised questions about their authenticity that caused others to call them spurious. Elizabeth at the time knew nothing of the controversy. She wrote later that if she had known of "the dispute about whether they were genuine or not," she would have made more inquiries than she did.

By September 22, she was back in London; Peters was at Stoke Poges with the Penns, urging her to join him there.[66] His servant, James, was in the city attending to Elizabeth's wishes. Peters gave her some shopping chores to do for him, gifts for his family.

While she was in Scotland, a young man from Pennsylvania, Nathaniel Evans, had arrived in London, sent by Dr. William Smith to be ordained. Evans was a very gifted unmarried Pennsylvania native five years younger than Elizabeth. He had attended the Academy in Philadelphia for six years and then become apprenticed to a merchant. A call to the cloth brought him back to the Academy for a masters of arts degree, earned in 1765. His intellectual accomplishments brought him to the attention of Dr. Smith, who encouraged Evans to take the final measures necessary to become a minister in the Anglican Church. Evans was a poet and published some of his poems in the *London Chronicle* while in that city. He called on Elizabeth in London, and they quickly found they had many common interests. He, too, was well read and liked literary discussion. His company would make the tedious ocean trip bearable and even amusing for the bereft woman.

Leaving England was not easy for either Elizabeth or Peters. It was especially difficult for Peters who had to say goodbye to all his relatives and the Thomas Penn family with whom he had such a close relationship, never again to see any of these people so dear to him. For Elizabeth, the leave-taking was ambiguous, since her family and closest friends were in Pennsylvania. She wrote that she hardly knew "what my Sensations were, when I went up the Ship side, a mixture of Pain & Pleasure, from my peculiar Situation." She wanted to see her family, yet she regretted leaving her new friends in England.

> I have receiv'd not only marks of Civility but real Friendship from People much my Superiors in Engld. . . . upon the whole I like Engld. much, ev'ry Art & Science, every particular Mode of Life, People may indulge the Hobby Horse to the utmost extent in, for the Number of People, create such a Variety of Pursuits, that London is the Mart for Knowledge & Pleasure, & Goodness & Virtue are by Individuals, as much practised here as any where. I love

Engld. because My dear Mamma was born in it, I love it because
it has given Birth to so many great & good Men, whose Writings
have helped to form our Education in America; & I love it because
I have been treated with Humanity, Respect & Politeness.[67]

Yet her enthusiasm for England was not without reservations. The
"Scenes of Pleasure & Disipation" had made her uncomfortable. "To be
sure if you have an unlimited Taste for Pleasure, have Health & Fortune,
here is the Place, but you must even then, have Moments of Doubt,
whether that Indulgence of Desires, is Consistent with Candidates & Pro-
bationers for Eternity." Even though Elizabeth "was delighted with a thousand things" in England, there was one characteristic of the country that
she did not like: its coal buring fires. Twenty years later, she wrote to
Benjamin Rush how much she enjoyed Pennsylvania's "snaping Crackling
Bouncing" hickory fires and how she had never failed to speak of them
"with Hyperbolical praise," when in England. One day, she had heard Dr.
Fothergill and some friends discussing the number of English suicides "in
the gloomy month of <u>November</u> When a french writer says Englishmen
hang themselves." Half joking and half serious, she told Fothergill that the
suicides were caused by the "<u>Gloom</u> of their Coal-Fires."[68]

The travelers sailed from Gravesend on October 7,[69] on the *Mary
and Elizabeth,* James Sparks captain, but did not arrive in Philadelphia until
December 26. The intervening two and a half months were spent navigat-
ing the Atlantic in what would be called today a very small ship, sails buffeted by prevailing winds or left empty by failing breezes. Before they even
had left English waters, the ship lay for three weeks off the Isle of Wight,
waiting for a favorable wind.

During the idle hours, Elizabeth and Nathaniel discovered that
they had many interests in common. To her Laura, he became Strephon.
Strephon proposed that they exchange poetry to wile away the time. Only
two of these productions remain, one of his and hers in response, copied
by Elizabeth into her commonplace book *Poemata Juvenilia.*[70] He wrote,
"<u>Lauras</u> sweet Notes shall still aswage / The rough winds and old <u>Time</u>
beguile." She agreed.

> Employment makes the Hours to smile
> And hastens Time away;
> My Pen my pensive Days beguile,
> While here we loitering Lay.

During this trip, Strephon fell deeply in love with Laura, and she might have loved him in return if he had lived to press his suit. He certainly would have been a fitting spouse, sharing her intellectual interests and having a quick wit and intelligence of his own.

Captain Sparks brought his passengers safely into Philadelphia on a Thursday, the day after Christmas. Elizabeth's reunion with Ann Stedman and her father after the eighteen-month separation was both tearful and joyous. Many hours were spent telling Elizabeth about her mother's last days, and Elizabeth opened the two letters her mother had left for her, "one, upon the choice of a husband, and the other upon the management of a family."

Only the first letter, written by Ann Graeme in 1762, remains in copy form. In it, she expressed her love for Elizabeth, telling her that she had always been a perfect daughter. Even in infancy, she had been "delightful," "a pleasant and quiet baby," and she had grown into someone "beyond [her] own or any bodies expectation." She reminded her daughter of her religious obligation to worship God and study the scriptures daily, to believe them explicitly and refuse to listen to skeptics. She was to cling to her family union and to marry a man who supported that union. About selecting a husband, she wrote:

> We women have it only in our power to deny, I cannot call it a choice, but I hope you will never bestow yourself on any other than one who is generally reputed a good and sensible man, with such a one a woman cannot be unhappy. When you meet with such a one take him with all his faults and frailties (for none are without) and when you have him expect not too much from him, for depend upon it this is like all sublunary things, the higher your ideas are the greater will be your disappointment.

She also charged her daughter to look after her father and, in an addendum written later, the grandchildren.[71]

Elizabeth could not be sorry for her mother, because she, too, believed her in a better place, but she was sorry for herself because of the void created by her mother's death. As Dr. John Morgan had written her in solace, "Happy are those who make a wise improvement of their Talents, & happy are they when the fiery Trial is over since they are thenceforward secure in the Enjoyment of their highest & only happiness through the endless Ages of time."[72] No one doubted that Ann Graeme was among the chosen.

If Elizabeth's loss had not seemed real to her in England, the familiar places where Ann Graeme had always been but was no more made her mother's death terribly real. The house empty of her mother's presence, the chair at the dining room table without the familiar person in it, the embroidery lying unfinished on the table, the book marked where Ann Graeme had last read—all brought grief to her even stronger than when she first had heard of her mother's death.

4

The Most Learned Woman in America

Shortly after Elizabeth's return from England, her only remaining sibling, Ann Graeme Stedman, died of a painful unknown disease, the air "pierced with her departing Crys." Elizabeth believed that she died of a broken heart, grieving for her mother. "She saw good Anna go: her gentle Soul / Dissolvd in Softenss could not Grief controul," Elizabeth wrote the following summer. These two deaths changed her life. From being the focus of family solicitude as daughter and younger sister, Elizabeth became the responsible person in the family, caregiver for an aged father, who would die soon, and for two small children, who would grow up and leave her wing. She saw herself as "an Exile left, forlorn, alone, / One antient Parent all I claim my own."[1] Grieving for her lost mother and sister, she was grieving for herself as well, as she entered upon a period of self-redefining.

Now twenty-eight years old, unmarried, and childless, Elizabeth had to decide what her life was going to be like and what kind of person she was going to be. Her options, however, were limited. The College of Philadelphia was not open to women and neither were the professions. Businesses were occasionally run by women, but more often they had succeeded to them upon the deaths of their husbands.[2] After years of helping run those businesses, they already knew how to manage them successfully. Elizabeth had had no such experience. Some thirty different trades in Philadelphia were followed by women,[3] but Elizabeth lacked the necessary training for such an occupation. In addition, she was the only heir of a father whose financial situation appeared to be quite sound. It was not necessary for her to support herself. For her to seek such a role only to occupy her time would have been so unusual, so startling, so outside the expectations of society for a gentlewoman of her economic and social position, that it never occurred to her that she might develop a business or learn a trade. But how was she to fill the hours to provide meaning and definition to her life? She had her sister's children to raise, since their father appeared incapable of doing it, but they would outgrow her care. The only answer available to her, considering her own inclinations and talents and the limitations imposed by society, was to bury herself in her books and her writing.

Her confusion is shown in her poem "Some lines upon my first being at *Graeme Park;* after my return from England," written August 16, 1766, and dedicated "To Memory." The poem begins with a call to memory to show her happier times "When Life was fresh; and all her Scenes were new." She remembers her childhood and her mother's teaching. If only she had known her mother was dying, she would not have gone to England, she laments. She would have been there to "snatch the mournful last departing Sigh." She had not forgotten her family, however, all the time she was in England and Scotland. No matter what wonders she saw, and she reviews some of them in the poem, still she remembered Graeme Park and her loved ones there. Then she asks what her future will be and considers various possibilities. "If Narrow Fortune prove my humble Lot, / Let me not Envy the luxuriant Spot." If "Gay Pleasure" and "giddy Mirth" should beckon, she hopes "With decent dignity" to "turn aside." But whatever happens, whatever new "Scheme" she pursues, she must "Still keep the great immortal part in view." The poem ends with a plea to God for her eventual salvation. "Place me Oh *God* at My *Redeemers* hand!" This is the troubled plea of a woman who though mature in years does not yet know who she is or what her place can be.

One of the first painful tasks for Elizabeth was to write an epitaph for her mother to be engraved on the family's gravestone in Christ Church graveyard. Before she finished it, Ann Stedman died. A poem, completed July 22, mourned both women:

Forgive, Great God, this one last filial Tear!
Indulge my sorrow on a Theme so near:
This Earth Born Strain indulge, that mourns the Blest,

Elizabeth Fergusson. From *The Pennsylvania Magazine of History and Biography* 39.3 (1915): 261. Courtesy of Rare Books and Manuscripts, Special Collections Library, The Pennsylvania State University Libraries, University Park, Pennsylvania.

And doubly mourns, because they were the Best.
Tho' Truth remonstrates, Self Love will prevail,
And sink the Beam in Nature's feeble scale,
A God incarnate once wept o'er Lazurus dead;
Tho power Divine recall'd his Soul when fled
A poor frail Being weeps a Mother gone;
The Tomb scarce closed before a Sister's flown.
Each was a Guide, a Pattern, and a Friend;
She prays to join when fleeting Life shall end.[4]

These two deaths coming so closely upon one another caused Elizabeth great suffering. But this was not the end of deaths to be mourned. Rev. Collin Campbell, minister at St. Mary's Church in Burlington and husband of Mary Campbell who was such a good friend of both Elizabeth and her mother, died later in 1766. Elizabeth had had many loving visits at the parish in Burlington. "What e'er he gave he freely did impart / And Shard his Blessings with an open Heart," she remembered in a memorial poem.[5]

What helped Elizabeth cope with her grief that spring was an extended visit to Graeme Park by Nathaniel Evans and his eventual settling nearby. His health was poor, and he needed to be near his physician, Dr. Graeme, and he also wanted to be near the doctor's daughter. While at Graeme Park, he wrote "An Ode" about the beauties of nature on the estate. One verse speaks flatteringly of its mistress:

Thus musing o'er the charming plains,
(Where *Graeme* the just and good retires,
Where *Laura* breathes her tender strains,
Whom ev'ry graceful muse inspires)[6]

When his health seemingly improved, the young minister took up his pastoral duties as missionary for Gloucester County, New Jersey, living at Haddonfield, across the Delaware River, not too far from Graeme Park. He and Elizabeth kept up their friendship, exchanging poetry. She seemed willing to enjoy his attention and to flirt with him, but not to commit herself when he began to approach too closely. During that summer, she wrote a parody on some lines from Alexander Pope's "Eloise to Abelard," which were about a country minister and which seemed obviously about

Nathaniel. A friend of hers told him they were, and he wrote an answer, which inspired another from her. In these bits of verse, the comic prevails, although Evans did not appreciate her wit at his expense. She wrote

> How happy is the country Parson's lot?
> Forgetting *Bishops,* as by *them* forgot
> Tranquil of spirit, with an easy mind,
> To all his *Vestry's* votes he sits resign'd:
> Of manners gentle, and of temper even,
> He jogs his flocks, with easy pace, to heaven.
> In Greek and Latin, pious books he keeps;
> And, while his Clerk sings psalms, he soundly sleeps.
> His garden fronts the sun's sweet orient beams,
> And fat church-wardens prompt his golden dreams,
> The earliest fruit, in his fair orchard, blooms;
> And cleanly pipes pour out tobacco's fumes.
> From rustic bridegroom oft he takes the ring;
> And hears the milk-maid plaintive ballads sing.
> Back-gammon cheats whole winter nights away,
> And Pilgrim's Progress helps a rainy day.[7]

He returned, "I lately saw, no matter where, / A parody, by Laura fair." A friend had shown him the verses and had identified him as the country parson. He denied that he smoked "*Tobacco* vile" or slept in church.

> As for the table of Back-*gammon,*
> 'Tis far beyond the reach of Damon;
> But, place right *gammon*[8] on a table,
> And then to play a knife I'm able.

He concluded the poem with a semi-serious proposal of marriage:

> Yet, if the happiness, fair maid,
> That sooths me in the silent shade,
> Should, in your eye, appear too great,
> Come, take it all and share my fate![9]

Laura wrote back, calling Nathaniel a "*saucy* friend" and denying that her poem was about him:

> 'Tis true, the moments I beguil'd,
> And at a country parson smil'd;
> Unhappy me! who ne'er could dream,
> That you should think yourself the theme;

And then she gave him a sharp reproof for presuming to have suggested matrimony.

> Yet, e'er I close allow me time,
> But just to add another rhyme.
> Since I esteem your bliss so great,
> In pennance you will chuse a mate,
> And tell me—"I may share your fate!"
> The scheme is good, I must confess,
> If you have bliss, to make it less!
> Yet, take a hint, before resolv'd,
> And in the *dragging chain* involv'd
> While youthful joys around you shine,
> Haste not to bend at Hymen's shrine;
> Let friendship, gen'rous friendship be
> The bond to fetter you and me,
> *Vestal, Platonic,* what you will,
> So virtue reigns with freedom still.
> But if, in matrimonial noose,
> You must be bound–and have a spouse;
> The faithful rib that heav'n shall send,
> I'll fondly greet, and call her friend[10]

Not to be outdone by his friend at Graeme Park, Evans continued the raillery, begging her forgiveness:

> Laura, for once excuse, I pray,
> The pertness of a rural lay;
> And I will ne'er again offend,
> Or need the name of saucy friend;

He excused his presumptuous behavior as the result of "a gay farce" carried on by their mutual friend "Stella" who had told him he was "the country parson." Determined to repay her ribbing, he had "seiz'd [his] pen." "And, in a fit of *warm regard*, / Dropt a few words-*quite off my guard*." When Cupid should incline to conquer him, it would be with "A *silken* cord," not a Dragging chain." He ended wishing her happiness "Whether in sacred wedlock join'd, / Or to the *Vestal* state inclined."[11]

What did this poetic exchange mean? Evans was testing the waters to see what kind of response he would receive to his jocular proposal. He was smitten with Elizabeth, encouraged perhaps by her father who would have regarded Evans as a good prospective son-in-law. Although he was just a poor "country parson," as Elizabeth had described him, he was well educated, intelligent, and moral, and, even more to the point, had interests in common with her. As for the young woman, her written denials cannot be taken literally. In her romance with William Franklin, she had denied any commitment to him, but her reaction to his marriage to someone else showed otherwise. Furthermore, if she had not been intrigued by the attentive young parson, she would not have bothered to send him poetry, and she would not have given him the same pseudonym, Damon, that she had given Franklin.

By August of 1766, Elizabeth, retired to Graeme Park, "over-whelmed With Grief for the Loss of [her] *Mother* and *Sister*," was looking for "a Rational and Pious Source of entertainment" for her "pensive mind." She believed that "the Mind was never so wretched as without a pursuit," yet she "had no relish for dissipated Pleasures." In her anguish, she found both solace and diversion in the Bible, her constant reading companion ever since her childhood. Her mother had used the Psalms as a teaching tool, requiring her to read them out loud. When Elizabeth had been troubled, Mrs. Graeme had suggested that she reread the Psalms, until they had become for the daughter "a very favorite Subject of [her] Medita-tions."[12] To assuage her grief that summer, she turned again to the Psalms, looking for peace in her faith, and then she applied her interest in poetry to her religion and began to paraphrase the Psalms in poetry, as an intellectual exercise, an "amusement."

The possibility of paraphrasing the Psalms had occurred to her as early as 1763, when her childhood friend Francis Hopkinson had published *A Collection of Psalm Tunes, with a few Anthems and Hymns,* for parishioners at Christ Church and St. Peters to join in singing. The following year he was commissioned to prepare the Psalms for a Dutch congregation, and these appeared in 1767. During this period, Hopkinson was a frequent visitor at Graeme Park. In July 1763, he and James Young were there together for a weekend, and the three friends experimented with rewriting the Psalms, trying different versions on each other.[13] It is reasonable to assume that Elizabeth and Frank must have discussed the Psalms again. They were good friends and saw each other often. After her return from abroad, she and Nathaniel Evans also had talked about the Psalms. In the book of Evans's poems that William Smith and Elizabeth edited and published posthumously, there are four Psalm paraphrases. That Evans had shared his attempts with her or with gatherings of their friends while he was alive is likely, since Elizabeth and the literary group about her frequently sent each other poems for discussion or read them when the group gathered.

In 1766, the versifying of the Psalms gave her something to do during her mourning period and helped her work through it to acceptance of her loss. In reviewing her favorites, she relived "all those Pleasures which [she had] experienced in that sweet period of Vernal youth; And [she] again [saw her] self with that dear Guide of [her] Infant Years accompanyd by those train of tender Ideas" which were returning too frequently to interrupt her peace of mind.[14] Trying to cope with grief and insecurity, she turned to the Psalms for consolation and answers. Without consciously planning to go through them all, Elizabeth was "Insensibly led in further, and Further . . . [as] the task grew every Day more and more pleasing" and as her sorrow began to lighten. Ultimately she paraphrased them all using classical iambic tetrameter.

This was a tremendous task. The paraphrasing and her annotations fill two thick quarto volumes, bound in red leather.[15] Ultimately there would be four of these volumes of identical size from this period of her life, an incredible output. The Psalm volumes were dedicated to Richard Peters, and she left the first on a table in his parlor to surprise him at the end of March 1767, seven months after she had begun. The volume starts with a long letter to Peters explaining why she had undertaken this project. She dedicated the volume to him, she wrote, because he was her religious teacher and adviser who had rendered "the most tender Care and friendly Attention to [her] welfare in this Life and happines hereafter."

In her letter to Peters, Elizabeth candidly admitted that some of her Psalms were "dull and lifeless to a great degree." This is largely true.

They do not have much literary merit. For example, here is the beginning of her version of the Twenty-third Psalm:

> The Lord supream doth Condescend
> My Path to guard, my Steps to tend:
> The heavenly *Shepherd* Guides my Ways;
> And Crowns with joy my Prosperous Days.
> He leads me to the Verdant Meads,
> And from the purest Pasturs feeds;
> Or by meandring Waters Sides;
> Where murmuring Fountains smoothly glides.

It would be very difficult to equal the soaring beauty of the version in the King James Bible: "The Lord *is* my shepherd; I shall not want. He maketh me to lie down in green pastures; he leadeth me beside the still waters."[16]

Sometime during this period, Peters returned the book to Elizabeth. He parted with it "as a Man subject to Cold parts with a good warm fire—he knows his Chilliness will return & continue till he can get again to the Comforts of it." Her fire "burns brighter as one sees more of heaven in it, & fainter as we see . . . an earthly nature contending with it." He suggests that the next time he is at Graeme Park, they discuss the Psalms "at such times as the other parts of the family are in Enjoyment of their own peculiar pleasure." The rest of his forwarding letter discusses people's right to freedom of expression. Peters was not always clear in his writing, and his message in this case is uncertain, but it does seem as though he was preparing her to receive some gentle criticism.[17]

Although the paraphrases are stilted and the rhyming forced, the exercise had accomplished what Elizabeth had intended for it. By March 1767, she was beginning to set aside her sorrow and take up her life again. Her grief, she wrote Mrs. Campbell, had "Exhausted itself," although her "Beloved Sisters Death had well nigh broke [her] Heart." To re-establish her social life, she had to return some "hundred and ten" calls made by her friends since her return from England. Even if this was an exaggeration, the visiting with her many friends would help complete the healing process, and the fact that she was ready to begin indicated progress already made.

After completing the Psalms, Elizabeth also paraphrased other sections of the Bible. For example, she did Augur's Prayer from Proverbs 30, verses 7, 8, 9, and the Parable of the Prodigal Son from the 15th chapter of

St. Luke, in November 1767.[18] There are nine existing paraphrases from this period and one other undated. Later she would publish three of these.[19]

Continuing her friendship with Evans, she exchanged poems with him in the spring of 1767, again inspired by a mistaken identity. Thomas Coombs, also a minister, had written a poem bidding farewll to the "Muse" in favor of "Reason." Elizabeth acquired this poem and, thinking it the work of Evans, wrote a poetic response, "The Dignity of the Muse Asserted," and sent it to him. Not knowing of the original poem, his answer was based solely on her lines. He denied that he was abandoning the Muse, "I too much in the Muse delight, / To bid her Ladyship good Night." If he had inclined to desert the Muse, however, Laura's "Song would Captivate [his] Soul."

But this romance was not to proceed any further. Evans's health continued a decline that the good Dr. Graeme was unable to stop. The young pastor died on October 29, 1767, supposedly of overwork as a missionary, but later diagnosis has blamed tuberculosis.[20]

Soon after his death, Elizabeth and the Rev. William Smith collected Evans's poems in a small volume and invited subscribers to pledge support for its publication. The list of 453 persons who responded to this plea is comprised of the names not only of prominent Philadelphians but also of men and women from other colonies and from Edinburgh, Nova Scotia, Halifax, Quebec, London, Bristol, Barbados. Lawyers, doctors, governors, ministers, the Speaker of the Pennsylvania Assembly, teachers, merchants, the attorney-general of Maryland, college professors, and representatives of many crafts all subscribed so that Evans's poems could be published. The list even includes the name Oliver Goldsmith, Esq., London. It is an amazing collection. Altogether they ordered 876 copies of the book.[21] How Elizabeth and Smith won this support is not known, but it could not have been by advertisement alone. They must have written letters all over the English-speaking world and perhaps persuaded pastors to announce the call for subscriptions in the Anglican churches as well. The resultant book, which appeared in 1772, begins with a preface by Smith and a poetic eulogy by Laura referring to Evans as Strephon and includes close to fifty complete and fragmentary poems and a sermon. Among the poems are several of Laura's that elicited responses by Evans or are responses to his. This may have been the first time any of her verses were published.

An interesting and unexplained feature of the book was Elizabeth's and William Smith's editing of the poems. Evans had published one of his efforts, "To Benjamin Franklin, Esq., L.L.D. Occasioned by hearing him play on the Harmonica," in *The London Chronicle* of August 31 to September 3, 1765. When Elizabeth and Smith included this work in the volume, they cut one third of the lines, from forty-eight to thirty, and changed the wording in several places. For example, the first line in the *Chronicle* reads: "Long had we, lost in grateful wonder, view'd" whereas in *Poems on Several Occasions*, it is "In grateful wonder lost, long had we view'd." The book acknowledges that editing had been done, but does not delineate specific changes made or tell by whom that editing was done. If editing of this dimension was commonplace, modern publishers of the poetry of this period need to reconsider the general practice of including the published version as the one most likely to have been the latest version of the author.

During this period, Elizabeth completed another large literary project: a verse translation of the prose work *Les Adventures de Télémaque,* shortened by Elizabeth to Telemachus. Written by François de Salignac de la Mothe-Fénelon and published in France in 1699, *Télémaque* in French was not published in America until 1784, but imported copies had circulated there. English translations had appeared in England and Ireland in 1719, 1725, and 1747, and Latin and Italian translations were published in 1742 and 1743. *Télémaque* was very popular in the colonies, a favorite with Elizabeth ever since her childhood. There had been no translations into English verse, however, before Elizabeth's undertaking.[22] Her work takes up two volumes of the same size as the two Psalms books and includes some 30,000 lines of poetry, a truly herculean task. Her introductory note is dated March 14, 1769, and was written around the time of the work's completion. She probably began it in 1767, when she finished paraphrasing the Psalms. In her commonplace book *Poemata Juvenilia*, she wrote that she "translated Telemachus from the original French into English verse in 24 Books; in the Space of Three years 67, 68, 69 when She was 29 and 30 31 years of age."[23]

In the introduction she explained how she had approached the project:

> The Translation is aimed at being as literal as the different Languages will admit, Added to the restraint of Verse, which unavoidable lengthens the performance. To prevent Obscurity: The present time is more frequently used than the Past or plu perfect; as In poetry by using the present tense the object described in a more lively manner comes in view than in the past.

"What the Critics call Personification," she continued,

> which is giving a personage to an inanimate thing is sometimes introduced here; when it is not in the original to prevent the Style being too Prosaic, which notwithstanding it is to be feared is still the Case, when the Translator has tryd to Shun Bombast, and Obscurity: and endeavord to introduce perspicuity.

She concluded the introduction by acknowledging that the work contains "ten thousand faults," but since it was done only to provide "a private amusement" and not intended to be published, they do not matter. The end was answered "when the translator was amusd . . . by the employment." Twenty years later, however, Elizabeth added marginal notes and at that time she wrote that if she lived long enough, she intended to write "a more correct Version," and if encouraged, she might have it printed. In the late 1780s, she did try to have it published, but her lack of money and her refusal to let her friends raise the necessary cost by subscriptions kept the manuscript out of print. The two manuscript volumes remain on the shelves of the Historical Society of Pennsylvania, a tribute to her dedication and intellect.

At the beginning of the translation, Elizabeth inserted a poem of her own, an "Invocation to Wisdom":

> Grave <u>Wisdom</u>! Guardian of the modest youth;
> Thou Soul of Knowledge! and thou Source of Truth,
> Inspire my <u>Muse</u>, and Animate her Lays,
> That she harmonious may Chaunt forth thy Praise.
>
> Passion and Wisdom hold perpetual strife
> Through the strange mazes of man's chequered life,
> Of all the evils our frail Nature knows,
> The most acute from Love's emotions flows.

This was perhaps inspired by Samuel Richardson's "Ode to Wisdom" in his *Clarissa*, a favorite novel among Elizabeth's women friends and often mentioned by her.

In addition to the paraphrases from the Bible and the verse translation of *Télémaque*, which would have been more than enough for any one else, Elizabeth wrote many other pieces. There are twenty-two other poems, one long "Allegory" narrative, and two prose articles that remain from the three year period after August 1766, and, of course, there may have been others now lost or undated. Among the poems, one, "The Dream," is very long, about 700 lines. She rewrote and expanded this in 1793.

This output was very diverse in subject matter. It included light hearted exchanges with Nathaniel Evans and Annis Stockton, elegies for Rev. Campbell, her mother, her sister, and Evans, words for two songs, an acrostic, a prayer, a hymn, a fable, and subject matter as varied as an easy chair, an eclipse, and the character of Richard Peters. Many of the poems, even the lighter ones, contain allusions to Greek mythology and classical writers, and there are literary references to the works of writers such as Pope, Locke, Milton, Thomson, and Shakespeare.

Two selections from this period are articles she wrote for the *Pennsylvania Chronicle* in 1767.[24] While in Philadelphia during the previous winter, she had read a report in a New York newspaper, reprinted in the *Chronicle*, about the desperate situation of imprisoned debtors. The two pence per day allowed for the support of each prisoner barely kept them alive. Their sufferings so moved Elizabeth that she sent her servant with a pot of broth to the Philadelphia jail, and she urged her women readers to follow her example and send their table scraps to the jail instead of to the waste heap. She reminded her readers that the name of their city meant "Fraternal Love." Her concern for others less fortunate lasted all her life even during the years when her small donations to charity entailed a substantial sacrifice.

The second article on "Benevolence" called for contributions to a subscription going around in Philadelphia for the victims of a fire at Bridgetown, Barbardos. It began with a story from the Greek historian Polybius about King Hiero who had had a magnificent galley built, "one of the wonders of that age," which the article described in engrossing prose intended, she wrote, to capture the attention of its young readers. Hiero had sent his galley loaded with provisions to Alexandria at a time of great famine and to Rhodes after it had been laid waste by a great earthquake. Elizabeth then drew an analogy between the problems of Egypt and Rhodes and the devastation in Barbados and wrote that Philadelphia had the means to help, not on the same scale as Hiero, but Pennsylvania could send some of its "fine wheat" to the Barbadan sufferers. "Public distresses require public Relief," she wrote, "There is a Season when Frugality is Parsimony, and Strict oeconomy meaness."

All her life, Elizabeth read constantly and widely. She read Latin, Greek, French, Italian, and probably German, as well. By 1778, her library consisted of 400 volumes on a great diversity of subjects. Among her favorites, and her mother's as well, were Edward Young's *The Complaint; or Night-Thoughts on Life, Death, and Immortality* (1742–45), a collection of essays in blank verse on religious and ethical conduct and James Thomson's *The Seasons* (1730), a nature poem in blank verse. She also regularly read colonial and English newspapers and magazines. As she grew older, she included more and more annotations in her pieces, explaining the allusions to a reader less well read. In the late 1780s and 90s, she heavily annotated some of her earlier works, such as her verse translation of *Télémaque*.

The Graemes, father and daughter, not only collected a large personal library but also supported the local circulating library in the nearby village of Hatboro. The Union Library Company of Hatborough had been started in 1755 by four local men to combat "black and dark ignorance."[25] The thirty-eight original members agreed to pay twenty shillings the first year to buy books to start the enterprise and ten shillings in future years. Thomas Graeme was never a member of the company, but both he and Elizabeth made occasional donations of books, beginning in May 1763. The gift titles reveal the catholicity of the Graemes' tastes in literature. There were six books identified in the records as "Barclay's Apology, Christian Obedience, Practical Astronomy, The State of the Protestants in Ireland, and Nelson's Justice," all donated by Elizabeth.[26] Three months later, Dr. Graeme sent the library "Jacob's Law Dictionary, Hawken's Pleas of the Crown, Civil Laws in 2 vols., Woods Institutes, Compleat Husbandry, Modern Husbandry, in 3 vols., Husbandry and Gardening, Stephen's on Potash, and Horsehoeing Husbandry."[27] These were books appropriate for a devoutly Christian community of farmers who often had to solve their legal as well as their agricultural problems without professional help. There are still at least four books in the holdings of the library that have Elizabeth's book plate in front: a Scottish history, an instruction book for the Church of England, a description of a system for ventilating mines, and a book on the British customs service, this last needed by Thomas Graeme in his capacity as Naval Officer of the Port of Philadelphia.

The year 1766 had brought not only the death of Ann Graeme Stedman, but also severe financial reverses to her husband and his brother.

Successful merchants, they had invested in iron works and land speculation. In 1758 they had become part owners of Elizabeth Furnace in Lancaster County and four years later in the Charming Forge. They also were active in the Anglican Churches in Philadelphia and in the new college. Both men began in 1765 to build large new houses for themselves in the city, appropriate to the level of their prosperity. But the houses were not finished when their fortunes began to decline, perhaps because of the boycott of British products in opposition to the Stamp Act, and they had to start selling off their holdings.[28] The waning fortunes of the Stedmans greatly concerned the Graeme family, and around this time, Dr. Graeme agreed to stand security for a debt of £800 contracted by the Stedmans.[29] This would become important during the settlement of Dr. Graeme's estate in late 1772.

Although Thomas Graeme had always been able to provide handsomely for his family, his income depended upon his medical practice supplemented by return from Graeme Park and his earnings from public employment. His savings had been invested in the estate. By 1767 Graeme was almost eighty years old and subject to increasing deafness, which forced him to limit his practice. By 1771, he gave it up entirely, only examining and giving medicines to poor people who consulted him.[30] The family's financial situation had been augmented over the years by the kindness of Thomas Penn, who had awarded a number of posts to Dr. Graeme that had increased his position and income substantially. In 1755, Graeme had thanked Penn for his patronage, without which his career would have stagnated and his plans for his family "been almost sunk."[31] By 1760, the appointment as Naval Officer was the only office he still held, and he held this position in name only. He drew the salary, but another man did the work for a small stipend. Yet the retained portion of his salary was a very important increment of the Graeme family income.

By 1768, this lucrative post was coveted by another man in Philadelphia, an old favorite of Thomas Penn, named Richard Hockley, the son of a one-time partner of Penn who had died. The widow and her three children had moved to Philadelphia where she had re-married. Penn was very fond of her children, especially young Richard, to whom he occasionally wrote letters and whom he had given an appointment to be Receiver-General of the colony. Over the years, Hockley's eyes had begun to bother him, and he wanted a less demanding appointment, specifically the one held by Graeme as Naval Officer, which paid £300 a year with no work required. Penn wanted to help Hockley, yet he did not wish to injure Dr. Graeme. The proprietor finally resolved to let Graeme keep the appointment and its rewards, while appointing Hockley auditor of Penn's accounts with a salary of £300 and the promise of Graeme's job in the future.[32] The loss of that much income would have cut considerable inroads into the standard of living of the doctor and his daughter. Their income then would have been limited to the earnings from Graeme Park, which Graeme ran more as a gentleman's estate than as a business venture.

When Ann Graeme was alive, she had managed the family household and supervised the servants. With her death, these jobs had fallen on Elizabeth, who did not enjoy the responsibility. "If I had not my Father, and the Children," she wrote, "I hate housekeep so much that I Never would encumber my Self with it in any degree; for I find it a very great Tryal to the temper." She had begun life with the belief that if she used people well they would react favorably, but she had found that servants, with whom she had continuing difficulties, were not responsive.

She also was finding her responsibility for her sister's children a great task. She admitted that she "never was so fond of Children As many People are," but since Providence had given her Anny and John she would try to do the best she could to educate them. Both children received their educations in Philadelphia schools, as well as from their aunt and grandfather. John attended the Academy during the winter, and his grandfather taught him Latin during the summers. Anny's school is not known. She was her aunt's particular province. Elizabeth taught her needlework and reading, choosing and explaining books to her, using the same general methods of instruction that her mother had used with her daughters. She intended to "keep her Steadily engaged in Learning till Sixteen at least."[33] No matter how she felt about children in general, Elizabeth and her charges would become very close; they developed a deep love and respect for her.

There is a story that when John was young, he was guilty of some infringement of the family rules. To punish him, Elizabeth is supposed to have confined him to his grandfather's library. The child was bored, and to relieve the tedium, he looked into one of the books there. Fortunately he chose one that would interest a young person. He became so engrossed in that book that for the rest of his life he was a devoted reader and scholar, at least according to family history.[34]

As word of Elizabeth's intellectual accomplishments spread, her number of correspondents and friends grew as people wanted to meet her. In September 1766, she received a poem from Annis Stockton of Princeton,[35] reporting that Elizabeth's "Fame" had reached her "calm retreat," and inspired her to seek Laura's friendship. She asked "fair <u>Laura</u>" to "kindly condescend / And to her Bosom take another Friend."[36] Although the poem implies that this was a new acquaintance, the two women must have known each other as children. Annis had been born in Philadelphia and had lived there until 1751. It is likely that their parents had known each other. Annis's pseudonym was Emelia, and the two women became fast friends, exchanging poems and visits for the rest of their lives.

Laura answered Emelia, welcoming her friendship, although disclaiming the "fame" Emelia had attributed to her as from a "partial Tongue." In spite of this "Error," Elizabeth was grateful for it because it brought Emelia's friendship. She mentioned the deaths of her mother and sister and implied that Emelia might take the place of a sister. She wished Emelia a happy life "Unruffled by Afflictions gloomy Storm," and concluded "Whether in *Verse* or *Prose* my thoughts combine / I am with gratful Ardor ever thine." This sort of sentimental communication was quite common among women.

Emelia answered Laura denying her own poetic skills while admiring Laura's. Her own mother, Catherine Williams Boudinot, had died the previous November, and her husband, Richard Stockton, was in England. Annis, by now with several children, had refused to leave her little ones to accompany him. She referred to her own emotional needs in her final lines:

A *Mothers* Death demands the filial Tear
An *Absent Husband* Claims the sigh Sincere;
But in My *Laura's* Friendship I shall find
A balmy Cordial for my Anxious Mind.[37]

While Richard Stockton was in England, he visited Alexander Pope's gardens at Twickenham, which had become quite famous ever since a plan of the gardens had been published in 1745. Apparently this book had not been available to Annis or she wanted more details because Richard took with him a man who could draw, to sketch the gardens for Annis. She was particularly interested in a picture of Pope's grotto to help her create one for their home, which she had named Morven from the Ossian epic. Her husband also sent her bulbs from England.

The friendship between Elizabeth and Annis, a year older, expanded to include the members of both families. Annis was the sister of Elias Boudinot, who was destined to take a very prominent role in the prosecution of the war and the development of a national government after independence had been won. Richard Stockton's sister Hannah had married Elias Boudinot to complete the circle of family entanglement. Elizabeth's friendship with Annis enlarged to include the extended Boudinot and Stockton families. This was a very important connection when Elizabeth during the war became embroiled in controversy with the Pennsylvania government. Boudinot became a highly respected member of the Revolutionary movement, first as commissary-general of prisoners, then as president of Continental Congress. As a brother figure to Elizabeth, he tried to protect her, to save her from financial disaster, and their correspondence continued throughout her life.

By early 1767, Elizabeth was back in Philadelphia. With her mother gone, Elizabeth became her father's hostess, and she began to keep regular calling hours on Saturday evenings when friends were invited to drop by the Graemes' Philadelphia home for conversation and exchange of ideas. These evenings grew into what several historians have called the first literary salon in North America. Such gatherings had begun in seventeenth-century France and had appeared later in London, where Elizabeth had encountered them.[38] Actually, Ann Graeme had held similar meetings when friends with shared intellectual interests had called on her. After her mother's death, Elizabeth continued and enlarged her mother's practice, making it a regular event. Many of the most literate people of the colony made regular attendance at Miss Graeme's a must when in Philadelphia. Dr. Benjamin Rush, Dr. John and Mary (Hopkinson) Morgan, Rev. William and Rebecca (Moore) Smith, Rev. Thomas Coombs, Rev. Jacob and Elizabeth (Hopkinson) Duché, John Dickinson, Francis and Ann (Borden) Hopkinson, the five Willing sisters, various members of the Stockton family when they were in the city, and many others. Single as well as married women came and perhaps met their future spouses there. Newcomers to Philadelphia were brought by friends to Miss Graeme's soirées. Her fame spread over the city as a gracious, perceptive, brilliant, and witty hostess. After her death, Benjamin Rush wrote an effusive description of how Elizabeth dominated these evening discussions:

> These evenings were, properly speaking, of the attic kind. The genius of Miss Graeme evolved the heat and light that animated

them. One while she instructed by the stores of knowledge contained in the historians, philosophers, and poets of ancient and modern nations, which she called forth at her pleasure; and again she charmed by a profusion of original ideas, collected by her vivid and widely expanded imagination, and combined with exquisite taste and judgment into an endless variety of elegant and delightful forms. Upon these occasions her body seemed to evanish, and she appeared to be all mind.[39]

Philadelphia at the end of the eighteenth century was an especially appropriate place for such a gathering to develop because it contained a large number of literary and scientific men and well read, informed women who were encouraged to express their own ideas. An intelligent woman was appreciated in that society. Quakers, from the early part of the century, had favored the education of women as well as men. Even though they were not permitted to attend the college, still girls were taught by parents or tutors to the standards of the Academy and the College of Philadelphia, and self-education carried them the rest of the way to equal the men in intellectual prowess. Sometimes professors from the college taught women privately in addition to their other duties, as did David James Dove.

Pre-Revolutionary Philadelphia was the largest and most culturally developed city in North America. A thriving port with a steadily growing population, it needed constant imports from other parts of the empire to answer the requirements of its citizens. To pay for these imports, Pennsylvania ships left daily for the West Indies, the British isles, ports in Europe, or colonial coastal cities. This meant regular contact with other places and the development of cosmopolitan interests. Many Pennsylvanians traveled to England and Scotland on business or for education. A continental tour became popular among well-to-do Philadelphia men. Newspapers, magazines, and books from other places were available. New ideas circulated in the city, stimulating native creativity. Citizens knew of the arts available in other places, and they wanted their city to have cultural opportunities such as concerts and plays. The affluent wanted and were willing to support services, such as dancing teachers, language instructors, and music teachers.

When John Penn, an amateur musician himself, came to Philadelphia in late 1763 to become governor of the province, among his party was a music master who soon established a music school where he taught various instruments. Elizabeth took music lessons from him the following winter, probably on the harpsichord.[40] As a result of her interest in the instrument, she commissioned Francis Hopkinson, who was a talented musician and composer, to select a harpsichord for her when he went to England in 1766. He wrote in February the next year, that he had finally shipped the instrument and that he hoped it would arrive safely.[41] There is no remaining mention of this instrument, whether Elizabeth learned to play it proficiently. We know that it was received because in 1778 when an inventory was made of Elizabeth's belongings, the harpsichord was listed among the parlor furniture.[42] It must have occupied a place of distinction and have been played by Hopkinson, if not by Elizabeth. Another close friend, Jacob Duché, played the organ and sang. He and his wife, Elizabeth, sister of Francis Hopkinson, liked to gather with friends around the harpsichord and sing songs written by local talents. We can imagine them all at the Graemes' home performing one of the popular Scottish ballads with words written by Elizabeth, perhaps "Content in a Cottage" sung to the music of "The Lass of Peatty's Mill" or "A Song" to the tune of "Tweed Side."[43]

Elizabeth and her friends would also have gone to any musical performances that were offered in Philadelphia. When she was in England, Betsy Stedman had written her a letter mentioning that "we have Concerts this winter [1764–65] as before where I generaly attend."[44] These were a series of concerts at the Assembly Room organized by Hopkinson and his teacher James Bremner, who composed music and played the piano, harpsichord, and other instruments. There had been seventy subscribers for a series of concerts the previous winter from January to May in 1764 before Elizabeth had left. The performers were the few professional musicians in the city and the gentlemen who were amateur musicians. Hopkinson played the harpsicord and John Penn, James Bremner, and others performed on the strings.[45] The first series had been so successful that Bremner had undertaken a second series the following winter, which Betsy Stedman was attending. Her wording implied that the Graemes were subscribers to both concert series. These concerts may have been the catalyst for Elizabeth's ordering of her harpsichord.

Another two series of concerts were given in 1769 and 1770. An Italian wine merchant and musician named Giovanni Gualdo, who had opened a music store in Philadelphia, gathered together local musicians for these performances. An unusual variety of instruments were played at the Gualdo concerts, "including the clarinet, which, invented about 1750, was still rarely played in Europe."[46] Again, Hopkinson and Penn probably performed. Sometimes the concerts, which began at six-thirty or seven, were followed by supper and a ball, with the concert musicians playing for dancing.[47] Although Gualdo held his final concert in February 1771 and died in 1772, Hopkinson continued to inspire occasional musical productions in the city until the war ended them. Private musical soirées also became popular among those who owned instruments and knew how to use them. Elizabeth, herself, once she received her harpsichord, may have held such gatherings, as did both John Penn and Francis Hopkinson.

In addition to concerts, theatre became popular in Philadelphia during the late 1760s. In the spring of 1767, it is likely that Elizabeth and her friends attended the first performance of Thomas Godfrey's play the *Prince of Parthia*. There is no remaining record by Elizabeth of her attending the theatre in Philadelphia and no mention of Godfrey's play, but we know that she attended plays in London. Richard Peters wrote to her when he was in Liverpool, asking her to write him how she spent "those tedious Evenings, when [she did] not chance to go to the Play." Later in life, she referred to seeing David Garrick perform and to seeing William Powell as Othello.[48] If she had not attended the theatre before her English visit, she had become a fan by the time she left England. Having lived near the Godfrey family as a child, having been friends with his sister and with Godfrey, and probably having read his play or even heard it read by him, she would not have missed the chance to see his play performed.[49]

Godfrey was the son of the Philadelphia glazier and mathematician who, it is said, invented the navigational instrument called Hadley's quadrant before Hadley. Elizabeth wrote disdainfully that Hadley "only made a few alterations on it."[50] The elder Godfrey and his family had shared a house with Benjamin Franklin when Franklin first established his printing shop, and Godfrey had became a founding member of Franklin's Junto, although he dropped out soon after.[51]

The son had been apprenticed to a watchmaker, whose craft he did not like, had tried soldiering with Forbes's expedition to Fort Duquesne, had worked as a mercantile agent in North Carolina and and in other unsuccessful jobs, and finally had contracted a "violent malignant fever" and died in 1763 at age twenty-seven. When he was young in Philadelphia, he had submitted poems to William Smith's *American Magazine*. Smith had recognized his abilities, taken an interest in him, and introduced him to some of his talented students. After Godfrey's death, Nathaniel

Evans, a good friend of Godfrey and protégé of William Smith, collected Godfrey's poems and published them,[52] just as Smith and Elizabeth later did for Evans himself.

Elizabeth, who was interested in education, especially for women, might have joined her callers on a Saturday night in debating the controversial issues about educational philosophy and particularly about the focus of the College of Philadelphia. By the 1740s, educational theory in Pennsylvania was divided into two main branches.[53] One emphasized a classical curriculum, the learning of Greek and Latin and the reading of books written in these languages. Usually upper-class families wanted a classical education for their sons as an adornment that would distinguish them from the lower sort and give them a common language with upper class people everywhere. Thus one young man in London wrote to his brother in Philadelphia "If you ever travel, you'll find how men of letters are everywhere respected. . . . Be a man of learning and you'll be a man of consequence wherever you go."[54]

This emphasis upon the classics was regarded by many middle- and lower-class parents as a waste of time. They wanted their children to receive a practical education to prepare them for a trade or business. They stressed the need for learning writing, English grammar, mathematics, accounting, French, and German. Schools that taught these subjects were called English schools as contrasted with the classical schools. This was the theory urged by Benjamin Franklin who wanted to provide young tradesmen with the tools for economic and occupational advancement. Franklin wrote in his autobiography that he had found it easier to learn Latin after he had learned some of the Romance languages. It was a mistake to start students with Latin first, he wrote, because if their education stopped after a few years, they had achieved nothing useful. If, instead, they learned French, and then moved to Italian, if they never learned Latin, they would have acquired some useful knowledge. To the many German speaking people in the state, a thorough grounding in the English language was more important than the teaching of the classical languages. The Quakers traditionally had emphasized a practical education to teach morality, to make good citizens of the many immigrants, and to give them the skills to support themselves. As a Quaker elite developed, however, they wanted their children taught the classics, and Quaker education changed to include both strains.

By 1762, the Academy, started in 1751 at Franklin's instigation, had expanded to three units. Franklin had envisioned it as being an English school, but in order to secure financial backing from the well-to-do, he had to agree to the inclusion of a classical school as well. Over the years, contrary to Franklin's vision, the classical school was emphasized. In order to obtain use of a building built for another purpose, the trustees of the Academy had to agree to include a school for indigent students. Therefore, a Free School was started the same year, where children of the poor were taught reading, writing, and arithmetic. Franklin had wanted to found an institution of higher learning as well. In 1755, William Smith became the first provost of the College of Philadelphia, which absorbed the classical school of the Academy. Therefore by 1762, the institution was structured with (1) the College, consisting of three Philosophical Schools and the Latin and the Greek Schools, (2) the Academy with its English and Mathematical Schools, and (3) the Free School.[55]

In 1765, the medical school opened. Philadelphia, the foremost medical center in the colonies, was a very exciting place for physicians in the 1770s. Dr. Graeme was not one of the leading doctors. He did not write medical tracts proposing new ideas or describing his own research. He was not the doctor who recommended and was instrumental in the creation of either the medical college or the medical society. He was, however, a competent physician for those times, well respected by his peers and patients. He knew all of the doctors who were leaders in the profession, and many of them were close friends, entertained in his home. Elizabeth as his daughter and, later, as his hostess, met these men, listened to their conversations, and struggled to understand their discussions. After the Revolution, she read medical tracts, corresponded extensively with several of the foremost Pennsylvania physicians as well as with Dr. Fothergill in England.

By the 1750s when Elizabeth was in her teens, Philadelphia doctors had already begun the professional developments that would come to fruition later. The Pennsylvania Hospital opened in February 1752, the brainchild of Dr. Thomas Bond assisted by the promotional skills of Benjamin Franklin. Newspapers publicized the new institution and the medical progress it represented, and the presses published medical treatises. Young men came from other colonies to study medicine under Philadelphia's noted doctors, thereby expanding Pennsylvanians' horizons as well as increasing their own knowledge. Dr. Graeme was connected with the hospital and, therefore, met all these new professionals and discussed medicine with them. Among the Graeme's closest friends were Dr. John Redman and his family. Graduated from the University of Leyden and trained at Guy's Hospital in London, Redman established a practice in Philadelphia in 1749 to 1750. Among his most famous students were John Morgan and Benjamin Rush. All of these families—the Bonds, the Redmans, the Morgans, and the Rushes—were close friends of Elizabeth and her family. Bond and Redman had trained abroad, and Morgan and Rush followed their lead. In addition, they took a tour of western Europe before returning home to establish their practices. Their ideas were cosmopolitan, their interests universal.

After the establishment of the hospital, other medical developments occurred. A medical museum, the first in the country, opened at the hospital and was expanded by donations from Dr. Fothergill. Dr. William Shippen Jr., presented bi-weekly public lectures based on the collection in the museum, and Elizabeth might very well have attended. In 1762, Shippen began a course of anatomical lectures. His first lecture in November is said to have been attended by a "large audience of local intelligentsia."[56] In May 1765, Morgan, now returned from his European training, proposed to the College's trustees that they establish a medical school in conjunction with their other facilities. Based upon the recommendations in Morgan's *Discourse upon the Institution of Medical Schools in America*, the College initiated the following fall the courses that led to the offering of a medical degree.

A major topic of conversation in the Graeme home would have been the controversy between Shippen and Morgan over which one had thought of the medical school. The competition between the two men led to a feud which would carry over into the subsequent establishment of a medical society and of a medical corps for the army during the Revolutionary War. All of these medical subjects were familiar to Elizabeth Graeme and inspired in her an interest in science in general, a topic she would write about occasionally in the future.

Another topic for table talk at the Graemes was William Smith, the controversial Provost of The Philadelphia College, who was determined to turn the institution into an Anglican school rather than the non-denominational school Franklin had conceived. The Quakers had largely refused to participate in the development of the Academy and College. This had left the schools in the hands of Anglicans, the majority of the trustees, and Presbyterians, the majority of the faculty. Since many of the Revolutionary leaders were Presbyterians and many of those who opposed independence were Anglicans, the schools became political pawns as the Revolutionary movement proceeded. Smith further aimed to become the first Anglican bishop in the colonies, and he constantly angled and politicized toward this goal. Thus the College and Smith himself became the subjects of gossip and speculation.

The Graemes had many close connections with members of the Anglican churches' congregations. All of the ministers had been familiars ever since their teens or had become friends upon their arrival in Philadelphia. Richard Peters was Thomas Graeme's closest friend. Jacob Duché and Thomas Coombes had both been born in Philadelphia and were graduates of the College. Elizabeth had known them and the women they married for years. When he arrived in Philadelphia, William Smith became a close friend of the Graeme family. Smith wrote after Graeme's death that "By a standing invitation [Smith had] spent every Sunday evening with him and his family, excepting in the Summer season, when they were at Graeme Park." On these evenings, usually there were five or six other friends "of congenial sentiments," including Rev. Peters.[57] The Stedman brothers were Anglican Church members, too; both had served terms as vestrymen of Christ Church.

The Graemes also had friends who were Presbyterians, Benjamin Rush, for example, and the Stockton family of New Jersey. Both Rush and Richard Stockton were graduates of the Presbyterian College of New Jersey in Princeton, where some Pennsylvania Presbyterians sent their sons to escape the Anglicanization of the College of Philadelphia.

Even though Elizabeth did not care for political discussions, they would have been more and more frequent as the clock hands completed their circles toward 1776. Elizabeth could protest and plead her dislike of politics, but she would have been unable to stop the discussions completely as her Saturday night guests expressed their concerns about the deteriorating relations between England and her North American colonies.

By the time she returned from England, the Stamp Act controversy had pretty well run its course, and a movement for the act's repeal was underway in England. Still, when Elizabeth called on Deborah Franklin the evening after her arrival in Philadelphia, her hostess would have related the story of her close escape in the fall of 1765 during the city's protest. Her husband's popularity had decreased during his long periods in England. His political enemies in Philadelphia had taken advantage of his absence to imply that he was responsible for the passage of the Stamp Act, had perhaps even written the measure. Although both accusations were untrue, still Franklin had not anticipated the colonists' reaction to the Stamp Act. He thought there might be some objection, but that the opposition soon would blow over. He even secured for his friend John Hughes an appointment as the Philadelphia stamp distributor, which looked like it would be a very profitable position.

Most Philadelphia citizens disliked the act because Parliament, in which the colonists had no representatives, had passed an act taking away some of their property, i.e., their money, without their consent. This was an extension of the argument they had long used against the claim of the proprietaries that their instructions had the force of law in Pennsylvania. The people had a natural right to life, liberty, and property, they believed. No one should be able to deprive them of any of these without due process of law, and the laws must be approved directly by the citizens or indirectly by their elected representatives. Even those in Pennsylvania who believed Parliament had the legal right to pass such laws believed that it was inexpedient for Parliament to do so and that the legalities should be changed to conform with the philosophy.

When word of the passage of the act reached Philadelphia, the first protest meetings were incited by the "Mobbing Gentry," as a contemporary called them.[58] They called and led public protest meetings, and they helped form public resistance to the British measures by writing newspaper articles and broadsides. Probably all of these men were known to the Graemes in varying degrees of intimacy. Among the early leaders were the sons of William Allen, the chief justice of the colony, and James Tilghman, newly appointed secretary of the Proprietary Land Office. Even John Penn did not approve of the Stamp Act. When disorder threatened in Philadelphia, the proprietary leaders took no action to prevent it, and when violence erupted, Allen's sons led the protestors.

To make the law unenforceable, leaders throughout the colonies encouraged crowds of people to threaten the appointed Stamp Act distributors to make them relinquish their appointments. The leaders of the opposition to British measures advertised in the newspapers that town meetings were to be held and invited all citizens to participate. At the meetings, speeches were made, decisions voted, petitions written, and persons delegated to draw them up and present them. In Philadelphia, no steps were taken by the government to stop these meetings. It was reported that "when the Mob were invited in the Morning to meet in the Afternoon at the State House to Oblige Mr. [John] Hughes to resign, the Governor Mayor Recorder and all the Majestrates save Mr. Shoemaker went out of Town."⁵⁹

Since Philadelphia had no police in those days to protect citizens from actions by individuals or by crowds, they had to protect themselves, and that is what Deborah Franklin had prepared to do. When William Franklin heard a rumor that the crowd would tear down his parents' new house in Philadelphia, he rushed to the city to persuade his mother to go back to New Jersey with him. His sister went to stay with friends, but Deborah refused to leave and prepared to defend her home. She "turned one room into a magazine" and "ordered some sort of defence upstairs," such as she could "manage" herself. One of her brothers and one of Ben's nephews armed themselves and came to protect her. John Hughes also loaded his gun the night "the mob made a bon-fire and burnt [his] effigy . . . and surrounded his house, whooping and hallooing."⁶⁰ What saved both houses from destruction was a crowd of about eight hundred mechanics and ship carpenters loyal to Ben, who preserved order and prevented property damage. When Elizabeth called on Deborah, her hostess would have related the story of James Allen "Sperriting up the mobe" and of her protection by the counter-crowd. And her listener might have shivered in fear when she imagined the crowd gathered at night surrounding the Hughes home, lighting up the night with their torches, and screaming invectives against the stamp distributor and his friend in England.

She also would have heard about the Stamp Act Congress that had been meeting in New York at the time her ship was idled off the coast of England waiting for a good wind and about the role played by Pennsylvania's own John Dickinson, lawyer and friend of the Graemes. Dickinson had been the chief author of the "Declaration of Rights and Grievances" published by the Congress, claiming the colonists' rights of life, liberty, and property. The colonies were not represented in Parliament, the address pointed out, and could not be since London was so far away that delegates from America would not know the wishes of their constituents. Only their own legislatures could lawfully tax them.

To force Parliament to back down, the merchants in the large cities had agreed not to import any more British goods until the act was repealed. From 1764 to 1765, the value of British exports to America had declined by several hundred thousand pounds sterling, and British merchants had formed a committee to persuade towns to petition Parliament to repeal the act. The first of the new year, Parliament began to debate the repeal, and in February 1766, Benjamin Franklin gave a very persuasive testimony before the House of Commons, which was printed in the colonial newspapers and helped to restore his reputation. The repeal bill was passed and became effective May 1. All this had been happening during the closing months of Elizabeth and Richard Peters's English sojourn and the first few months of their return to Philadelphia.

By the time Elizabeth was beginning to put her grief behind her, a new ministry had come to power in England and was urging Parliament once again to tax the colonies. The subsequent Townshend Acts passed in June 1767 put import duties on paper, glass, lead, paint, and tea. The money raised was to be used to defray "the charge of the administration of justice, and the support of civil government . . . [and] the expenses of defending, protecting and securing" the colonies. Colonial opposition again arose, urging the reinstatement of the nonimportation of British goods to force another British retreat. In Boston, Providence, Newport, and New York, nonimportation agreements were drawn up, but merchants in Philadelphia were dilatory. Many of them had suffered economic losses during the Stamp Act boycott, and they argued that they were being unfairly penalized when others were burdened not at all. Among this group were Alexander Stedman and his brother, Charles, who had been the husband of Elizabeth's deceased sister, Ann.

In December 1767, to mobilize public opinion, John Dickinson began publishing his famous "Letters from a Farmer in Pennsylvania to the Inhabitants of the British Colonies." The "Letters" were an explanation of the principles behind the rights claimed by the colonists in the "Declaration of Rights and Grievances." While conceding Parliament's right to pass laws regulating the trade of Great Britain and all its colonies for the "general welfare" of the whole, Dickinson denied Parliament's right to pass laws whose only purpose was to raise revenue in the colonies, without the consent of the colonists. He reviewed various laws that had been passed by Parliament that had affected the colonies since their beginning. None, he wrote, had been designed solely to raise money. Therefore, both the Stamp Act and the Townshend duties were innovations, "dangerous" innovations. The Townshend duties were on products that the colonists were required to buy from Great Britain, and the taxes were to apply to those products only when they were shipped to the colonies. He posed the question "whether the parliament can legally impose duties to be paid *by the people*

of those colonies only FOR THE SOLE PURPOSE OF RAISING REVE-
NUE, *on commodities which she obliges us to take from her alone*; or, in other
words, whether the parliament can legally take money out of our pockets,
without our consent."[61] Moreover, he objected to the act's proviso that the
tax money would be used to pay the salaries of the British administrators in
the colonies. He pointed out that historically the people's only way to
control unsatisfactory rulers had been through their pocketbooks. Without
the responsibility for paying the salaries of the British administrators, the
colonial assemblies would have no way to protect the people from a venal
British agent. He warned the British people that although no one then
wanted the colonies to separate from the mother country, they should not
push the colonists too far. "A people does not reform with moderation."[62]

Dickinson not only told the people what was wrong with Parliament's measures but he also told them what to do about it. Do not be
disorderly, he advised. Use "constitutional modes of obtaining relief." Try
petitions and complaints to the proper authorities. But if these do not win
redress, then do not hesitate to deprive Great Britain of "all the advantages"
she had been receiving from the colonies.[63] In other words, reinstitute the
boycott. Dickinson's "Letters" were very popular; they were reprinted in
local papers all over the colonies and in England. After the last was published, they were gathered together in a book. His opinions were very
influential in winning people over to the resistance movement. Finally, the
merchants in Philadelphia in early 1769 agreed to resume nonimportation.

Throughout this period, Elizabeth was busily writing poetry. But
she also kept up with what was happening. Her father and his friends discussed the growing difficulties between the mother country and her colonies when they dined together at the Graemes on Sunday evenings and
commented on Dickinson's letters as they appeared each week. Soon after
the "Letters" were published as a book, Dr. Graeme gave his daughter a
copy and told her "to atend to the arguments there made use of, as they
contain points very serious." He said that "evry woman was capable to
take in their force and that he much aprovd."[64]

In the middle of October 1768, Elizabeth wrote a long poetic response to Dickinson's "Letters." Entitled "The Dream" or "The Philosophical Farmer," it took Dickinson's ideas one step further.[65] It addressed
the individual colonists and told them what their patriotic duty was. It
urged its readers to forgo the manufactured goods of England and to adopt
the rural life. The dreamer first sees an angry England announcing that she

shall be obeyed. The clouds part, revealing a figure identified as William Penn, who reminds England that no matter how great her power, it must be limited by law. The founder of Pennsylvania unrolls a scroll, which John Dickinson reads to waiting listeners. He tells them to turn to nature who will provide bountifully. Shun British wealth and manufactured goods. "Turn then from *Commerce* your too blind eyes, / And learn your Countrys own produce to prize." He reminds them that liberty is dear, "Dear to your Souls as *Ophirs* purest Gold, / And for no price, be sacred Freedom Sold." America can make its own manufactured goods from its many raw materials, such as iron and wool. A section devoted to women tells them to spin and weave their own wool and linen for their families' needs.

> To show proud *Albion* [England] that you can resign
> Her *Manufacturers*; and her *Trade* decline:
> When weighty *Taxes* do each Good invade
> And strike at *Liberty* that lovely Maid!

This is a call back to the simple rural life, a romanticized version of the farmer's life, telling the reader to learn from nature. The busy bee builds its cells; the spider weaves its web; the beaver builds his home. "The happy Farmer views with honest joy, / The Growth luxuriant of his late employ." As the seasons change, the poem shows that "a rural Life is Best." The farmer is his own master, more independent than most other beings. Ultimately Great Britain will change, but until she does, Pennsylvanians must give up their luxuries and return to the simple country life. The last advice that Dickinson reads from the scroll is to "fear God alone, but never *Albion* fear." And the dreamer awakes.

By 1770, Great Britain was ready to back down again. Nonimportation had cut the colonists' orders for British goods markedly. Furthermore, the ill will of the colonists toward the British administration was increasing. In some colonies, blows had come between the people and British troops. Throughout the colonies, citizens had formed themselves into groups called Sons of Liberty who tried to intimidate British appointed officials into neglecting to enforce the new laws. In January 1770, there was a pitched battle in New York City between soldiers wielding bayonets and citizens with clubs and cutlasses. Two months later, violence broke out in Boston. On March 5, 1770, soldiers fired into a crowd that refused to disperse, killing five people. In addition, war was threatening in Europe, and Great Britain did not want to face a war with discontented, angry colonists at her back. Since full repeal would indicate weakness, the bill that ended the Townshend duties left the tax on tea, and the ministry promised not to lay any new taxes on the colonists. For the next year or two, there would be relative calm in the colonies. Elizabeth and her friends hoped for peace with the mother country.

By 1770, Elizabeth had made a place for herself in Philadelphia society. Her Saturday night salons were recognized as gatherings of the intellectual elite. The proprietaries, their families, and their senior appointees were among her intimates. She was highly educated, she knew several languages, she was informed about art and music, and she probably played the harpsichord. She had published articles in the newspaper, and several of her poems were due to be published in the book of Nathaniel Evans's poems that she and Dr. Smith were putting together. Her father was well-to-do, and she was his main heir. Only marriage and children were missing from her life, and she seemed to have filled those empty spots with other interests. Life was fulfilling and people appreciated her talents. The future looked secure and as trouble free as her chronic health problems would let her be.

Nevertheless, Elizabeth's own self-image was not so sanguine. By her thirty-third birthday, she viewed a woman's temporal life as a period to be endured, the few pleasures enjoyed and the pain tolerated, a vision that reflected the feelings of her mother during Elizabeth's formative years. In consoling a mother who had recently lost a daughter, Elizabeth explained her view of women's lives and their connections to men. She wrote that she understood the great loss the woman had suffered;[66] she had always believed that the "softest And fondest" tie "the Human Heart could experience" was that between a mother and daughter. Male connections promoted women's "pride and ambition," but "Our Domestic Comfort receives its most balmy sweets from the female branches of our family." The role of men in the family, thus, was to provide material objects and community status by their successes. Women could not entertain the same sort of ambitions for themselves or take pride in their own accomplishments; these reactions came to them by reflected glow from the men in their lives. There is no mention of love and emotional support to be expected from a husband; that came from daughters.

She consoled the bereaved mother by reminding her of what her daughter fortunately would miss. She would not have to suffer:

the anxiety atending a large family and that particular painful part that the Almighty in his wrath has assigned as a punishment to our Sex; Hard and painful even with a kind and tender partner; but if it is our fate to be conected with A Tyrant; it is then a temporary Hell; in exchange for all this what has your child got? by her youth and innocence at least a habitation of rest; if not a mansion of Glory.

Death had brought her peace and absence of unhappiness.

And, after all, what did life really amount to? For "minds of sensibility, and strong affections," there were "keen disappointments and a constant struggle to submit those passions and feelings to the Ground rules and Laws of Religion and Philosophy." "People of Calmer spirits" found in "all the Enjoyments of the World" an "insipidness . . . that scarce amounts either to positive pleasure or pain; but a kind of vacant state arising from a privation of both." As for herself, she was not "averse to the enjoyments of Life." She was "more than ever determind to cultivate upon principle every species of innocent chearfulness" that she encountered. But in retrospect, "the happiest thing that could have [befallen her was] to have been taken of[f] the stage of Life in [her] infancy, because the most difficult trials in life are "dreadful indeed; the midling one Insipid; and the happiest not worth the wish of an immortal Spirit."

In discussing a friend's approaching second marriage, Elizabeth made a telling analysis of her own character: "All the world will get matrimony in to their Head" before she. The older she grew, the more objections she had, and because of these growing objections to marriage, "less pain will be taken by others to remove those Objections." She recognized that her beliefs were hardening, her flexibility lessening, and her appeal, therefore, declining. Yet in little more than two years, she would be married, and marriage for her would be the disaster she had described in the letter to her friend.

During the summer of 1770, the fever returned to the household at Graeme Park, striking Elizabeth with virulence.[67] She recovered her good health, however, and resumed her usual social life in time to entertain William White, future rector of Christ Church and first American bishop of the Episcopal Church, at Graeme Park in September. White was going to England in October to be ordained as an Anglican clergyman, and he asked her to write letters of introduction for him. He especially wanted to meet Lady Juliana Penn, because "the Company of the fair" was more agreeable to him than that of his own sex. It would make him happy, he wrote to Elizabeth, if he "could be admitted . . . into an agreable female Circle" while he was England. He feared, however, that Lady Juliana's "Rank" placed her too far above him to "expect any thing more than a very distant Acquaintance." From England in January, White would thank Elizabeth and report that he had delivered her letters to Lady Juliana and that he had "seen few Women in England equal to her in Person."[68] White would remember Elizabeth's kindness when misfortune struck her during the war. Elizabeth, herself, would remember these days as halcyon compared to the stormy trials that soon would consume her thoughts and energy for the rest of her days.

5

---◌◟---

Very Tender and Painful Emotions

On August 14, 1771, a man named George Steptoe penned a letter to Dr. Benjamin Rush, whom he did not know, a letter that would change Elizabeth Graeme's life forever. Steptoe wrote from Westmoreland, Virginia, that he was a physician, settled in practice there, and that he, too, had studied medicine at Edinburgh, perhaps at the same time as Rush. The purpose of the letter was to introduce its bearer, a young man named Henry Hugh Fergusson, whom Steptoe called "an ingenious young Gentleman" who had "travelled through many Parts of France & Flanders." Steptoe asked Rush to show Fergusson "any thing *Curious*" in Philadelphia.[1]

In mid-November, while Fergusson was traveling to Philadelphia, the Graemes returned from Horsham to the city, although where they stayed is not entirely clear. They had been renting a house on the north side of Chestnut Street, between Sixth and Seventh, from John Smith of Burlington, but in March 1769, Smith had proposed building another structure on the property. Dr. Graeme had objected and wrote Smith that he could not agree because access to the house would be cut, a grassy area and the garden he used for "Raising Sallading and Other Kitchen Herbs" would be eliminated, and he would have to suffer the "Brick dust & lime flying over" during the construction. Smith persisted, and Graeme asked to be released from his lease.[2] There is no record of the Graemes renting another property in Philadelphia, yet the settlement of Dr. Graeme's will indicates that they did. Wherever it was, by early December, Elizabeth was once again holding her Saturday night calling hours, "at her father's house in the city."[3]

On December 7, Benjamin Rush brought Henry Hugh Fergusson[4] to the Graemes' home. Fergusson, born in Scotland March 12, 1748, was eleven years Elizabeth's junior. Little is known of his background except that he was the son of a man who had served for thirty years in the British army and retired at the end of the Seven Years' War. Fergusson Sr. had bought property in Scotland, probably in the west Highlands, where he had extensively altered the house, enlarging and improving it, and had beautified the grounds. This much is known from a poem Henry wrote.[5] Where the estate was located, his father's full name, and other details are missing from the record.

Henry had the appearance and characteristics of a gentleman, but he apparently owned no property of his own nor was he eligible to inherit any. He had had a classical education, although we do not know where or from whom. His handwriting was well formed, his grammar and spelling indicated training, and he seemed to be able to match Elizabeth quotation for quotation from literature, classical or contemporary. Fluent in French, he also spoke Italian and Spanish, and he had traveled extensively on the continent.[6] It has been said that he was a relative of Sir Adam Fergusson, the philosopher,[7] who wrote a recommendation for Henry after the war to the British Commission on Loyalists' Losses, but the relationship is not supported in any known manuscript source. In 1769, Henry had gone to Virginia, where his brother Robert lived with his wife and five children, and then in the fall of 1771, he had traveled to Philadelphia with Steptoe's letter introducing him to Benjamin Rush.

Tall and handsome, Henry had light brown hair, blue eyes, and dimpled cheeks. Three years after they had met, Elizabeth described him in a poem as very comely in appearance, yet, at the same time, she had reservations about his "mental part," as she called it. Actually, what she described was what we would call character. She wrote that she wished to be objective, yet she found the task hard, "For Light and shade so close unite."

> His Modesty I there may dwell
> For sure in that he does excell
> But yet a certain careless air
> Makes all His merits seem less Fair

A kind of apathy is joind
With Indolence of mien combind.

Her poem continues with a picture of a young man not always careful of the feelings of others, even tactless in his relations with friends. She blames these failings on his youth and says that time will mellow and smooth away the faults, refining his virtues "like generous Wine." In spite of her assurances, however, Elizabeth was a perceptive woman who saw through the handsome exterior to a flawed character. Even though this was written over two years after they were married, some of this must have been apparent beforehand and have accounted for her hesitation.[8]

The courtship had to be clandestine because Dr. Graeme, more concerned with suitability and property than with a handsome face, opposed the match. To him, Henry was not the most desirable suitor for his daughter. The age difference was likely to cause personality problems between them, and Henry's lack of personal fortune made her future appear insecure. It was true that Dr. Graeme's estate, if it continued to be properly managed after his death, could provide comfortably for the couple, but there was nothing to indicate that Henry was capable of such management, especially if he was inclined to "indolence." Dr. Graeme undoubtedly shared the suspicions of a descendant who called Fergusson an adventurer "who had come to America in search of a rich wife."[9] Elizabeth may have entertained such suspicions herself, which would have explained her reluctance to leap precipitously into the marriage,

But leap she did, despite her reservations. On March 4, 1772, Elizabeth confessed her love for Henry and agreed to marry him, although she did not set a date. At the end of a poem, "A Pastoral Ballad, Love and Alexis," given to Henry that day, she wrote "Given to my Dear Dear Hug Fergusson with a heart glowing with the most unfiegnd Truth and affection."[10] Still, reluctant to go against her father's wishes, she saw herself as caught "between *Sylla* and *Charybdas*," and refused to make the marriage date definite. Henry was urging her to marry him secretly and accusing her of leading him on when she had no intention of marrying him. Henry sighed that she had "it in [her] Power to ruin him Soul and Body." She wrote Dr. Rush that she did not want "the vile imputation of giving false hopes and unmeaning encouragements."[11]

Henry wrote her a letter two days before their marriage asking her "Why Tremble to embark on a voyage with Such fair prospects of a pleasant voyage?" One wonders if Elizabeth, or anybody else, had indicated concerns about his character because he assured her that since he regarded "Moral Rectitude of conduct . . . as the most rational Source of happiness," he would never "Swerve from it." Why would he make such a statement unless his "moral rectitude" had been questioned in some way? He further guaranteed: "If in [his] pursuits [he could] in any thing Contribute to the Ease, quiet and Enjoyment of the worthiest of her Sex, And through Life merit her Love and Esteem [his] ambition [would] be fully gratifyd." Elizabeth wrote on the letter "God grant the writer of this letter may be such as he describes in marriage."[12] It seems she was having serious misgivings, even as she loved him and agreed to marry him. Perhaps his sexual attraction was so strong that she put aside her objective analysis of his character. Or perhaps she was willing to gamble because she did not want to miss what might be her last chance for the kind of life considered the norm. Letters written about him later indicate that he was attractive to women, and this may have given Elizabeth some uneasiness, especially considering that she was thirty-five to his twenty-four.

His ardor overrode her qualms, however, and they were married April 21, 1772, in Swedes Church, Philadelphia, at nine o'clock in the evening, without the knowledge of Dr. Graeme.[13] She spent the hour between one and two in the afternoon at the bedside of her old childhood friend Rebecca Moore Smith, who was recovering from the birth of a daughter, Rebecca, on April 11,[14] undoubtedly discussing the ceremony to take place that evening. Rebecca may have tried to calm Elizabeth's uneasiness by telling her that misgivings on a wedding day are common to most couples. As for the marriage ceremony, those present have not entirely been identified. Later, Benjamin Rush would point out to Anny Young the spot in the church garden where Elizabeth stood to be married,[15] so we know that Rush was there and that it was a pleasant day for an outdoor wedding. One wonders whether Dr. William Smith attended, considering his deep friendship for Dr. Graeme and the doctor's disapproval. This kept away John Dickinson, who was invited but declined to attend. When the news leaked out, Mary Sober Redman, wife of Dr. John Redman, wrote Elizabeth that she was sorry Elizabeth's marriage had become the subject of gossip, but she was certain no one who was there was responsible.[16] Probably the Redmans were also present, since they, too, were old friends. As the couple left the church after the wedding, family tradition relates that Elizabeth "stumbled in the churchyard and fell on a grave," prompting someone in the party to remark prophetically that this was an "ill omen for the future."[17]

Throughout the following spring and summer, the spouses were separated, and the marriage was kept secret from Dr. Graeme, Henry all the while urging Elizabeth to tell her father. He had to return to Scotland on family business, but he did not want to leave with his marital situation still secret. Dr. Graeme had been persuaded to give his consent to Elizabeth and Henry's marriage, against his better judgment, but he had insisted that they wait until Henry returned from Scotland. This had been the same restriction he had applied to her relationship with William Franklin. He probably hoped for a similar result. At some point in early summer, Henry left, but he was not happy about the secrecy still maintained by his wife.

Subsequently, Elizabeth, Betsy Stedman, and Dr. Graeme adjourned to Graeme Park for the summer.[18] Elizabeth's marriage would have been the main subject of whispered conversation between the women. No matter how they looked at her dilemma, there was no good option. She must tell her father before Henry returned from Europe or her husband would do it himself, and that might create a disagreeable confrontation. If Elizabeth told him, Henry would be pleased, but her father still might be angry. He was going on 84 years old, beset with the failings of old age, and she hated to distress him with her news.

This was a difficult summer for Elizabeth, even though it saw the first publication of any of her poems. Elizabeth and Dr. William Smith brought out their edition of Nathaniel Evans's poems, which volume also included four of her own verses. It must have been very exciting for her to see her pieces in print and to know that copies of the book that contained them were to be sent all over the English-speaking world. The only existing new poetry from her pen during this trying period is her "Farewell to the Muses written by a young Woman soon after marriage," a long romantic work in fifty-seven ballad stanzas. That summer, people came and went at Graeme Park, as usual; Thomas Coombe and Benjamin Rush dropped in one evening and left at five the next morning.[19] Rush would have created an opportunity to take Elizabeth aside and ask her about Henry and whether she had told her father yet. Elizabeth, as her father's hostess, coordinated servants and meals to provide for these guests. At the same time, she continued to supervise the education of her niece and nephew. Anny was sixteen, while John was fifteen, a handful in any period.

Finally on Friday, September 4, Elizabeth determined to reveal her marriage to her father. He always took a walk before breakfast, and she decided to tell him when he returned. She sat in the window seat looking out toward his path. When he came into view, she became more and more apprehensive. "I was in agony," she reported later. Every step brought him nearer. "It was a terrible task to perform." Suddenly he was stricken and keeled over, never regaining consciousness. Had she told him the day before, as she had thought of doing, she would have blamed herself for his death "and gone crazy," she wrote.[20]

Dr. Graeme was buried two days later in Christ Churchyard in the family plot that already contained his wife, eight or more children, two grandchildren, and mother-in-law. The funeral service, attended by many people, was conducted by Dr. Smith.[21] Elizabeth wrote the lines engraved on his tombstone:[22]

> The Soul that trod within this mouldring Dust
> In every act was Eminently Just!
> Peacefull thro' Life, as peacefull too in Death
> Without one Pang he renderd up His Breath

Elizabeth did not mourn her father's death with the same intensity that she had shown for her mother and sister. She respected and admired him, and "lov'd him tenderly," but the same depth of affection and grieving was not there. She believed that his "favorite child" had been her sister Ann Stedman. When he saw Ann's corpse, Thomas Graeme had said "there is the Child who never gave me pain till this Moment," and Elizabeth believed that he "never got over her Death." Fourteen years after her father's death, Elizabeth wrote Benjamin Rush that Ann Stedman had been her father's "deservedly favorite Child."[23]

By September 21, Elizabeth was expecting to hear of Henry's arrival at his destination since he had left Philadelphia a month or more before Dr. Graeme's death. She was also beginning to cope with the legal problems caused by both her father's death and her clandestine marriage. Although she would have preferred to keep it a secret until her husband returned, she was advised that she had to make public her marriage for legal reasons. On September 21, she sent lawyer John Dickinson, a copy of her father's will, asking several questions about what she should do.[24] "Under a variety of very tender and painful Emotions," she informed Dickinson that her father's death had flung her "into a thousand perplixitys." She was land poor, she wrote, with no money. No matter how valuable the land was, for her it would never "bring in anything equivalent to Money put out to interest." It was her experience that a large farm was "to be Suported not a Suporter." Furthermore, she really did not like living in the country. At that distance from Philadelphia, she would have to "live quite excluded from Society," or if she wanted to see company, it would be "atended with more trouble and expense than [she] Could see the same number of people in a City." She also had "found [her] time more at [her] own Command in a City than in the Country." What she wanted to do was to sell all the land at Graeme Park except for the house and one hundred to two hundred acres. She would then invest the capital and live off the return.

Henry's approval, however, was needed for any sale of the property. When a woman married, all of her personal property became her husband's, even the clothes she was wearing. He also controlled her real property, with some restrictions. He made all the decisions about managing the property, but he could not sell or mortgage it unless his wife signed the deed. In order to protect wives from coercion from their husbands, the southern colonies required a private examination of the wives by a judge to make sure that they understood the conditions of the sale and that they freely agreed to it. Pennsylvania, however, had not imposed this examination until 1770 when the Assembly had passed a law requiring it.[25] Although this law was not yet fully enforced by local courts, Elizabeth would have been very aware of this restriction since the law had been passed and published only two years before her marriage. Furthermore, under common law, if the couple was childless and he died first, his wife's real estate did not become part of his estate; it remained in her possession. If she died first, he did not inherit her property; instead it went to her heir, in this case, John Young.

In the fall of 1772, Elizabeth wanted to sell Graeme Park, but she could not do so without her husband's approval. Since Henry's "Affairs would be much injurd by a precipitate return" from England, Elizabeth asked Dickinson if there was some way Fergusson could provide her with a power of attorney to act in his absence. In a few days, Dickinson answered her letter, providing the form of power of attorney for her to send to Fergusson. Unfortunately, none of the Fergusson letters from this time, his or hers, remain, and so we do not know how Henry reacted to his wife's preferences. The land, however, was not advertised for sale until after Henry returned, so either he refused his permission or the distance that separated them slowed communication.

In the weeks after Thomas Graeme's death, word of his daughter's elopement leaked out and the gossips began to chew it over. Elizabeth was concerned that her dearest friends would hear of it from others before she had a chance to inform them herself. John Dickinson had advised openness,[26] and she hastened to declare her marriage to her closest friends. One of her principal concerns was Richard Peters, who had not been told at the time of the marriage because of his deep friendship with Dr. Graeme. That also accounted for the marriage being held at the Swedes Church rather than at Christ Church where Peters was the rector. In late September when Elizabeth heard of the "public Conversation" about her marriage, she wrote Mary Redman, asking her to inform Peters as soon as possible, but before Mrs. Redman could show Elizabeth's letter to Peters, Rev, Jacob Duché had told him. Elizabeth was concerned about how Peters would react, but he took the news very sensibly. He sent her the message not to give herself "one moments pain with respect to his oppinion of the affair." He acceded to her reasons for not informing him sooner, and he wished her happiness. Apparently, the gossips were criticizing Elizabeth for having kept her marriage secret from her father, because Mrs. Redman assured her that she thought Elizabeth's conduct was motivated by "duty and affection" and the desire to make "his declining years hapy & Comfortable" by hiding from him news that "would have given him pain."[27]

Under the terms of her father's will, Elizabeth was left the 837 acres of Graeme Park, all that was in the ground or on it, and all of the household furniture and plate in his city house, subject to the payment of a legacy of £1,000 to James Young and his children. She was permitted to choose the most convenient time to pay this legacy unless she sold the plantation, at which time the legacy was to be paid out of the proceeds. Young and his children were also left two tracts of land, one of 1,000 acres and the other of 500 acres, in Northampton County.

If Graeme's evaluation of the Horsham property at £10,000 had proved accurate at sale and if there had been no debts or if Elizabeth and Henry could have taken over its management competently, they would have been comfortably settled—a number of "ifs" that did not materialize and that were further complicated by the Revolution. Graeme Park was a prosperous, fertile farm, well equipped with a large quantity of tools and

Elizabeth Graeme Fergusson's country home, Graeme Park. Courtesy Friends of Graeme Park.

livestock. In addition, there was a twenty-acre orchard with "a collection of the best grafted fruit trees."[28] There were crops on the ground, employees and slaves to harvest them, and a nearby city in which to sell them. Debts could have been negotiated and payment postponed. She should have had an income. But that fall Henry was three thousand miles away, and she soon broke with her one living adult male family member, James Young, over the terms of the will. She was unable to take over management of the farm herself, because her father, unfortunately, had not trained her to be a plantation manager, and there was no time for her to learn. Furthermore, she had no interest in learning.

There were many debts, whose payment the will did not anticipate adequately. Dr. Graeme had specified that a lot he owned in the Moyamensing area of southern Philadelphia was to be sold to pay his debts with the residue being divided between his heirs. Since the lot was worth about £300 and the debts totaled about £1400,[29] most of the debts had to paid by other means. The law required all the debts to be paid out of the personal estate first. This meant that Elizabeth's share of the estate paid all the debts, while the Youngs' share paid none. Since she had little cash, she had to sell property, but even if she had sold all the personal property, its value barely equaled the extent of the debts. In early October, she sold some of the livestock for £91.13.5,[30] but this sum did not make much of a dent in the debts. Furthermore, such a sale decreased the income producing potential of the farm. She wrote Dickinson,[31] who had refused to be her lawyer as a hired professional but had volunteered to help her as a friend, that she was sure her father never intended for all his debts to fall on her. She must have discussed this disparity with James Young about this time, asking for the "true Spirit" of her father's "will to be complyed with," but he insisted upon the letter of the law. Despite having lived at Graeme Park much of the time since he had married Jane Graeme and despite the Graemes' raising of his children, James Young paid none of the debts in Horsham "that he could avoid," leaving it all for Elizabeth to absorb, even the costs of his own personal neighborhood purchases charged to Graeme Park. This caused their relationship to deteriorate. She wrote that "As for Mr Young I hold the Whole of his Conduct in such Contempt that I shall not trouble my self to speak about him; only that I am well rid of him."[32] At the same time, Elizabeth was concerned about Henry's reaction when he discovered the state of Dr. Graeme's assets. She assured Dickinson that she knew "my dear Mr. Fergusson did not Marry me with sordid views," but there was a nagging doubt in her mind, or she would not have denied the possibility.[33]

The settlement of the will was a great burden for Elizabeth. Probate took place shortly after her father's death, leaving her no time to recover from the shock and to grieve. Two men began assessing the estate at Graeme Park within a week of Dr. Graeme's funeral, and they continued until mid-November. The assessment of personal property in the house the Graemes rented in the city was made on September 16, which meant two men listing all their possessions, not a very pleasant occurrence. When they finished, Elizabeth questioned the accuracy of the assessments, which she believed too high. Although six persons were named as executors of the will, only James Young and Elizabeth actively carried out that responsibility, according to the papers filed in the office of the Register of Wills, and Elizabeth appears to have done most of the work.[34]

The disagreement between Elizabeth and James Young was so intense that he took his children from her care to live with him in Philadelphia. Anny Young, aged sixteen, was very unhappy at being separated from her aunt. Her father had not remarried after the death of her mother, so that Anny would be expected to become his hostess. Anticipating that she would be unable to control her distress in person, Anny wrote Elizabeth a very pathetic leave-taking note thanking her for the years of tender care. "You took me," she wrote,

> at an age totaly incapable of giving you Pleasure, too old to Divert you with innocent prattle And too young to be Company for you, you waited my growing reason with patient Care And Still instructed me both by your precepts and Example in the practice of every Virtue And now that I am of an age to know and Return your tenderness I must leave you.

She was upset about living with her father. "I tremble when I look forward in the Situation . . . I am about to be thrown into[.] I know that it requires a prudence that is inconsistent with my tender years." Referring to "the terrors of [her] new Situation," she deeply regretted leaving Graeme Park where she had spent the happiest part of her life.[35] For Anny, this separation meant being taken from the female closest to her, her surrogate mother. Always there had been her aunt to turn to with problems; now she would have to find her own answers under totally new circumstances, and she was frightened. For Elizabeth, the separation meant living with only servants, for the first time in her life, except for a short period in London, or persuading Betsy Stedman to join her.

In February 1773, Henry was still abroad, and Elizabeth was coping as best she could with her inheritance's deficiencies. She was making arrangements to sell the Moyamensing lot to pay a bond her father owed to the estate of Samuel McCall, now deceased. "It was the Clear purport of the Will that it Should goe for that use"; therefore, she wanted "to take any Steps or Sign any papers" necessary to expedite its sale to settle the bond as quickly as possible. She paid the rent for the house in town and all the debts in Horsham, including salaries owed workers on the plantation. Although she had not received "a Copper" from the people in Philadelphia who owed her father money, the estate's creditors expected her to pay immediately. Even the local miller, who had had the business of Graeme Park for many years, would not let her charge the bread she needed; he told her "he could not Support his Mill without Cash."[36]

That winter, Elizabeth acted as farm manager in her husband's absence. She put her coachman and gardener to work repairing fences, and she worried about long-time employees, such as Old Joseph, who had been in her father's employ many years and whose care for the rest of his life was her father's desire. She was reluctant to discharge any of the six personal servants maintained by her father, although the estate could ill afford their salaries. In addition to Old Joseph, there were two housemaids, Sam, Andrew Bodin, the gardener, and John Jenny, the coachman. There were also two slaves Alex and Mars listed in the inventory of Graeme Park. At first she thought she would sell the crops in the ground unharvested, but neighbors told her that it would be much more profitable to harvest them herself and then sell them. The only problem with this was that she would have to hire people to do the harvesting, as there were insufficient workers on the estate, and this would be difficult for her to manage in her tight cash situation.[37] Apparently, she did not act fast enough in the matter of the Samuel McCall bond. McCall's executor, Archibald McCall, brought suit against Thomas Graeme's executors and secured a writ of execution ordering the sheriff to sell the Moyamensing lot. This was done, and the lot sold for a disappointing £233, not the anticipated £300.

A further problem was the bond for £800 that her father had co-signed for the Stedman brothers. Alexander Stedman had gone bankrupt and was unable to pay anything. Elizabeth wrote that she was willing "to Submit it to the determination of Sensible Impartial Judges," if Charles Stedman would agree.[38] The precise details of the solution to this debt are not available, but she did pay part or all of the bond, even though Charles Stedman was solvent and could have been made to pay the debt himself. After the war, when Henry Fergusson filed a claim with the British government for his losses in America due to his loyalty to the crown, the settlement of Dr. Graeme's estate was considered in detail. At that time, Philadelphia lawyers, who had fled the city during the war but who had been familiar with Dr. Graeme's property, testified that although Elizabeth was not required to pay the bond, she had "conceived it a matter of conscience" to do so.[39] Charles Stedman had remarried in September 1767, eighteen months after the death of Elizabeth's sister Ann. His second wife was Margaret Abercrombie, the widow of James Abercrombie, a ship's captain who had been lost at sea in 1760. The Abercrombies had been very close friends of the Graeme family for many years. It was Margaret to whom William Franklin had written his letter ending his romance with Elizabeth. Unwilling to endanger this friendship, Elizabeth may have contributed to the repayment of the bond to make sure their closeness continued.

All of these decisions were very difficult for her to make by herself.

We do not know precisely when Henry returned from England. The Hatboro Library elected Fergusson a member on February 6, 1773, he having bought the share of another man, but Henry was not present at this meeting. He was back before early May because he carried a letter from her to Dr. John Redman in Philadelphia and the doctor's answer back to her. Her problems had been complicated further by an attack of urinary discomfort, a condition that troubled her all her life.[40]

In order to circumvent the restrictions on Henry's ownership of Elizabeth's inheritance, he persuaded her to sell Graeme Park to him in 1773 in fee simple.[41] Before the deed was completed, however, James Young heard about it and demanded his inheritance from his father-in-law's estate. Under Thomas Graeme's will, Elizabeth could pay the Youngs' legacy at her convenience. Since she was very short of cash and alienated from James Young, she had done nothing about the legacy. But the will required her to pay it if she sold the estate. Therefore, if she conveyed it to Henry, the couple would have to give Young and his children £1,000, money which they did not have. Henry had to be content with managing the estate and give up the idea of owning it outright until such time as he had accumulated enough money to pay the Youngs.

After Dr. Graeme's death, Elizabeth gave up the rented house in Philadelphia, and she and Henry, when he was there, lived year round at Graeme Park. In spite of all her romantic poetical descriptions of nature and her often declared love for Graeme Park, she did not really want to live there year round. She did not enjoy farming and its responsibilities and much preferred city life. Moreover, after Anny and John were taken by their father to live in the city with him, the empty house was lonely.

Although she supposedly bid farewell to the muses in April 1772, Elizabeth did not abandon poetry. While Henry was abroad, Elizabeth's pen was busy. During the spring of 1773, she wrote a series of poems, which she sent in a packet to Annis Stockton in Princeton.[42] Four of these were odes to the seasons. The ode to spring would be published in 1776 and the odes to summer and fall in the early 1790s. She also wrote lyrics to five Scottish ballads, among them her favorite "A Hymn to the Beauties of Nature" to be sung to the music of "The Birks of Invermay," also later published.[43] The first stanza of this last poem is typical of the lyrics Elizabeth was writing:

> The glorious sun, with lustre bright;
> And sparkling stars, a dazzling sight,

As through their azure fields they roll,
The wondrous works of God extol.

By October 1773, Henry had agreed to sell most of the Graeme Park land. An advertisement appeared in the *Pennsylvania Gazette* on the October 27 for 700 acres, altogether or in several tracts. The property was described as including "300 acres of wood, 100 acres of meadow (the greatest part of which is excellently watered), 280 of arable land, 20 acres in good orchards, filled with a collection of the best grafted fruit trees." The estate contained "valuable improvements," the land had been manured, and the whole was well fenced. The description was very tempting, but apparently there were no takers because Graeme Park was not broken up for several years. Since this effort was unsuccessful, the Fergussons had no recourse but to continue to live there.

The year 1774 was a very stressful one for Elizabeth who had many adjustments and decisions to make. Other than a poem celebrating Henry's twenty-sixth birthday on March 12, there are only three other existing poems from that year. The first two, written in May, are very melancholy. "The Ode to the Evening"[44] begins with the day ending. It says: "The Soul feels harmony'd to Love; / What thrilling Joys delighting." But we soon learn that she is not referring to connubial bliss but to spiritual salvation.

O Waft me to those pure abodes!
Where holy Spirits blessed
.... In Vision let me join the Blest!
Their Sacred Haunts discover.

The fifth stanza is very revealing of her inner state:

That foretaste of Superior Joy;
Lifes dreary vale Shall Brighten,
Shall dark Coroding Doubts Distroy;
And Deaths drear path Enlighten.

Corroding doubts? This is hardly the sort of verse a happy wife would write only two years after she had married the man she loved.

In the second of the poems written in May, entitled "The Recluse," Elizabeth bid farewell to "Light pleasure," "vain Charms," and "the flutter of Follys alarms." When taken in conjunction with her sentiments about country living given in her letter to Dickinson, we can see that she regarded herself as exiled away from human company. As far as her relationship with Henry, the fifth stanza declares mortal love overrated:

> Believe me, Oh try it! The Passion of Love
> When fixd in a Mortal or raised far above;
> To such a Sweet Contrast so worthy the Soul!
> That no human language its worth can Extole
> The first is all flutter uncertain And paind!
> And Keen Disapointment as soon as obtain,
> The Second is lasting Seraphic And pure!
> And will in the End perfect Joy procure.

Elizabeth thus refers to human love as uncertain, painful, and disappointing.

Furthermore, her marriage was not making up for her isolation at Graeme Park. John Young wrote to her from Philadelphia about her solitariness in the country. He sympathized with her because of her exclusion "from the Joys of Society."[45] Sometime during this period Elizabeth wrote to Margaret Stedman about her isolation. Her letter is gone, and only a short quotation from the original response of Stedman remains, but Elizabeth's feelings are clear. Margaret commiserated with her complaints about country living: "I am truly sorry my dear Mrs Fergusson to find by the tenor of your letter you still dislike pastoral life. I was in hopes time joined to the engaging companion you have would have reconciled you to it."[46]

But Henry was not as "engaging" as Mrs. Stedman had suggested. Either he liked farming and took a real interest in making the estate succeed or he used his agricultural responsibilities as an excuse to spend less time with his bride. Sometimes he stayed out on the farm until eight o'clock at night, even though he had promised to return earlier. Elizabeth wrote a friend that she kept a novel at hand, something like *Banford Abbey*, "in order to pass away a salutary hour." She did not mind her husband's tardiness, she wrote, but her mind must have longed for the intellectual companionship that she had had all of her previous life. Her correspondent regretted that Elizabeth was not as fond of farming as Henry because if she had been, he was certain "it would turn out to good account."[47]

It is true that Elizabeth could have become involved in the business of the farm. She certainly was intelligent enough to understand and contribute to her property's management. Since her father's library contained many books on the latest agricultural techniques, and he had been deeply interested in agronomy all his life, Elizabeth must have heard these subjects discussed and have had information available to her. But the odds were against a woman of her background with a living husband taking an active interest in the management of their farm. This was considered man's work, and for her to interfere might have signified a distrust of her husband's abilities. In addition, the management of Graeme Park was not her prerogative. When she married Henry, under Pennsylvania law the estate became his responsibility.

Marriage for Elizabeth meant loneliness and boredom. She had no children. Since Anny and John were gone and Henry was home only a few hours in the early afternoon for the midday meal and in the evening before bedtime, there was no one around during the days for her to talk to except servants. Most of her friends were nineteen miles away in Philadelphia. She enjoyed reading, but she was accustomed to having other well read persons with whom to discuss the books that she enjoyed, especially her women friends. To invite people to come to Graeme Park meant having them for one or more nights. Since her father's death, she did not have enough money to entertain guests in the style her parents had set for the estate. She enjoyed needlework and weaving, but her requirements were easily met. The days were long and ways to fill them few. If she was complaining to friends, she probably was complaining to Henry, too. Loneliness would make her possessive of her husband's time. This made the marriage less attractive to him, as well. If he had courted her because she appeared to be a prospective wealthy heiress, he, too, must have been disappointed with his bargain.

The following November, Henry escaped to Philadelphia for a week of fun. He told Elizabeth he was going to the city for the day, but he did not return for a week. Meanwhile, his wife did not know where he was, and no explanation remains today for his absence. This occasioned the third poem she wrote that year. It is called "An Advertisement." Written in a facetious tone, it nevertheless reveals the heartache she was experiencing. She begins "Lost, Strayd, or Stollen from my arms!" and then describes the physical appearance and character of her husband who is lost. Disclosing her wry acknowledgment of the difference in their ages, she writes

His years too few, I wont them tell
The numbers would not sound so well,
If eer the writer should be known
At least I would conceal my own.
But let that little Error pass
I cant forget I keep a Glass![48]

She concludes by offering a reward to whoever will return her husband, but she has no gold and can only give her love. If a young man should bring him back, she hopes for him as faithful a spouse as she is to Henry. If a woman should return him, Elizabeth wishes her as much truth from her spouse as Henry boasts. This last wish is a two edged sword. If Elizabeth believes Henry faithful, then it is a true reward, but if she believes him unfaithful, then it is a penalty to be incurred by a woman who has distracted his love.

Her unhappiness with her isolation and marital disappointments may have silenced her pen. Except for a verse Elizabeth wrote commemorating the death of Thomas Penn on March 21, 1775, there are no remaining new poems until July 1777. Even her letter writing was curtailed; John Young scolded her in March 1775[49] for her silence. He was concerned about her withdrawal and encouraged her to take up her pen, reminding her that at Graeme Park she had "all Advantages that any Poet can wish for." The "Season of Poetry" was fast approaching, and he expected to "see something of the Pastoral Kind" in "the next Magazine." Young would get his wish in April when one of his aunt's poems appeared in *The Pennsylvania Magazine; or, American Monthly Museum,* published in Philadelphia by Robert Aiken and edited by Thomas Paine. This new periodical, begun in January, provided the only opportunity for American authors to see their work in print outside of newspapers or books. No other magazine was published in British North America at the time.[50] Elizabeth's poem was entitled "To a Young Lady who asked her friend (a married lady) to describe the marks of a real passion to her."

The printed version of this poem is considerably shorter and different from the manuscript original, written the previous year.[51] In the original, she referred to herself as Laura, her well-known pseudonym. In the version offered to Philadelphians, she changed her name to Delia. The first poem points out that people react differently. The "pensive Maid: / Courts *moonlight, Sentiment,* and *Song* / . . . Hates *Crowds,* and *Visits, Dress and Forms.*" The "gay *coquet,*" in contrast, "disdains the Sigh Sincere / The heaving breast and heart felt tear." She craves society and public acknowledgement of her love and beauty. A third type is the woman, obviously Elizabeth herself, with

> the Candid open heart
> Where Sense and passion bear a part;
> that knows its weakness yet Essays
> The truth to prove by various ways.

The published poem only discusses "love in gentle bosoms." Such love "gleams with melancholy light." The "tender maid" seeks "the gloomy shade," "listens to the wood-dove's song," and courts the moonlight. She "sheds a tender tear, / Responsive sheds a trembling sigh." The original does not have this Gothic sense to it. It is more realistic about the anxieties of the maid toward the man who has declared his love for her, and it also includes several lines describing the "virt[u]ous Swain." In print, Elizabeth was careful to express herself in conventional literary terms, but her true feelings were disclosed in the original.

Even though James Young had removed his children from Elizabeth's care, nevertheless, her relationship with them continued, although restricted by distance. Anny continued to look to her aunt for advice and love. When Elizabeth was in Philadelphia, they visited, and when she was at Graeme Park, they exchanged letters and poetry. Anny continued to write poems and send them to Elizabeth. One of the most interesting of these poems was Anny's reaction to the treatment of women by Jonathan Swift, the Irish author of *Gulliver's Travels,* whose works she had been reading in 1774. She asks Swift,

> Say when you Dip your keenest pen in Gall
> Why Must it Still on helpless Woman fall?
> Why Must our Dirt and Dullness fill each Line
> Our Love of Follies and Disire to Shine?
> Why are we Drawn as whole Race of Fools;
> Unswayd alike by Sense or Virtues Rules?

She calls his satire harsh, "Rude Severe, unjust" and tells him that it just awakens "our anger or Disgust." Although admiring Swift's "Wit allmost Divine," Anny tells him that even while readers laugh, they mourn his "Wits abuse," and while they praise his talents, "Scorn their use."[52]

That year Anny fell deeply in love with physician–druggist Dr. William Smith, a graduate of the University of Pennsylvania Medical School, but no relation to the provost of the university. In September Anny wrote him a poem[53] while he was away. It begins with a sad picture of Anny in ill health, with "pain and Sickness" hovering round her bed, pining for Damon [William}. "Where art thou *Damon* whither art thou flown / While thy lovd *Sylvia* [Anny] Sighs unheard unknown!" Even though his presence might make her better, she doesn't want to trouble him. "To Save Thy Bosom but one anxious Groan / Content Id bear each Sorrow of my own," she writes. Should heaven not permit their meeting again and Fate should "gently lay [her] in the Arms of Death," he must not grieve but let religion "Calm [his] Bleeding heart." In that event, she hopes that he will find another woman who will love him as she does and that they may meet again on "that Blissfull Shore."

Elizabeth's later reaction to the poem is revealing. In 1787, she sent Annis Stockton, copies of fifteen poems of Anny's. After this one, Elizabeth wrote that she did not approve of "so free a Declaration of attachment to any Man howevr Worthy Before Marriage: at least so long as a twelfth month." Because many reasons might have arisen to break the connection and make the return of letters desirable, Elizabeth thought this "a mighty foolish piece of Business."[54] In other words, one cannot trust a relationship, no matter how deep, to last a year and, therefore, must protect oneself from possible future embarrassment. Elizabeth was not willing outwardly to commit herself completely to a man but always held back. This had been true in her relationship with William Franklin, and it was true with Henry. There was a lurking presentment that it could not last based on a distrust of men or perhaps a deficiency in her self-image.

In June 1775, Anny sent Elizabeth a letter reporting that she and friends had been walking in the garden of the Swedes Church where Elizabeth and Henry had married. She enclosed a poem "Lines Occasioned by Wallking One Summers Evening in the Churchyard of Wicacoe Church in the Environs of Philadelphia." This, Elizabeth wrote Annis Stockton, was, in her opinion, Anny's most "mature" piece, although "none can tread with advantage in a Church yard after the Celebrated Mr Grey."[55] In the 1790s when Elizabeth was submitting her own work for publication, she also arranged to have several of Anny's poems published, and this one appeared in the *Universal Asylum and Columbian Magazine.*[56]

Just as Anny reacted to the anti-women contents of Swift's satire, her brother, while otherwise "charmed," with *Lord Chesterfield's Letters,* complained that the author treated women unjustly and severely, even with "Contempt."[57] The similar reactions of these two young people to examples of the disdainful treatment of women may reflect their sensitizing by their aunt during their formative years. Even if she made no verbal comments about the position of women, her own talents would have denied the classification of all women as inferior. This, however, was the prevailing view about women. For three months in 1768, a series of sixteen articles by the "Visitant" had appeared on the front page of the *Pennsylvania Chronicle,* written by one or two men who signed their work either "C." or "L."[58] Their reason for writing, they said, was "to examine, in a moral view, the sentiments and manners of the world." Seven of the articles were almost exclusively about women, and their gist was to tell women how they should behave in order to please men.

The assumption underneath these essays was that women were inferior to men. They were designed to be "an help-meet for men," their sole reason for existence to please the opposite sex. When the authors complimented women, it was for characteristics that accomplished this aim. When they criticized them, it was for their failures to do so. Women's only choice was whether to seek admiration for their physical attributes or to seek esteem for their mental ones. Men were still the center whose approval women must earn. And, furthermore, according to the authors, this was what women wanted.

Under these conditions, Visitant wrote, turning to men, it behooves a man of honor to treat women with respect.

> The delicacy, the timidity, the beauty of the fair sex, require that they should be respected, protected, caressed. . . . Every principle of honour demands that they should not be losers by those, for whom they were made—that they should be treated with all imaginable tenderness by those, to whom something would still be wanting in creation, *without this last—best gift of Heaven.*[59]

God had given women to men for their pleasure; hence a gentleman would never mistreat these helpless beings under his control.

There were only three printed responses to these articles, one from a man who found the authors much too kind to women. He told the authors to point out how vain women were, how prone to slander, how envious of others. The second response was a satirical poem from a group of women, and the third was an essay from one who signed herself "Aspasia."

The women's poem was written in answer to the third article, in which Visitant had argued that "a maxim generally received" was that "women have little minds, that they are narrowly vain, and disposed to be pleased with trifles." These faults the Visitant had blamed on female education, which was based on the principle that "the cultivation of the mind is of less importance than the external accomplishments of person and behaviour." Yet women must not go to the other extreme," he had written, and become "sentimental, learned, and bookish." "When good sense, improved by reading, is united with the amiable virtues of modesty and submission," the article continued, "with a desire of being rather than appearing to be wiser than others, I cannot but think it must engage universal respect."[60]

Calling the author a "gen'rous man" with more irony than gratitude, the women answered his comments:

> You, Sir, with better sense, will justly fix
> Our faults on *education*, not our *sex*;
> Will show the source which makes the female mind
> So oft appear but puerile and blind;
>
> .   .   .   .
>
> But that the odium of a *Bookish fair,*
> Or *female pedant,* or *"they quit their sphere,"*
> Damps all their views, and they must drag the chain,
> And sigh for sweet instruction's page in vain.
> But we commit our injur'd cause to you;
> Point out the medium which we should pursue.
> So may each scene of safe domestic peace
> Heighten your joys, and animate your bliss.[61]

The author of this poem has been identified by Professor Carla Mulford as Annis Stockton.[62] Whether this was written by Stockton alone or by a group of women is not known. In later life, Stockton would deny Mary Wollstonecraft's claim in her *A Vindication of the Rights of Woman* that women were generally accepted as slaves of men, inferior to them in mental ability.[63] Hence this poem should be read as satire rather than as a true statement of her beliefs.

The identity of the person using the pseudonym Aspasia is not known, although it could very well have been Elizabeth Graeme. She would have known that "Aspasia" referred to an Ionian courtesan who moved to Athens and became the mistress of Pericles. The Greek Aspasia had been noted for her charm, talent, and intellect. A strong woman, she had become involved in the politics of Athens and was said to have influenced Pericles. Whoever the Philadelphia Aspasia was knew the identity of her namesake and chose that pseudonym as part of her statement.

She began her answer to Visitant as had the group of women with thanks to the author for pointing out "both the errors and perfections of the female sex."[64] This sort of introduction in the poem as well as in this essay may have been neither sarcasm nor sincerity but simply a polite way to lead into her subject without alienating her male readers. She turns then to the nature of the Visitant. She cannot determine whether he is one person or two or whether he is unfeigned or "the reverse of every thing he says."

In any case, he must "correct some faults in [his] own sex, before [he] can brighten the shades of" women's. For example, men say one thing about women but often act the opposite. Visitant said that women should educate their minds so that they will be pleasing to men but not so much that they will become female pedants. Men, however, really do not appreciate a good mind as much as they do a pretty face, wrote Aspasia. If she is beautiful, she is judged "brilliant," even if her repartee is "what Pope calls 'the pert low dialogue.'" Although all men do not say, "Give me a wife who can make a shirt and a pudding," nevertheless that is the "sentiment [that] runs through the major part of the lordly race."

She called on men to think what they are saying when they complain about educated women, what it says about themselves when they conclude that education lowers women's esteem for their husbands.

That the more a woman's understanding is improved, the more apt she will be to despise her husband—that the strengthening of her reason will weaken her affection—That the duties of tenderness and attention, and all the social train will be disregarded in proportion as her knowledge is increased—that to teach her *God* and *nature* will, in the end, destroy all order and domestic comfort. Good Heavens! What a subversion of truth are all these assertions!

Aspasia argues that education, to the contrary, makes a better relationship between husband and wife, not a lesser one.

In addition no matter how "pleasing timidity and implicit submission in [women] may be to" men, there are times when strength is absolutely needed by women to survive. "As maids, as wives, and as widows," women "meet with a thousand occasions in life where fortitude and resolution are absolutely necessary." Perseverance is necessary for single women who have nothing else to do but accept or reject lovers. "After marriage, it is necessary in the education of children, and in regulating the more subordinate members of a family. For as to a husband, it is virtue never to peep out, where his lordly prerogative is concerned. And sure equally essential is it in the lonely widowed state, where we have to act in so many different capacities."

Elizabeth and Annis visited during 1768 and this series of articles and the responses to it undoubtedly were discussed. There is no evidence of Elizabeth's feeling, but it is difficult to see how she could have reacted otherwise than to agree with Aspasia, considering her own intellectual level and her determination to keep Anny "Steadily engaged in Learning till Sixteen at least."[65] The fine line that women had to toe between some education and too much, between interest in current events and meddling in them, was shown in a letter Elizabeth wrote to John Dickinson. It transmitted to him a copy of a poem she had written in 1768 about the tension between England and her North American colonies, in which she had included his name as author of the Farmer letters. She wrote, "As the theme is treated quite in a domestic Manner; I hope the author will not be accused of Styring into Subjects improper for her Sex; For a female pedant is a most disagreeable Character."[66]

Elizabeth's contacts with John were not as frequent as hers with Anny, but nevertheless they maintained their connections. The situation for John under his father's wing was very different from his prospects at the Graemes. There he had attended the Academy and the intention would have been for him to pursue advanced education at the College. His father, however, ended his schooling and put him to work as an apprentice for a

Philadelphia dry goods merchant, a Mr. Carmick. Yet his work was not strenuous, and he had plenty of spare time to read, which he devoted mostly to histories of England and Scotland. By July 15, 1774, Carmick had died, and within a month, John was apprenticed to John and Peter Chevalier, import/export merchants.

It was more difficult for Elizabeth to visit with John when she was in Philadelphia than with Anny because she usually stayed with Charles and Margaret Stedman. The brothers-in-law, James Young and Charles Stedman, had become estranged after Thomas Graeme's death, probably over the doctor's will, and Young forbade his son to enter Stedman's home. Apparently he did not lay the same injunction on his daughter. When Elizabeth was at the Stedman's on one occasion, she had Anny deliver presents from her to John. He wrote thanking her especially for a "pocket Book" that had belonged to Dr. Graeme and apologizing for not having written more often.[67]

In July 1774, John asked his aunt her "sentiments on the times." If they should turn out to be the same as his, she could furnish him with arguments to support his opinions in conversation. If different, her opinions would show him where he was wrong.[68] She must have answered affirmatively because in an August letter, John wrote that he was glad that her "Sentiments on Politicks" agreed with his.

The politics that John questioned and that were on the tongues of everyone in Philadelphia involved the colonies' reactions to their treatment by Great Britain. The relationship between the mother country and her colonies had reached the boiling point in the years 1773 and 1774. Soon to erupt, the controversy would change Elizabeth's life forever.

6

Everybody Is a Whig or a Torie

In Pennsylvania, there had been almost universal dislike of the Stamp Act of 1765, but disagreement over the proper way to win its repeal had developed. As crowds of citizens had gathered to express their opposition and to recommend action, and as these crowds had claimed an extra-legal, sometimes violent, life of their own, threatening those who disagreed with them, the society had fractured over the question of its proper response to British measures. The Quakers, a large minority, and other pacifists disapproved of any violence, and many other people while opposed to British taxation feared uncontrolled mob actions. They believed that the educated and qualified should rule and that government should be reasoned and dispassionate. When crowd actions challenged this belief and enforced actions in the name of all inhabitants, these people cried anarchy and worried about the dissolution of the society. They preferred to negotiate with the mother country, to use patience and conciliation rather than mass meetings and threats.

Confrontation with Great Britain was not what they wanted. The mother country was too powerful; if war broke out with her, the colonies would surely lose, they argued, and be deprived of the privileges they had developed over the years. If the colonies by some remote chance should win, they would forfeit all the advantages of being a part of the British empire. Furthermore, they could not survive separately because they were not economically or militarily viable units. Strong European nations taking advantage of their weakness would pick them off one by one or play them off one against the other. Yet, they would be unable to unite because they were so different. A future independent of England would be bleak, indeed, and a future tied to England after defeat in a civil war would mean complete suppression. The preferred response to British legislation, therefore, should be respectful negotiation.

Any recommendations for moderation, however, soon incited unpleasant consequences against the people who made them. As early as 1770, it had become very uncomfortable to oppose the escalating colonial anger toward Great Britain or, for that matter, even to remain uncommitted. There were many examples of people being treated rudely if not violently when they expressed reservations about colonial actions. Abigail Coxe asked Benjamin Rush, "Who can live quietly among you that shews ye least Dislike to y^r Methods or Measures? You do not Tar & feather 'em indeed, but you make very free with their Principles & Characters, which is an injury in ye worst way."[1] Later, Pennsylvanians would violently manhandle those who dared to speak out against American opposition to the mother country, forcing them to retract their opinions publicly.

Parliament had repealed first the Stamp Act and, four years later, all of the subsequently passed Townshend duties except the tax on tea. Many Americans had responded to the remaining duty by boycotting British tea, using the smuggled Dutch product instead. By 1773, the East India Tea Company was having financial difficulties. In order to help the company recover its North American business, Parliament passed the Tea Act permitting the company to bypass the previously required stop in England and to ship its product directly to the colonies, thereby eliminating the costs of middlemen handling. This would lower the price of English tea to the point where, even with the Townshend duty, it would be cheaper than smuggled Dutch tea. Parliament thought that frugal colonial housewives would buy the cheaper tea, thereby helping the East India Company recover. The colonists, however, believed that there was a deeper motive for the measure—to establish the precedent of colonists paying a Parliament tax.

When the Company announced that it planned to ship tea to selected consignees in Philadelphia who would sell it, citizens objected as they had before, with outcries, newspaper articles, and pamphlets. Benjamin Rush, by now deeply involved in the resistance movement, wrote articles signed with the pseudonym "Hamden," arguing that the British measure was a trick that would deprive Americans of their liberties. In October, he wrote, "Let us with ONE heart and hand oppose the landing of it. The baneful chests contain in them a slow poison in a political as well as a physical sense. They contain something worse than death—the seeds of Slavery."[2] John Dickinson, accusing the East India Company of "Rapine, Oppression and Cruelty," recommended that "if a Person assists in unloading, landing, or storing the tea he shall ever after be deemed an Enemy to his Country, and never be employed by his Fellow-Citizens"[3] The inflammatory wording of these messages raised the level of invective and encouraged violence against those who opposed colonial resistance.

Boston had dumped three shiploads of tea in its harbor on December 16, but Philadelphia citizens managed to prevent a ship intended for that city from docking. When word was received in December of the imminent arrival of a ship loaded with tea, the Delaware River pilots were warned not to guide it to the port, and the Captain was sent a broadside threatening him with a halter around his neck and tar and feathers should he bring his ship to Philadelphia.[4] When the captain proceeded up river without a pilot, following another ship, a committee from Philadelphia met the ship at Gloucester Point and escorted the captain to the city. There he attended a town meeting on the twenty-seventh where nearly eight thousand people told him that the tea must not be landed. On December 28, the ship sailed for England.

An angry Parliament, its patience ended by Boston's action, began passing in the spring of 1774 a series of four acts, which the colonists dubbed the "Intolerable Acts." In March, the first of these, the Boston Port Bill, closed the port of Boston until its citizens paid for the tea. Two other punitive acts followed in May: the Administration of Justice Act permitted the Massachusetts governor to move certain trials outside Massachusetts whenever he believed that English officials could not get a fair trial in the colony, and the Massachusetts Government Act made many changes in Massachusetts's charter government, strengthening the powers of the royally appointed governor. The fourth measure was the Quartering Act of June 2, which legalized the quartering of British troops in private dwellings. In addition, a British general, Thomas Gage, replaced the governor of Massachusetts, and British troops were moved into the city.

The Philadelphia town meeting on December 27, 1773, had resolved to send its approval and thanks to Boston for destroying the tea, but this was not the opinion of all Philadelphians. Many people disapproved of the destruction of private property and believed that Boston should reimburse the East India Company. If Elizabeth had been living in the city instead of at Graeme Park during the uproar, she would have been buffeted by the conflicting views of her friends and family. While Rush and Dickinson strongly supported the resistance, other friends opposed it. Even her family was split. James Young, Anny, and Anny's suitor, William Smith, were warm supporters, or Whigs, whereas the Stedmans, John Young, and Henry had grave reservations.

The only remaining contemporary statement by Elizabeth of her opinion about the British colonial crisis is the poem she wrote in October 1768 after reading John Dickinson's farmer's letters. At that time she believed the colonies justified in their reaction to the British tax laws, and she strongly supported the boycott of British manufactured goods. She pictured Great Britain as haughty and demanding, and she reminded the mother country of her power's limitation: "Great is your Power; but still that Power has Law; / And <u>God</u> and <u>Reason</u> certain Limits draw."[5] During and after the war, Elizabeth often wrote that she always had supported the colonies' position. There is no reason to suspect that she believed differently in the period immediately before independence when hostilities were increasing.

Her nephew asked her July 15, 1774, about her "sentiments on the Times." Her response no longer exists, but John's next letter states that he was "glad" that her "Sentiments on Politicks" agreed with his own. He judged the "proceedings of the British Parliament . . . tyrannical to the last degree," but at the same time he also believed that the Bostonians had gone too far.

> If the Oliverian Spirit of the Bostonians could be curb'd without endangering the Liberties of America in generall [he] should be glad to see them punished for their insolence in destroying the property of the East India company, which unwarrantable act but too much resembled the oppostion of their Ancestors to the measures of the Court of King Charles the first.

Young wanted the colonies to reinstate their non-importation boycott and include non-exportation to the West Indies, as well.[6]

By the summer of 1774, the colonies had called for the meeting of a Continental Congress in Philadelphia in September to coordinate help to

Boston and opposition to Great Britain. A conservative group of delegates had been chosen by the Assembly from its members to represent Pennsylvania, and Young was distressed that John Dickinson was not one of them. Actually, John Young's views at that time were quite in line with those of the resistance leaders who also expected the Congress to renew the boycott, whereas the cautious citizens, including Henry, wanted the Congress to petition the King for redress and to negotiate before taking any actions.

The more defiant position won out, and Congress created the Continental Association committing all the colonists to non-importation, non-exportation, and non-consumption of British goods. Most important, the Association contained an enforcement procedure. In previous boycotts, the merchants had controlled enforcement, but this time, enforcement was taken out of their hands. Committees that might or might not include merchants were to be set up in every county, town, or city to assure that all citizens obeyed the sanctions. Violators were to be punished by having their names published in the newspapers as enemies of their country and by having their businesses boycotted by other citizens. This committee enforcement led to conflicts with cautious citizens who had not agreed to this provision and who regarded committee tyranny as worse than British.[7] The First Continental Congress adjourned but agreed to meet again in May 1775, if Parliament had not repealed the "Intolerable Acts."

Very little is known of the Fergussons' activities during this time. Only one of Elizabeth's letters remains from the period February 1773 to August 1777. She may have stopped writing to her friends because she had little to say and did not want to disclose her marital discontent. Or her friends could have obeyed her later request to burn all her letters. In March 1775, however, John Young wrote that it had been so long since he had heard from her that he was afraid that their correspondence was "in Danger of dropping."[8] As for Henry, after the advertisements failed to produce a purchaser for Graeme Park, he apparently tried to make a success of the farm and became involved in community affairs. He had become a member of the Horsham Library in 1773; in November of 1774 and 1775, he was elected one of its directors.[9] In 1774, he paid a county tax of £4.17.6 on property assessed at £65;[10] in February 1775 he was appointed to be justice of the peace for Philadelphia County;[11] and he signed as witness to an apprentice agreement the next month.[12] These are the only records of his activities that remain.

While Elizabeth and Henry pursued their pastoral lives at Graeme

Park, their newspapers reported that hostilities between Great Britain and her North American colonies had escalated. The Battles of Lexington and Concord occurred on April 19, 1775, in Massachusetts, and Parliament having not repealed the Intolerable Acts, the Continental Congress reconvened May 10 in Philadelphia, according to the terms of its previous adjournment. That same day, British Fort Ticonderoga on Lake Champlain was captured by a colonial force. Cannons from the Fort were subsequently hauled across country and used to force the British army to evacuate Boston in March 1776. On June 15, 1775, Congress named George Washington Commander-in-Chief of the Continental forces, but before he could reach Boston, the British attacked American soldiers on Breeds Hill located on Charlestown peninsula across the harbor from Boston. The British won a tactical victory in what would be called the Battle of Bunker Hill on June 17, but they paid for it with tremendous losses.

Before the battles of Lexington and Concord, Pennsylvanians had cautiously supported the resistance movement, forming committees first to communicate within the colony and with other colonies and then to enforce the Continental Association or boycott formed by the Continental Congress, but they had refused to arm and form militia companies. After April 19, this changed. Although Pennsylvania had not been affected directly by the actions at Lexington and Concord, nevertheless many people believed that what had happened in the Massachusetts towns could happen in their localities. News of the event reached Philadelphia on April 24, and the next day about eight thousand Philadelphians gathered at the State House where they agreed "to *associate*, for the Purpose of defending with ARMS their Property, Liberty, and Lives,"[13] and they determined to meet force with force. Out in the counties, committees began to assemble, to agree with the Philadelphia resolution, to form militia companies, to choose officers, and to arm the men. After the battle of Bunker Hill, Congress gave its approval to what was already happening by recommending that all able-bodied men between sixteen and fifty immediately form militia companies and telling the colonies to accumulate arms for them.

As the Whigs began arming and preparing to defend their liberties, the position of those who differed from them grew precarious. The committeemen extended their responsibilities from their original charge of enforcing the boycott called for by the Congress to identifying and ostracizing their opponents, called the disaffected or Tories, who would now be silenced or punished. Reinforced by newly organized and armed Associators, committee members picked up Tories, carted them about the city, and forced them to recant publicly. In early May, for example, a shoemaker, Thomas Loosely, was brought to the Coffee House where he was forced to apologize for his criticisms of the Whigs.[14] Since there was no police force responsible for preserving the peace, there was no one for the disaffected to turn to for protection. Philadelphia's less than thirty constables were responsible only for carrying out court business. The unarmed Tory had to be very courageous, or foolhardy, to stand up to a crowd of angry armed militiamen determined to make him recant. Even the freedom of the press was stifled by Whig enthusiasm. Quaker Jabez Maud Fisher was summoned to appear before the Philadelphia committee and forced to disclose the name of a man he had quoted anonymously in a newspaper article.[15] The most respected citizens were subject to intimidation. Joseph Galloway, attorney and ex-Speaker of the Assembly, received threats and feared for his life because he tried to slow Pennsylvania's reaction to British measures.

Elizabeth and Henry were concerned about the Charles Stedmans, whose disaffection to the resistance was well known. In May the Fergussons urged their friends to leave the city and retire to Graeme Park before they were driven out by crowd violence. Stedman thanked them, commenting that he thought soon the city would "be too hot." Affairs seemed to him to "have a dismal appearance": the port was shut, people were arming everywhere, and many would be ruined, he wrote.[16] Ten days later, Stedman's wife, Margaret, wrote Elizabeth describing the arrival of John Hancock in Philadelphia for the opening of the Second Continental Congress. "Many hundreds went out to meet him (nay it is said thousands) two men rode before him with drawn swords in their hands, and the whole city seemed to be in a tumult, flocking from all quarters to get a peep at him, as if he had descended from the celestial abodes and had been different from other mortals."[17]

On June 20, Henry wrote a letter to Benjamin Rush explaining his position about the burgeoning war with the mother country. Claiming his right to speak his opinions freely about the controversy, Henry urged patience and negotiation. He believed that England was "disposed to a reconciliation" and that her colonies should "give her an oppertunity to be reconciled." He asked Rush,

> Are then our resentments so high, is revenge so sweet a thing, that to distress Britain in a few particulars, we will expose ourselves to

every horror the imagination can paint?—Our cities destroyed, our fields uncultivated, our plains strew'd with death and ruin and to what end all this? Why to be enslavd at last: for depend upon it when things are reduced to the utmost extremity, not only England and the other powers in europe will squeeze and harness us, but demagogues among ourselves will spring up to tear the vitals and suck the blood of this once happy happy country.

Instead, if the colonies should stop their fighting immediately, because of what they already had accomplished and of their importance to England, they "should be able to obtain . . . peace, liberty, and encreasing greatness." The two men had argued about this problem before, and Rush had written Fergusson urging him to renounce his "present system of politicks." Henry concluded his reply by offering to send a carriage for his friend and another man so that he could hear the latest news from them.[18]

In June, Anny Young, while asking to be remembered affectionately to Henry, regretted "that a Gentleman so Formed by nature And Education to take part in the present Disputes with Honour to Himself And advantage to the Community should unfortunately possess Sentiments which . . . Condemn His talents to Rust in Obscurity."[19] Obviously this subject had been argued at family gatherings, further troubling Elizabeth.

Anny's brother was indecisive at this point, leaning toward the American cause but not committed. He was pleased that Washington had been appointed Commander-in-Chief of the army outside Boston. "It is happy for America," he wrote his aunt,

> that the Person promoted to that high Dignity has allways borne the Character of a Man of Honour, & is remarcable for his Honesty & Integrity; for he certainly has it as much in his Power to raise himself on the Ruins of his Country as old *Oliver* had.

He reported to Elizabeth July 1 that many young men of his acquaintance were heading to the American camp at Cambridge, Massachusetts. Young envied his friends because they had the necessary means to "maintain the Character of a Gentleman Volunteer." If he were so lucky, he "would follow them immediately." But the young man's motivation was not strongly ideological. He had "allways had a Desire for a Military Life," he wrote his aunt.[20]

Elizabeth may have expected during the preceding two years that she would become pregnant, since her mother and her sister Jane had known little time during their reproductive years when they were not pregnant. But this did not happen, or at least there were no pregnancies carried to term, and by summer 1775, Elizabeth was two years short of forty. She may have decided that she was not intended to become a mother and that she needed to fill her life with other expectations.

In any case, that summer, Elizabeth increased her close ties with her women friends, even if their meetings were difficult to arrange and she could only see a few at a time, and renewed her interest in handwork. By sending her carriage to town, she could entice visitors to come to Graeme Park. Mary Redman and Abigail Coxe came to Horsham in mid-June for a week, and even before they arrived, Elizabeth had made plans for her coachman to pick up Rebecca Smith when he took the other two visitors back to Philadelphia. Mary Roberdeau was prevented by illness from going to Horsham soon after, but two other women did keep their commitment. Elizabeth was also filling some of her empty hours with a variety of handwork. The wool from the sheep on the farm, she carded, spun, and wove. She wrote Rebecca Smith that she would weave fringe for Rebecca's sister Williamina, if someone would send her the dimensions Willy desired.[21] By September 2, there had been so many visitors at Graeme Park that Margaret Stedman congratulated Elizabeth "on a little cessation from company." She commented upon the hospitality of the Fergussons and wrote that "the natural sweetness" of Henry's "temper" made him "so very engaging that it is impossible not to be pleased where he is."[22] One wonders how Henry felt about this invasion of women without their husbands. Perhaps he was glad to have other people around to relieve him of Elizabeth's expectations for attendance upon her. For her part, Elizabeth had found a way not only to alleviate her loneliness but also to bring her husband home at reasonable hours to entertain their company.

From Abigail Coxe and Rebecca Smith, Elizabeth heard great opposition to Pennsylvania's resistance to the British. Mrs. Coxe, a widow, had been appalled at least since 1770 by the intimidation measures used by the Whigs to silence and discredit their opposition, and she was a very outspoken woman. Rev. William Smith agreed with John Young that the colonies were right to oppose taxation without their representation, but, at the same time, their violent resistance measures were dangerous and unwarranted. There is no indication that his wife did not agree with him.

He had been in the forefront of the early Whig movement, but by the summer of 1775, he had "wholly declined being of any new Committee or taking any public part in affairs" concerning Great Britain. He was not allowed to withdraw completely, however, because as an Anglican minister, he was expected to preach to and commend the patriotism of the militiamen, called Associators, who were volunteering to fight the enemy. As he pointed out to the Bishop of London, if the colonial clergy were seen as "Enemys to the principles of the Revolution," they would soon lose their congregations, and the church would decline.[23]

Other friends would have given Elizabeth another story. In July, Mary Roberdeau was planning a visit. Her husband, Daniel, a long time Graeme friend and one of the executors of Dr. Graeme's will, was very active in the colonial cause. He was so "engrossed by publick business," his wife commented, probably with more truth than humor, that she considered herself as "an encumbrance," free to leave town and visit friends.[24]

Elizabeth was growing concerned about Henry's safety on those occasions when he visited friends in Philadelphia, and she tried to convince him to be more circumspect. He argued privately with Benjamin Rush and family members, believing that he had the right to express his opinions, but such behavior could be dangerous when public. In tavern meetings, Elizabeth feared that he made no secret of his disaffection to colonial measures and that committeemen might decide to silence him, as they had others.

Finally, Henry decided to go back to Great Britain, ostensibly on family business with his brother in Scotland. Although Elizabeth left us no record of her feelings upon the occasion, she may have encouraged him to leave for his safety from rebel reprisals. Once he had arrived, she constantly urged him to remain abroad until the imperial crisis was settled.[25]

On September 10, 1775, Henry left for Bristol on a merchant ship, accompanied by Richard Stockton's brother Samuel W., who was going to enroll at the Inns of Court, but never did. This was the last time that Henry Fergusson was ever at Graeme Park. Henry and Sammy had a difficult journey to the ship, picking their way through debris. The week before they left, the area had suffered a terrible wind and rain storm of hurricane force that had destroyed almost all the bridges between Newcastle and Philadelphia. Water Street in the city had been flooded, with great loss of dry goods, such as salt and sugar. Ships had been "thrown so far upon Land" that it was doubted they could ever be launched again. Henry and Sammy must have been shaken by the sight of "the Devastation in the orchards, woods meadows and Indian Cornfields,"[26] as they traveled toward their embarkation point.

After the war, Henry filed a claim with the British requesting reimbursement for the losses he had incurred because of his loyalty to the mother country. Henry wrote the commissioners that in September 1775, just before he left the country, he had induced Elizabeth to agree to an arrangement whereby he, rather than her heir at law, John Young, could inherit Graeme Park should she die during his absence. Supposedly, the estate was placed in the hands of a trustee, Dr. John Redman, to convey to Henry in the event of her death. The conveyance was left with Richard Stockton, Henry asserted, but never registered legally. It had subsequently disappeared, he maintained, but he produced what he said was a copy of the original and presented it to the British claims commission in 1784.[27]

When Elizabeth heard from John Young that some of the émigrés in England had seen such a paper, she vehemently denied that such a conveyance had ever existed. She wrote that "the Fee was not vested in Mr. Fergusson nor never had been."[28] If, indeed, Henry told the truth, the paper might have disappeared when the Stocktons' home was destroyed by the British army at the time of the Battle of Princeton. Since Elizabeth was noted for honesty, it is more likely that Henry was embellishing his claim of losses in order to win a larger settlement from the British, and that such a paper never had existed.

What was executed, without a doubt because it still exists,[29] was a power of attorney from Fergusson to Richard Stockton allowing the attorney to dispose of Graeme Park as he thought best and to give the proceeds to Elizabeth. Under Pennsylvania legal practices, except in cases of the husband's long absence or desertion, a woman could not buy, sell, or manage property without her husband's permission, not even her own inherited property.[30] Elizabeth was determined to sell the estate and put the money out at interest so that she and Henry would not have to be dependent on agriculture for their support. Apparently she was able to convince Henry, although reluctantly, to give her the ability to sell the estate while he was gone. But he dragged his feet about executing the document. Before Henry left September 10, he had already discussed this matter with Richard Stockton, and Stockton wrote his brother October 31 to present his respects to Fergusson, from whom he expected "to hear by the first ship."[31] A gentle reminder of a promise not yet kept! By letter dated November 20 from London, Henry wrote Stockton that he had sent Elizabeth a power of attorney for Stockton to act in his behalf in his absence.[32] This was not true, however, as the eventual letter of attorney was signed by Fergusson on December 19, 1775, in London.

In England, Henry seems to have had a pleasant vacation, although we know little of his activities. He had taken with him a letter of introduction written by Benjamin Franklin to Jonathan Williams Jr., in London. Franklin had also encouraged him to call on Margaret Stevenson, which he did frequently. She held visiting hours every Wednesday, and Henry and Samuel Stockton were attending most weeks in the fall of 1775.[33] Although none of Henry's letters back to Pennsylvania remain, Elizabeth abstracted one written March 25, 1776, from London in which he assured her of his fidelity. He wrote that "neither the evil passions, Corrupt Customs nor Caprices of this metropolis have in any Degree tainted the morals or manners of your Husband." One wonders why he felt the need to assure her that he "would be more Happy with you [,] from my Soul I would [,] in a Cottage on the Apalachian mountains of America than rolling in all the Disapation and Luxury of London without you."[34] If true, why was he in London rather than in Pennsylvania helping her manage "their" estate? And why did he feel the need thus to reassure her? Had rumors of dissipated activities reached Pennsylvania?

Back in Philadelphia, gossip concerned the courting of Julia Stockton, daughter of Annis and Richard, by Benjamin Rush. He visited Morven, the Stocktons' Princeton estate, in August and became smitten. Shortly after, he asked the Stocktons if he could visit. Apparently in mid-October he wrote or told Elizabeth of his feelings, and this disclosure had gotten back to Julia, who complained of his indiscretion. He wrote his intended that Elizabeth was the only person he had confided in, although this seems unlikely given Rush's gregariousness.[35] The couple married the following January 11. Elizabeth's close friendship with Benjamin Rush lasted all her life, seemingly closer to him than to Julia, to whom Elizabeth sent regards in her letters to Benjamin, but did not write directly.

The newspapers were full that fall of the activities of the various Pennsylvania committees. Each one of the Pennsylvania counties elected its own committee to carry out the edicts of Congress, and Philadelphia's group coordinated their activities. Since the committees constituted an extra-legal government, they could not enforce their will using the proprietary courts and jails. To punish violators of the resolves of Congress, they had to use public ostracism and group persuasion. Frequently, this led to physical abuse when Tories refused to be intimidated and to conform to Whig demands to keep their views to themselves. Since Governor John Penn did nothing, or could do nothing, to protect them, Tories had little defense against the violence their criticism incited. In addition, the Assembly appointed a twenty-five man Committee of Safety to coordinate the colony's defense measures, to regulate the Associators, and to equip them. This group would become a Council of Safety in July 1776.

By fall of 1775, Pennsylvania was being ruled by two governments. The proprietary government consisted of the governor, his appointees, and the elected unicameral Assembly. For ordinary domestic business, the legally constituted Assembly passed measures and sent them to the governor for his approval or rejection. If approved, they were sent to England for the king's approval or veto. For the business of the resistance to Great Britain, the Continental Congress, meeting in Philadelphia, recommended action to Pennsylvania, as to all the colonies. The Assembly responded without consulting the governor, acting by resolves. The county committees reported to the Philadelphia Committee, to the Committee/Council of Safety, or to the Assembly by petition. To complicate matters further, the Associators soon selected committees from among themselves to further their interests.

All of these committees disliked Tories and freely took it upon themselves to convert the disaffected, by whatever means were necessary, and the armed Associators were available to help them. Both groups resented Tory criticism. If the Tories should prove to have been correct and if the British should put down the rebellion or even if reconciliation should take place, they could be accused of and prosecuted for breaking the law, at the least, or committing treason, at the most. Furthermore, there was a good possibility that the Associators might have to risk their lives for principles that, if successful, would advantage everyone; therefore, everyone should contribute. And so they deeply resented Tory criticism and refusal to participate. Their intimidation may have silenced most of the Tories, but it did not change their minds.

What happened to Dr. John Kearsley Jr. demonstrates how dangerous it was to challenge the prevailing views. Kearsley and about fifty other men had begun gathering in the spring of 1775 in a support group for Tories where they sang Tory songs, toasted the health of the monarchs, drank success to the British, complained about Whig activities, and in general tried the limited patience of the committeemen and the Associators.[36]

In the fall of 1775, a crowd that included Associators seized Kearsley and carted him through the city, announcing to one and all that Kearsley was an enemy of the people and their liberties.[37] Not intimidated, Kearsley decided to let the British ministry know how their loyal colonists were being treated. He and three other men prepared a report on the conditions in Pennsylvania to send to the ministry, but a servant informed the Philadelphia committeemen who confiscated the incriminating papers and arrested the dissidents.[38]

The committeemen had their captives, but they had no legal authority to arrest, imprison, or even detain people. When they asked Congress what to do, that body resolved that anyone who endangered the colony's safety should be secured but left the method up to the committeemen to determine. Congress's resolve enlarged the powers of the committeemen, who from then on used it as authority to punish Tories by jailing them. To the Tories, this was a dangerous decision because it vested tremendous power in extra-legal groups with no constitutional foundation. To give the Philadelphia committeemen some measure of authority, Congress told them to deliver their prisoners to the Committee of Safety because that group at least had been appointed by the province's Assembly, although it had not been given the powers of a court. Kearsley was subsequently tried by the Committee of Safety and sentenced to jail, but this turned out to be a death sentence. The jails were terribly unhealthy places, and he died in the Carlisle jail in 1777.[39]

The Kearsley family was well known to the Graemes; Kearsley Sr. had come to Philadelphia six years before Dr. Graeme. There were few physicians in the province in those years, and the two doctors had cooperated to establish the medical profession in Philadelphia. Called "the founder of the medical profession of Philadelphia,"[40] Kearsley had become the teacher and mentor of many doctors of the next generation, including Drs. Thomas Bond and William Shippen, both friends of the Graemes. The Kearsleys were staunch Anglicans, as were the Graemes, and Kearsley Sr. had served as a vestryman of Christ Church, along with the Stedman brothers. He was also an architect, the principal designer of Christ Church, an assistant architect for St. Peter's, and a contributor to the design of the State House. The treatment of Kearsley, the younger, his nephew, would have been the subject of many conversations at Graeme Park, and Elizabeth would have been very distressed about his fate.

One pleasant subject of other conversations that fall of 1775 was

Anny Young's approaching marriage to Dr. William Smith scheduled to take place at Graeme Park the end of November. The details do not remain, but family tradition says that Richard Peters performed the ceremony even though he was in such ill health that he had resigned the rectorship of Christ Church in September and would die the following July. We do know that at least Hannah Griffitts and a Miss Rhea were bridesmaids and that Benjamin Rush was a groomsman.[41]

A few days after the wedding, Hannah Griffitts wrote Elizabeth a letter thanking her for hospitality at Graeme Park. From this letter, we gather that after the ceremony, the newlyweds had to go into the city to church to finalize the marriage, possibly to sign papers. Traditionally, the bride would have ridden in the carriage with her bridesmaids, but Anny rode with Smith until close to the city, and then she changed places because of "Bashfulness." Hannah was glad inclement weather gave her an excuse not to go to the church with the bride because she did not like to be a public spectacle. She knew that Anny, probably still in her bridal dress, would attract unwanted attention "most disagreble to a Woman of Delicacy." Hannah, at this point unmarried and forty-eight years old, ten years older than Elizabeth, commented that she was "picqued" because Dr. Rush did not pay any attention to the bridesmaids. She wrote that she would never again "officiate as Bridesmaid where an engaged Gentleman is Groom's man."[42]

Hannah commented that Anny was too busy with company to write. It was the custom for the first week after the wedding that the groom's male friends would come every morning to pay their respects and drink punch. Just before they left each day, the husband would escort his bride to the roomful of men to be introduced to and kissed by them, and she would sit with them while they drank her health. No other woman would be present except for her bridesmaid, an uncomfortable situation for some women. When Grace Galloway had married less than twenty years before, she had "Upwards of seventy Men to do [her] the honour of a Kiss which [she] would have given the world to be excused from." In the afternoons for the first month, the bride was expected to stay home, dressed in "a white satten Night gownd," to receive women visitors, while her bridesmaid was required to make and serve tea and entertain the guests. Each woman as she left was handed a large piece of cake wrapped by the bridesmaid in white paper. After the bride's tour as hostess was over, she had to return all those calls she had received.[43] Hannah's participation in her friend's wedding had given her the opportunity of "forming an acquaintance with" Anny's aunt. The friendship between Elizabeth and Hannah Griffitts would continue over the years. Hannah, too, was a poet, leaving over 200 unpublished poems. She and Elizabeth and Susannah Wright corresponded and exchanged poems in a network of women poets.

Elizabeth's poetic muse may have been quiet during this period, but Anny's was active. In 1775, she wrote "Ode to Sleep," and "Lines Occasiond by Walking One Summers Evening in the Churchyard of Wiacoe Church," which Elizabeth believed to be Anny's most "Mature piece."[44] The next month she wrote "An Ode to Damon," addressed to her future husband, and that fall, she presented him with the gift of a small writing desk and letter case, the subject of another poem. Anny was a strong supporter of the American cause, which she commemorated in several poems. "An Elegy To the Memory of the American Volenters Who fell in the Engagement between the Massachessttes-Bay Militia and the British Troops: April 19 1775" was written May 2, and on June 28, 1775, the day after the announcement of Joseph Warren's death at the Battle of Bunker Hill, Anny wrote "An Elegy to the Memory of Doctor Warren." She also wrote a sixteen stanza "Ode to Liberty" in 1775. The following September she commemorated the anniversary of her grandfather's death with a poem in his memory. None of these was published during her lifetime, but Elizabeth in the nineties managed to have several of them published.[45]

The following January, Thomas Paine published his famous, influential pamphlet *Common Sense,* arguing that the colonies should declare their independence from Great Britain. Paine said nothing particularly new, but he put his arguments together in a very persuasive essay. Everyone, in England as well as America, he wrote, agreed that someday the colonies would separate from the mother country because it was absurd to suppose "a continent to be perpetually governed by an island." The only difference was a matter of timing, and he argued that the proper time was then. It was senseless to hope for reconciliation with a king who would order his troops to shoot his own citizens in America. Even if England would agree to reconciliation, it was not worthwhile to expend millions and to sacrifice many lives only for the repeal of tax laws. The only sensible move was separation and the establishment of a republican government dedicated to protecting its citizens rather than killing them. Many readers were convinced by his arguments. Some people had already reached these conclusions by themselves. Still others were shocked by such a suggestion. Even some Whigs who had supported every resistance measure up to that point drew back in horror from the final irrevocable step. The William Allen family, Thomas Willing, John Dickinson, and Rev. William Smith all recoiled from independence. All of these men and their families were friends of Elizabeth, and all had given some support to the early American resistance. None approved of Parliament's measures, but none wanted separation.

In Pennsylvania, the leading spokesman against Paine was Rev. William Smith who published eight essays in the *Pennsylvania Ledger* beginning March 8 under the pseudonym "Cato." Smith reminded the colonists that being Englishmen had meant prosperity, protection from France and Spain, and mild English government. North America, he argued, was too big an area for a democracy, which could only exist in a small town. Smith blamed the colonies' difficulties on revolutionary leaders who had usurped powers not assigned them.

One person who was not convinced by Paine's treatise was John Young. Against Elizabeth's advice, he went to New York in January 1776 and boarded his majesty's ship *Phoenix*, lying in the harbor. Lt. Gen. Tryon accepted Young's offer to serve the king and sent him on a ship to Boston to join the royal army as a volunteer. En route, he was shipwrecked and made a prisoner by the Americans. Fortunately for him, his father was an active and influential Whig. In March, the Continental Congress granted James Young's request that his son be paroled in the custody of his aunt and confined at Graeme Park, where he remained for the next eighteen months before he broke his parole and once again joined the British.[46]

In May, Pennsylvanians had the war brought close to them. The British man-of-war *Roebuck* and the frigate *Liverpool* started up the Delaware River. They reached as far as modern Wilmington, Delaware, when Pennsylvania's small fleet of newly built gondolas intercepted them. As the forces exchanged cannonading, thousands of people lined the shore to watch, while others, fearing that the ships were the vanguard of an invasion, fled Philadelphia for the interior of the province. Much to the Americans' glee, the gondolas damaged the British ships enough so that they retreated to the Chesapeake Bay. The battle made the Whigs even more determined to separate from Great Britain.

Meanwhile, each fall the people of Pennsylvania had chosen Assemblymen who were much more cautious in responding to British actions than the committeemen. The Assemblymen had to be pushed every inch of the way toward independence, taking the least action they could. The representatives selected Pennsylvania's delegates to the Congress and, in November 1775, had instructed them to work for reunion with the mother country and not to vote for independence. Finally, on May 10, 1776, the Continental Congress passed a resolution recommending that colonial governments not competent to deal with the exigencies of affairs should be replaced with ones that were. The independents in Philadelphia called a mass meeting ten days later to consider Congress's recommendation. The meeting agreed that Pennsylvania's government should be replaced and directed the Philadelphia Committee to arrange for the election of a Provincial Convention to devise a method to create a new government. The Committee called for the election of delegates and ordered them to assemble on June 18.

The anti-independents, determined to prevent the replacement of Pennsylvania's government and the separation of the province from Great Britain, prepared a remonstrance to be signed by Pennsylvania citizens and sent to the Assembly to stiffen that body's resistance to the colonies' independence and its own dissolution. Active in this Tory movement were the Stedmans and Rev. William Smith. Anti-independents met at the home of Alexander Stedman, prepared copies of the remonstrance, and sent them out into the counties with Charles, the lawyer son of Alexander. Despite some six thousand signatures procured by the anti-independents on their remonstrances, letters of support for the resolves of the May 20 Philadelphia meeting deluged the desks of the Assemblymen from militia companies and from county committees. The Assembly finally succumbed to all the pressure and gave Pennsylvania's congressmen new instructions permitting them to vote for independence.

This step did not save the old Assembly, however. The Provincial Convention gave its support for a declaration of independence and called for the election of a constitutional convention to devise a new government for Pennsylvania. This convention would meet July 15 and create a new government similar to the old but also in some ways very different. Before this would happen, the Continental Congress took the step Paine had called for over six months before. It had been emotionally wrenching to cut the cord to England, yet by July 4, 1776, there was no other reasonable alternative. Independence was declared.

Actually, the tie had been severed on the battlefield long before

Congress had acted. In the summer of 1775, the colonists had heard that Great Britain was raising an army in Canada to attack New York, and Congress had launched a preventive attack against Canada. Colonial forces had captured St. John's and Montreal, but their assault against Quebec had ended disastrously, and the city's subsequent siege also had been defeated by a combination of winter, smallpox, and British reinforcements. Early the following year, British General Henry Clinton had taken an expeditionary force to the south, planning to invade North Carolina. When that had proved inexpeditious, he had tried to land an army at Charleston, South Carolina. Rebel fire had damaged his ships so badly that they had had to retire. In March 1776, guns from the captured Fort Ticonderoga, arduously dragged across country, had been mounted on Dorchester Heights overlooking Boston. General Howe had recognized the impossibility of his position and had withdrawn British forces from the city on March 17, 1776. This warfare on top of the vitriolic messages sent back and forth across the Atlantic had destroyed the affection of many Americans for England and had made it possible, if not easy, for them to accept disunion.

Still, no matter how righteous people felt about their provocations for separation, England was a powerful nation, whose wrath was dreaded by all sensible people. By the summer of 1776, Pennsylvanians feared invasion. The Continental Congress, the rebel government, was sitting in Philadelphia, making that city a logical target for British attack. People planned what they would do if they had to flee before an invading British army. Thus, Dr. John Redman kept a supply of ready cash at hand, rather than put it out at interest as he would have done in the past.[47] The Redmans planned to make Trenton, the home of their daughter Sally and her husband Daniel Coxe, "their retreat in Case of danger." Mary Redman sent off "a few necessaries" that she might "not be quite destitute should [she] unhapily be obliged to fly." "Allass," she wrote Elizabeth, "in such an event how much must the Scene be changed from peace plenty and security to be obliged to leave them all and perhaps never know the heart felt joy again of a peaceful Home."[48]

Pennsylvanians' fears were reinforced by Washington's string of defeats on the battlefield late that summer and fall. When Howe had evacuated Boston, he had taken his troops first to Halifax and then to New York City, landing about ten thousand troops on Staten Island on July 2. By August Howe had at his command about thirty-two thousand soldiers, including about nine thousand Hessians, and on August 26, Howe began a series of moves that would chase Washington's army from Long Island, New York City, White Plains, and across New Jersey. By December, it appeared that the British were headed for Philadelphia, and Congress fled to Baltimore.

Meanwhile, on June 24, Congress had passed a resolve that would be of great significance to Elizabeth. All persons living in any of the colonies owed allegiance to that colony and its laws, the Congressmen had declared. Anyone waging war against that colony or helping the king or other enemies of the colony was guilty of treason. Congress's resolve had asked the colonial legislatures to pass their own treason laws. The Pennsylvania Assembly, while still meeting, often without a quorum, ignored and powerless, had ended its existence on September 26. In the legislative vacuum, the Pennsylvania Constitutional Convention had assumed legislative powers, while it was preparing a constitution for the new state. In response to Congress's resolve, the Convention passed an ordinance against treason on September 5. Under that ordinance, anyone living in Pennsylvania owed allegiance to the state. Any persons found guilty in a Court of Oyer and Terminer of waging war against Pennsylvania or aiding the king or other enemies would be punished by imprisonment for the duration of the war and forfeiture of all of their lands and possessions to the state. All the courts in Pennsylvania were closed, however, so that no one could be tried under this ordinance. By the time they reopened, a new legislature would have passed its own treason law.[49] This subsequent law would catch Henry in its net.

The Convention finished a draft for a new state constitution, issued it to the public on September 5, and unanimously adopted it on September 28. Elections for a unicameral legislature were called for November 5. This constitution, the most democratic issued by any of the colonies, would be controversial until it was finally replaced in 1790. Supporters and opponents quickly formed into groups to defend or change it. The Whigs split into constitutionalists and anti-constitutionalists, arguing their differences in mass meetings, petitions to the new Assembly, and elections.

There is no record of how Elizabeth reacted to all the local political turmoil. As a faithful newspaper reader, she would have been familiar with the controversy about the new Pennsylvania constitution. Since her friends were in both camps, Benjamin Rush, for example, an anti-constitutionalist and Daniel Roberdeau a constitutionalist, she would have heard both sides.

Perhaps her personal life was in such confusion that she ignored the political strife, which she disliked anyway.

On July 10, Richard Peters died, after four days of very painful illness. Rev. Jacob Duché, his successor as Rector of Christ Church, was with him and respected Peters's last minute wishes for "no funeral Sermon preachd over him" and no obituary in the papers. His body was buried in Christ Church with only his brother William and William's sons present. Hearing of Peters's death after his burial, Elizabeth was upset that no one had notified her, but Anny assured her that since her old friend had died at his brother's home, it would have been impossible for Anny to have notified her aunt in time for her to have attended his interment.[50] Although not unexpected, this must have been a terrible blow to Elizabeth. One by one she was losing all the people in her life upon whom she had counted. Her husband was in England; she had no children nor much likelihood of ever having any; her parents and all her siblings were dead; and she had to live nineteen miles from Philadelphia and her closest friends. Only the presence of her nephew, John Young, captured by the Americans and paroled in her custody, and Betsy Stedman, who had come to live with her after Henry left, softened her loneliness. The two women's companionship persisted until Elizabeth's death.

By the summer of 1776, Elizabeth's financial affairs were becoming quite troublesome. Henry had left her in a strained financial situation. She employed an overseer for the farm and tried to make it earn her living, but times were difficult. Furthermore, she was saddled with the repayment of a loan for £100 borrowed by Henry. The interest and principal for this loan were overdue, and John Redman, sensing her distress, offered to pay it for her.[51]

Thomas Graeme's legacy to the Youngs and the debt of the Stedmans that Graeme had signed also bothered Elizabeth. Her father's will had stated that if she alienated Graeme Park, she must give the Youngs their legacy immediately. Otherwise, she could pay them when it suited her convenience. Friends advised her to wait until land and currency in Pennsylvania were more stable, but she wanted to erase these obligations, especially the part owed to James Young from whom she had become estranged while executing the will. John Young later would deny that anyone had been pressuring his aunt for money, but his memory may have been faulty. It is likely that he was importuning his aunt for his legacy of £400. He had no job, and his income from the unimproved land his grandfather had left him could not have been very large. In addition, he wanted to purchase a lieutenancy in the British army. Furthermore, Henry wanted her to turn over the estate in fee simple to him, but she could not do that without paying the legacy.

The arrival of Henry's power of attorney that spring or early summer made it legally possible for her to act. She began, therefore, to search for buyers for Graeme Park land. On August 14, 1776, she sold thirty-seven acres of Graeme Park located in Bucks County for £400, although the letter of attorney was not registered with the Pennsylvania government until August 22.[52] The following November 26, John Penn bought two hundred acres for £2,000.[53]

Elizabeth used the £2,400 that she received to pay the legacy of £1,000 to James, Anny, and John Young and to pay the £800 debt of the Stedmans and the £100 debt of Henry. This was contrary to the advice of Dr. Redman who told her that the land was worth £10 per acre in Spanish dollars, whereas she accepted the current depreciated paper money. If she would wait, the price of land and the value of the money would increase, Redman argued. Since she used most of the money, however, to repay debts, the biggest losers were the Youngs and the creditors of the Stedmans and of Henry, since they received the depreciated money rather than hard currency. As events transpired, of course, she would have had a long wait for the currency to increase in value. Redman argued additionally that she was not required to pay either debt at that time. The Youngs were not suing for their legacy, and Charles Stedman was solvent and capable of repaying his own debt, even though his brother was not. Despite the truth of that argument, Elizabeth considered both debts to be commitments made by her father, which she must fulfill for him. Henry agreed with Redman and did not approve of the sale, but once he had empowered Elizabeth with the letter of attorney, the sale was perfectly legal, and there was nothing he could do. He admitted later that he had known when he signed it that it could be used to sell the property, but that he did it "to comply with her wishes and Feelings."[54]

Her major personal concern that summer, other than her own financial affairs and her husband's future prospects, was Anny's pregnancy with her first child. Four days before the child was born, Anny wrote her aunt a letter full of fear for the approaching delivery. She was convinced that she would suffer "Pain Violent And Sever," more so than she had ever known. In case she should die in childbirth and this should be the last letter she should ever write her aunt, she thanked Elizabeth for all the care she had taken of her niece's education and "the numberless proofs of [her] tenderness." Should the "dear unborn . . . Survive its mother," she hoped Elizabeth would give it the "affection which is now the portion" of its mother.[55] Because of their fear of the unknown and the lack of preparation, women were terrorized by the prospect of the birth of first children. Undoubtedly, this made the labor of the tense and frightened mothers longer than it had to be. Anny lived to describe her travail to Elizabeth as "the severest pangs that the Human Frame Could Suffer." Her thirty hours of labor, attended by a midwife, ended in the birth of a daughter, one day short of nine months since her marriage. The upper-class mother could expect at least a month of predominantly bed-rest and of solicitations from her women friends after her delivery. As a result, a month after the child's birth, Anny was still in "Confinement," feeling "Languor and Weakness." She wanted the child to "Pay her Respects to her Grandaunt," but she did not expect it to happen until November 30, when she would celebrate her anniversary at Graeme Park. Then Anny would claim her "Bacon Flitch."[56]

The reference to the flitch of bacon is from the *Spectator* of October 15, 1714.[57] Elizabeth frequently quoted from the *Spectator* and had exposed Anny to it as part of her education. The article related that a certain Sir Philip de Somervile was required to keep a flitch of bacon prepared in case it should be claimed by someone who could meet the following requirement. He or she must swear, and bring two witnesses who would confirm, that he had been happily married for a year and a day and that he would not change his spouse for any other person. Either man or wife could make the claim. The next issue of the *Spectator* reported that during the first century of the bacon's availability, only two couples had claimed it successfully, one of whom was a sea captain and his wife who had not seen each from their marriage to the day they made the claim. Elizabeth's and Anny's letters often contained literary references, both women having read deeply in eighteenth-century English literature.

Since none of the letters between Elizabeth and Henry during his absence have survived, we can only surmise a few of his activities from other sources. From March 25, 1776, when Henry was in London and wrote Elizabeth a letter extracted by her into a commonplace book, until the following September, his actions are unknown. In early September, he was in Paris, carrying a "Seal" from Edward Bancroft to Silas Deane.

Connecticut native, Yale graduate, and enthusiastic Whig, Silas Deane had been sent by the Continental Congress to France to negotiate with that country for aid to the American colonies. He was charged to buy arms, clothing, munitions, and artillery for twenty-five men, preferably on credit. But he spoke no French. He arrived in Paris in early July, and he immediately wrote to Dr. Edward Bancroft in London, whom he had been told to contact. Bancroft had been born in Massachusetts, had been an early student of Deane, had received a medical education in England, was a fellow of the Royal Society, and was intimately familiar with the ins and outs of European diplomacy. In addition, he spoke French and was a friend of Franklin and other American leaders who considered him to be a patriotic American, loyal to the cause. Upon receipt of Deane's letter, Bancroft hurried to Paris to help Deane through his negotiations with the French. Sometime after his arrival, however, Bancroft decided to offer his services to the British as a double agent.[58]

In mid-August, Bancroft returned to London where he met Henry Fergusson, perhaps at one of Margaret Stevenson's soirées, and arranged for him to carry his message to Deane. Henry had traveled extensively on the continent and spoke French fluently. Whether he had planned a trip to Paris for other reasons or whether Bancroft sent him there to make his delivery is unknown. Margaret Stevenson wrote Franklin in Pennsylvania on September 3 that Fergusson, who was leaving soon, would deliver the letter she was then writing. A letter written by Bancroft to Deane on the 13th says, "I sent your Seal as promised last Saturday by Mr Ferguson."[59] It is likely that the Mr. Ferguson who served as Bancroft's messenger was Henry. It is unlikely, however, that he knew of Bancroft's spying for the British. Bancroft would not have confided in a man with Fergusson's relations in Pennsylvania, even if Henry opposed the American cause. Furthermore, Henry did not mention this service in his claim for compensation from the British after the war. Once in Paris, Henry may have made himself useful to Deane because of his language fluency.

Henry either stayed in Paris until the end of the year or later, or he went back to London and then returned to Paris in December. In any case, he was in Paris when Benjamin Franklin arrived from Pennsylvania on December 22. Congress had sent Franklin and Arthur Lee, already in Europe, to Paris to help Deane negotiate treaties of amity and commerce with the French government. Henry sent his compliments to Franklin and asked for an interview to inquire about "Mrs. Fergusson and his friends in Pennsylvania."[60]

Elizabeth meanwhile was writing Henry to remain in Europe. Later, when the Supreme Executive Council challenged Henry's behavior at this time, Elizabeth explained that it had been "plain to see" that "nothing but the Sword" would settle the imperial controversy. "Still as a wife it was natural for [her] to wish [her] husbands absence at so Critical a juntor[juncture] of time."[61] This disingenuous answer covered her real reason for wanting her husband to stay away: she desperately feared that his opposition to the Revolutionary governments would bring severe punishment, either legal or extra-legal.

By 1777, Henry was convinced that the British were going to put down the uprising and that therein lay opportunity for someone who supported them. In addition, although Elizabeth must have sent him some money, he was probably running out of funds. It is not known how he managed to support himself during his protracted stay in Europe. Perhaps he also wanted to see Elizabeth. Washington's coups at Trenton and Princeton, clearing western New Jersey of the British, should have given Henry pause, if he knew of them. Unaware of or not concerned by these victories of the Americans, Henry took ship for Jamaica and, after a month there, for New York.

In Jamaica, he undoubtedly stayed with relatives, either his or Elizabeth's. Two of Sir William and Lady Keith's children had settled there while their father was still in Pennsylvania. Son William died in Jamaica without issue, but his sister Jane had married William Yeeles and had six children before she died around 1760. Her daughter Deborah married William Senior, and Elizabeth and she corresponded intermittently. Elizabeth never went to Jamaica, but two of Mrs. Senior's sisters and possibly Mrs. Senior herself traveled to Philadelphia in the mid-seventies. In addition, two sons of Henry's brother Robert, John and Robert, both lived in Jamaica.[62] Henry would have been welcomed by either the Seniors or the Fergussons.

After a month of enjoying Jamaica's lovely climate and scenery, Henry enbarked for New York where he arrived the night before Lord Howe's fleet sailed for Philadelphia. He inquired for the best way to travel to Graeme Park and was advised to go with the fleet. At Head of Elk, he marched overland with the British army to Brandywine Creek where he proposed to cross over to Graeme Park. Friends told him, however, that by having traveled with the British navy and army, he was "renderd too Equivicol in his Political Character To pass through the County with Safety." He, therefore, rejoined the British. Elizabeth had no knowledge of his return or of the mode he had chosen until he managed to get word to her on September 25, the day before the British entered Philadelphia.[63] When she heard of his association with the enemy, she was beside herself with fear for his person and for their future.

7

Attainder

While Henry was working his way back to Philadelphia via Jamaica and New York, Elizabeth was anxiously coping with her problems in Pennsylvania. The state was also trying to solve the many problems created by its separation from Great Britain. Pennsylvania's solutions in turn added to Elizabeth's problems.

The Pennsylvania constitution of 1776 created a three-part government, giving almost all power to the legislature, a unicameral General Assembly popularly elected annually. Administrative functions were to be carried out by a Supreme Executive Council, headed by a president, who had no special powers. A presiding officer only, he was to be chosen by the members of the Assembly and the Executive Council from among the Council's members, who were also to be elected by the people. Neither he nor the other members of the Executive Council could veto laws passed by the Assembly. Supreme Court members were to be chosen by the Supreme Executive Council for seven-year terms. Amendment of the Constitution was possible only after seven years, if two-thirds of a specially elected Council of Censors agreed that changes were necessary and called a convention to make them. The constitution was declared in force by the Constitutional Convention; it was not subjected to popular vote.[1]

The new General Assembly met for the first time November 28 and immediately was embroiled in controversy. Anti-constitutionalists boycotted state offices at all levels because they believed that the oath of allegiance required by the constitution would prevent them working for constitutional changes. In the Assembly, there was a minority of anti-constitutionalists, enough to prevent a quorum by absenting themselves, although not enough to prevent measures from passing when they were present. In both the city and county of Philadelphia and in Bedford County, the people had refused the oath required of electors, had not chosen Councillors, but had elected only assemblymen, who were instructed to prevent formation of a government and to consider the Assembly as a convention to revise the constitution. It would not be until March 4 that all the counties had chosen their councillors and that the Executive Council and Assembly could finally meet together to choose a president and vice-president. Thus, Pennsylvania was without a complete government from July 4, 1776, until March 4, 1777, and even then the courts were not functioning properly. In spite of this delay and all the critical problems facing the state, the Assembly adjourned March 21 until May 12, once again leaving the state without leadership.[2]

While the government vacillated and quarreled, the problems of the state multiplied. Courts were not open; therefore the state could not punish its enemies nor protect its friends. In Philadelphia, the city government had ended with the Declaration of Independence and no Quarter Sessions court met between March 1776 and September 1777. Inflation had sent the prices of necessities soaring. Furthermore it became increasingly certain that General Howe intended to capture Philadelphia. A man named James Molesworth was convicted as a spy for trying to hire men to pilot the British navy up the Delaware River. He was court-martialed and hanged by the army, the first man in Pennsylvania to die as a traitor to the new government. Yet there was no government to prepare the city's defenses. Even the militiamen who had associated so readily the year before were balking at further service under the prevailing regulations, and desertion became a problem. They resented risking their necks when so many people were doing nothing and the pay was so low. When General Thomas Mifflin called out Philadelphia militiamen, they refused to march. Confusion, disorganization, and party squabbling drained the state of its potential to act.[3]

In the absence of a legally constituted government, extra-legal groups held impromptu courts at which they examined persons they accused of being traitors to the American cause and decided what to do with them. In November 1776, for example, seventy-three citizens met at a Philadelphia tavern and questioned several men. They decided that they should collect the names of people who might be "Tories & unfriendly to the cause of America" and meet again. Two men were subsequently taken by the group to the Council of Safety for that body's examination. One of these men spent five months in jail, before the British freed him.[4] The Tory poet and merchant, Joseph Stansbury was also imprisoned by this meeting, although he was articulate and persistent enough to win his release.[5] Mass meetings and committees ruled Philadelphia, instead of a legally constituted government.

Around this time, rumor reported that a list was being prepared of some two hundred suspected Tories who would be sent to North Carolina. Supposedly, the names of the four sons of William Allen were on this list. Allen, a very well-known figure in Pennsylvania, and his family members were friends of the Graemes. A wealthy man, he was for many years an assemblyman and chief justice, and by his daughter Ann's marriage, he had become the father-in-law of John Penn. His sons had strongly supported all resistance short of independence. They had served on committees and lent their voices to speeches and petitions. Andrew helped found the First Troop Philadelphia Cavalry. William Jr., served in the American army in Canada in 1775, rising to lieutenant colonel. But the brothers did not approve of separation from the mother country, and as soon as independence was declared, William resigned his commission. Under the threat of exile, the brothers went to the Union Iron Works in New Jersey, in which their family held interests. Soon after, Andrew, William Jr., and John fled to Trenton, then occupied by the British, and from there to New York. When General Howe landed at Head of Elk, Andrew and William Jr, as well as Henry Fergusson, were with him.[6]

In order to deter persons who might consider helping the British or to punish those who did, the Constitutional Convention, acting in lieu of an established government, had passed ordinances to deal with the problem of treason. But since the courts were not functioning, there was no way to enforce the Convention's measures. There were also doubts about the legality of these ordinances because the convention had been elected solely to form a constitution, not to legislate. In any case, the ordinances would expire at the end of the first session of the new Assembly.[7] Therefore, that body passed its own treason law on February 11, 1777. Residents of Pennsylvania, the law claimed, owed allegiance to the state. Persons convicted in a court of Oyer and Terminer of any one of seven listed crimes against Pennsylvania or the United States were guilty of treason and punishable by death and confiscation of their property. The law also listed five crimes, any one of which constituted misprision of treason, punishable by imprisonment during the war and forfeiture of half of the convicted person's property.

The combination of legal and extra-legal measures taken in Pennsylvania against persons disaffected to the rebel cause terrified Elizabeth for Henry's safety. She thought, of course, that he was out of harm's way in England or France. She knew that if he returned and continued to talk the way he had before he left that he would come under the Assembly's definition of misprision of treason, which broadly included speaking or writing against the colonies' defense and trying to persuade others to return to their allegiance to the king. She did not know, and probably never knew, that his actions after he began the march from Head of Elk with the British army would also be included in the definition of treason under the Assembly's act.

After the British forces landed at Head of Elk, Henry marched with them toward Brandywine Creek and the battle with the American forces. On the way, Henry was considered by the British to be a "very active and zealous" volunteer. On the morning of the Battle of Brandywine, a British unit needed to be warned of a topographical condition that could be seen from across the river but not on the spot. Fergusson volunteered to swim the river and warn the officer in charge. He was not allowed to take the risk, however, because if he should be caught he would be shot immediately. During the occupation of Philadelphia, Henry "frequently procured intelligence, of considerable consequence . . . upon which the Kings troops acted," reported a British officer after the war. Henry used his acquaintance with Philadelphia disaffected persons to sound out the possibility of forming a corps of light horse made up of Americans to fight with the British. He and a British officer wrote General Howe in November 1777 that such a corps could be raised speedily to take the lower Delaware River counties and the eastern shore of Maryland, and they proposed themselves as its field officers.[8] None of these attempts to fight with the British army was told to Elizabeth.

With or without his treasonous actions, however, once Henry elected to enter the continent via New York City and travel with the British army, his continued acceptance as an American was doubtful. Elizabeth's later argument that he could not travel across country from New York to Philadelphia safely was probably correct. This would have been very difficult without the proper passes to cross the lines and without extensive knowledge of the countryside and of safe hiding places. But his mistake was choosing New York City as his point of entry. He should have found transportation from Europe to one of the southern colonies, to Virginia perhaps, and then have traveled overland by horseback or by foot to Graeme Park, thus avoiding any connection with the British and the stigma that association brought. When Elizabeth's friend Elias Boudinot received word that Henry had left London in early March, Boudinot guessed that Henry was coming by way of New Orleans.[9] It does not appear that such a difficult route ever occurred to Elizabeth's husband.

Before the battle of Brandywine, while Washington's forces were near Neshaminy, about a mile north of Elizabeth's home, General Anthony Wayne and part of his division stayed at Graeme Park for about ten days in August. The men camped on the grounds, and Wayne and his staff were accommodated in the mansion, entertained by Elizabeth, John Young, and Betsy Stedman. John's sister, Anny Smith, sent out of the city by her husband after Howe's forces landed, was also there with her one-year-old daughter. When the army left Graeme Park, after having abused the grounds extensively, two of Wayne's sutlers persuaded Elizabeth's slave to abscond with them, appropriating her wagon and two oxen. They drove the beasts unmercifully on a very hot day, causing one of them to drop dead along the way. This was a substantial loss that Elizabeth's straightened financial condition could not absorb easily, so she asked Wayne how to apply for compensation.[10] But he was busy with "the Manoeuvres and hurry, ever incident to the eve of Battle" and did not respond until September 14. The man who had stolen her cattle had left the army and gone to Carlisle, Wayne wrote, but he promised "to take hold of him as soon as he" returned.[11] She did not care whether the thief was punished or not; she only wanted the state to reimburse her, but there is no record that it ever did. Although Elizabeth and her family enjoyed the excitement of having Wayne and his staff as guests, Elizabeth owned she should prefer seeing him next time "without quite as large a Retinue as composed his train when he was last" there.[12] Caring for the men was a tiring job for the three women with the estate's decreased staff. As for the damaged grounds, they would never be fully repaired by Elizabeth.

News that a British army had debarked from New York, its destination unknown but probably Philadelphia, had caused the Continental Congress to recommend to the Supreme Executive Council of Pennsylvania that it arrest all the late crown and proprietary officers and send them and any other disaffected persons into the back country.[13] Accordingly, the Council on August 1 had issued a warrant for the arrest of some forty men who fit the description and then released them on their paroles.[14] The list included the names of Alexander Stedman and his son, Charles, the Rev. William Smith, and other friends of the Graemes. The two Stedmans would flee behind the British lines and eventually to England. Smith, his wife, Rebecca, and his younger children went to an island in the Schuylkill River, called Barbadoes Island, that he had bought in 1776 as a refuge. They remained there until the British left the state.[15] John Penn, the last proprietary governor of the province of Pennsylvania, and Benjamin Chew, ex-chief justice and member of the Governor's Council, refused to sign paroles. When Congress reacted by ordering the two men into exile in Fredericksburg, Virginia, they changed their minds and decided that they wanted to sign after all. Congress first refused and then, after some debate, released them on parole.[16]

Howe's landing at Head of Elk on August 25 and march north caused a renewal of attention toward persons believed to be threats to the American cause. Congress recommended that Pennsylvania authorities disarm and secure all persons "notoriously disaffected" and search their houses for guns, bayonets, and swords to be given to Pennsylvania militiamen without arms.[17] Before this could be done, Congress issued another recommendation listing specific names of persons to be detained. Acting on information, now believed spurious, that the Quakers were spying for General Howe, Congress included eleven prominent Quakers. The Executive Council expanded the list to forty-one names, most of them Quakers. For four days, thirty men were confined in the Free Masons' Lodge, a large building used for concerts and other public functions, the Council not wanting to put them in "the Common Goal" or "the State Prison." The charge against them was that they had shown "in their General conduct & conversation . . . a disposition inimical to the Cause of America."[18] Many of them had been offered a chance to promise to remain in their houses and not do anything injurious to the United States, but they had refused, citing long years of service to Pennsylvania and their innocence of any crime, likening their treatment to the arbitrary practices of the British. After some shuffling between Congress and the Executive Council over which body was responsible for the men who refused to make this promise, twenty prisoners were ordered into exile at Winchester, Virginia.[19] Benjamin Chew and John Penn were not among these prisoners, but they, too, were ordered out of the state by Congress. They were allowed to spend their exiles at the Union Iron Works in New Jersey, on the estates of family members. The following May, Congress discharged them from their paroles, and they returned to Pennsylvania, to spend the rest of their lives there.[20]

Elizabeth probably knew most of the people on the list. The Quakers were prominent men who had been active in the development of the city. If not personal friends, they certainly were acquaintances. Among the non-Quakers well known by the Graemes were Alexander Stedman and his lawyer son, Charles. Council had added their names to Congress's original list. Both were picked up and at first confined with the rest in the Free Masons' Lodge. They, however, were considered more dangerous than the others and less deserving of considerate treatment. On September 2, both were sent to the State Prison.[21] Thomas Coombe's name also was added by the Council. One-time student of Rev. William Smith, cousin of Benjamin Rush, and childhood friend of Elizabeth, Coombe was an assistant minister of Christ Church. His friends worked out a deal with Council whereby Coombe would surrender to the governor of Virginia as a prisoner of war as soon as possible, and from Virginia go to St. Eustatius in the Leeward Islands.[22] Rev. William Smith's name was also on the list, but he signed the parole before leaving for his island sanctuary. The lawyer Phineas Bond, a nephew of Rebecca Smith, whose mother was an intimate of Elizabeth, was also proscribed. He signed the parole but renounced it when he discovered the narrowness of his circumscription. Council then confined him with the rest in the Free Masons' Lodge until they could all be sent to Virginia. The day before the prisoners left, however, Bond worked out an arrangement with the Council similar to that of Coombe. He, too, was freed on his promise to go to Virginia and from there to the West Indies.[23]

The next day, firing from the Battle of Brandywine could be heard in Philadelphia all day from seven o'clock in the morning. Margaret Stedman, writing Elizabeth about noon that day was so frightened that she trembled and had to stop writing until she could restore her composure. By three o'clock, a man had been sent through the city "ringing a Bell and ordering all Houses to be immediately shut up." "General Howe is advancing," he cried. "Every man who can carry a Gun must appear on the Commons." Philadelphia citizens were terrified, every face looked "wild and pale with fear and amazement, and quite overwhelmed with distress Some flying and some moving one way some another." It was reported that eight hundred Americans had fallen, but as the wounded were being brought into the city to be cared for, people began to suspect that the slaughter had been much greater than what they had been told. Rumors were everywhere and certainties non-existent.[24]

Their fears were fed by a proclamation issued by the Council the previous day that beseeched the people to take their weapons and join Washington in defense of their homes against the "cruel & perfidious enemy" who had committed "wanton ravages, Rapes, Butcheries" in the states of New Jersey and New York. "Consider," the proclamation warned,

> the mournful prospect of seeing Americans like the wretched inhabitants of India, stripped of their freedom, robbed of their property, degraded beneath the brutes, & left to starve amid plenty, at the will of their lordly Masters, and let us determine once for all, that we will *Die or be Free.*

The proclamation ended with the prayer "GOD SAVE THE PEOPLE."[25]

That afternoon, the twenty remaining detainees were sent off to Winchester under guard. Bystanders whose sympathies were with the exiles had tears in their eyes at the injustice of men innocent of any crime being so severely punished for what they might do. Among the prisoners were elderly men, and people feared that they could not survive the difficult trip. Several of the bystanders confessed that "their eyes had never beheld so moving a scene before." When a militiaman insulted Thomas Wharton as he was being pushed into a wagon, the compassion of one of the onlookers was so raised that he flew at the tormentor "and swore he would thrust his hands down his throat and pull out his heart if he dared abuse a Prisoner." The detainees would be kept in Winchester for over seven months, and two would die there. Only two would join the British.[26]

In the confusion, neither Thomas Coombe nor Phineas Bond went to Virginia. Coombe pleaded illness and remained in his home the day the others left, while Bond hid out in a friend's house The Executive Council was too busy to worry about them. The Councillors, as well as the rest of the Pennsylvania government and the Continental Congress, left Philadelphia for Lancaster on the 19th of September. But first, all their records and the treasury of Pennsylvania had to be moved out of the city.

No one had time to worry about the two men, who would still be in Philadelphia when the British entered on September 26.

While Coombe and Bond were hiding from the members of the Executive Council, Howe was headed toward Philadelphia, with Washington in pursuit, and citizens were predicting that "the last effort will be at Schuylkill," one boundary of the city. Instead, the last stand was at Paoli, in Chester County, where Wayne's division waited to attack Howe's flank. The British learned of Wayne's projected ambush, however, and launched a night bayonet attack on September 21 that surprised Wayne and took 150 more American casualties. From then on, Howe's way was clear, and his forces entered the city on September 26.

During the two weeks between Brandywine and the fall of Philadelphia, its citizens had had to decide what to do. There was to be no street by street defense of the city, which would have destroyed it. Therefore, should its citizens remain in their homes to protect their possessions from looting and hope the British would not accuse them of treason? Or should they flee to the countryside to save themselves and their families from possible punishment? The warm patriots who had most eagerly furthered the American cause were afraid for their necks and left while they could. Others who had been either neutral or opposed to the independence movement felt safe in staying. Margaret and Charles Stedman remained. Dr. William Smith went to Graeme Park to pick up his wife, Anny, and his daughter, and they spent the winter in Allentown, about forty-five miles north of Philadelphia. James Young, Anny's father, who had been a very active participant in the independence movement, went to Lancaster. Elizabeth and Betsy Stedman remained at Graeme Park.

When Wayne's brigade first appeared at Graeme Park, unannounced, its occupants were very fearful. There was only one eighteen year old male to protect three defenseless women and a toddler. Apparently something amiss was said about the occupation because Elizabeth later apologized. "Rest assur'd Sir," she wrote Wayne, "that if in the Hurry of your first comeing, any thing might have Occurd that you could have wishd Otherwise; nothing was intended. I wish the general Cause of America most Sincerly well." Perhaps John Young was responsible. At the end of August he petitioned the Congress for release from his imprisonment at Graeme Park and for permission to to leave the continent. Both were denied.[27]

The controversy must have been at a high level at Graeme Park between the young man and the women, who wanted him to remain. His sister had been a "warm Whig" from the beginning of the Revolutionary movement. Elizabeth, too, was a strong supporter of the American cause and wrote later that she had tried to stop his enlisting with the British. After the war, he would bitterly regret his decision, but in September 1777, it hardly seemed possible that the British could lose the war, an occasional battle, perhaps, but not the whole war. In September, he broke his parole and joined Howe's army at Germantown. There he was made a Lieutenant in the Pennsylvania Loyalists, a troop of cavalry raised and led by William Allen Jr. Young remained with Allen's corps until August 3, 1778, when he switched to the British 42nd Regiment as an Ensign. He obtained a Lieutenancy in that regiment in May 1780 and fought with it until the end of the war.

Elizabeth by now knew that Henry had left London the previous March headed for home, but she had no idea by what route he would arrive. On September 25, as she was entertaining Vice-President George Bryan and other visitors, a stranger delivered a note to her door. It was from Henry announcing his presence near Philadelphia and asking her to meet him the next day in the city. They met in Germantown, as Elizabeth said later, because she "could not bear to see the British Troops in posses-sion of the Capital." But all the joy of seeing him was "blasted by the Mode of his Return."[28] Henry probably was not aware of the actions taken both by crowds extra-legally and by the state government legislatively dur-ing his absence, but Elizabeth could not forget and knew how his actions would be seen by the pro-independence majority in the state.

Both Henry and Elizabeth requested their respective commanders for permission for Henry to return to Graeme Park, and both were refused. Howe's secretary responded with surprise at his request and guaranteed that it would not be granted. Elizabeth wrote George Washington on Septem-ber 26, asking him to give Henry "a probation for a month to stay in his own House: And he will [give] his parole that he will not give any informa-tion to the enemy. He will be confin'd to such Limits of Space as will be thought proper by your Excellency."[29] Washington's reply was not surpris-ing. He wished he could say yes, but her request for her husband "to come out and remain at Graeme Park for thirty days, implies his intent to return at the expiration of that time into the Quarters of the Enemy." Further-more, it appeared to him "very odd, that a Gentleman who has been so long absent from his family should wish to remain so short a time with them."[30] This thought must have been troubling Elizabeth herself before the general mentioned it. Washington's irritation at receiving such a request when the enemy had just occupied the capital after giving his forces a severe drubbing is evident in the draft of his letter. It is the same as the final copy, except that at the beginning he says, "I wish the Nature of your request was such that I could with propriety comply with it, but you must be sensible."[31] This sentence was omitted from the copy sent Elizabeth, probably because the general did not want to hurt the feelings of a woman whose unhappiness seemed to be clouding her reason.

The exodus of disaffected persons from Pennsylvania to the British reached a peak during the occupation of Philadelphia, particularly in the fall and winter when the American situation looked especially gloomy. As many as six thousand persons may have defected to the British while they were in the city,[32] in addition to those who had left earlier. Although the act passed by the Assembly in February covered the actions of these people, they had to be caught first and tried in a court of Oyer and Terminer before they could be convicted and punished.

Yet many of these persons left behind valuable property. Confiscating and selling their estates would make them help pay the costs of the war. This had been suggested the preceding May 6 by "A Civilian" in the *Pennsylvania Post* who had called these defectors outlaws. He had argued that "all property held under that tenure is considered as *British property*, and subject to the same fate as if at sea." If this property could be confiscated by the state, it not only would provide desperately sought additional sources of revenue for prosecuting the war but also would help answer the complaints of those who were sacrificing their occupations and risking their lives for the cause they believed would benefit everyone in the state, while fair weather friends had deserted their fellow citizens and sought safety with the enemy.

In June, the Executive Council had asked Chief Justice Thomas McKean if the law of Pennsylvania provided any means for outlawing and confiscating the estates of people who could not be caught for trial. McKean had replied that the February act had made joining the enemy's army a treasonous act. Persons indicted of treason who could not be apprehended could be outlawed and attainted under an act of May 31, 1718. In such cases, the court could order the sheriff of the person's home county to bring him before the Supreme Court. If the accused could not be found, the sheriff could proclaim at the Quarter Sessions court that the accused must appear at the Supreme Court on a specified day. If he did not appear, he would be attainted of treason, and the state could confiscate his property, reserving half for the accused's family or next of kin.[33]

At this point, Elizabeth had had but slight concern; she thought Henry was safe in England and that the law and McKean's opinion did not affect her. In her copy of the *Post* on August 23, she read that New Jersey was considering a law to confiscate and sell the property of those who went to the British, but still as far as she knew, her property was not in danger. All of her confidence was shattered on September 25, when she learned that Henry had returned with the British army. "A Civilian" had shown that Pennsylvania had just as much incentive for such a law as New Jersey; it was only a matter of time before the Assembly would get around to passing it.

After his victories at Brandywine and Paoli, General Howe kept an advance post of about nine thousand men at Germantown. This is where John Young joined the British forces. On October 4, Washington tried once more to drive the British out of Pennsylvania by attacking this garrison. He came close to victory, but a dense fog and a too complicated plan combined to give him another defeat with heavy losses. Howe next turned to clearing the Delaware of American fortifications so that British ships could sail up river to Philadelphia, after which both sides settled down for the winter, Washington's forces at Valley Forge, west of Germantown, and Howe in the city.

Thomas Coombe was not the only Episcopal minister to be troubled by the separation from the mother country and the split in the Anglican Church that ensued. Because there was no Anglican bishop in the colonies, American ministers had had to travel to London to be ordained before they could officiate in the Anglican churches. Peters, Coombe, William White, William Smith, and Jacob Duché all had made this trip. American Anglicans had longed for the establishment of an American bishop, and leading colonial ministers had dreamed of filling such an office. After independence was declared, Anglicans asked what would happen to the American branch of the Church, if separation was achieved. This religious problem caused Anglican ministers to behave equivocally. They simply did not know what was the correct stance for them to take. Even if politically they had applauded the resistance movement, still religiously they were troubled by its final resolution.

Elizabeth's friend Rev. Jacob Duché, who had become rector of the combined Anglican churches of Christ Church and St. Peters upon the retirement of Richard Peters, was led by his distress to take an action that ruined his successful career in Pennsylvania and jeopardized Elizabeth's situation as well. From a wealthy Philadelphia family, he had graduated from the College of Philadelphia in 1757 in the same class as Francis Hopkinson, his best friend. After graduation, Duché had married Hopkinson's sister, traveled to England in 1762 for ordination in the Anglican Church, and returned to Philadelphia where he became known for his eloquent sermons. Mrs. Graeme, before her death, had found his sermons particularly inspiring and had copied them into her commonplace book. Duché and his wife, Elizabeth, were frequent visitors at Graeme Park.

At first Duché strongly supported the American resistance movement, as most people did. When the first Continental Congress had met in September 1774, its members had asked Duché to be their chaplain. He had opened both the first and the second Congresses with an eloquent prayer, and he had published two patriotic sermons. One of these, dedicated to George Washington and sent to him with an effusive letter, was entitled "On the Duty of Standing Fast in our Spiritual and Temporal Liberties." At the end of his transmittal letter Duché had written, "My prayers are continually for you, and the brave troops under your command."[34] This sermon he had preached at a service on July 7, 1775, for the First Battalion of Philadelphia. Even after the Declaration of Independence, he had seemed to be wholeheartedly behind the American cause. He had eliminated the prayers for the royal family from his service, and he had accepted the appointment as chaplain of Congress, officiating every day for the next three months.[35]

By October 1776, he was having second thoughts. He resigned his post as Congress's chaplain, citing health problems and the demands of his position as Rector, and he donated his salary to the dependents of Pennsylvania officers killed in the war. When the British took Philadelphia, Duché put the prayers for the royal family back into his service the next Sunday. As he was leaving the church, however, he was arrested by the British who did not realize that he was no longer a rebel. Jailed for his services to Congress as its chaplain, he remained there only one day before his friends convinced the British that Duché had had a change of heart, and he was released.

On October 8, 1777, Duché wrote a long letter to Washington urging the general to defect to the British. He wrote that he had always opposed independence, as had all "the most respectable characters." The possibility of French help was a delusion, and previous friends in Great Britain were no longer sympathetic. The contest was unequal and the bloodshed fruitless. Congress was made up of "illiberal and violent men. What can you expect of them?" He insulted the members of Congress from Massachusetts, calling them "Bankrupts, attorneys, and men of desperate fortune. . . . chosen by a little, low faction." The American army, too, was composed of the dregs of society. "How very few are there that you can ask to sit at your table!" The cause was lost. Washington should recommend to Congress "the indispensable necessity of rescinding the hasty and ill-advised declaration of independency." If Congress did not declare "an immediate cessation of hostilities," the general should take matters into his own hands and "Negotiate for America at the head of [his] army."[36]

Having written the letter, how was Duché in Philadelphia to deliver it to the general at Valley Forge? He considered this problem for a while and then remembered his old friend Elizabeth Fergusson who lived outside the British lines and whose social position would make it easy for her to approach Washington, already an acquaintance. Furthermore, her husband was a British supporter living in Philadelphia. Although General Washington did not allow Henry to go to Graeme Park, as Elizabeth had requested, he had sent her a pass so that she could go through the American lines to see her husband. Duché knew that the Fergussons were meeting and that she could take the letter to Washington. He contacted Henry to see if he would be willing to persuade Elizabeth to undertake its delivery. Fergusson, of course, agreed with all the letter's contents. Enclosing a note from Duché asking her for a favor, Henry wrote Elizabeth that she must meet him immediately at the Rising Sun tavern at the forks of the Germantown Road and the Old York Road. At that meeting, Henry gave Elizabeth Duché's October 8 letter to Washington and another shorter transmittal letter dated October 13, and she agreed to deliver them.[37] Whether she knew their specific contents and, if so, whether she agreed with them is not known, nor is what passed between husband and wife.

It is easy, however, to reconstruct her feelings. She was a forty-year-old childless woman married to a twenty-nine-year-old attractive man who had just spent two years in Europe yet was not willing to come to her unconditionally without permission from the American commander-in-chief to be able to return behind British lines if he chose. As Washington had pointed out, his behavior was very strange. It did not indicate overriding love for her, in spite of what he might say. Furthermore, he was not deterred by the strong possibility that his behavior might cause her property and their only livelihood to be confiscated by the state. If that should occur, what would happen to them? Neither one of them had had any preparation for earning a living. Henry had been educated to be a learned gentleman, yet he had not been given the wherewithal to pursue such a life. If they moved to England, how would they live? Selling Graeme Park to raise money was probably impossible. She had only been able to sell a portion of it under more favorable circumstances. Now, the state was at war, and the British occupied Philadelphia. It was highly unlikely that anyone would buy real estate at that unsettled period. Even if she could find a buyer, she would have to accept continental money, which would be useless in England. In addition, she had been born in Philadelphia and, except for a year and a half abroad, had spent all of her life there or at Graeme Park. It is true that she had friends in England and Scotland, but her childhood friends were in Pennsylvania, and all of her memories were there. In England, she would be an interesting minor colonial transplant, that's all, whereas in Philadelphia, she was recognized as a learned, intelligent woman, the most prominent in the city. She had many friends there, not the handful she had in Great Britain.

Yet she loved Henry, and he was her only chance to lead what was considered the normal life for a woman. He was a charming man, well educated, witty, a good companion for a woman with her intellectual interests. As far as her personal life was concerned, she would be better off if the British were able to restore the colonial status of the province. Many Pennsylvanians were wishing with her, over the winter of 1777 to 1778, that the imperial relationship could be turned back to what it had been in 1763. At the same time, she also loved her country and wanted what was best for it. If the British should win, what would happen to all the people who had started or supported the colonial resistance to British law? Many of her friends and some of her family were in that group, possibly threatened with treason charges by the British should they prevail. Further, she believed that the British tax measures had been unacceptable. And so she was torn.

If, as Duché was suggesting, the Americans led by Washington should lay down their arms and negotiate a settlement now before the controversy grew any worse, perhaps the British would be willing to return to happier times. Perhaps they would repeal the tax measures and agree to a different relationship with their North American colonies, one that would recognize the colonial legislatures as equal to Parliament under the king. This was the only solution that held any potential for solving her personal problems in a way that would not hurt her native land. In fact, by saving all the lives to be lost in future battles, it would help her country. Was such a scenario reasonable? Of course not, but Elizabeth was not in a condition to be rational. And so, importuned by her husband, confused and distressed, she agreed to go. It was a mistake, a big one, which she would regret.

Washington was encamped near Kulpsville on October 15, when a woman was announced. Surprised, he received Elizabeth, whom he had met before, in his tent. As she sat waiting, he read Duché's letter carefully and then "rising from his seat, walked backwards and forwards upwards of an hour without speaking. He appeared to be much agitated during the greatest part of the time." Elizabeth's own agitation must have equaled the General's, especially if she had not read the letter before handing it to Washington. Finally he stopped pacing and addressed Elizabeth. There are at least two versons of what he said to her. Benjamin West, the artist, heard from Pennsylvania émigrés in England, possibly Duché himself, that Washington had addressed her in some version of the following:

> Madam, I have always esteemed your character and endowments, and I am fully sensible of the noble principles by which you are actuated on this occasion; nor has any man in the whole continent more confidence in the integrity of his friend, than I have in the honour of Mr. Duchey. But I am here entrusted by the people of America with sovereign authority. They have placed their lives and fortunes at my disposal, because they believe me to be an honest man. Were I, therefore, to desert their cause, and consign them to the British, what would be the consequence? to myself perpetual infamy; and to them endless calamity. The seeds of everlasting division are sown between the two countries; and, were the British again to become our masters, they would have to maintain their dominion by force, and would, after all, retain us in subjection only so long as they could hold their bayonets to our breasts. No, Madam, the proposal of Mr. Duchey, though conceived with the best intention, is not framed in wisdom. America and England must be separate states; but they may have common interests, for

they are but one people. It will, therefore, be the object of my life and ambition to establish the independence of America in the first place; and in the second, to arrange such a community of interests between the two nations as shall indemnify them for the calamities which they now suffer, and form a new era in the history of nations. But, Madam, you are aware that I have many enemies; Congress may hear of your visit, and of this letter, and I should be suspected were I to conceal it from them. I respect you truly, as I have said; and I esteem the probity and motives of Mr. Duchey, and therefore you are free to depart from the camp, but the letter will be transmitted without delay to Congress.[38]

Washington sent a shorter, more terse, version in his letter forwarding Duché's letter to Congress:

I yesterday, thro the hands of Mrs. Ferguson of Graham Park, received a letter of a very curious and extraordinary nature from Mr. Duché, which I have thought proper to transmit to Congress. To this ridiculous—illiberal performance I made a short reply, by desiring the bearer of it, if she should hereafter by any accident meet with Mr. Duché, to tell him, I should have returned it unopened, if I had had any idea of the contents; observing at the same time, that I highly disapproved the intercourse she seemed to have been carrying on, and expected it would be discontinued. Notwithstanding the Authors assertion, I cannot but suspect, that the measure did not originate with him, and that he was induced to it by the hope of establishing his interest & peace more effectually with the Enemy.[39]

Elizabeth's thoughts as she traveled the fifteen miles or so back to Graeme Park were certainly disturbed. Her situation, unstable before, was now immeasureably worse. Even if she did not know the contents of the letter she had delivered, Washington's reaction would have told her that its transmittal had been unwise and was going to have unfortunate consequences. If she knew the letter's message, perhaps she realized, now too late, that a general of Washington's known integrity who had refused a fairly innocuous request for permission for Henry to come to Graeme Park was not going suddenly to lay down his arms and sue for peace just because a Philadelphia minister had suggested it. When Washington sent Duché's letter to Congress, he would have to disclose how he had received it. If Washington was upset, Congress would be, too. What had she done!

Once Congress received Duché's letter from Washington, the whole sequence of events became public knowledge along with Elizabeth's role as courier. Both Washington's letter to Congress and Duché's letters to Washington were read in Congress on October 20, 1777.⁴⁰ Although Congress's journals contain no other mention of Duché, we can be sure that the letters were received with shock and anger. It had been suspected that Duché had not been happy with the Declaration of Independence, but no one had guessed the depths of his disapproval. Congress was meeting by then in Yorktown, but the Pennsylvania Assembly in Lancaster soon knew of Duché's insulting comments. The letter was copied many times and circulated about the countryside. Eventually it was published in the *Royal Gazette* in New York on November 29. People in Philadelphia, if they had not heard already by word of mouth, found out shortly thereafter when the next British ship from New York brought copies of the newspaper.

Francis Hopkinson, signer of the Declaration of Independence, had seen a copy of the letter by early November and was appalled. On November 14, he wrote his brother-in-law a caustic renunciation. "What Infatuation," he asked Duché,

> could influence you to offer his Excellency an Address fill'd with gross Misrepresentations, illiberal Abuse & sentiments unworthy of a Man of Character. . . . You have by a vain and weak Effort attempted the Integrity of one whose Virtue is impregnable to the Assaults of Fear or Flattery. . . . You have drawn upon you the Resentment of Congress, the Resentment of the Army, the Resentment of many worthy and noble Characters in England whom you know not, and the Resentment of your insulted Country.

Hopkinson sent his long impassioned letter to Washington to be forwarded to Duché if the general approved. Washington replied that he would try to transmit the letter to Duché. He explained why he had sent Duché's letter to Congress. If he had kept it secret and if in the future "any accident have happened to the Army entrusted to my command," he wrote, and the letter became public, it might look as though he had betrayed his country.

The general, having never found an opportunity to forward Hopkinson's letter, would return it to the writer in January.[41]

When Duché's letter became public knowledge, he was through in Philadelphia. His promising, even brilliant, career there was ended. On December 9, he told his congregation that he was leaving for England, and he sailed shortly thereafter. He was attainted by the state, and his beautiful house on the corner of Pine and 3rd was confiscated. It was assigned to the Chief Justice in December 1980 and bought by Thomas McKean from the state the next August. In England, Duché was appointed chaplain and secretary of the Asylum for Female Orphans in Lambeth Parish. His living there was comfortable, but he always missed his homeland. In 1792, he returned to Philadelphia to live out the last few years of his life.

Before the Assembly had adjourned to Lancaster, the representatives had appointed a committee to draft a bill confiscating the estates of people who had defected to the enemy or who might do so in the future.[42] The legislature met in its new location on September 29 without a quorum until October 6 and adjourned again for the elections that would select a new body. In the interim between meetings of the first and second Assembly, a special Council of Safety was established to exercise the powers of government.

This Council, consisting of the members of the Supreme Executive Council and others, would take the next move to confiscate the property of the defected. The day after Washington's and Duché's letters were read in Congress, the Council acted. On October 21, the members passed an ordinance naming commissioners for each county to seize without a prior trial the personal property of any one who had joined or would join the British army or who had given or would give the enemy intelligence or aid. These commissioners were given wide powers to confiscate, to store, or to sell this property, to question witnesses, to break open doors, and to jail resisters. It also empowered the state to take produce being carried to the British in Philadelphia by local farmers.[43] But it did not call for the confiscation of realty, and therein lay the greatest potential revenue for the state coffers. Congress recognized this potential, however, and in November recommended that the realty also be confiscated and sold. Congress suggested that the money be used to buy continental loan office certificates rather than be kept by the states, a suggestion not likely to be adopted by the financially strapped states.[44]

Meanwhile, the Pennsylvania General Assembly was acting to legalize the confiscation of émigré property for the state. On December 23, a committee brought in a proposed bill for confiscating the estates, both real and personal, of those who had gone to the enemy. That same day, "An Act for the attainder of diverse traitors, if they render not themselves by a certain day and for vesting their estates in the Commonwealth" was read a second time and ordered to be printed for public consideration. It was then set aside, as required by the state constitution, until the next session of the Assembly. If Elizabeth had not heard from friends what was being considered, she discovered it when this proposed act was published in the newspapers, and she realized the full potential for ruin that Henry's actions had brought upon them, and especially upon her. If she lost Graeme Park by confiscation, she would have no way to survive.

By this time, Henry, living in Philadelphia, had accepted a job under General Howe, making their connection to the new nation even more tenuous. He had no income, and Elizabeth had no money to send him. She was living by borrowing from friends because she had not restored the full productivity of her farm. Henry, therefore, accepted the job of Commissary of Prisoners, offered him by General Howe after Howe had turned down Fergusson's proposal to raise a corps of cavalry for the British army. Elizabeth would argue later that Henry did not "have a regular Commission made out, nor did he take the Oath customary on those Occasions." Hence, technically, he had not been in the British army. She also maintained that he accepted the job largely "from a principle of Humanity" to help American prisoners who were suffering "most severe hardships."[45] This may have been what Henry told her, but his other conduct makes this motivation seem unlikely.

Even she doubted that others would believe her and became very fearful once she learned of the Assembly's plans to confiscate the property of those who helped the enemy. She began to solicit the help of influential friends in the new government. The day after the Assembly began considering the bill for confiscating the property of émigrés, General Daniel Roberdeau asked the Executive Council to protect Mrs. Fergusson's property from confiscation. His "worthy patriotic friend" had displayed "heroism" in alienating herself from "a beloved husband" because of his part against America, and Roberdeau did not want her to be involved in the same predicament as her husband.[46] The letter's content was also "favored" by Col. Elias Boudinot. The plea of two men of such outstanding and unquestioned devotion to the American cause had some weight.

In December, Elizabeth poured out her troubles and unhappiness to her friend Annis Stockton: bereft of all her immediate family, her nephew gone to the British, her husband likely to be proscribed, and she left all alone with only one other woman, Betsy Stedman, to console her and keep her company. Her letter was so affecting that Benjamin Rush, then visiting his mother-in-law, wrote a letter offering to speak in her behalf to the Executive Council, most of whom he knew, to prevent them from confiscating her property. As to Henry's behavior, the only consolation Rush could offer was that when peace came perhaps acts of indemnity would forgive him. "His office will enable him to show mercy to our countrymen in captivity," Rush pointed out, "and this may prepare the way for his future reconciliation with his country."[47]

Rush's mother- and father-in-law had themselves had a year of terrible crisis and uncertainty. On November 11, 1776, the Stocktons and their children had fled Princeton and taken refuge from the British in Monmouth County, New Jersey. But this was not a safe haven. Two days after their arrival, Tories broke into the house, dragged Richard Stockton from his bed, and took him to the British, who were delighted to have in their custody one of the signers of the Declaration of Independence. They put him in the Provost jail in New York, a dreadful place. There he was abused, kept in irons, and denied adequate food. When the Howes offered pardon and protection of property and life to anyone who would swear to obey the king and not take up arms against him, Richard, sick and worried about his family, signed the oath. He was released, and by early January, he and Annis and their children were back at Morven. The house had been sacked and much of it destroyed by the occupying forces, the contents stolen or ravaged, the east wing burned, and family portraits slashed. Richard resigned from Congress because of the oath, but there is no indication that he was denounced because of his apostasy. People seemed to understand the pressures upon him at the time. In late 1777, however, Annis and Richard could not have been certain how the new government of New Jersey would treat them. They were potentially in just as serious a situation as Elizabeth.

Henry's opposite as Commissary of Prisoners for the American army was Elias Boudinot, his wife's dear friend and Annis Stockton's brother. He and Henry first met as opponents rather than friends on December 1.[48] Boudinot had come to their encounter from visiting Graeme Park bringing with him two army officers and, for some unknown reason,

Betsy Stedman. The two men met often during the occupation, but their relationship was never smooth. On their first meeting, Henry had to concede to Boudinot's charge of British cruelty toward American prisoners, which he said "should not happen again." The chances of Henry alleviating the conditions of American prisoners of war, however, were slight. He found his humanitarian orders often countermanded, and he was able to do little.[49] In March, he was given the job of arranging for the exchange of Governor William Franklin who had been confined by the Americans in Connecticut since the summer of 1776. But his efforts were ineffectual, and Franklin's exchange was not accomplished until the following September.[50] By April 1778, Elias Boudinot was at the end of his patience. He wrote Henry a very sharp letter complaining of the cruelty to jailed American prisoners of war by Provost Marshall Cunningham who had beaten prisoners with the heavy key to the jail and had killed two of them. "You must have had an Opportunity by this Time of knowing this Man's general Conduct," Boudinot commented critically, and he threatened that if this behavior did not stop, he would not be able to prevent retaliation against British soldiers imprisoned by the Americans.[51]

During Christmas week, 1777, Graeme Park was once more invaded by part of the American army. Major General James Armstrong went into winter quarters at Graeme Park, and on New Years Eve, Brigadier General James Potter and his brigade joined Armstrong's command. At one point there were nearly two thousand men bivouacked there. This number decreased rapidly as enlistments ran out and the men went home in the new year. Both officers were replaced by Brigadier General John Lacey Jr., who reported that on January 24, there were only seventy men at Graeme Park. On that day, Elizabeth and Betsy were badly frightened when six or seven thousand cartridges, stored in a tent, blew up. Fortunately the ensuing fire was extinguished before it could spread. The next day, Lacey moved his remaining men to Warwick in Chester County, much to the relief of Elizabeth and Betsy,[52] although the mess left behind by the army was extensive. Valuable timber had been cut down to build log huts for the men. The drawing room of the mansion had been occupied as a guardroom, and most of the furniture usually on the first floor had been moved upstairs to the third floor. Elizabeth was reimbursed only £106.4 for 2360 pounds of beef slaughtered, and that not until the end of March.[53] How the two women survived after the army left is hard to imagine. No cattle or horses were left and other food must have been pretty well consumed by the army.

That winter, when not coping with unwanted visitors, Elizabeth put her fingers to work spinning flax to be woven into linen cloth for the American soldiers. In March, Elias Boudinot made arrangements to have it collected and sent to the American prisoners of war in Philadelphia, whose sad plight Henry had reported to her.[54] She also is reputed to have entertained General Washington on several occasions. No documentary evidence of this remains, but when William Buck was collecting information about Elizabeth in the 1850s there were still people alive who remembered having seen letters written by the general thanking Elizabeth for her donations to the soldiers and having heard Betsy Stedman say that the general once spent a night at Graeme Park while he was encamped at Valley Forge, nineteen miles away.[55]

Elizabeth also went into Philadelphia to see Henry as often as she could secure a pass, very carefully observing all the rules. These visits were very painful, as she tried to persuade Henry to quit his job with the British and take his chances on securing a pardon from the Americans, and he tried to persuade her to move into Philadelphia and commit to the British position. Altogether in the fall, winter, and spring, she managed to spend about two weeks with him.[56] When she worried about the confiscation of Graeme Park, he countered that the British would undoubtedly win, and their supporters would be rewarded with lucrative jobs after the war ended. She in turn would point to General Howe's lassitude in preferring Philadelphia's social life to the battlefield and ask what would happen if the Americans won.

Elizabeth wrote only one poem during the period of the British occupation of the city, and this was in response to Henry's urging her to forsake Graeme Park for the city. It is entitled "Country Mouse" and addressed to

> a gentleman in Philadelphia, written in the month of November *1777* when the British was in possession of the City. The gentleman to who these lines were adressd; asked the writer, to leave the country and partake of the winter Pleasures of the City and the entertainments given by the military gentlemen.

The poem draws an analogy between the predicament of the country mouse in an Aesop's fable and her own. The rural mouse is enticed by the lady mouse to leave her home under a shed and enjoy the fine life in a luxurious house in the city. At first she is dazzled by what she sees.

> But Ah the Scene is soon reverst;
> Her mind is filld with dread!
> She longs to Bite a Barly Crust,
> Beneath her Humble shed.
> No friendly hand, no little track;
> Points out her late left Shed;
> No light gleams forth to lead her Back
> Where Peace and safety tread.

Warned by the fate of the mouse, Elizabeth refuses to leave Graeme Park.[57]

Elizabeth's agony reached the ears of her niece, Anny Smith, in Allentown who was distressed to learn that her aunt was "in Some Respects more unhappy with Regard to Mr F n" than when she last saw her. She had heard of "the pathetic letter" Elizabeth had written Henry to "draw Him of[f] from British Conections." She commiserated with Elizabeth's situation, her husband unable to come to his home after a separation of two years and both spouses attached to opposite sides. "Oh my dear aunt I See you are Compleatly wretched But a few months ago with an independent fortune . . . Superi[o]r talents And uncommon Virtues."[58]

Elizabeth's wretchedness, however, was only beginning. On March 6, the Pennsylvania General Assembly passed an act ordering thirteen men suspected of having joined the British to report for a treason trial by April 20 or be attainted of high treason. This meant that they would be declared guilty without a trial. Among the names on the list were many men whom Elizabeth had known most of her life: the three Allen brothers, Andrew, John, and William, Joseph Galloway, Jacob Duché, and others. Her friends had managed to keep Henry from proscription, but they could not protect him forever in the face of his continued allegiance to the British. The act also empowered the Executive Council to proclaim additional names of persons suspected of helping the enemy. They were required to report before a fixed date, forty days after the date on the proclamation, to stand trial for treason. If they were caught or reported late, the judge could not order a trial to determine their guilt. He could only ascertain that they were the persons listed in the proclamation and that they had not reported on time. He then had to sentence them to the obligatory death penalty. After the deadline, their real and personal estates were to be seized by the state and sold and the proceeds put in the state treasury.[59]

Two months later, Henry's name was on the first proclamation issued by the Supreme Executive Council on May 18, and three days after that, John Young was proscribed. Henry had to report before June 25 and John before July 6, or their property would be confiscated by the state, and they would risk execution if caught. By then, it was apparent to all that the British would be leaving Philadelphia soon. Elizabeth begged Henry to make his peace with the Americans and not to go with the British army. But he adamantly refused all her entreaties.

8

Confrontation and Confiscation

Philadelphia was not a nice place to be in June 1778. A heat wave made people uncomfortable and tempers short. Lightning flashed across the sky in erratic patterns at night but brought no cooling rain to allow people to sleep. Gnats on the river were "as large as sparrows,"[1] and the usual mosquitoes made life miserable for everyone. The city was filthy, garbage in the streets and flies so thick that people found that they could not drink a cup of tea without having its surface covered with the insects.

On Saturday, June 6, three peace commissioners arrived in the sweltering city from England committed to an impossible errand. After the Battle of Saratoga, a movement toward reconciliation had gained support in England. Although the English ministry was not willing to grant absolute independence, it was willing to discuss almost any other concessions that might bring the states back into the British empire. By March 1778, a peace commission had been organized to go to Philadelphia and negotiate with Congress. The head of the commission was the Earl of Carlisle and the other appointees were William Eden, George Johnstone, and the two Howe brothers, Richard and William, who were already in America. Neither of the Howes would serve; General Henry Clinton, who had succeeded General Howe May 8, took their places. It was a futile undertaking, doomed to failure before the commissioners were even appointed. Unfortunately, the machinations of Johnstone would implicate Elizabeth in his scheme to win American leaders to the British desire for reunion, further damaging her relationship with the new national and Pennsylvania state governments.

Before the commissioners left England, copies of the treaties between the United States and France, negotiated by Benjamin Franklin and his cohorts in Paris, had arrived in America and been signed by Congress. With French help now assured, the American leaders made it quite clear that without the one concession the commissioners could not discuss, there would be no peace treaty. As long as the American people remained behind their government in its demands for recognition of United States independence, the commissioners' junket was useless, and they could have saved themselves their trans-Atlantic trip. Furthermore, the one big stick they could have used to force Congress to the negotiating table had been taken from them: Philadelphia was to be evacuated and left without major destruction by the British army. When Congress refused to discuss the situation until Great Britain withdrew her army and navy from these shores and recognized United States independence, the commissioners did not have the power to make these concessions, and they had nothing to offer or threaten to make Congress back down from its stand. The only possibility of success for them—however remote—lay in weaning Americans, especially the leaders, from their support of independence. And the British were not above attempting to bribe Americans to return to their loyalty to Great Britain.

When Johnstone arrived in this country, he wrote a letter to Colonel Joseph Reed, a member of Congress and a friend of Washington, and sent it to Valley Forge along with a packet of newspapers and a letter from Reed's English brother-in-law, Dennis De Berdt, introducing his friend Johnstone. The commissioner's letter to Reed appeared innocuous enough until subsequent events revealed Johnstone's real design. He first introduced himself to Reed, whom he had never met, and told of his efforts on behalf of America and his desire that "every subject of the Empire might live equally free." The letter concluded with a wish to open a "line of communication" with Reed. "The man who can be instrumental in bringing us all to act once more in harmony," he wrote, "and to unite together the various powers . . . will deserve more from the King and the people . . . that ever was yet bestowed on humankind."[2] Reed's reply of June 14, cleared first with Washington and a few other men, spoke flatteringly of Johnstone's "unavailing efforts to prevent the dismemberment of the British empire," but he held out no hope for reunion and recommended that

"Great Britain give up her visionary schemes of conquest and empire" for the benefits of friendship and trade.[3] This letter never reached Johnstone, or perhaps he would not have tried to pursue this line further. Soon after, Reed sent Johnstone's letter to the President of Congress and then forgot about the commissioner.

When the commissioners arrived at Philadelphia, they discovered what they had not been told before they left England, that the British army was evacuating Philadelphia and moving back to New York. The withdrawal had already begun, and the commissioners, too, would have to leave very shortly. By June 10, Lord Carlisle was already on board the ship that would take him to New York. He reported that there were three thousand "miserable" disaffected persons on ships waiting to be evacuated because they thought that "they would receive no mercy from those who [would] take possession" from the British.[4]

Among those who left with the British were several of Elizabeth's childhood friends, such as Phineas Bond. In July, Bond sent a feeler back to Philadelphia asking whether he could return without being punished for breaking his parole. He was advised that if he would take the oath of allegiance to the state, probably his conduct before the British occupation would not be considered. His leaving the state with the enemy was another matter. As a lawyer, Bond would have to decide himself, he was told, whether that act would be forgiven upon his taking the oath. Apparently, he decided that the dangers of returning were too great, and in November 1778 he sailed for England where he would establish a legal practice. After the war, he would be forgiven, and he would return to Philadelphia as a British consul.

Another old friend who left his native city was Thomas Coombe. After the British left, Coombe asked for his parole, which he had not kept, to be discharged, but he was refused. On July 6, the Council gave Coombe permission to leave the state, and the next day he told the vestry of Christ Church that he had decided to go to England. A few days later he left for New York where he could procure passage, leaving his wife and child in Philadelphia until he became settled in England. She died the following October, and his son lived with his grandmother until December 1781 when she sent him on his way, a boy of seven years, to make the long trip from Philadelphia to New York to London, to join his father. Coombe spent the rest of his life in England. By 1787, he had become one of forty-eight chaplains to the king. He died in London in 1822.[5] Except for

Coombe and Bond, everyone else who had signed a parole before the British entered Philadelphia was discharged from it the end of June.[6] This included Rev. William Smith, who now returned to the city from his retreat on the Schuylkill River, where he had retired after taking the parole.

On his last day in Philadelphia, June 16, Johnstone, not having any answer from Reed, wrote a similar letter to Robert Morris, making the offer of a bribe even more precise. Once more he introduced himself to Morris and wrote that he wished to meet him in person. Of course, he wrote, "the men who had conducted the affairs of America [were] incapable of being influenced by improper motives." But he thought that "Washington and the President [Henry Laurens, President of Congress] have a right to every favour that grateful nations can bestow, if they could once more unite our interests."[7]

Johnstone, who had been governor of Florida for a period and who was known for his sympathetic and outspoken opinions about colonial rights, had brought with him letters from England to deliver to Americans. His friendly comments about the American cause infuriated the loyalists in the city who wondered why he had been appointed to the commission. He was reported to have asked "about the Value of Lands & landed Security in this Country, & expressed his Intention of selling what he [had] in England & sitting down" in Pennsylvania. Among the communications he had brought from England was a snuff-box with Washington's picture in the lid to deliver to Elizabeth Fergusson from a friend in England.[8]

On the same day that he sent his letter to Morris, Johnstone had a private conversation with Elizabeth at Charles Stedman's house, where Johnstone was living while in Philadelphia. Elizabeth had come into Philadelphia to say goodbye to Henry who was leaving with the British, and she was staying there, too, during most of Johnstone's visit. It was there that he gave her the gift from England. His acquaintance with her English friends and his well-known sympathetic inclinations toward the American cause made his views appealing to her own. Twice previously she and he had talked. Johnstone wanted to converse with influential Americans, to try to convince them that the best path for America lay in reunion. Congress did not represent the views of the majority of the people, he believed, and was keeping them uninformed about the true situation. If the commissioners could only reach the people, Johnstone thought, they could convince them to demand the repeal of the Declaration of Independence. To Elizabeth, the commissioner seemed a reasonable man, "a friend to

America, who wished some person would step forth and act a mediatorial part, and suggest something to stop the effusion of blood." But she told him that his analysis of Congress as a non-representative body was "a delusive idea" and that the people favored independence.

At this time, Elizabeth's thoughts were consumed with Henry's proscription deadline. He had to report before June 25 for treason trial or be declared guilty, punishable by execution if caught and by confiscation of all his (her) property. That date was rapidly approaching, yet she had been unable to convince him to conform to the law. He was going to leave with the British army, regardless of her reluctance to leave her home and regardless of her situation, left in Pennsylvania to suffer the penalties of his actions. He wanted her to go with him, but that seemed to her to be a foolish move, since he had no way to support them. How would they live? She had been advised by lawyers—Richard Stockton and others—that Henry could not be guilty of treason against Pennsylvania since he had been born in Scotland and was not in the colony at the time independence had been declared. The Assembly's own definition of treason supported her argument. On February 11, 1777, the Assembly had passed an act that said that anyone then living in Pennsylvania or coming into the state thereafter to live owed allegiance to the state, but Henry in February 1777 was somewhere in the British isles or on the continent. Elizabeth was leaving shortly to go to Lancaster to present these arguments to the Supreme Executive Council, and she again urged Henry to stay in Pennsylvania and fight the charge against him.

Johnstone had heard her speak of her errand and decided she could be used to communicate his ideas to Joseph Reed. About fifteen minutes before his departure, between ten and eleven in the morning, she met him in the Stedmans' tea-room to return a manuscript journal he had sent her a few hours earlier. The journal listed the many advantages for the colonies of reuniting with England, but the time was so short that she had read but a portion of it. As she was leaving the room, he started a conversation. He said that he had heard that Robert Morris and Joseph Reed were influential in American politics and that he wished he could see them. He would be "particularly glad of Mr. Reed's influence in this affair," since he was an intimate of Washington.

> If Mr. Reed, after well considering the nature of the dispute, can, conformable to his conscience and view of things, exert his influ-

ence to settle the contest, he may command ten thousand guineas
and the best post in the government, and if you should see him, I
could wish you would convey that idea to him.

Elizabeth reported later that she had been "hurt and shocked" at this "indelicate hint." Johnstone then turned to go, but she stopped him, register-
ing "disgust" on her face, and asked him, "Do you not think, sir, that Mr.
Reed will look upon such a mode of obtaining his influence as a bribe?"
Johnstone then assured her that such a "method of proceeding is customary
in all negotiations; and one may very honourably make it a man's interest
to step forth in a cause." Elizabeth, while admitting that she knew little of
such negotiations, pointed out that if Reed believed reunion desirable, he
would say so without reward, and if he believed the contrary, no reward
would change his mind. Johnstone said he disagreed with her analysis and
abruptly left the room, perhaps regretting his overture.[9]

Sometime within the next four days, Elizabeth wrote to Reed asking for an interview with him the following Monday.[10] She was planning
to go to Lancaster to present a petition to the Supreme Executive Council
about Henry's proscription. She would pass Valley Forge, where she
thought Reed was, and she proposed to visit with him en route. She enclosed a letter from General Roberdeau urging her to attend the Council
soon. She also enclosed a letter from Richard Stockton arguing that Henry
could not be prosecuted for treason to Pennsylvania since he had never
been a citizen of the state. Elizabeth asked Reed to consider Stockton's
letter and give his advice when they met. Since Reed was a prominent
leader among the new rulers of Pennsylvania, she desperately wanted his
voice in her favor.

On Thursday, June 18, the British left Philadelphia, and Reed returned to the city. He received her letter on Sunday, while dining at a
friend's home. The bearer told him that Elizabeth had just come to town
that morning and told him where she was staying. Apparently, she had
gone back to Graeme Park after her conversation with Johnstone and had
returned to Philadelphia to plead for Reed's intercession on her behalf
before going to Lancaster. Reed sent word that he would wait upon her
that evening. When he arrived, he found her much agitated about her
husband's attainder and wanting his advice about what she should do. This
was her main concern. How Reed advised her is not known, but he did
not offer any help in her crisis.

The conversation then became more general and turned to the subject of the British commissioners, especially Johnstone. Elizabeth told Reed that she had been at the Stedmans' while Johnstone was lodged there and that she had had several conversations with him. She related that the British commissioners mistakenly believed the American people opposed independence and that she had informed Johnstone of his error. When she told Reed that Johnstone had expressed favorable sentiments about him, the general told her that he had received a letter from Johnstone at Valley Forge. Elizabeth then repeated Johnstone's desire to see Reed and his offer of a reward to Reed if he could accomplish a reunion of the colonies to Great Britain. Reed responded that he "was not worth purchasing, but such as [he] was, the king of England was not rich enough to do it."[11] With that the meeting ended. Reed went off to fight with the army at the Battle of Monmouth on June 28, and Elizabeth hastened to Lancaster.

There she presented her petition to the Supreme Executive Council on June 26, the day after Henry's proscription date. She had written the petition herself, although someone with a more legible handwriting had copied it for her. In it, she related the sequence of events involving Henry's leaving in September 1775 to attend to family matters in Scotland and his returning with Howe's forces two years later. Henry had accepted the position of commissary of prisoners, she wrote, to try to alleviate the terrible conditions under which American prisoners were suffering. Her estate afforded only a frugal support, but her wish was to remain unmolested there in "retirement." She concluded with the plea that any digressions or omissions would be forgiven as due to "the Ignorance of a Female, whose Line of Writing has been confin'd to Epistolary Subjects, in a careless Way, unsuspicious of the Eye of Criticism or severe Examination." If her petition should shed new light on her situation and cause the Council to prevent her estate from being forfeited, she would be grateful; if not, she would consider it her "Duty cheerfully to bear a Link of the Chain of heavy Calamities incident to a Civil War."[12]

The day that Elizabeth presented her memorial, the councillors were not very sympathetic. Her old friend George Bryan, vice president of the state and acting president ever since Thomas Wharton Jr. had died May 23, presided over the meeting, but none of the other members present was well known by Elizabeth. Their minutes record that the petition was presented and read but report no action taken on it. Perhaps her involvement as the carrier of Duché's letter to Washington dulled any natural compassion they might have felt for a woman in her situation. If the Council continued to ignore her petition, the confiscation of her property would proceed according to order, because Henry had not reported for treason trial before his deadline.

On July 15, Reed returned to his seat in Congress, again meeting in Philadelphia, and found that by the previous week, knowledge of Johnstone's letters to several American leaders had become public. Congress had ordered on July 9 that "all letters received by members of Congress from any of the British commissioners or their agents . . . of a public nature, be laid before Congress." Robert Morris immediately had complied, producing Johnstone's letter of June 16. On July 16, Francis Dana turned over a letter from Johnstone to him, and on July 18, Reed, who had already given Henry Laurens Johnstone's letter to him of April 11, told the story of a bribe offer transmitted to him by a lady, whose name he withheld, although he described her as "a married lady of character, having connections with the British army." Congress ordered the letters to be published, and the next day William Henry Drayton, the president of Congress, told Reed to write his recollection of his meeting with the lady and sign it. On July 21, Drayton had Johnstone's letters published in the newspapers, along with a letter of his own to the commissioners that included Reed's account of his meeting with the still unidentified lady.[13]

When Elizabeth received her copy of the *Pennsylvania Evening Post* on July 26, she was horrified to see what to her had been a conversation with Reed about her husband's attainder described as the transmittal of a British bribe attempt. Frightened and unhappy, she took her pen and wrote to Reed, for four hours pouring out her agony. Although the paper did not mention her name, it might just as well have done so, she wrote Reed. The details he had given clearly had identified her as the lady involved. How could he have caused "an innocent and . . . almost friendless woman to be exhibited in a common news-paper" in a manner that portrayed her as "an emmissary of the Commissioners." His story implied that the only reason she had met with him was to convey Johnstone's business. But that was not true. She reminded Reed that he had told her he had received a letter from Johnstone, and she had assumed that Johnstone already had presented his proposal in that communication. "I am sensible, Sir," she wrote,

> that the political opinions of women are ridiculed among the generality of men, but I own I find it hard, very hard (knowing the

incorruptness of my heart) to be held out to the public as a tool of the Commissioners. . . . How far, at this critical juncture of time, this affair may injure my property is uncertain; that I assure you is but a secondary thought.[14]

It could not, however, be a "secondary thought." She was fighting to prevent confiscation of her property because of Henry's attainder, and she could not afford to be characterized as a tool of the British commissioners.

Still waiting for the Supreme Executive Council to act on her memorial, Elizabeth found her identity at the center of an outcry of anger over Johnstone's crude attempts to blackmail America's leaders. Incensed about the episode, the councillors, on July 24 had called for the name of the woman, her name, to be made public. Their call was seconded by "C—S" in the *Packet* on July 30, who wrote that the name of the lady should not be concealed. Attempted bribery was treason and should be treated as such. Elizabeth, at Graeme Park, trembled for fear of her life, remembering that execution was the punishment for traitors under the treason law of February 1777. The Continental Congress, already annoyed because the Commissioners had arrived without authority to negotiate independence, was now furious at Johnstone's clumsy bribery effort. On August 11, the congressmen, in high dudgeon, expressed "the highest and most pointed indignation against such daring and atrocious attempts to corrupt their integrity" and resolved that they would have nothing more to do with any of the Commissioners.[15] With condemnation of Johnstone's actions coming from all sides, Elizabeth's connection with him made her position very tenuous.

The whole business was further complicated by Johnstone's reaction. On August 26, he published his answer to Congress's resolution. He began by saying that he did not find Congress's condemnation offensive; to the contrary, he found it a "mark of distinction." He then proceeded with a diatribe against Congress, whose actions, he wrote, were "injuring their nearest and dearest friends and relations, [and] forgetting all the principles of virtue and liberty." The letter did not address the question of the attempted bribery at all, except to say that he reserved the right to defend himself before leaving North America. In October, he sailed for England leaving with Adam Ferguson, secretary of the commission, a letter, which Ferguson published in Rivington's *Gazette* on October 8. Johnstone claimed that he had left with Adam Ferguson complete, indisputable evidence, that no act of [his], by word, writing, message, or conversation with any person whatsoever, could have been conceived by the Member of Congress, Joseph Reed, Esq., previous to the 19th of July last, as an attempt or as having a tendency . . . to corrupt his integrity.[16]

Because of his respect for private correspondence, this "evidence" would not be revealed to the public.

It is suspected that his so-called evidence was probably a letter that Reed had written to a woman friend planning a journey to New York the end of July, shortly after the first publication of the affair. Reed had asked her to pick up any letters from his brother-in-law in England addressed to his family. If she ran into any difficulties, he had told her to apply to Governor Johnstone for help. Johnstone heard of the woman's inquiries, came to see her, saw the note Reed had written her, and confiscated it. Johnstone might have claimed that if Reed had believed his integrity had been challenged, he would not have authorized someone else to ask a personal favor of the man who had thus insulted him. The careful wording of the denial supports this interpretation because Johnstone did not say that his conversation with Elizabeth never took place.[17]

Meanwhile, Elizabeth's situation was becoming increasingly precarious. The Philadelphians who had fled the British had returned to find their possessions plundered or destroyed, the city filthy, and public buildings damaged. Many of these sufferers were calling for government action against the disaffected who remained. Joseph Reed was one of those who called for retribution. He and his friends wanted the laws enforced to the letter, for without punishment, laws were useless and government appeared foolish, in his opinion.

Their views, however, were countered by those of Vice President George Bryan and Chief Justice Thomas McKean who spoke for Pennsylvanians who wanted to treat the disaffected with tolerance. They believed that there should be harsh laws to prevent crimes but that they should not be fully enforced except against people who actually endangered the state and its citizens. McKean wanted people accused of treason to be treated with mercy, except for "some men of property" whose estates should be confiscated as examples, although their lives should be spared. He reasoned that "The application and interest that will be made by the relatives & friends of the culprits for mercy will create respect to the Rulers, and their granting it on every reasonable occasion will reconcile & endear men to the Government." "Pardoning is a God-like power and a God-like virtue," he wrote in early June 1778.[18]

By the end of June, three proclamations had been issued by the Supreme Executive Council charging 332 persons, in addition to the 13 originally charged by the Act of Assembly, with treasonous behavior and ordering them to report for trials or be declared guilty. McKean and the two other justices of the Supreme Court began sitting every day in early July to receive those persons who wanted to turn themselves in for trial. By July 7, almost 40 of the persons proclaimed had appeared, but the justices had released them all on bail because of insufficient evidence.

The actions of Philadelphians about the disaffected were very ambiguous. Although in general they wanted the people who had destroyed or stolen their property punished and the disaffected to be forced to contribute to the Revolution because they, too, would profit from a victory, nevertheless when it came to specific individuals, they were reluctant or unable to produce any evidence. Furthermore, and perhaps more important, the people calling for revenge were the most vociferous Whigs who had left the city before the British had arrived and, therefore, probably had no evidence to present. Those who had stayed and observed their neighbors' actions did not want to be responsible for the execution of a friend or, even worse, feared possible self-involvement.

Yet the state officials were under a real dilemma. They certainly did not want to set loose a period of bloody revenge, but if they did not do something, the people might take matters into their own hands. There was a very vocal minority who demanded vengeance. "Casca" writing in the *Pennsylvania Evening Post* on July 16 warned those who had helped the British that "the day of trial is close at hand when you shall be called upon, to answer for . . . your *treachery* to this country." A front page article in the *Post* two days later told citizens to collect evidence against the disaffected and present it to the magistrates. A statement on July 25 signed by about 100 men said that the "notoriously disaffected" were trying to hide the evidence of their treasonous activities and pledged to do everything to uncover them. Elizabeth, accused of being the carrier of a British bribe, read these cries for revenge in her newspapers and worried about her safety.

The position that was taken by the government was that proposed by General John Armstrong, among others, who believed in mercy and "as little sacrifice to the passions & prejudices of the populace as possible." "A few examples ought to be made," however, very quickly to satisfy the public demand, he suggested. The most notorious "examples" sacrificed to the popular outcry were two Quakers, Abraham Carlisle and John Roberts, whose crimes were no worse than those of many others who escaped punishment. Probably they were guilty of the charges against them, of helping the British during the occupation, but so had many others. Both men turned themselves in before their deadlines, were tried and found guilty, and sentenced to death. Public opinion largely opposed the sentence; "most good men wished for an act of oblivion," it was said. Memorials flooded the desks of the councillors begging them to pardon the men. Included among the petitioners was Chief Justice McKean, even though it had been he who had tried and sentenced the two men. To him, the threat should have been enough; he had not intended the executions to take place. Roberts's wife and children threw themselves on the floor of the Council chamber begging for mercy. But the cries for clemency were unheeded. The men were executed on November 4. Joseph Reed, one of the prosecutors in the case, was disgusted by the outcry in favor of Carlisle and Roberts. "Treason, Disaffection to the Interests of America & even assistance to the British Interest is called openly only Error of Judgment, which Candour & Liberality of Sentiment will overlook," he complained.[19]

On July 8, Andrew Robeson, a young attorney and friend, wrote her that both Colonel Elias Boudinot and General Daniel Roberdeau were using their influence in her favor. Roberdeau had assured Charles Stedman that "no further immediate Steps will be taken." The next day, however, the Supreme Executive Council ordered the agents who had been appointed to seize, inventory, and sell the estates of persons who had gone over to the enemy to proceed without delay. Unless Henry's attainder was removed, Elizabeth's property would soon be sold. Three days later, Robeson was less sanguine. He had since talked to Roberdeau and did not want his earlier letter to have "lulled [her] into a Supposed Security and prevent [her] taking other and more proper Measures for the preservation of her Interest." Roberdeau now believed that she should petition Chief Justice Thomas McKean to reserve a portion of her estate from confiscation for her support. Under the attainder law, the Chief Justice was given the power to make such an allowance, at his discretion.[20]

Sometime in the next six weeks, Elizabeth took this advice and applied to the Supreme Court for the allowance of furniture for a living room, bedroom, and kitchen, 400 books, and the grain and flax stored at

Graeme Park, all of which the Court granted. Until the remainder of the estate was sold, Elizabeth was allowed to remain there, although she must pay a rent to be determined by the agents for forfeited estates. The chief justice had assured Francis Hopkinson and William White in informal conversation that after the value of the estate and the debts against it had been determined, the court would withdraw from sale and give to Elizabeth, such of the estate that her "Station in Life" required. McKean sent her the message that if a rent was set high above the property's value in order to make her leave it, she could obtain redress from the court.[21]

On September 17, Dr. Archibald McLean Jr. and his brother-in-law Col. Robert Loller (or Lollar), neighbors and long-time acquaintances of Elizabeth, appeared at Graeme Park to inventory her personal property. This was a very distressing job for them as well as for Elizabeth. Their sympathies were with her, yet they knew that they would have to swear under oath that they had appraised the goods honestly. The inventory remains and shows that her clothing and any jewelry or plate she may have had were not included, even though in colonial Pennsylvania a man secured complete ownership of all the personal property of a woman upon their marriage, and hence these would have been confiscatable as Henry's property. Four hundred books were in her library. Most were not inventoried by name, but among those that were three volumes of Shakespeare, two of David Hume identified as his *History of the Stuarts,* six volumes of Herbert Spencer, two volumes of Montesquieu's *Spirit of the Laws,* four volumes of Henry Fielding's *Tom Jones,* three volumes of *Tristam Shandy* by Laurence Sterne, nine volumes of the *Spectator,* four volumes of Edward Young's works, and several Bibles. Many of the books were not bound, as was customary, and one hundred and thirty of those that were belonged to others whose names were in them. Another interesting item was the name of a slave, Alexander, who was not listed on subsequent lists, neither allowed to Elizabeth nor sold in the forthcoming sale. Alexander had been inherited by Elizabeth from her father who had expected her to care for him in his old age. In 1783, one Negro was listed in her tax assessment, valued at £250. This must have been Alexander.[22]

This was a terrible day for Elizabeth. Her property was being inventoried. If it was all sold, how would she live? Her husband was proscribed and demanding that she join him in New York, although he had no prospects for supporting them. Her closest living male relative, John Young, also attainted of treason, was fighting with the British army against her country. Her nearest relative in Pennsylvania was Ann Young Smith, a young woman with pronounced Revolutionary principles, who although very sympathetic was not able to help her aunt. Betsy Stedman was still living with Elizabeth, and day after day the two women went over Elizabeth's situation, trying to decide what, if anything, she could or should do. What would become of them if the state should take Graeme Park away from her?

In her petition to the Supreme Executive Council, Elizabeth had pointed out that Graeme Park had been willed to her by her father in fee simple or "without any condition, limitation, or restriction." Henry, through his marriage to Elizabeth, had secured the right to manage and profit from that property but only during her lifetime. At his death, it did not become part of his estate but remained in her possession. At her death, since they had no children, it would descend to her family heirs, John and Ann Young, not Henry's.[23]

In late September the Council asked the Attorney General about the status of such estates held by husbands who were traitors, whether the state could confiscate them. Upon being informed that this kind of property was forfeited by acts of treason, the Councillors ordered the agents for seizing forfeited property to take these estates. Pennsylvania, however, would only have the use of them for a limited time until either the attainted husband or the owner-wife died.[24]

Although the justices of the Supreme Court officially decreed in early October that Elizabeth could keep the household items she had requested until they decided differently, the sale of the rest of her personal possessions was rapidly approaching, and she had little money to buy back her own property. On October 15, Agents for Confiscated Estates, George Smith and John Moore, sold her property at auction. The sale had been advertised in the Philadelphia newspapers and was well attended; forty-nine persons, besides Elizabeth, bought items. Local historians reported that her Quaker neighbors were so distressed by the injustice of the sale that they refused to attend. This is born out by the names of the purchasers. Of the 134 names on the 1779 township tax list, only eight men, whose religions are unknown, made purchases; this represented very substantial neighborhood support. General Daniel Roberdeau, a prominent Whig, attended the sale with her to lend moral support. Elizabeth herself was able to buy a few items, among them four rush bottom chairs, an easy chair, four beds, a tablecloth, and four pigs, but then her resources were exhausted. There is no record that any of her friends bought items for her, although perhaps some of the eight did. The sale brought £537.11.8 into the state's coffers of which Elizabeth contributed £53.8.6.[25] After everyone had left, Elizabeth and Betsy sat among her remaining possessions, hoping that she would have better luck keeping her real estate. Her only hope for their future was to be able to sell part of it and invest the proceeds in an annuity that would provide them with a steady income.

On the day of the sale, Vice President George Bryan advised the Agents for Forfeited Estates for Philadelphia County to let Elizabeth continue in her home. Council had ordered that the widows or wives of traitors be allowed to rent their former homes, and he pleaded that "The laws should be excuted without any rigor." Although Elizabeth was allowed to remain at Graeme Park, the rent was set at £260, a sum she would be hard pressed to raise, even though this was in depreciated paper money.[26]

As if this was not enough distress for any one woman to tolerate, Henry, now in New York City, was planning to leave the continent, and the Pennsylvania authorities were refusing permission for her to go see him one last time. Although she had made up her mind that she was not going to go to England despite his insistence that she accompany him, she at least wanted to say goodbye to her husband. When she applied to the Council for a pass to go within the enemy lines and return, her request was denied. The Council was readily permitting wives of Pennsylvania refugees to leave, but return was another matter. Richard Stockton made a second application for her, but the Council remained adamant. By the end of December Elizabeth was desperate. She had received six or eight letters from Henry telling her that he planned to leave immediately. At her wit's end, she wrote Benjamin Rush for help. The Board of War, Congress, and General Washington all could give passes, and she planned to address them all, if necessary. She did not like to bypass the Council, but she could not reconcile not taking leave of Henry. Two days later, she received another letter from Henry advising her that, having waited since October to see her, he intended to go the beginning of the new year. She wrote to Rush enclosing a letter for him to transmit to Washington asking the general for a pass. Although the general did not receive this request, he discovered her need through an intercepted letter and voluntarily sent her a pass. Elizabeth was able to meet Henry at Elizabeth Town point, New Jersey. She wrote

Mrs. Campbell that she had been gone six weeks, but it must have been less than this because she returned to Philadelphia on February 3 and presented a petition to the Assembly three days later.[27]

On her return journey, she spent a week at the home of Annis and Richard Stockton in Princeton, New Jersey. There she heard about Richard's recent surgery to remove a cancer from his lip and their hope that the doctor had removed it all. During surgery, without any anesthetic, he "did not utter a sigh, or move a muscle," Annis proudly reported to her friend. He was finally given a painkiller when the wound was being stitched.[28]

Back in Philadelphia, Elizabeth learned that her brother-in-law, James Young, had died. In his last years, he had been totally separated from both his children and was attended during his last illness by hired people. When his children were little, he had been "a very fond father . . . and a good husband," but the death of his wife had been "an ireparable Loss." He had opposed Anny's marriage to Dr. William Smith and John's adherence to the British and never had become reconciled to either.[29]

No sooner was Elizabeth at Graeme Park then she was once again embroiled in the Johnstone affair. Reed still had not named her publicly, although her identification was generally surmised. Shortly after the turn of the new year, Reed heard that Rev. William Smith had asserted that the conversation between Reed and Elizabeth had never taken place, that it was all fiction. Reed talked to General Roberdeau about the matter, suggesting in a not very subtle threat that this was a dangerous statement for her to make. He received in return a message from Elizabeth that she had never disavowed their meeting or empowered anyone else to make such a disclaimer for her. It was found that the story had started with a third party who had misunderstood a conversation with Elizabeth and passed on his misinterpretation to Smith who had then informed a "few" of his friends. Since Smith had not talked previously to Elizabeth about the story and since they had been friends for a long time, he undoubtedly had been delighted to believe it false. Within a few days of the unraveling of the gossip, Smith met Reed and explained to him what had happened.

Around this time, a newspaper report caused Elizabeth to announce publicly her identification as the woman innocently involved in the Reed-Johnstone affair. Johnstone had spoken to the House of Commons on November 26, 1778, to defend the "honour of the Commissioners," and a summary of his speech appeared in the Philadelphia newspapers. Beginning by blaming the commissioners' failure on the ministers who had sent them to America without adequate information, he continued that "he never made any overtures, as it is asserted, to Joseph Reed. There was no lady authorized by him to make any offers to him [Reed], and this he solemnly protested to be true." A month later a more complete transcription of Johnstone's speech appeared in the *Packet*, in which Johnstone did not deny that his conversation with Elizabeth had taken place. He only claimed that he had not given anyone authority to make an offer. Once again he repeated that he had "perfect proof . . . that Mr. Reed never understood any message or writing of mine as liable to that construction." He concluded that if Congress really had had a case against him, it should have made Reed reveal the woman's name, questioned her, sent her testimony to Johnstone for his reply, and then made a judgment. Since Congress did not go through this process, it was clear that the delegates knew they did not have a case.[30]

In early February, Elizabeth had presented to the General Assembly of Pennsylvania a petition asking that Graeme Park be restored to her. In her petition, she had repeated her arguments that Henry was not and never had been a subject of Pennsylvania. Therefore, he could not be guilty of treason to the state. Second, he had done nothing against the state. Furthermore, her father had left her Graeme Park in fee simple, which meant that any purchaser of it would only have its use during her lifetime. If it was confiscated by the state, her health, always fragile, would soon deteriorate and her life "be of short duration." No purchaser of Graeme Park would pay much to have the estate for only a few years. Therefore, in return for very little reward, the state would subject her to great suffering. During the previous adjournment of the Assembly, she had presented a petition to the Supreme Executive Council, she wrote, but that body, although disposed "to commiserate and assist her," had declared that the matter was not within their power. Therefore, she was asking the Assembly "to restore her to the use and absolute possession of her patrimony, which she [had] never forfeited by any act of her own."[31] After her petition was read and tabled, Elizabeth was informed by several members of the Assembly that the members who supported her and would like to help her were afraid that they would be censored if they spoke in her favor while she stood suspected of helping a British commissioner's attempt to corrupt a Pennsylvania official. The need to put to rest any ambiguity about the affair and to correct errors she saw in Reed's account convinced Elizabeth to go public with her own story.[32]

She began her explanation, published February 16, with the declaration that her statement was totally without political bias of any kind. She was "not influenced or directed by any person or persons in office, or expecting to be in office" in either the United States or Great Britain. Not one line of it had been "seen by, or read to an individual of either sex." She then narrated the story of her conversation with Johnstone. A copy of her letter to Reed of July 26 followed, but only after she berated Reed for his treatment of her. She had been given no inclination that he meant to publish the affair, she wrote. It is true that he had not disclosed her name, but his description clearly had identified her. She "was immediately pointed out," "obliged to hear a hundred rude and impertinent things said by people," and her reputation was tarnished. Among the most "mortifying insinuations" that she had had to endure was the intimation that she had acted to win a post or preferment from Johnstone for Henry. She did not deny that she had told Reed about Johnstone's conversation, but she challenged him now to say whether or not she had encouraged him to accept Johnstone's offers. Her letter then followed with its explanation that she had told Reed about her conversation with Johnstone only because Reed had first told her that he himself had received a letter from the commissioner. She had thought that that letter had already transmitted Johnstone's offer to Reed. The newspaper account concluded with a notarized oath that all of this had been written by her alone and was entirely true.

Elizabeth would have been better off to have softened her published criticism of Reed's behavior toward her. Her implication that he was no gentleman angered a very influential and vindictive man. Reed, chosen president of the Supreme Executive Council the previous December 1, now wrote to the General Assembly on February 23, challenging the truth of that part of Elizabeth's recent petition to the Assembly in which she had described the reaction of the councillors to her petition to them. He informed the representatives that the councillors present on June 26, 1778, remembered that the petition had been "barely read," and they had "expressed nothing." Furthermore, "it was not considered as beyond the reach of the Executive authority to restore her husband, both as to person & Estate, but it was very distant from their intention to do it." They did not refer her to the Assembly; they "gave no answer whatever to her memorial."[33]

The next day, Reed sought further revenge in the *Pennsylvania Gazette*. Annoyed with Elizabeth's accusing him publicly of treating her in an insensitive, cruel manner, he insisted that he had tried to protect her by concealing her name. Now that she had made her identity known, he wanted to present the whole story. He described Johnstone's letter to him of April 21, 1778, and his response, cleared with General Washington, which had probably never reached Johnstone. He then reprinted Elizabeth's letter to him asking for an interview and advice about her husband's situation. He agreed that her first words at their subsequent meeting were about Henry's proscription, but he went on to state that he had thought that question was secondary to Elizabeth's true reason for requesting the interview, i.e., Johnstone's proposition. In this version he quoted Elizabeth as praising Johnstone as a man of "great abilities and address" with "many amiable qualities." He repeated the same narrative he had given in the story published in July 1778 about their meeting. Answering her request, he granted that she had said nothing approving the proposition, but then he added that she had also "expressed no unfavorable sentiment of Governor Johnstone" either. He told of his note to his woman friend who was going to New York but included more of the woman's conversation with Johnstone, this time disparaging Elizabeth. He claimed that Johnstone had said that Elizabeth's "misfortunes had so affected her mind and spirits, that he never thought her capable of a confidential conversation." Reed also claimed that he was not responsible for Elizabeth having been identified as the woman involved. She herself was to blame. She had dropped the note Reed had written her agreeing to their meeting, and it had been read by several people before an acquaintance had retrieved it.[34] He ended with the narrative of Dr. Smith's involvement stressing that Smith had been "very active and diligent" in denying Elizabeth's conversation with Reed. He had spoken to General Roberdeau about it rather than to Smith himself because he did "not often converse with" Smith. Nevertheless, Smith had sought him out and explained how his misunderstanding had arisen. Reed had felt himself "embarrassed by the conversation" and was "not sorry when it closed." All in all, it was a very nasty letter.

　　　Reed's uncalled for reference to Elizabeth's possible mental instability and his superfluous inclusion of Smith's involvement so angered the provost that he wrote a reply.[35] His conversation with Reed had been, "upon a point of honour in our private capacity as gentlemen," Smith wrote, implying that a gentleman would not have repeated it in a newspaper. Furthermore, there had been no point in publishing it. Since he had, however, Smith must give the details to correct Reed's story. He then explained painstakingly about his misquoting Elizabeth, her correcting him, and his subsequent explaining of this to Reed. He denied that he had been "active" in propagating Elizabeth's supposed rejection of any conversation between herself and Reed. He elaborated why Reed's account was unkind to both Elizabeth and himself and promised that he would publish another letter defending his own patriotism.

The last word on this subject was had by Reed. In September he published *Remarks on Governor Johnstone's Speech in Parliament with a Collection of all the Letters and Authentic Papers* . . . , a long collection of documents written by himself, Elizabeth, and Johnstone relative to the affair. Perhaps Reed realized by then that both his and Elizabeth's letters published in February had not been to his credit because he omitted them.[36]

This confrontation with Joseph Reed not only had been embarrassing for Elizabeth but also had made an enemy of a very unforgiving man at a juncture when she needed his help, not his opposition. Reed had become the leader of one of the two political parties that had developed since the British left Pennsylvania. For the next two years, he would use all his influence to prevent any government action at all merciful toward her.

9

Between Constitutionalists and Anti-Constitutionalists

By February 1779, Pennsylvania was entering upon one of the worst periods in its history. Class divisions had intensified. War profiteers were becoming rich while laborers and small businessmen were suffering from runaway inflation. Prices soared as the value of paper money, both continental and Pennsylvania, slid downward toward oblivion. Meanwhile, the government passed ineffective and unenforced measures, which did nothing to improve the situation. Not understanding what was causing their problems, many Philadelphians blamed those they perceived as Tories. They reasoned that since the faltering economy prevented Pennsylvania from prosecuting the war effectively, those who favored the British must be responsible for the economic difficulties and should, therefore, be prosecuted to the fullest. Angered by a do-nothing government, the poor, bolstered by the militia, took to the streets, threatening people they perceived as Tories or war profiteers. The twin questions of what to do about the economy and how to treat the Tories remaining in the state divided the two political parties that had coalesced around the Pennsylvania state constitution of 1776. Because of Henry's actions and because of her own connection with a corrupt British commissioner, Elizabeth's efforts to win the return of her property became involved in the party strife, and she had to play politics to succeed.

By 1779, the state's leaders, the Whigs of the pre-independence period, had split into supporters and opponents of the Pennsylvania constitution of 1776. Joseph Reed had become a powerful supporter or constitutionalist. Because Elizabeth had angered this influential political figure, Reed would oppose her every move for the next two years. When he was in power, he tried to punish her. When he eventually lost power, she was able to have her real estate revested in herself. But even then, he managed to throw a small roadblock in her way.

During October 1778, while Elizabeth was suffering the seizure and sale of her personal property, a heavily contested election had chosen a legislature consisting of over half new members. This Assembly contained a third or better anti-constitutionalists, and the political divisions over the constitution, which had lain dormant during the occupation of Philadelphia, once again became acrimonious. The anti-constitutionalists were numerous enough to persuade the Assemblymen to schedule a referendum to decide whether another constitutional convention should meet to revise or rewrite the document. The constitutionalists then stirred up a campaign that covered the Assemblymen's desks with petitions containing over ten thousand names, urging them to cancel the referendum. Arguing that they were responding to public desires, the constitutionalist majority in the Assembly rescinded its previous decision, and a constitutional convention would not be scheduled again during the war.

Eventually, in 1790, a new constitution would be written for the state, but meanwhile, the issue sundered state politics. In February 1779, the opponents of the constitution, led by lawyer James Wilson, formed the Republican Society, whose members blamed Pennsylvania's difficulties on the constitution and its supporters. Among the Republicans were many of Elizabeth's friends: George Meade, Benjamin Rush, Robert Morris, Henry Hill, Francis Hopkinson, and Thomas Smith, brother of the Rev. William Smith. Daniel Roberdeau, George Bryan, Thomas Paine, and other constitutionalists responded by forming the Constitutional Society. Its members argued that the Republican call for a constitutional convention was an act of disaffection because it was dividing the society and distracting the people from the war effort. Hence the Republicans must be Tories. Their reasoning was tortured, of course, since the Republican anti-constitutionalist leaders had been as strong proponents of the Declaration of Independence as the Constitutional Society leaders, but they argued that the Republicans were fair-weather friends who had changed their minds when the going became difficult.[1]

The men who opposed the constitution generally urged more leniency toward the disaffected than did the constitutionalists. They recognized gradations of objectionable activity by the disaffected ranging from pacifism to fighting with the British, and they wanted corresponding gradations of punishments administered. Pacifists, for example, should be punitively taxed to help pay war expenses, but they should be permitted to remain in the state as productive citizens with their civil rights protected. The constitutionalists, in contrast, tended to lump all their opponents together. All who had opposed independence or the Pennsylvania constitution, who were pacifists or neutrals, who wanted more merciful treatment of the non-dangerous disaffected, or who were war profiteers were put in the same package with traitors charged with serious offenses. And the constitutionalists tended to call them all Tories or disaffected and to demand harsh punishments for them. "All who were less violent and bigoted than themselves, were branded as Tories," complained a contemporary.[2] Whenever the Assembly had a large minority or a majority of anti-constitutionalists, the government's treatment of the non-violent disaffected tended to be tempered with mercy, although this was not always true. It was also influenced by where the British army was operating and what the public pressure was demanding.

The Assembly of 1778–79 would probably have been more sympathetic to Elizabeth's petition had she never been involved with Johnstone's duplicity. During the following year, it would pass special acts alleviating punishments for three attainted persons, but the legislators stalled when it came to helping Elizabeth Fergusson. She and her friends were unable to win enough votes to give Graeme Park back to her. This was to a large extent the legislators' reaction to public pressure. On the same day that Elizabeth had submitted her petition to the Assembly, February 6, 1779, "A Whig Citizen" in the *Packet* took the Assembly to task for measures it had passed relieving two men of their attainders. Reynold Keen and Albertson Walton both had been ordered to report for treason trials but had failed to appear by their deadlines. On August 21, 1778, they had applied to the Assembly for mercy, but the Assemblymen had dismissed their petitions. A proper response, agreed "Whig Citizen," because it was the responsibility of the executive, not of the legislature, to grant pardons. After the new more Republican Assembly had been elected in October 1778, the men had applied again. This time bills for their relief were read and passed into laws, to the great disapproval of the letter writer.

"Whig Citizen" explained how the Republicans were able to win these measures in the face of their minority status by comparing the two Houses of Assembly. The previous legislature, he wrote, had been composed of "an unleavened body of determined Whigs," "plain men without the advantage of refined education." The Republicans in the new Assembly (of 1778–79) were able to win the assent of the majority by their "superior address" which enabled them to carry these acts through, under the "acquiescnce of the . . . unsuspecting, country gentlemen." "Whig Citizen" further suggested that these acts were designed to be precedents for the return of all the refugees, among whom were many friends and relatives of the Republicans.

Such a condemnation of their proceedings added to the reluctance of some Assemblymen to grant Elizabeth her petition. The legislators who had just been called country bumpkins for allowing the city slickers to put one over on them in the cases of Keen and Walton could not turn around and give another act of mercy to Elizabeth. Furthermore, her involvement with Duché's letter and Johnstone's proposals made even friendly Assemblymen less willing to help her than they otherwise might have been because they did not want to be tarred with the same brush.

The majority in the Assembly of 1778–79 was also influenced by Joseph Reed who was seeking revenge. At the end of February 1779, only a few weeks after Elizabeth published her version of the Johnstone affair, James Abercrombie advised her that her petition to the Assembly would be "in vain" because Reed, her "professed enemy," controlled the decisions of the constitutionalists in the Assembly. He told her to come to town immediately and consult a lawyer. Her application should be made to the Supreme Court, he wrote, which would be more sympathetic to her plight.[3]

Confirming Abercrombie's opinion, on March 16, the Assembly had Elizabeth's petition read a second time and decided not to refer it to a committee for further consideration. The legislature adjourned on April 5 without taking up her request again. This meant that it would carry over to the next session, scheduled to begin on August 30. Since it had not been completely rejected, Elizabeth continued to hope for a favorable decision when the Assembly reconvened, provided Graeme Park was not sold before then. Before it adjourned, however, the Assembly had passed a law on March 29 that ordered the President, Vice President, and Council to sell "by public auction to the highest bidder all the forfeited estates of traitors" and deposit the money in the state treasury. Claimants against these estates were given six months to file their claims.[4] Time was running out. Graeme Park might be lost to Elizabeth before the Assembly met again.[5]

Unfortunately for Elizabeth, the new Supreme Executive Council, consisted largely of constitutionalists also under the control of Joseph Reed, its new president.[6] Although George Bryan, the new vice president, had indicated friendship for Elizabeth in the past, there was little he could do, even if he wanted to help her, and there is no indication that he did. In accord with the law passed March 29, the Council ordered its secretary, who was also the keeper of the register for forfeited estates, to give notice that a group of estates would be sold soon by public auction. To Elizabeth's despair, the list included Graeme Park. Since the estates were to be "exonerated & discharged of all former claims or demands made under any of the said Traitors," creditors were called upon to make their demands promptly.[7] The secretary wasted no time posting a notice of the impending sale and warning to creditors in the *Pennsylvania Gazette*.

Elizabeth read every word trying to determine how she could prevent Graeme Park from being sold. Two parts of the order were of special interest. One provision required any claims against the estates to be made to the Supreme Court and specifically mentioned claims of a "femme covert," or married woman. Richard Stockton advised Elizabeth to apply to the Supreme Court immediately under that provision, knowing that the Chief Justice would be more inclined to favor her claim than either the Assembly or the Council. Rev. Smith, however, advised her to address the Council again because Reed's letter to the Assembly of February 23 had implied that "the power of Redress lay with the Council." In desperation, Elizabeth wrote Smith that she did not know where to apply for redress because she could not tell "where the Power is lodged." She had not seen Reed's letter, so she could not "write a Memorial hinging on the contents of it."[8] At the same time, she knew that she had few, if any, friends in the Council, so that applying again to that body seemed hopeless. The second part of the order that might help Elizabeth was its schedule. The Assembly's act allowed creditors six months to present their claims, so that Graeme Park would not be sold immediately. During the elapsed time, more appeals could be made or perhaps the Assembly might decide after all to revest her property in herself. The following October a new Assembly would be elected, and more anti-constitutionalists might be chosen. Any delay was a possible advantage for Elizabeth.

But events in Pennsylvania were proceeding to a climax in ways that would not benefit the desires of one frightened woman. Matters would become much more threatening before there was a turn around in Elizabeth's favor. The Assembly in 1778 had passed various laws to curb hoarding and market manipulation, but the laws had not been enforced effectively. Meeting in January 1779 to demand higher wages, nearly 150 sailors had rioted and unrigged several ships.[9] In March, four petitions containing over 1,000 signatures had been presented to the Assembly complaining about house rents and monopolistic practices. One of these petitions had blamed the disaffected. Before adjourning April 1 for the summer, the Assembly had passed a law forbidding forestalling and regrating of food products, but there were no provisions for enforcement of its stiff penalties. The Assembly also had done nothing further about the disaffected still in Pennsylvania whom the people blamed for their troubles. Between April 1 and May 1, 1779, the continental currency depreciated in relation to specie from 17 to 1 to 24 to 1. Angry citizens, whose wages were not increasing in proportion to the decline in the value of money, saw their purchasing power fall disastrously and took matters into their own hands.

During the Assembly's adjournment, Philadelphia militiamen, who had complained a year earlier about their low pay and the economic situation for their families, addressed President Reed and the Supreme Executive Council. They reviewed how they had answered the call to arms ever since 1776, only to return each time to find inflated prices and their businesses taken over by others. All the Assembly had done was pass laws permitting the hiring of substitutes and fining those who did not answer the call. Fines were no use, however, because the trade manipulators could pay their fines for a year with the proceeds of one deal. "The Midling and poor" had no choices; they either were ruined by heavy fines or answered the call to arms and risked their families' starvation while they were away. The petition warned the Council that the militiamen had arms and knew how to use them. They wanted the Council to persuade the Assembly to enact stiffer laws.[10]

Without an avenue for governmental redress until the lawmaking body reconvened August 30, the suffering poor and the militia gathered in the streets in uncontrolled crowds, milling around and distributing threatening handbills. Angry people rounded up suspected Tories ominously menacing them until the authorities jailed the frightened victims for their protection. There they remained sometimes for days, until the Council, trying to put some order into these illegal arrests, ordered the magistrates to investigate. Men with clubs visited storekeepers whose prices were deemed too high in order to force them to lower their charges. A major riot threatened.

At a large public meeting May 25, 1779, Daniel Roberdeau, Elizabeth's friend and Constitutional Party leader, told the people that they had a right to defend themselves against those who were "getting rich by sucking the blood" of the country. Led by Roberdeau, the crowd blamed the merchant Robert Morris, a leading member of the Republican Society, for some of the price increases, demanded that the price of necessities be rolled back to the level of the previous January 1, and declared that anyone "inimical to the interest and independence of the United States" should be expelled from Pennsylvania.[11]

After the meeting, a Philadelphia committee joined by local committees in all the counties tried to roll back prices, month by month, to January's level,[12] taking extra-legal measures against those who refused to cooperate. The militiamen threatened that if the committees should fail, the militia's "*drum shall beat to arms*,"[13] but the effort was doomed to failure. The Assembly had already considered and rejected price controls because products for sale would flow where the prices were better in neighboring states, leaving Pennsylvanians without the necessities. By mid-September, the committees, too, would reach the same conclusion, but until then, crowds harassed the merchants and anyone else they considered to be Tories.

The average citizen did not understand that the major cause of the economic distress was the continued printing of worthless paper money. Reed and others asked the Continental Congress to decrease its issuance, but the Congressmen replied that they had to print the money to pay the costs of war and that the real causes of the problem were selfish individuals. Many people agreed with Congress that the economic situation was due to businessmen who refused to accept continental money at face value or who manipulated the market.

At Graeme Park, Elizabeth read about the unsettling events in her newspapers and heard about them from visiting friends. Adding to her many fears, the Grand Jury for the City and County of Philadelphia on June 10 recommended that the wives and children of exiles with the British be forced to leave the state. Many of the absent husbands were in New York City, and the correspondence of their wives in Philadelphia was believed to transmit valuable information about the conditions in Pennsylvania. The Grand Jury argued that the best way to end the correspondence was to end the separation of the spouses. But Henry was no longer in New York City nor was anyone else Elizabeth knew well. She certainly did not want to be sent there.[14]

Although Elizabeth's memorials contained the expected disclaimers acknowledging her ignorance and incompetence as a woman, she was becoming quite knowledgeable about the law as it pertained to her sex. She read all the published minutes of the Assembly and Council and their various laws, orders, resolves, and proclamations, remembered what she read and the appropriate legal vocabulary, and learned from discussions with lawyers. Thus in a letter to Rev. William Smith in early June, she said that she would take Stockton's advice and write the Chief Justice, but she wanted to word her appeal to differ from the various appeals she had written to the Assembly and Council. In these memorials, she had "beg'd as a Matter of favor" from her "peculiar Situation": Henry was not a citizen; he had done nothing wrong; she had resided continuously on the premises and was not planning to leave; she had always been devoted to the colonial cause. She had "hop'd they would be content with the Movables already Seiz'd" and abstain from taking her real estate.

In writing to the Chief Justice, however, she wished to accomplish something different. The Assembly's law relative to attainder had given the Chief Justice the power to make provision from the confiscated estates "for the Wives and Children of the Attainted." But Elizabeth did not want, at that stage, to ask for this concession. To do so, she believed, would weaken her position. She argued that the Assembly's provision only applied to the women who owned no property in their own names, so that they "and their unhappy posterity were left entirely to the Mercy of the Court." She believed that her case was different from theirs because her father had willed her Graeme Park in fee simple. She wanted the Chief Justice to recognize this distinction. To do so, she proposed to ask him only to explain her rights under the law: "Namely that He will be good enough to Answer to this plain Question. Have the States or the State of Pennsylvania a power to sell an Estate of a Woman (the Fee-Simple Vested in Her) for the Attainder of Her Husband?" By asking him this question, she would be forcing him to recognize what she already knew, the rights of a woman who owned property. Under Pennsylvania law, Henry, by marriage, had acquired the right to manage and profit from the estate, but its ownership remained with her and her heirs. He could not sell it without her permission. When she died, it would descend to her heirs, not to Henry or his heirs. This meant that the state had acquired by attainder only Henry's right to occupy and manage Graeme Park as long as she lived, and that was all the state could sell. This would weaken the property's attractiveness to prospective buyers. She had concluded that her case was not "so dark and Dreary" as that of propertyless women, and she did not want to be identified with them.[15]

Elizabeth's letter to Chief Justice McKean, presented by William White, the rector of Christ Church, does not survive, but White's report to her relates McKean's reaction.[16] He said there was no question about her owning the property in fee simple and agreed that this condition should be clearly stated in the advertisement for the property; an order for that purpose should be given by the Supreme Court. Since all the justices would not meet until September, he intended to block a sale before then. He told her to send the court a claim in legal form setting forth her father's legacy to her in fee simple and relating her marriage with Henry Fergusson. Elizabeth wanted the advertisement for Graeme Park to be accompanied by this information because she hoped that no one would want to buy property he could own only for the lifetime of a middle-aged woman in poor health. Furthermore, the law governing such purchases forbade the buyer "to commit waste." Having to preserve the property would make it even less attractive. If the worst happened and the property was sold, she hoped to be able to buy it herself at the lowest price possible.

White had also asked McKean two questions for Elizabeth. First she wanted to know whether her applying to the Supreme Court would preclude her applying elsewhere for redress. The Chief Justice said "by no means" and referred her to the Assembly, which would meet in September. Elizabeth also wanted to know whether the Assembly or the Supreme Executive Council had the power to return her property to her, but McKean did not know the answer to this question. He said that such confusion would arise in a new government. If she should apply to the wrong place, "none can be offended" because her "object is not to decide on the merits of such a Question."

McKean sent Elizabeth the message that for the cases of women whose husbands' property was confiscated and for whom the law had stipulated that the Supreme Court should provide, the Court had "adopted the rule prescribed by law in the cases of those who die intestate." In such circumstances, the law "allows to the widow one-third & in case of no children, one half. . . . From this rule they deviated in certain circumstances & [he] mentioned the Education & rank in life of the party concerned as causes that had induced the Court to allow more than" that. This practice was contrary to the understanding of the Supreme Executive Council, which informed the Agents for Forfeited Estates in Chester County in August that "Dower at Common Law is Forfeited by the attainder of the Husband." The dower itself might have been forfeited, but the Supreme Court was giving back to such women at least an equivalent sum and in some cases more.[17] Elizabeth had also asked about some oats and wheat that the Court had set aside for her use and that had been sold inadvertently with her personal property by the state. She certainly could use the £134 they had brought at the sale. McKean reassured her that if she did not receive the profit the Court had intended, the justices "would rectify the mistake."

In June, Annis Stockton, who had known Joseph Reed ever since he had been a law clerk in Richard Stockton's law office from 1758 to 1763,[18] wrote him reminding him of their many shared memories and asking for his favorable consideration of Elizabeth's predicament. He responded that he "sincerely pit[ied] & sympathize[d] with her," but if he could not do what Elizabeth wanted, it should be "imputed to the Restraints of publick Character which sometimes clash with private Feelings." He then commented that Elizabeth was lucky that the power to provide her relief was "lodged in the Hands of gentlemen of Tenderness & Consideration who have in all Cases hither to shown the most favourable Attention to Distress like hers, & it cannot be doubted they will show a proper Liberality of Sentiment when her Case comes judicially before them." Although this sounds as though he was commending the Supreme Court for its merciful interpretation of the laws, this was an ironic statement actually criticizing the Court. His true feelings had been expressed not two months earlier, when Reed had chided the Chief Justice for the Supreme Court's giving "too easy an Ear . . . to the Applications of those who are dissafected to their Country." The Court's "Error of extreme Compassion . . . had a Tendency to weaken Governmt, & encourage the political Sinners of this State," Reed had written. McKean, however, had paid no attention to Reed. The Supreme Court discharged about twenty men accused of treason only three days later.[19]

Annis Stockton had taken time from caring for her husband to write the letter to Reed. Richard Stockton's lip cancer had spread to his throat, and primitive medical advice was subjecting him to a very uncomfortable treatment. Morning and night, Stockton had to stand over a burning concoction of "strong spirits, set on fire with a quantity of salt in it." Annis thought that the swelling was caused by "his very low diet in the winter." She asked Elizabeth to send her a "treatise of the Effect of Salt water in such cases."[20]

Throughout the summer, crowds roamed the streets of Philadelphia carrying out their own justice, while the government did little to control the extra-legal activity. After a particularly unruly meeting interrupted by men armed with staves, an observer commented that "we have no government, and, . . . no laws, for every man who takes a club in his hand to town meetings . . . undertakes to be governor: and our executive powers submit very patiently to their new masters." The "executive powers" or Council submitted because they had been elected by constitutionalists who were inciting and leading the crowds in their mischief. The constitutionalists hoped to blame the economic crisis they had been unable to stem on Republican merchants, such as Robert Morris, so that the people would reject the Republican members of the Assembly in the fall elections, thereby ending all question of revising the constitution.[21] There had been "riot for some time past," the observer complained. "There are few unhappier Cities, on this Globe than Philada.," reported another.[22]

Meanwhile, in an unrelated case, the Chief Justice rendered an opinion that also supported Elizabeth's arguments about Henry's attainder. The Council had asked McKean about ex-Pennsylvanians who had been captured at sea on privateers commissioned by the British to prey upon United States shipping. Should these men be treated as traitors or pirates? He ruled that "all those who did not, on the Eleventh of February, 1777, [when formal government started in the independent state of Pennsylvania] or since, owe any allegiance, are to be deemed Prisoners of War; . . . those falling within that description, may be proceeded against as Traitors." The principle of determining allegiance as due from all Pennsylvania inhabitants on and after February 11, 1777, would have released Henry from attainder, since he had left Pennsylvania long before that date. Elizabeth had argued all along that Henry was not a citizen of Pennsylvania and hence could not be accused of treason against it, but there is no indication that she or her friends ever quoted McKean's opinion in her case.[23] Since it was not published in the newspapers, she probably never heard of it. Nevertheless, if

Henry had reported for treason trial before his deadline, he probably could have won his release, just as Elizabeth had tried to persuade him.

Adopting McKean's advice, Elizabeth had a lawyer, probably Andrew Robeson, draw up a claim to be presented to the Supreme Court. This was the only remonstrance that was not written by Elizabeth herself. In it, she asked the Court formally to confirm her fee simple title and her husband's very limited right in it. This would require the Agents for Forfeited Estates to advertise Graeme Park with the proviso that possession would only be for Elizabeth Fergusson's lifetime.[24]

She was beginning to think that there was nothing she could do to stop the sale from taking place and started asking friends for advice as to how she should go about trying to buy the Park herself. Roberdeau wrote warning her not to interfere in any way with the agent selling the estate. Recently, the nephew of an attainted person had tried to persuade an agent to sell his uncle's estate to him for a much reduced price. This became known, and it was suspected that the nephew really was acting for his uncle in New York. As a result, the nephew could not buy the property. Roberdeau also told Elizabeth not to have any "Tories" present at the sale with her if she attended. "The very shadow of any of them would tend to obscure [her] Patriotism." He extended the term Tory even to "Whigs not of the first Growth."[25]

Trying to touch all bases, Elizabeth wrote to the Assembly when it gathered in early September 1779. She reminded the members that the petition she had presented in person to that body in February had been set aside to another session. She asked them to revive and give it favorable consideration, stressing again that Graeme Park was hers in fee simple and that Henry was not a citizen of Pennsylvania.[26] Over and over again she drove these points home to anyone who would listen.

Searching for any influence she could possibly extend to her case, she wrote John Dickinson, whom she had known for years but had not seen since she had visited him in December 1776 at his home, Fair-Hill. She sent him copies of all the various papers pertinent to her case, her petitions, and writings of other people favorable to her, asking him to read them and "say something in [her] behalf" to members of the Assembly. The seizing of her personal estate and the inflation had made her affairs "so Embarassed" that if she was "not Speedily Redressed; Want and Distress must compose the Remaining part of [her] Days." She was already assured of the support of the assemblymen from the city and of neighbor and friend

Robert Lollar, a representative from Philadelphia County. But it was the back-country members whose votes she was unsure of. She referred to her political situation, caught between the two parties: any point made by one party would automatically be opposed by the other, no matter how valid it was. Dickinson answered sympathetically but begged off, saying he had no influence. Elizabeth took this as a polite way of declining her request.[27] Actually, Dickinson may have been speaking the truth. Roberdeau had warned her against Whigs "not of the first Growth," which included Dickinson who had opposed both the Declaration of Independence and the Pennsylvania constitution. Given the political situation, his support might have done her more harm than good, but she would not forgive him for not trying.

The Assembly adjourned on October 10, without taking any action on her petition and once again referred it to the next Assembly, which would meet after the election. Elizabeth knew that "referral" was not as good as "recommended" would have been, but it was too much to expect the legislators to do anything about her plea during the Assembly's final weeks of existence. They were absorbed in trying to provide legislation to answer the bitter complaints of the people, but the legislators' process moved too slowly for the militiamen. They wanted action, not debate. On October 4, the months of crowd activity, the distress of the people about the inflated prices and depreciated money, the constant complaints about the government's ineffective action, the vehement denunciation by the constitutionalists of their political rivals—all finally had come to a head in a violent encounter called the Fort Wilson Riot.

The Philadelphia militiamen, blaming the disaffected for the economic distress and despairing of the courts ever punishing them, had taken matters into their own hands. They chose one man from each company to be a Committee of Privates whose job was to "take up all the Tories & Quakers." They also resolved to send away "the wives and children of those men who had gone with the British, or were within the British lines." Focusing on James Wilson, prominent Pennsylvania lawyer, member of Congress, and signer of the Declaration of Independence, who had started the Republican Society and who had successfully defended many men accused of treason, the militiamen covered the city with broadsides threatening Wilson. On October 4, a crowd of militiamen picked up four Quakers whom they accused of opposing price controls and led them about the city with the drums beating "The Rogues' March." As they marched, the militiamen passed Wilson's house. It is not clear what happened next, but someone fired a shot, both sides exchanged bullets, and six or seven people were killed. The militiamen broke into Wilson's house and reached the stairs leading to the second floor where Wilson and his friends had retreated. Only the appearance of President Joseph Reed and others on horseback stopped further bloodshed.[28]

After this shocking attack on James Wilson, who was not a traitor, the Assembly acted quickly to calm the people before another outbreak took place. Even if the Assemblymen had had the time to consider Elizabeth's petition, they would not have dared grant her request for fear the militiamen would think them too lenient with the disaffected. Instead, they passed a strict measure against forestalling and engrossing, thus empowering the Councillors and the Supreme Court justices to investigate suspected disaffected persons and bind them with a security guarantee or banish them, and then increased the fine for not turning out for militia duty. A few days later, a new government was elected, one completely controlled by the constitutionalists, Assembly as well as Council. Reed once again was chosen president. George Bryan resigned the vice presidency and later in the year became a Supreme Court justice. Elizabeth's one friendly voice in the Council was now gone. Robert Lollar was re-elected to the Assembly, however, and continued to be her supporter.

Elizabeth wasted no time addressing the new House. On October 27, she sent Lollar a new memorial to present if he thought desirable. It was a short communication, mentioning her previous petitions, which had been referred to the new House, and asking the members to "give her full Power over her own Patrimonial Property."[29] To make sure that Graeme Park would not be sold while the Assembly was considering her petition, she wrote again to the Council, asking them to prevent its sale while the Assembly was considering her case.[30]

Although the new assemblymen ignored Elizabeth's memorial, one of the first measures they took indirectly helped her cause. They passed an act appropriating the College of Philadelphia to the state and turning it into a university. To pay the salaries of the administrators of the college and to support the Charitable School, the act reserved to the university enough of the confiscated estates to create an annual income of £1500. The Council then ordered the Agents for Forfeited Estates to postpone further sales until the councillors had set aside the necessary estates. Any postponement of sales gave Elizabeth and her friends more time to win support for her petition. In addition, since the state had to guarantee the titles to all estates sold under its authority, the agents were ordered to describe fully all property sold to prevent future litigation. This implemented Elizabeth's wish that Graeme Park be clearly described as available only for her lifetime.[31]

Unfortunately, the Council countermanded the postponement of sales of certain estates, including Graeme Park. On March 10, the Council discussed the question of property, like Elizabeth's, that had been acquired by attainted persons through marriage. Since the ownership was not freehold, they had been more "burdensome" than "profitable to the State." Instead of simply giving them back to the wives, the Council ordered the Agents for Forfeited Estates to proceed with sales of all estates held by attainted persons in less than fee simple. By May 8, the Council was ready to resume the sales of all the estates, at least in Philadelphia City and County, and on May 12, they extended the order to all the counties.[32]

Elizabeth was frantic. On May 16, 1780, George Meade, Thomas Franklin, and William White presented a petition to the Council reporting that Mrs. Fergusson was in "utmost distress." When her personal property had been sold, she had been allowed to live on her estate, paying an annual rent for it. But the high rent, the sum equivalent to the current cost of one hundred bushels of wheat, together with the taxes were more than she could pay. In addition, she had been given the use of the furniture for two rooms, upon giving security for its value. General Roberdeau had bound himself to the state as her guarantor, but now she was not able to pay for the furniture's deterioration. Roberdeau had told the petitioners that it would be useless to apply to the Council, but the petitioners trusted to the Councillors' "Justice & Mercy." Roberdeau, unfortunately, was a better predictor. The Council refused to do anything, saying that the case of Mrs. Fergusson had been repeatedly before the assemblymen, "who are best entitled to dispose of the property of the State,"[33] and they had not thought proper to make special allowance for her. The Council referred her to the Agents for Forfeited Estates for mercy.

Two days later, five friends of Elizabeth appeared before the Assembly asking that body to favor Elizabeth's petition. These were the men who most consistently tried to help her: Elias Boudinot, Thomas Franklin, Rev. William White, George Meade, and someone identified in the minutes as Mr. Hopkins, probably a misprint for Francis Hopkinson. Their description of the precariousness of her situation was so moving that the Assembly finally acted, and quickly, before the Council could have its agents sell Graeme Park. Within a week, they read her petition a second time, referred it to a committee, and then adopted the committee's recommendation that the sale of Graeme Park be deferred and that she be permitted to live on the estate rent free, paying the taxes. But the assemblymen did not pass a law making this provision for her. They only resolved to recommend to the Council that it be done.[34]

Even though the councillors had told her that the Assembly had proper jurisdiction, they were furious that the legislature had recommended relief. When the Council heard the Assembly's recommendations for mercy, the members sent to the legislature a very harsh objection, signed by Reed. The message began by objecting to the "interference of [the] Hon'ble House in matters merely of an Executive nature" that the Council had already taken care of; this, in spite of the Council's minutes that said the responsibility for disposing of the state's property belonged to the Assembly. Accusing the assemblymen of being moved by pity and the search for popularity, Reed warned them that they would attract an "insupportable burthen" from the cases that would be laid before them.[35] It was a stinging rebuke, Reed's anger revealed in every word.

Chastened, the Assembly resolved on September 17 that the constitution had separated the powers of government, and one branch should not infringe upon the powers of the other. The matter of petitions pertained correctly to the executive department. If the House dispensed with the punishments of the laws in individual cases, all complaints would be directed to House, diminishing the courts and the Supreme Executive Council. It would violate the principal of free government by which punishments should be few and moderate but certain. In spite of this promise to be good, the Assembly would, on occasion, continue to relieve petitioners of the full force of the laws.

The Council had reprimanded the Assemblymen for being moved by "the importunity of the petitioners" and weakening the force of the laws by making exceptions to them, implying that any pardons should be made sparingly, if at all. The Council itself, however, used its power frequently to grant pardons. For example, on July 10, 1780, the councillors used the authority that the Assembly had recognized as constitutionally vested in them to pardon two men attainted of treason. These two young men had joined the British during the occupation of the city as troopers and then deserted upon the evacuation. They had been tried and sentenced to death, but Council decided that since they were "young" and had "good characters," clemency was justified.[36] Certainly, Elizabeth was more deserving of mercy than these men, yet her requests were scorned by the Council, clearly reflecting Reed's enmity.

Elizabeth was having trouble just living from day to day. She was not farming the land herself, and the sum her tenants paid was hardly enough to cover the interest on her debts. Yet she had to pay both rent to the state and taxes, because the Council refused to abide by the Assembly's recommendation that she not be required to pay rent. The tax bill for Graeme Park in 1780 was £464. This was the highest tax assessed in the county by £200, possibly intended to force her to leave.[37] George Meade appealed to the tax assessor, who lowered the rate to £300 to be paid in two monthly installments.

Meade and William White also had gone to see the Chief Justice about Elizabeth's problems. McKean had told them that he and George Bryan, now a justice of the Supreme Court, would discuss the disposition of the furniture and the wheat. McKean had intimated to Meade that the Court's decision about both would be favorable. They had also discussed the possibility of the Assembly revesting Graeme Park in Elizabeth, where-upon the Chief Justice had indicated that he thought there would be no difficulty in securing this, if Elizabeth would promise not to sell it.[38] Therein lay a problem for Elizabeth. Her only potential way of earning enough to live was to sell the estate, invest the return, and live on the income. By then, she had borrowed so much money that it would take two-thirds of the proceeds of a sale just to pay her debts.

As some of her problems were being eased, another even worse threat arose—the possibility of being sent behind the British lines. The continued presence in Pennsylvania of the wives and children of men who were in New York had caused problems for the state government for several years. Officials, both national and state, feared that communications between husbands and wives would transmit intelligence or counterfeit money, and they had tried unsuccessfully to discourage them. The letters that seemed so dangerous to authorities, however, were links between loved ones and to stop them entirely would seem insensitive and cruel. The government, therefore, had issued warnings, but had taken no enforcement steps. In June 1779, the Grand Jury for the City and County of Philadelphia had pointed out that the best way to solve the problem was to put families back together so that communications would not be necessary. Send the wives and children to New York, the Grand Jurors had recommended. That will stop the correspondence.

Nothing was done until the following March when the journals of one of the wives were intercepted and revealed that she had helped prisoners go to New York. On March 7, 1780, the Supreme Executive Council announced that the wives of men with the British would be given passports to go within the enemy lines to their husbands before April 15. If they did not go, further measures would be taken for this purpose.[39] Henry had long since gone to England, and Elizabeth had no desire to leave Philadelphia. She stayed at home very quietly, hoping she would be forgotten.

Since most of the wives followed suit, by June, very few had left the state. The Council on June 6 ordered that the wives and children of men who had joined the British must leave within ten days or "be proceeded against as enemies of the state." Elizabeth, panic stricken, took the step that must have been hardest for her; she wrote to Joseph Reed, pleading for leniency, and asked Dr. William Smith, husband of her niece, to deliver it. Humbling herself, she begged the President to exert his influence in her favor. Since she knew no one in New York, she was not guilty of carrying on dangerous correspondence with anyone there. She had made no friends among the British military when they were in Philadelphia. How could she survive? She had no resources. Pennsylvania was her home. When Smith presented her letter to Reed and told him who it was from, his first reaction was impatience. Mrs. Fergusson and her "friends had been too importunate with respect to [her] affairs in general," he told Smith. After reading Elizabeth's letter, he said he would present it to the Council, but that nothing could be done. He explained the reasons for the order and said that exceptions could not be made even for those innocent of any political correspondence. Other gentlemen to whom Dr. Smith had talked about Elizabeth's case were of the opinion that the Council really did not mean to send her away, that they wanted to get rid of "some of the more obnoxious characters," but that she should not expect any formal relaxing of the order for her or else no one would leave. Smith advised her to "remain quiet" where she was.[40] On June 12, Elizabeth's letter to Reed was presented to the Council, and her friends actively applied themselves in her behalf.

She also wrote to Chief Justice McKean, who responded very sympathetically that, contrary to Reed's opinion, "in all cases of this sort discrimination should be made." The Chief Justice even talked to Reed urging that Elizabeth be allowed to remain on her farm, that the innocent should not be punished with the guilty, but he received a cool reception from the president. McKean could not have expected much from Reed, considering their strong differences over treatment of the disaffected. The only encouragement the Chief Justice did receive was from Dr. Smith, who said he had heard that her stay "would be connived at," in other words, not formally allowed but tolerated nevertheless.[41]

Rev. James Abercrombie, son of Margaret Stedman, wrote Elizabeth a very revealing letter in mid-June.[42] He had been to visit her and upon his return had delivered all her letters. A morning or two later, a man identified only as Mr. B. waited upon him and communicated the Council's decision with regard to her. Mr. B. first spoke scornfully of the Assembly's resolution of May 26, the one permitting Elizabeth to live at Graeme Park rent-free but paying taxes. She had assumed that the resolution had reversed the attainder's effects on her, but she was mistaken, B. said. The resolve was considered by the Council as having "no weight or validity. It cannot be a Law, because agreeably to the Constitution it has not the enaction stile of a Law, viz: Be it enacted & . . ." The Council, therefore, was "under no obligation." Furthermore, they

> are not disposed to shew that lady any particular favour, because she has already received many favours; and she has risen in her requests, and has been troublesome and importunate, both in her own name, and by her friends; and she not only corresponds with, but has also constantly remitted to her husband such sums at different times, as she may have saved by the lenity of government; that their authority for this will be founded on a former act of the Assembly suspending the Habeas Corpus act, and putting it in the power of the Council to send away suspected persons.

B. continued, however, with his own opinion, which gave Abercrombie and, through him, Elizabeth a lesson in political realities. Neither she nor her friends should bother the Council with any more petitions. She should wait

> untill the government shall proceed to put their resolve with regard to her into execution; untill which time she will seem to know

nothing about it, to suppose that the resolve of the Assembly had operated to reverse the attainder and Confiscation of her Estate. It will then be left between the Legislative and Executive branches of the government.

The Council might not consider the resolve as law, yet he did not think they would dare ignore it entirely. Their only recourse would be to order her under guard to the British, but this would be difficult to execute because public opinion would be outraged. In addition, the Council had established martial law, using the authority of a resolve of the Assembly. Therefore, it would not "suit the Council altogether to despise the authority of such *Resolves*." Nevertheless, he recommended that Elizabeth be ready to leave if such should be the final resolution of her case. Before B. left, he swore Abercrombie and Elizabeth to secrecy. Abercrombie ended his recitation of this conversation by telling Elizabeth to "*remain on the farm at all events*."

On the back of his letter, Abercrombie added a few postscripts. The Chief Justice had "interested himself *warmly* in [her] favor" and had spoken to Reed, but without effect. He was so incensed that he would call the court the next week and give her the furniture outright and make an allowance for the wheat. Everything that he could do, he would. Abercrombie added that he had heard from a private channel that the Council had "no serious intention of sending [her] off & mean[t] to wink at [her] remaining on the farm after the ten days are expired." His mother, he wrote, was very distressed for her, and Charles Stedman had "lost the power of speech on that subject & [could] only raise his hands & Eyes to heaven."

True to his promise, McKean called the court the next week, and on June 17, he and Justice Bryan decreed that the furniture for two rooms and kitchen were hers "absolutely and as her own Property."[43] McKean, although willing to make an allowance, was unable to do anything about the wheat that she was supposed to have been able to keep but that had been sold instead. Wheat was not obtainable at that time of year, and money was very scarce. Since she was receiving the furniture, McKean hoped that "the Wheat might be dispensed with." Although she was very grateful to have full ownership of her furniture, the loss of the wheat was a big disappointment. The proceeds of its sale or the money she might have received in its place would have helped meet her expenses.

Elizabeth remained at Graeme Park, as she had been told, and things came to pass as her friends had predicted, although other wives were not as fortunate. Not until the tenth day did ten of the wives request passes to New York, and by the twentieth at least three of them had left. By July 16, some of the worst offenders were still in Pennsylvania, and the Council ordered four wives detained in the workhouse until they gave security to leave the state and not return.[44] Throughout the war, the question of the families of refugees would surface, the Council would threaten them with exile, perhaps a few would leave, some returning later, but wives with influential friends often won exception or were ignored. Elizabeth would not be troubled again with fear of banishment. An interesting sidelight to Elizabeth's troubles was the reaction of Benjamin Franklin. James Abercrombie wrote Elizabeth, "A Certain *great personage*, says, Nothing ever wounded his Sensibility so keenly, as the Consideration of the distress in which Mrs. Fergusson is involved" to which Abercrombie skeptically responded "Fudge!"[45]

Throughout 1780, economic problems continued to upset Pennsylvanians. At the beginning of the year, continental money was worth 40 to 1; by July, it had depreciated to 64 to 1. By May 2, 1781, its value would fall to 175 to 1, and it would be almost impossible to find anyone willing to accept it.[46] As the people became more and more discouraged with the failure of the constitutionalist Assembly to master the situation, their support for that party waned. In the election the following October, the Philadelphia mechanics abandoned their previous loyalty to the constitutionalists, and the city elected Republican assemblymen by a three to one vote. The Republicans also won overwhelmingly in three of the counties, winning almost as many seats in the Assembly as the constitutionalists. It would take another two years for the Republicans to garner enough votes to take the Executive Council, as well, but their voices were strong enough to push through many of their measures.

In November, Elizabeth consulted her friends in Philadelphia to determine their opinion on her chances of persuading the new Assembly to vest Graeme Park in her. She was advised that it was too early to tell what the complexion of the House would be since its members had had no occasion to debate anything of substance. She should wait a while.[47] In December, however, the Assembly passed a law, which once again made Elizabeth tremble for her future support. The problem was that the Pennsylvania treasury was empty, and the state was unable to pay the salaries of the officers and men in the Pennsylvania Line who were in great need. The legislators decided to give each man a certificate stating how much was owed him in specie. These certificates would be accepted and considered as equal to specie in purchasing forfeited estates. To speed up this process, the Assembly ordered all forfeited estates remaining unsold to be sold at public auction by July 1, 1781. Since the Council had announced that it did not consider the resolve of the Assembly about Graeme Park obligatory, Elizabeth feared that the Council would now order it sold.

Once again she took up her pen and wrote a petition to the Assembly and letters to her many friends in Philadelphia. She spent days copying the letters she had received supporting her to send to other people whose influence might be enlisted. In the past, she had played off the Chief Justice against the president; this time it would be the legislature against the executive. She reminded the legislators of her situation married to a non-citizen of Pennsylvania, who nevertheless had been attainted of treason to the state even though he had done nothing against the state. All of her property had been seized and her personal property sold. She had applied first to the Council "who afforded her no kind of relief." She had then applied to former houses of the Assembly, one of which had seemed disposed to answer her petitions. When a committee had reported favorably, the Assembly had passed a resolve "*recommending* to Council to Grant the prayer of her Petition." Council, however, did not consider the Assembly's resolve as obligatory. "She [had] since remained in a State of the greatest Uncertainty and Distress subject to the Terms which an Agent [might] dictate and at present is subject to the payment of a Rent as well as the publick Taxes," in spite of the Assembly's resolve to the contrary. She reminded the assemblymen that because the estate was hers in fee simple, it could be sold only for her lifetime. For this reason it would not bring a large sum at auction, yet sale would "destroy the sole Support of One who . . . [would] not be found to have deserved Evil at their Hands."[48]

This time, Elizabeth had many friends in the Assembly, and her petition was acted upon speedily in order to prevent the Council from interfering. It was presented February 28 and referred to a committee on March 13. A bill was presented by the committee, read twice, published for public consideration, and enacted into law on April 2.[49] Before it was finally enacted, the Council again berated the Assembly for overriding decisions of the Council. Reed was still President, and his animosity toward

Elizabeth clearly showed. The Council, he wrote March 27, had no intention to

> intercept the kindness and liberality of the House to petitioners of any character, but . . . the introducing special and particular laws to repeal the acts of the Executive branches of Government, without any conference with, or information from the Board . . . disturb the harmony of Government.

This way of conducting business would result in the House acting upon partial and "often erroneous ground." If the laws are wrong or if the Council is believed to have too much power, then the laws should be changed.[50] As a result of Reed's message, the two branches met on the 29th to discuss the Council's scolding. No records remain to tell us what happened, but on the same day, the Assembly read for a third time the bill giving Elizabeth her estate and ordered that it be engrossed. The act passed April 2, and the Assembly adjourned on April 10.

Reed had received partial revenge, however, in the wording of the act. It vested the estate in Elizabeth "during her natural life," rather than giving it to her in fee simple, as she wished.[51] For some time, until she figured out that this was a meaningless restriction, she was very distressed. This wording implied the same sort of condition upon her sale of Graeme Park that had been upon the state's sale: if Elizabeth wanted to sell the estate, and she did, it could be only for her lifetime, for at her death it would revert to the state. Without this act, if the state sold Graeme Park, upon her death, it would revert to her heirs. In neither case could a purchaser own the estate in fee simple, it seemed. If this reasoning had been correct, the measure actually benefited the state in the long run because Pennsylvania would end up with the Park, whereas without this law, Elizabeth's heirs would finally own it. She believed that this law would make it very difficult for her to sell her property, and she could make very little from the sale. Yet she desperately needed to sell the land to provide for her future.

The estate contained six hundred acres, and ever since Thomas Graeme had died, she had wanted to sell all but two hundred and the residence. She expected to be able to sell the land at from £12 to £15 per acre. "Think what an Income this would be compared to what I get," she wrote to a friend.

> It is Rented at a hundred and twenty five pounds hard money: And I pay all the Taxes, the land Exhausting, The timber Cutting down; and I altercating A hundred trying points with the tenants that I have no turn for: and as to farming it my Self it is the last Mode of Life I Would ever fall into. I love the Country: and Retirement but it is a Philosophic Repose Not the Bustle of an Extensive Farm which Suites my taste.[52]

The measure, as she understood it, presented her with a real dilemma. She did not know whether to turn down the act and take her chances of buying the estate at a sale with a fee simple title or to take it on the terms of the act that she thought made her a tenant for life. Friends advised her that the words in the bill "during her Natural life" were "void of efficacy a mere sound." Several members of the Assembly declared at its passing that "the true design of the Bill" was that she "should be enabled to dispose of the lands at pleasure."[53] Reed's hand was undoubtedly present in these negotiations because friends reported that it would have been impossible to pass the bill without this qualification. There were Assemblymen, who did not want her to be able to sell the property, for fear that she would send some of the money to her husband. After much self-questioning, she decided to accept the Assembly's presentation, but this phrase would trouble her, discouraging possible buyers, until she found out how to interpret it correctly.

10

The Deserted Wife

After Elizabeth and Henry had had their last meeting in Elizabethtown, Henry had left for England as soon as he could book passage. Even though the deadline of the proclamation ordering him to report for a treason trial had passed and the state, therefore, had declared him guilty and punishable by death, Elizabeth had begged him to throw himself on the mercy of the court and plead innocence of treason. Henry adamantly refused to consider such an action, giving conscience and duty as his reasons for leaving, but there was another, perhaps stronger, reason why Henry wanted to turn his back on Philadelphia as quickly as possible. The Stedmans' maid Jane, or Jenny, was pregnant and had claimed that Henry was her seducer. During the British occupation of Philadelphia from September 1777 to June 1778, Henry had lived at the home of Charles Stedman and his second wife, Margaret, while Elizabeth continued to live at Graeme Park. Whenever she could get a pass to cross the American lines, she had visited Henry there. Shortly after he arrived in Philadelphia, Henry had become enamored of Jane. Mrs. Stedman's son, Reverend James Abercrombie, reported later that he had heard Henry at Jane's door importuning her thirteen months before the child was born.[1] Young Abercrombie offered to take an oath that Jane had told him before she became pregnant that Henry "was after her."[2]

Three days before Henry left Philadelphia in June 1778, Jane asked Dr. Thomas Bond, who was attending a family member at the Stedmans', for "medicine for female Complaints." Bond recognized Jane's condition, refused to give her any "forcing Medicine," and accused her of "making too free with some of those Red Coats." Denying having relations with a British soldier, she named Mr. Fergusson as the father. The shocked Bond urged her never to let Mrs. Fergusson know, but Jane responded that she did not care whether or not Elizabeth knew.[3]

Several other of Elizabeth's friends also knew of the charge against Henry months before Elizabeth did and tried to keep it from her. Thomas Coombe, Anglican minister, cousin of Benjamin Rush, and old friend of Elizabeth, left Philadelphia in July. The night before his departure, Mrs. Stedman went to his house at midnight with a message from Jane for Coombe to take to Henry. Jane, "poor and Penny less," had gone to the Yellow Springs, in Chester County, where she had grown up, to have her child. She had named Henry as "her seducer" and begged him to send her "something to Defray the expences." Coombe was so upset by the disclosure that he broke down in tears for "poor Mrs F." "All her happiness is destroyd," he predicted, quite accurately. Whether Coombe ever delivered the message to Henry is not known, but it seems likely, since the two men met almost every day in New York.[4]

After Henry left Philadelphia, he settled on Long Island near other Pennsylvania émigrés, waiting for his wife to join him for the trip to England. He already knew of Jane's condition, having been informed by several people: by Jane herself before he left the city, by Elizabeth's maid Sally (or Sukey) who had been sent by Mrs. Stedman to inform Henry in August 1778,[5] and also probably by Coombe when he arrived in New York. All had told him that Jane had named him as her seducer. He probably hoped that if he could persuade Elizabeth to go to England with him soon enough, she would never become aware of Jane's charge.

Elizabeth's ignorance and her happiness ended when she was informed of Jane's pregnancy and the charge against Henry sometime before September 6. On that date, she went to Yellow Springs to talk to Jane. Mrs. Stedman was present at the interview and confirmed the story about Coombe being asked to inform Henry.[6] From that point on, Elizabeth's relationship with Henry was embittered, and her whole life changed.

In September, after her interview with Jane, Elizabeth wrote Henry that she knew the charges against him. On November 12, Henry replied denying in very strong language that he had had "any Conextion with that woman of a nature to render her pregnant." He assured her that he had always "behaved with proper fideltiy in the Conjugal State."[7] None of Henry's original letters to Elizabeth survive; all we have are fragments from those letters that Elizabeth copied to send to friends. Assuming these copies were accurate, Henry made a very convincing case of injured, traduced innocence.

Throughout the fall, Henry wrote Elizabeth begging her to join him in New York and reminding her of a wife's duty to follow her husband. By the end of the fall, Henry was planning to leave the continent for England and again urged Elizabeth to forsake her country and go with him. She continued to refuse and argued that he should return to Philadelphia and turn himself in to the authorities, since she believed him innocent of the crime of treason. He believed that the British would ultimately win the war and could see no reason for accepting any punishment, capital or otherwise, from the rebels. Also, of course, Henry must have been reluctant to face the sexual charges against him, although he denied that Jane's accusation, which he called false, had anything to do with his refusal to return to Pennsylvania.

At the end of the year, before General Washington had sent Elizabeth a pass to meet Henry, she had decided in desperation to go anyway and take what punishment might befall her. In a revealing aside, she compared the depths of her and Henry's separate commitments to their marriage. She wrote that she could not bear the thought of Henry leaving the country without seeing him. But she added bitterly, "I do not believe that he would face the Resentment of His own party to see me; And be Suspected as I am in Consequence of Such a Step, while I love my Country as Dearly as he can do His."[8] Finally, Washington sent her permission to meet Henry in Elizabethtown, New Jersey, where they had a short painful farewell visit in mid-January. This was the last time they ever saw each other.

The night before they parted, Elizabeth gave her husband a copy of one of her favorite books, Young's *Night Thoughts*.[9] On a blank page, she had written a poem for Henry, which begins:

> If e'er thy Laura to thy soul was near;
> If e'er her sorrows claim'd one manly tear;
> If e'er amidst her numerous errors you
> One latent virtue fondly could pursue;
> If e'er she pleasd, if e'er her form appear'd

But one soft moment to thine eye endeard!
If e'er congenial transports warmd thy mind,
And fondly whisper'd that our souls were joind,
Peruse this book, with candour scan the *page*,
And shun the vices of a fallen age![10]

Elizabeth then related the truths shown in Young's poem about "Life, death, eternity." These transported her "to the skies" and removed all other thoughts from her mind, even thoughts of Henry. As to their meeting again sometime, she held out no hope for an earthly reunion:

If right we weigh *time's* worth whilst here below,
If right we measure our last *weal* or woe,
We yet shall meet where neither joy nor pain
In ebbs or flows shall short admission gain!

The rest of the poem relates the everlasting joys they would find in their heavenly meeting. Hope and its companion fear would be banished, and husband and wife would part no more. Unfortunately, this was not the way their earthly lives were to be.

In 1780, 1781, and 1782, Elizabeth wrote a long, very revealing poem about her marital situation called "The Deserted Wife."[11] In its four divisions, the poem shows the development over those years of her suspicions of Henry's guilt: "Hope," "Doubt," "Solitude," and "Adversity." In the second part of the poem she described in her words Henry's early denials after she had written him of the charges:

Be every Tye that Binds the Human Race
My Conscience Clears me of this Foul Disgrace . . .
By pure Conubial Love I Solemn swear,
And void of guile I can with truth Declare
By me that woman never was betrayd
Nor through my means a blushing mother made . . .
And since I took the sacred marriage vow
I no loose Pleasures to my self allow!

At first Elizabeth either honestly believed him innocent or wanted it so badly that she convinced herself of it, against her better judgment:

I read exulting in an Honest Pride!
And the low malice of her [Jane's] art Defyd
My tottering Fortune was at once forgot
And Hope Illumined all my future Lot
A virtuous man tho' poor and Lost to show,
To me was treasure in my Wallk below;
My spirits Cheerd . . .

The reactions of her friends in Philadelphia, however, those closest
to the situation, who knew Jane, began to create doubts in her mind. The
Stedmans, for whom Jane had worked eleven years, believed their maid.
Charles Stedman was quoted as saying that the child was Fergusson's
"Without Doubt."[12] After Jane's daughter, Margaret, was born, Jane went
to live with the Walls (or Walns). Both couples gave her "a most extr[a]or-
d[i]nary Character for Regularity of Conduct And behavior," Elizabeth
had to admit.[13] Both believed Jane's story that Henry was the father of her
child, and both condemned Henry for not supporting his daughter. Jane
was able to report several conversations with Henry with details that it
seemed impossible for a simple uneducated servant woman to concoct. An
interview with her also convinced childhood friend Mrs. Campbell, and
these friends "urged a cool Delay; / For Doubts and Dangers Strewd the
Briary way!"

But Elizabeth brushed off their cautions, believed Henry's letters,
and went to Elizabethtown to bid him goodbye. She tells us in the poem
that

. . . all was yielded to a Husbands call:
He Seemed the Poll Star that attracted all.
I went, I saw, I all the weakness Showd
Which is on Womans poor frail Sex bestowd!

They stayed in the home of old friend Elias Boudinot for what must have
been a very difficult interlude.[14] While Elizabeth begged Henry to return
to Philadelphia to answer the moral and political charges against him,
Henry urged Elizabeth to go with him to England, arguing colonial fault
in the dispute that led to the war and personal innocence of the charge of
infidelity. Nevertheless, his soothing denials of all accusations brought her
peace, she wrote, "And drew the poison from the festering wound, / Shed

a soft requiem oer my bleeding Heart / Which long had Struggled with Suspicions Dart." She then began to blame herself, "To think my Bosom had Indignant Burnd / With Jealousys Ignoble yellow Flame; / Which Made me thus My honest Henry Blame." And so Henry went back to New York to take ship for England, and Elizabeth went back to Graeme Park to defend her property from state confiscation for Henry's "treason" and to await infrequent letters from her husband.

With Henry three thousand miles away and letters seldom reaching Philadelphia, those nagging doubts once more began to challenge Elizabeth's faith in him. She wanted to believe and relinquished her loyalty with great reluctance. "Beware! Beware" she told herself,

> be not again unjust
> Least you as Supliant plead and Plead in vain,
> And never more a Conubial Peace regain. . . .
> Loves Lamp Extinguishd never can revive
> Reasons too cold to keep the Flame alive.

But distrust did come to rule her feelings for Henry. She says in the poem that she will not tell how the flame was snuffed, but she mentions "apathy and Cold neglect" and says that "The Reed she leaned on proved a pointed Spear / To pierce her Soul with agony severe."

To add to the agony of Henry's infidelity and the threat of losing Graeme Park, in April 1780, her last adult relative in Pennsylvania died. As Elizabeth was working on the first part of "Il Penseroso" to send to Henry with Mrs. Duché, who was leaving soon to join her husband, an express came from Philadelphia calling her to the home of Dr. Smith. Her niece, Anny Young Smith, was dying from the complications from the birth of her third child. She found Anny "*Blind*; And nearly *Speechless*."[15] To have to close the eyes of the lovely young woman who had been like a daughter was one of the most distressing acts Elizabeth ever had to do. After the funeral, burdened with grief, she returned to Graeme Park to confront her husband's probable unfaithfulness.

Through her letters, mainly those to her old friend Rebecca Smith, the wife of Rev. William Smith, we can trace the outlines of what happened after Henry left. First Elizabeth awaited Henry's actions to defend himself. But letters that Henry said he had sent did not come; after Henry went to England, Elizabeth received only three letters in the first three years. Henry adopted the stance that he had denied the charge, he would not lie because he was an honorable man, hence his wife and friends should believe him. He was the victim of a plot to deprive him of his reputation, and anyone who loved him should be able to recognize his innocence. To expect him to investigate, to confront, to explain Jane's details was to damage his already injured pride.

When it became apparent that Henry planned to ignore the charges and expected her to accept his denial as fact because it came from her husband, Elizabeth was torn between conflicting reactions. At first, Henry wrote that he would not further discuss the issue. On the establishment of peace, he would "Return to refute the Base accusation which I Shall ever reprobate as repugnant to Truth and possibility."[16] By July 1783, the date of his last letter to Elizabeth of which we have record, Henry was vowing never again to live in North America. Even if the attainder against him were to be lifted, he would not return, and he swore his decision had nothing to do with Jane's charges, which would not "deter me from going to any place where my interest or inclinations call me." During this period, three close friends of Elizabeth, Mrs. Stedman, the Reverend Abercrombie, and the elderly Mrs. Campbell interviewed Jane and sent Elizabeth individual letters reporting on the encounter.[17] All three found Jane very convincing. Elizabeth sent Henry their letters, but he never responded to their contents. Whether guilty or slandered, Henry wanted Elizabeth to join him in England, but she seems never to have considered this move seriously. Pennsylvania held her by ties of childhood, kinship, and loyalty. Furthermore, she believed the colonies had been right to throw off their connection to England, and she was proud of their accomplishments.

Yet conflicting arguments pulled her in both directions. After the peace, her friends in England and Scotland wrote her wondering why she did not join her husband. They thought Henry an honorable man, and they believed his denials. Anyone who talked to Henry believed him and found Elizabeth's behavior incomprehensible. They urged her to forget Jane's slanderous charges and to remember her wedding vows. Sarah Coxe, a Philadelphia native who went to England with her husband, Daniel, wrote Elizabeth in 1788 that "It is . . . impossible that a man who conducts Himself as Mr Fergusson does with Uniform Conduct, Friendship, and Benevolence and good will towards all who know him, can be other than a good man."[18] This sums up the reactions of Elizabeth's friends in England and Scotland. At the same time, the Stedmans, Rev. Abercrombie, the

Walls (Walns), and Mrs. Campbell maintained Henry's guilt and condemned him for not assuming his proper responsibility for the child.

Elizabeth's first reaction was to try to prove Jane unreliable, hence unbelievable, to prove her capable either of making up the story to protect the real father or of seducing Henry, as she had others before him, in other words to prove Jane a liar or a whore. In order to do this, Elizabeth was driven to take actions she never would have conceived before 1778. Rebecca Smith wrote her of hearing that a man had suggested that Jane had had a prior illegitimate child, and Elizabeth went looking for proof of this rumor. The day after she received Mrs. Smith's letter, Elizabeth summoned her driver and carriage to take her to Yellow Springs, where Jane's child had been born. There she planned to find the midwife who had assisted at the birth to ask her if she thought Jane "had ever before been a Mother."[19] When she arrived at the inn where she had planned to stay, she discovered that Mrs. Smith's parents, the William Moores, were currently in their home a quarter of a mile away. Since these were people she had known closely from her childhood and since this was such a small settlement that they would soon know she had stayed in a public hostelry, she went to their home for the night. Of course, she had to explain why she was there, and Mrs. Moore warned her that such a determination was "quite beyond" the skill of the midwife. This proved to be the case when Elizabeth posed her question. Furthermore, Elizabeth could discover nothing derogatory about Jane's prior character, and the people in Yellow Springs only named Henry as the child's father.

Not deterred, Elizabeth ordered her coachman to take her to the city. There, she stopped for three days at the home of Mrs. Bond, who was Rebecca Smith's sister and the mother of Phineas. In each place, Elizabeth was so obsessed by her errand that she could talk of little else. In the city, she talked to a Mrs. Sommers, the source of the rumor about Jane. Sommers told Elizabeth of hearing a man named Isaac or Nathan Harris say that when he had been in the hospital with a sore leg, Jane had been living there and had cared for him. He said that "she came in just after She had had a little one." Not being able to find Harris, Elizabeth went looking for his sister to find out where he lived. "She is the Wife of the Man that Herds the Cows to the people who keep Cows in town," and "appeared a very low vulgar Woman," Elizabeth wrote to Rebecca Smith. She recognized that her actions would appear out of character to her friend and commented, "A pretty Plebian Set, I am Dancing after to be Sure!" The sister reported that Harris then lived near Baltimore and added that "she did not believe he had ever said such a Thing . . . [because] Jenny was a Virtuous Girl."

So the rumor remained still a rumor, and Elizabeth's attempts to clear Henry by blackening Jane had been thwarted. Now Elizabeth turned to her friends for help in her quest. In the letter to Rebecca Smith reporting her frustrating journey, Elizabeth begged her friend to ask relatives in Baltimore to take up the search for the missing Harris. If the story should turn out to be true, Elizabeth wrote, "it would have a prodigious tendency to invalidate the principal part of her Story." Jane would no longer be the innocent servant girl seduced by the handsome gentleman visitor in her master's home. He would not have seduced her or, perhaps worse, forced her! The records show only the word "seduction," never "rape," but the sexual misuse of poor servant women by men having power over them has not been uncommon. There is a hint of more than seduction in a later letter to Mrs. Smith in which Elizabeth said that some people in Philadelphia who had heard Jenny's story had "concluded Some thing of a Criminal nature had passed."[20] The phrase "Criminal nature" is not explained, but certainly implies rape.

At first friends were sympathetic, but as the possibility of resolution became more and more remote while Elizabeth's obsession became deeper and deeper, they tired of the subject and refused to help where they felt their interference not appropriate. Rebecca Smith responded immediately to Elizabeth's letter. She pointed out to her friend the futility of her search and told her she must reunite with Henry because her religion, her reason, and her love all demanded it. Her marriage vows, Rebecca reminded Elizabeth, bound her to Henry, and no separation was possible. Elizabeth responded three months later that her religion provided one justification for separation, and if Jane's story was true, she would have that justification. Reason, Elizabeth continued, answering Mrs. Smith, "is a faculty of the Intelligent Mind, that draws Conclusions and determines from Experience and Observation from within and Without." Her reason told her that "there can be no Happiness without Confidence, . . . If What Jenny asserts is true no future Confidence Can take Place Between my friend [Henry] and me" and neither could her love. "Reason Religion Love are all against the reunion," she concluded.[21]

But Elizabeth still hoped for proof that would clear Henry and reverse that conclusion, and her investigations did not stop. Jane, by this time, had had enough of Elizabeth's accusations and refused to talk to her anymore.[22] Therefore, Elizabeth turned to Mrs. Smith for aid. In her letter to Rebecca, Elizabeth asked her friend to visit Jane and interrogate her to find out whether her story was true. Mrs. Smith had already declined this request, but Elizabeth repeated it in person and in letters over and over, until her friend in exasperation stopped visiting and writing.

Shortly before this exchange, Elizabeth had heard from a friend about a discovery of the doctor of the Wall (Waln) family where Jane was currently working. He had had occasion to be in the nursery where the children, including Jane's daughter, were. There he saw, conspicuously displayed, Jane's Bible with the child's name, Margaret, entered, her date of birth, and the last name Fergusson. The doctor said that he felt "affront" for Elizabeth, but her response was quite different. For Jane to write that name in her Bible gave the story credence to Elizabeth, who never would have lied in a Bible.[23]

By this time, Elizabeth was trying to involve in her marital difficulty her Pennsylvania friends who had left the state during the war and gone to England. The expatriates in England remained in close touch, saw each other frequently, and helped one another as witnesses in their claims to the British government for reimbursement for their losses. Some of these people had known Elizabeth for many years and had come to like Henry since her marriage to him. One man in particular, lawyer Phineas Bond, the nephew of Rebecca Smith, had become a close friend of Henry. Since Henry refused to answer any queries and to discuss the problem further, Elizabeth asked Bond, Thomas Coombe, Jacob Duché, and others to question Henry and report to her. But these men, after initial inquiries, resisted her blandishments to become further involved in another man's possible indiscretions, especially when they liked that man as they did Henry. When she pressed Bond in spite of his stated reluctance, he became angry and refused to discuss the matter with her further. But Elizabeth would not give up. She sent Bond messages by Mrs. Smith, by his mother, and by other friends, begging him to answer her questions. He maintained that he already had and refused additional involvement.

Her biggest dispute with Bond involved an oath that Henry claimed he had taken and sent to her in a letter dated March 1782. Supposedly, in order to convince Elizabeth of his innocence, Henry had written a statement that he never had had carnal knowledge of Jane and was not responsible for her child. He attested to this oath before a notary in England

and sent the oath to Elizabeth. At least this is what he told her. For Elizabeth, a very religious woman who believed Henry would never perjure himself, such an oath would have carried much weight. The problem was that she never received it and was unable to track it down. Refusing inexplicably to tell her how he had sent the oath, Henry made her search impossibly difficult. He maintained that he had told her he had taken the oath and that that should be enough. She should believe him and put the matter out of her mind. But it was not enough for his wife, whose childhood friends believed Henry was lying. Since her other letters had come via New York, she enlisted the help of her friend Mrs. Coxe who was in New York before she left for England. When her friend's efforts were unsuccessful, Elizabeth herself even tried to get permission to go to New York to look for it, but she was refused both by John Dickinson, president of the Pennsylvania Supreme Executive Council since fall of 1782, and by General Sir Guy Carleton, commander-in-chief of the British forces in New York.

By fall 1782, Elizabeth had been informed that the oath had been sent to her enclosed in a packet of letters from Phineas Bond to Philadelphia. But in a packet received in October, there had been no oath enclosed, and letters from Phineas to both Mrs. Bond Sr., and to Elizabeth did not mention any deposition having been forwarded, even though both letters discussed the Fergussons' marital difficulties. Bond's letter to Elizabeth forbade her ever again to "address him as a Mediator." Meanwhile, Henry maintained that he had done all that he could and refused to repeat the oath and rewrite its transmittal letter or answer any questions about these documents. In a letter to Mrs. Smith once again asking her friend to interrogate Jane, Elizabeth described the situation about the oath and concluded that Henry's behavior was very strange: "A Child of seven years old of a Common Capacity would in Such Case Cry out Could not Mr F n write over what he had Said?" In exasperation, she continued,

> For a Man of Common sense, Common Humanity, or Common Affection, to declare He would not repeat what He knew by some Accident was not Arrived . . . shows that he either wished to Evade the Subject, or he was totally regardless of His Own Character and my peace of Mind.[24]

What she did not say but must have been thinking was that Henry was trying to deceive her. By this time, Elizabeth had come to believe that Henry was the father of Jane's child.

Still, she would not let go of the subject. Haunted by doubt and indecision, she could neither forgive nor forget him. In December 1782, by an acquaintance going to England, Elizabeth sent Henry a long letter explaining the importance of the oath and its particular wording. Jane's story was so convincing that Elizabeth needed a strongly worded oath to be able to confront the woman and her supporters in Philadelphia, who were beginning to suggest that a crime had been committed. Jane's "Detail was long and Contained Some points that was of a Most extraordinary Nature." She begged him to write in such a way that she could convincingly refute the woman's story. "An Oath that guardedly said He was not the Father of Her Child was not Sufficient to Confute the long and many Conversations she [Jane] told." The following April, Henry wrote but did not address Elizabeth's concerns. All he said on the issue was that he had received her December letter and read it "with attention." Curtly, he replied, "I shall make a very short Reply to a very long Letter: As to the affair of the Child when I sent you the Oath I told you I never more should enter on it, which I shall solemnly adhere to."[25]

In July 1783, Henry wrote his wife an ultimatum, either join him in England or he would consider her refusal a "Renunciation" of her husband, a total contradiction of "every Law human and divine." Any other suggestion she should make would be "a mockery and Insult to one against whom you have no just cause of complaint but that of having followed the line of His Duty And the Dictates of His Conscience." Henry brushed off Elizabeth's concerns, refused to sympathize with her feelings about his possible adultery, and called her behavior "a Breach of Duty." He softened his denunciation by assuring her that she had his "whole and entire affection and I declare from the Bottom of my soul, that I prefer living with you to any woman upon Earth." But Elizabeth had trouble believing these declarations. She had received only three letters from Henry in the previous three years. Each had referred to other letters, which Henry claimed he had sent her but which she had not received. She realized that these letters could have been lost, especially during wartime, but Henry's refusal to repeat his answers to her questions was incomprehensible to her.

Determined to discover the truth, one way or another, Elizabeth enlisted her nephew in the investigation of the oath. John Young arrived in England sometime in 1783, located the justice of the peace who had taken Henry's oath, and forwarded to Elizabeth a letter from this man, Thomas Wiggens, dated January 6, 1784.[26] Wiggens wrote her that in early

1782, Mr. Fergusson, whom he knew very well, called upon him with a paper "to which he wished to make an affidavit." Henry had told Wiggens that it was "a private family concern . . . intended only to Satisfy the Doubts of a Gentleman of the name of Bond." Henry did not let Wiggens read the paper, so that the justice did not know its contents, although Henry had indeed sworn to the truth of those contents, whatever they were. Henry must have lost the paper or have refused to show its contents to Phineas Bond because soon after this, Bond had written Wiggens to find out if Henry had indeed taken such an oath, and Wiggens had replied in the affirmative.

When she received Wiggens's letter to her, Elizabeth did not know what to think. John Young had written her that Bond had sworn that he had seen the original. Elizabeth, however, would accept nothing but Bond's own written statement to her, and he refused to answer her letters. So she sent Rebecca Smith a copy of Wiggens's letter and begged her reluctant friend to write Bond, asking him if he had ever seen the original oath.[27] It is not known whether Rebecca ever wrote her nephew, but Elizabeth's question remained unanswered.

With the coming of peace between England and the United States, the return to Pennsylvania of John Young and Henry Fergusson became a possibility. At first there was a public uproar against the émigrés, but as the months passed, indifference replaced anger, and people began to come back. Phineas Bond enlisted the aid of Benjamin Rush, who, without any controversy, persuaded the Supreme Executive Council to suspend the attainder of Bond and two other men in October 1786. Elizabeth asked Rush whether she should encourage her nephew to return to the state. By all means, responded Rush. "There will be no difficulty in getting his attainder taken off." Rush offered to write John Young to encourage his return. "He will be happy, useful, and respectable among us."[28] How Young responded to this suggestion is not known, but he did not return.

The same judgment also applied to Henry's possible return. Elizabeth may have tried to communicate to him that there were no longer any legal obstructions preventing his return, none, that is, except any instigated by Jane against him. Elizabeth would not have mentioned such a possibility, although he would have been well aware of it. In June 1787, John Young wrote her answering a letter she had written him the previous February, no longer available. Young's answer referred to her "Disposition to be reunited to your Husband" and advised her to communicate this sentiment to Daniel Coxe because he knew Henry's whereabouts and corresponded with him.[29] Without Elizabeth's letter, it is impossible to know her intentions. There is no indication, however, that any contact was opened with Henry ever again. By this time it was doubtful that Elizabeth really wanted a reunion with her husband, no matter what gestures she made. The conflict and compromises that such a meeting would have entailed would have been too painful to endure. Jane's child was now ten years old, and there had been no deviation in her story about paternity. If anything, her charge against Henry may have been increased to rape, forcing civil authorities to take action against him had he appeared in Pennsylvania. No, the whole situation was better left alone, unresolved.

Those who felt she ought to join Henry in England, however, were continuing to promote him. In early 1788, Sarah Coxe sent Elizabeth a copy of a letter Henry had written to her oldest son. Jacob Duché's grandson was being sent by his parents to the continent for his health, and the sixteen-year-old son of Daniel and Sarah Coxe was going with him. Henry Fergusson, who had lived in France intermittently for many years, had written young Coxe a letter advising him how to behave during his stay in that country. It was indeed an admirable letter, stressing that the boy's main activity should be to study the language. He should spend at least four hours every morning learning French, and nothing should be allowed to infringe upon this time. "History and the Belles Lettres," Henry wrote, "may be Cultivated for two Hours more to advantage, and Books of the same Language which will be at the same time improving your mind and still acquiring the Speech of the Country." After instructing him to keep a journal of his activities, Henry warned him against "Indolence and Intemperance." He concluded the letter with a statement that must have seemed to Elizabeth very hypocritical. Henry wrote,

> There certainly is a *Retribution Justice* and Dispensation of Providence through Life, which Punishes every Deviation from the Standard of Truth and moral Rectitude: . . . the only sure means of Being happy in your Self and a Comfort to your Friends and respected among mankind is to steadily persevere in the Paths of virtue.

Mrs. Coxe concluded her transmittal letter stating that Henry's behavior proved him to be a moral man.[30] The contents of this letter fed Elizabeth's ambiguity about her husband and condemned her as the guilty spouse for not believing him.

Meanwhile, Elizabeth's friendship with the Smiths was crumbling under the weight of her insistence that her friends listen interminably to every nuance of her evidence about her husband, sympathize endlessly, and help her investigation even when they had already refused several times. One of the most troubling aspects for the Smiths was Elizabeth's demands that they talk to Phineas Bond, Rebecca's nephew, about the oath Henry had taken. By the end of 1786, Bond had returned to Philadelphia as British consul. The Smith's son Thomas Duncan, then twenty-six, needed a job, and the Smiths were asking Bond if he could employ Thomas as his representative in Baltimore, New York, or any other capital.[31] They could hardly expect a favor for their son at the same time they were harassing Bond about Elizabeth's situation. Yet they could not explain this to their friend.

When Thomas died July 9, 1789, Elizabeth wrote Rebecca a letter of condolence, but even in such a communication, she was unable to forget her own problem and concentrate on her friend's sorrow. After expressing her sympathy, she relapsed into her own situation. She accused Rebecca of advising her to be silent and of giving her "Little *lectures* as to a Child at a *Boarding school* Rather than your Equal in years And some small pretensions to understanding." She concluded her letter by telling Mrs. Smith that "Living Sorrows are worse than dead ones." People who had lost friends two years ago had found peace, and she hoped that the Smiths' sorrows would be healed "long before that period has half Elapsed."[32] In spite of Elizabeth's insensitivity, Mrs. Smith visited her at Graeme Park in September. The occasion must have been strained because the following June, Elizabeth wrote Mrs. Smith complaining that they had only exchanged two letters since that time. With her June letter, Elizabeth returned to her friend a communication Mrs. Smith had written her some years before which had caused the recipient "a flood of tears." She also gave Mrs. Smith a lesson in friendship.

If their roles were reversed and if she was in Mrs. Smith's shoes, Elizabeth wrote, she would not treat her friend's complaints about her husband's conduct as coming from "a mind whose ideas are near deranged with poring over one idea and the same train of thought till the distinction And accuracy of rational perception become Clouded and her once tolerable understanding bewildered And led astray." She would not tell her that it was God's will she never know the truth. She would not advise her to ask her husband's pardon for ever doubting his fidelity. She would not change the subject when her friend's "heart is ready to burst with Anguish And mortification," and when she became bored with the topic, she would not "tell her it is quite an old Story And nobody talks of it." Instead, she would "let friendship speak a softer sound, and tell her [friend] she has cause for sorrow." She would not point out "the weakness of her [friend's] wishing to hear of Him as I would not Hurt her by too pointed an Observation On That Head." Elizabeth concluded that "the Heart and not the Head has dictated This Epistle."[33] Elizabeth and Rebecca had been intimate friends for nearly forty years; Rebecca might have shed a few tears herself when she read Elizabeth's cry for empathy and true friendship. But the cost of that friendship was very high in patient understanding.

Too high, apparently, for the friendship did not improve. In December 1790, Mrs. Smith's daughter died after childbirth, and Elizabeth wrote her several letters of condolence in January, which went unanswered. In April 1792, when Elizabeth wrote three letters, she began the third of these, "you will no doubt think that you are to be overwhelmed with my Epistles: Nor have I much reason to think they are welcome as you never have written to me this two years."[34]

Meanwhile, Elizabeth had received more evidence of Henry's unfaithfulness. A man named Christian Fesmire, who lived near Oxford Church, came to help new tenants move onto Graeme Park after Elizabeth succeeded in selling it. While there, he visited with Elizabeth and Betsy Stedman for an hour. During their visit, Elizabeth, who shamelessly told her troubles to anyone who would listen, must have told Fesmire about Henry's supposed fathering of Jane's child. Fesmire then described to them something that he had seen happen between Henry and Jane at the home of Jacob Duché before Henry left Pennsylvania. The details of what he had observed do not remain, but they incriminated Henry further because Elizabeth wanted Bond to hear Fesmire's story and ask Henry whether it was true. She begged Rebecca Smith in her April letters to ask Phineas Bond either to meet her and Fesmire at a tavern in Frankford or allow her to bring the man to Bond's home so that he could hear the man himself and, when he got to England, relate the evidence to Henry. Elizabeth also had four other questions she wanted Bond to put to Henry.[35] There is no record that Bond actually talked to Fesmire. After a decade of reluctant involvement in the Fergussons' marital troubles, it is inconceivable that he would not adhere to his decision to refuse further mediation duties. Elizabeth, however, could not see this but regarded his behavior as disloyal to someone he had known since childhood and unfeeling toward a dear friend of his mother and his grandmother.

Elizabeth also told Mrs. Smith at this time that her relatives in Scotland had written to ask "the Reason of this fatal Separation." They had been "shocked and astonished to hear that" she was not "Convinced of the worth of a Man who [had] so Sedulously taken pains to convince [her] by an oath that he never had the least knowledge of the person of His accuser." She had suffered their condemnation without explanation, but she told Mrs. Smith that she was giving Henry until January 1793. If by then he had not answered her questions satisfactorily, she would write to friends and relations in England, his as well as hers, who had "Condemned [her] without knowing the Facts." She would explain her conduct in detail, all about the oath she never had received, about his refusal to repeat or even describe the oath, and about the evidence she had of Henry's duplicity. She wrote that "in vindication to [her] own Character," she would no longer "Sit down Branded as a poor weak Jealous Wife."[36] Although January 1793 passed without any communication from Henry, Elizabeth did not follow through on this threat until 1799.[37]

In spite of the lack of communication during the previous two years, Elizabeth, lonely and facing the impending move out of her home of so many years, urged Mrs. Smith to spend a few days with her in Graeme Park and to bring her sister Mrs. Bond, the mother of Phineas. Rebecca Smith must have been very reluctant to commit herself to several days trapped with Elizabeth's interminable speculations about her husband's adultery and her requests for assistance. But she did answer Elizabeth's letter in May. Unfortunately, no copy remains; it would be very interesting to see how she responded.[38] Elizabeth was in Philadelphia the following September where she had a short visit with Rebecca devoted entirely to the subject of Elizabeth's marriage. It probably was not an amiable discussion. This was their last visit. Rebecca Smith died of yellow fever in the terrible epidemic of fall 1793.

Rebecca may have relented, nevertheless, and spoken to her nephew or persuaded his mother to speak to him. Before he left Philadelphia for a visit to England, Bond did send Elizabeth the letter he had received from Thomas Wiggens, the English justice of the peace who had taken Henry's oath and who, at the instigation of John Young, had written Elizabeth in January 1784. In spite of her hopes, this communication brought no peace to Elizabeth. Neither the original nor a copy of this letter survives, but Elizabeth believed the two Wiggens letters contained a conflict in dates and that "a Cruel Deception had been practiced" on her. The Wiggens–Elizabeth letter said that Henry had taken the oath in 1782. The letter Wiggens had written to Phineas Bond was dated with only the day of the week. The wording of this letter, however, convinced Elizabeth that Fergusson had taken the oath in 1783, not in early 1782, as he had told her. It would not have been the first time Henry had lied about dates. When he was in England in the fall of 1775, Henry had written Richard Stockton November 20 that he had sent Elizabeth a power of attorney. When the document finally had arrived, it was dated December 19.

After receiving the Wiggens–Bond letter and discovering the contradictory dates, Elizabeth again tried to enlist the aid of others to solve the enigma. She wrote Bond a long letter explaining her belief, but he did not reply or tell her whether he had shown her letter to Fergusson. She then "applied again and again to Mrs. Cadwalader [Bond's sister] to speak to him." But he would not explain. She commented in 1795 to Rev. William Smith "How hard I take it that the Child of a family I ever loved as my own relations should treat me so."[39] It was impossible for her to understand that whether Henry took an oath in 1782 or 1783 was simply not important to her friends.

In October 1792, Mrs. Bond, her daughters Mrs. Travis and Mrs. Cadwalader, and her granddaughter Frances Cadwalader visited Graeme Park. In a confusing, disjointed letter to Benjamin Rush describing the visit, Elizabeth referred to a letter she had sent Phineas Bond, which must have been very unpleasant. He had informed his mother of Elizabeth's letter, and this had created an uncomfortable tension during the women's visit.[40]

Elizabeth's friendship with William Smith, Rebecca's widower, also of long duration, was sorely tested during the two years after Rebecca's death. He paid her a visit in early September 1794, and she went over the whole problem with her husband: what had happened, the evidence of his adultery, her attempts to determine exactly what had or had not happened, and her beliefs that her old friends who should have helped her instead had thwarted her efforts with indifference or even obstacles, as in the case of Phineas Bond. That same fall, she encountered Smith at church and gave him "a number of Papers and Letters, relative to the Subject," after which she "waited in almost daily expectation to See or hear" from him. What response she expected is not clear, but he made no attempt to meet her expectations. Five months later she wrote him of her surprise at his silence. Still she received no reply. Finally, in June 1795, she wrote what would be their final communication.[41] In it she accused him of flinging "the Packet into [his] Desk and seeing it long and intricate tossed among old rubbish, quite Obsolete" of forgetting it. To compound his error of neglect, Smith had not delivered a business letter of hers until two months after he had volunteered to deliver it. As far as her marital problem was concerned, she described his reactions probably quite accurately:

> [Y]ou Sir found it a tiresome entangled piece of Business And so continually procrastinated it and the Stimulus being weak like the first rebound of a Stroke grew fainter And fainter till a Dying Pulse preceded a total Stagnation. . . . It is very easy to Say why do you always pose on one Subject? But to a Female what Subject can be more natural? we have no Character but as Wives and mothers: in the Latter it has pleased God not to place me.[42]

In this same letter, Elizabeth commented bitterly on her deteriorated relations with her old friends. Jacob Duché and his wife, the sister of Francis Hopkinson and another childhood friend, had returned to Philadelphia in May 1792, but they treated her with "a Coldness that Freezes [her] heart." While they were in England they, too, had received many letters from Elizabeth about her husband, whom they defended, yet when they returned to Philadelphia, they refused her request to interview Jane, and they never had said "one word to Mr Fn [about] his most Scandalous Conduct," she wrote to Smith. Once again she asked Smith to speak to Bond. "For the love of Truth and Candor get something Sensible and Manly and rational out of Mr. Bond," she begged Smith. "There is but one way to Silence me, no other Sop for *Cerberus* but one apple plucked from the golden Bough of truth."

Elizabeth's obsession with Henry's infidelity not only cost her friendships but also made her believe that she was the center of everyone's gossip. Friends could not convince her that her failed marriage was not the subject of public discussion, that Philadelphians had long since moved on to more contemporary topics. This self-consciousness kept Elizabeth from the city she loved. She explained to Benjamin Rush in June 1795,

I think I am ill used all round and treated truly with a want of Candor my soul Disdains. . . . The afair has banished me as tho I was the offending Party from a City Dear to me once with filial Love and where I have done nothing to cause a Blush. . . . To think I know no more of the Duché famly than if they lived at the Antipodes.[43]

That same month, she received a letter from another old friend urging her to visit Philadelphia. "Do you not my dear Madam intend ever to see your Friends in town again," asked Anna Maria Clifton.[44] But Elizabeth had come to believe that she was widely seen either as a jealous wife mistrustful of an honorable man or as an admittedly deceived wife unable to forgive and forget her husband's indiscretion and fulfill her sacred marriage vows. That she might be the one blamed instead of Henry, that she might be the subject of public scorn was galling and unacceptable.

In April 1796, almost twenty years after Elizabeth had discovered Henry's faithlessness, she still searched for news of him and was upset when friends refused to help her investigations. She had written three times to Sally Bard in England to ask her friend, a Miss Kemp, who was friendly with Henry, to find out from him whether he had received a box of books Elizabeth had sent him in 1793 along with a sealed packet, but she had never heard an answer. "Indeed," she wrote, "I am treated beyond all hopes of reconcilement" as though she thought that she and Henry might still be reunited. "Mrs. Bard always treated me in a Careless way as to this affair," she wrote, and then concluded "He is not worth a Line from my Pen: yet a man one once Loved and expected to have passed ones Life with . . . cannot be the object of Indifference."[45]

In May 1799, to Dr. Rush, her faithful correspondent, she wrote of her "Shame, sorrow, Suspence and every fatal Passion that can Knaw a female heart of Sensibility." She was still living the old hurt, never having proceeded in life beyond that date in 1778 when she heard of Henry's possible adultery. Still also, she was blaming Phineas Bond for not answering her questions about the oath.

How must I appear to Mr Fergussons friends when I State the Strange Oath, that Mr. Bond can only fix, and that I have not influence enough to obtain one hours audience with him, nor have even influence enough with any friend male or female to enter into a Conversation, and entreat of him to Search His memory to fix the true Date of that time he Sent to the magistrate.

Henry's nephew had visited Philadelphia earlier in the year, but Elizabeth had had no opportunity to see him. She said that she would have insisted that "he Should have [heard] the Story from Janes own Lips; that I might have been vindicated in my Reasons for my Conduct [and] my Separation."[46]

Of Henry's life after he left New York City, we know little, except that he could not find a job and was pressed for money. None of his letters to America survives, and we can only piece together a few fragments of his life from public documents in the Public Record Office in England and from the few references Elizabeth made in her extant letters.

When Henry reached London in early 1779, he discovered a very active group of loyalists trying to persuade the British government to compensate them for their losses in America. As early as winter 1775, the Lords of the Treasury had begun awarding small sums to loyalists whom crowds had driven from their homes. By 1779, the Treasury was giving pensions to refugees it deemed worthy. On March 2, Henry submitted a memorial asking for support and work, pointing out that he read and spoke three foreign languages: French, Italian, and Spanish. The following June, he was notified that he would receive a pension of £100 per year, which was the usual sum that the Treasury thought sufficient to support single persons.[47] Henry, however, was helping support his brother Robert's widow and five children and found this sum insufficient. By the time he reached England, he already had accumulated debts because of his stay in New York for over six months without employment, and while in London, his debts continued to climb.

As soon as he discovered the amount of his pension, he wrote to Sir Adam Fergusson complaining of its size and asking the noted Scottish philosopher to intervene in his behalf. He needed at least £200 per year, he wrote, to be able to

> afford any relief for Mrs. Fergusson who by her husbands [*sic*] conduct is reduced from ease and plenty to wretchedness and want. My inability to bring her with me was the cause of my leaving her in America when I left it, and unless I recieve [*sic*] the above mentioned sum I shall still be unable in any degree to assist her, which

is an agonizing circumstance to one who on every account owes her as much love support and protection as husband can to wife.

In June 1782, Adam Fergusson certified that Robert Fergusson, Henry's brother, had died insolvent leaving a widow and five children, whom Henry was helping. Henry also wrote in 1782 to Henry Strachey asking him to speak to the Lords of the Treasury. In this letter Fergusson said that he had received a "smaller Allowance than any Refugee from Philadelphia" because he lacked "Patronage." Later that same month, Henry applied formally himself to the commissioners for an addition to his allowance, but he was denied. The commissioners recommended that his allowance should be continued until he was "otherwise provided for."[48]

There is no indication that Henry ever thought seriously of sending Elizabeth any money. Quite the contrary was true. She probably took him money when she met him in Elizabethtown in January 1779 and sent him money in England after he discovered that his pension was less than he had hoped. Again in the summer of 1784, she received a letter from him "imploring a remittance to relieve his distressed condition." The following September, George Meade recommended that she stop giving money to charity because her husband and nephew needed every penny she could spare. He suggested that she come to Philadelphia, and they would "fall on some method of sending a temporary supply to them both."[49]

The pension system provided the loyalists the means to live, but what they really wanted was to be reimbursed for their losses in a lump sum. Finally in July 1783, Parliament passed a compensation act, creating a commission to investigate the refugees' claims. The commissioners began their work on August 30, and shortly after, they advertised in the London newspapers telling loyalists where to submit their claims before the following March deadline. Henry Fergusson presented his memorial January 6, 1784.[50] In his claim, Henry reviewed his arrival in North America in 1769, his marriage to Elizabeth Graeme, his departure in 1775 "to avoid temporizing or taking a part with those who acted repugnant to his principles," and his return with General Howe in 1777. He reported that his property, which he had obtained by marriage, had been confiscated and sold by the state. Although his wife had won the return of the real estate, he stated that he could not benefit from this because the act forbid it and because "unhappy differences" with his wife precluded his return to Pennsylvania. He asked to be reimbursed for all the personal property that had been sold in

October 1778, claiming its value at £1402.12.6, and for Graeme Park, valued at £7303.

The deliberations of the commissioners moved slowly, and it was not until February 1785 that Henry appeared before them to answer their questions and give further evidence verbally. At this time, Henry said that Graeme Park had been turned over to him in fee simple before he left the country in September 1775 so that in case his wife died during his absence, her heirs would not have been given possession. He said that the settlement paper had been left with Richard Stockton, but that he had a copy of the draft, which he presented to the commissioners. He claimed that Elizabeth had destroyed the original document when she applied to the Assembly for the act to revest the estate in her. Three Pennsylvania loyalist witnesses appeared in Henry's behalf: John Young, Daniel Coxe, and Phineas Bond. All more or less supported Henry's claim, although they were vague about the existence of any settlement upon Henry of the fee simple in Graeme Park. All agreed that the differences between Henry and Elizabeth were irreconcilable and that he never could return to Pennsylvania to recover the estate. The examination by the commissioners must have been very rigorous because the next day Henry sent a letter to their secretary explaining two points that were not clear in his testimony. He blamed these discrepancies on "the Embarrassment occasioned by [his] Examination." In the course of his explanation, he wrote that he owed "between three and four hundred pounds Sterling contracted since [he] left America."[51]

Before deciding to award a sum of money to a claimant, the commissioners required that he prove the extent of his losses and his loyalty throughout the war. In order to prove that their claims were valid representations of their true losses, the loyalists needed documentation from the United States. In August 1785, John Young wrote his aunt asking her to secure from the state comptroller's office a description of James Young's estate sold after his death and an account of the sale of Henry Fergusson's personal estate "expressed in the money of the time as sold without reduction or alteration of any kind." Elizabeth asked George Meade to present John Young's request to John Nicholson, the comptroller, who sent Meade's letter to the Council along with the notation that he had been refusing such requests because John Dickinson, when president, had ordered him to do so. Meade had done as Elizabeth requested, although he thought it a waste of everybody's time since James Young had owed more at his death than his estate could cover. The Council, now under the leadership of President Benjamin Franklin, told Nicholson to "follow his own opinion."[52]

Apparently he did as he was requested because around the first of March 1786, Henry presented the necessary documentation to the commissioners. This report, however, forced him to explain the difference between the sum he had claimed—£1,402—and the actual sale result—£537. He wrote that the amount in his memorial was the value when he left Graeme Park in September 1775 before the depredations first of Wayne's brigade and then of the Pennsylvania militiamen. He also stated his belief that the sales of loyalist property were "shams" at which belongings were not sold for their true value.[53]

In addition to detailed proof of the value of the estates lost in America, the commissioners required evidence of the applicant's loyalty to England. Therefore, Henry also included in his claim letters from two British officers attesting to Henry's eagerness to help the British while he traveled as a volunteer with them from Head of Elk to Philadelphia. They wrote that on several occasions he procured guides for them and gave intelligence upon which the British army had acted.

The British government at first refused to make any payments until all of the claims had been examined carefully by the commissioners, a time consuming process. In June 1785, however, the Pitt government agreed that £150,000 be dispersed to those whose claims already had been decided. Anyone who had fought with or helped the British army was to receive 40 percent of his claim. All others were to be given 30 percent. Apparently Henry was not considered in the first category because he received just about 30 percent. The commissioners had granted him £1853 , and he received £555.18.[54]

A new compensation act of Parliament passed in 1785 provided for representatives to go to Canada and the United States to collect information on the justice of the claims. As a result of these investigations, many of the compensations were augmented. Henry's was revised to £2,304, a substantial increase.[55] The sums were paid in sixteen installments over a period of eight years. For Henry, this amounted to a little less than £225 per year since he already had received £555. This was not a bad compensation for someone who had arrived in Philadelphia with no known income and no job and who had earned this largess simply by marrying and living with his wife in comfort on her estate for about two years.

Although Elizabeth had provided the documentation necessary for her husband to receive this dispensation, his claim to ownership of Graeme Park caused her extreme embarrassment when news of it reached Philadelphia. She heard from John Young in early 1788 that he had seen a paper in Richard Stockton's handwriting vesting fee simple ownership of Graeme Park in her husband. This was the unsigned draft that Henry had included in his claim to the Loyalist Claims Commission. She was upset about this news because she had "with truth again and again told all the people in power collectively and individually that the Fee was not vested in Mr. Fergusson nor never had been." Any rumor of Henry's possible ownership of Graeme Park challenged her honesty and decreased the likelihood of a profitable sale of the estate, which she desperately needed.

Little else is known about Henry's life in Europe. Historian William Buck believed that in 1793 Henry went into the British army and was sent to Flanders.[56] This was at the end of the eight-year disbursement period, so that Henry, once again, would have needed a job. He probably had left the army by 1797. The records show that he received a small annual allowance of £40 from the British government from 1797 to 1801, to which he would not have been entitled had he still been in the army. After 1801, however, his name disappears from the lists. What happened to him is not known.[57]

In September 1799, Elizabeth wrote Mrs. Frazer[58] that she did not know if Henry was dead or alive. She had not seen him in nearly twenty years, nor heard from him in eleven years, nor heard of him in three. She guessed that Phineas Bond corresponded with Henry, but Bond would not tell her if he did. Although there was no further contact between husband and wife, to the end of her life, Elizabeth never gave up the possibility of Henry's name being cleared and of him returning to her side in Pennsylvania.

11

Femme Savante

For the rest of her life, Elizabeth Fergusson lived as a semi-recluse. Until December 1793, she continued at Graeme Park. After that, she boarded successively at the nearby homes of widow Mrs. Todd and of farmer-clockmaker Seneca Luken. Without the domestic duties of women who were wives and mothers, how was Elizabeth, educated beyond her opportunities, to fill her hours? There was nothing much for her but to continue her habits of reading and writing and to make her literary creations provide the status denied her as wife and mother. She spent the rest of her life composing new verses, annotating and revising old ones, and sending others in commonplace books to remaining friends. When a new magazine began publication in Philadelphia, she aggressively submitted her writing for publication. It seems obvious that she expected her work to be read by other people even after her death, or she would not have bothered to revise, annotate, and publish. Seeking a more lasting and widespread intellectual recognition, she reached out to the world through her writing and created the record that gave her lasting renown.

At the same time, her social life narrowed, friends one by one falling away as they died or were alienated by her obsession with Henry's intransigence. She still invited people to visit her at Graeme Park as long as she held the estate, although she had so little money that entertaining in her previous style was out of the question. When others urged her to visit them in Philadelphia, she refused, except on rare occasions, because she still believed herself to be the subject of ugly gossip. To the end of her life, Elizabeth was obsessed by what she called her desertion, by the unhappiness it had caused her, and especially by her friends' refusal to interfere as she wished them to do.

She could have ended her marriage, had she wished, because divorce was obtainable in Pennsylvania,[1] but Elizabeth never entertained such an option. Her religion forbade it, although she did manage to find in her faith sanction for separation from an adulterous husband, and so did her position in society. Even though it seemed obvious that Henry never would return, she always rejected anyone else's implication that her marriage was finished. Women, she wrote, in a poignant comment to Rev. Smith, had "no Character but as Wives and mothers: in the Latter it has pleased God not to place me."[2] She could do nothing about her childlessness, but at least she could hold on to the title of wife, even though it was in name only.

Elizabeth continued to see herself as blameless in her separation from Henry and bitterly resented people implying that she should have acted otherwise. Her friends in Pennsylvania and in England all stressed her duty as Henry's wife to follow him, ignoring his duty as her husband to be faithful, which to her was equally important. Rebelling against this double sexual standard that ruled male-female relations, she rejected being characterized as the villain in the story while Henry was pictured as the mistreated spouse even though he probably had committed adultery.

By the late-1780s, the Smiths and their extended family members had lost all interest in the subject and refused to become involved any further. They believed that whether Henry was guilty or innocent, she should abide by her wedding vows and join him in England, no matter how painful the transition would be. If she decided to stay in Philadelphia in spite of her religious commitment to her husband, then she should stop talking about the subject. They had heard all the known details many times, and neither she nor they could do anything to discover the truth about Henry's possible unfaithfulness. Elizabeth insisted to the end of her life that they could help her in her investigation, if only they would.

Her friends in England and Scotland who knew Henry as a charming, seemingly moral man believed him innocent and her a disloyal wife who had not stood by her traduced husband, as she ought. He had taken an oath of innocence, and she, as a loving wife, should trust him. Even if he was guilty, she had overreacted. Her religion told her to forgive and to remain faithful to her husband no matter what the provocation. Therefore, she was violating her marriage vows and thus violating her religion by not joining Henry in Europe. It all came down to her being the spouse at fault. Elizabeth, in contrast, believed herself to be the injured party and her husband to be behaving very strangely for a man who claimed to be innocent. She also could not be persuaded that Philadelphians no longer were concerned about her husband's infidelity. And if they were not, as Mrs. Smith told her, at least her closest friends ought to be if they really cared for her because that was the main concern of her life. As she cut the ties of friendship with more and more childhood friends, her social life narrowed in constricting circles. She even refused invitations from the Rushes and Boudinots, who begged for her company and promised that she would be the only guest.

Yet, as her social person was contracting, her intellectual person was expanding, challenging contemporary opinion about the learned woman. Philadelphians believed that women should be educated but only to a point and that they should not flaunt their abilities. This had been clearly argued by "Visitant" in 1768, and opinions had not changed since then.[3] People made the distinction between a savant/e, a learned or scholarly person, and a pedant/e, one who excessively displays his or her learning. It was admirable for a man to be a savant, but not a pedant; a woman was to be neither, at least not publicly. John Adams made this distinction very clearly in a letter to his wife, Abigail, in 1776. "Your sentiments of the importance of education in women are exactly agreeable to my own. Yet the *femmes savantes* are contemptible characters. So is that of a pedant universally, how muchsoever of a male he may be." But then he continued with historical examples of men whose successes had been shaped by women with "knowledge and ambition above the ordinary level of women."[4] Women should educate and help the men in their lives, but this should be done inconspicuously and not to win prominence for themselves. Although Elizabeth gave this argument lip service on occasion, the reality of her last fifteen or so years contradicted it. She no longer made any attempt to suppress her erudition but, on the contrary, actively stressed it.

When younger, she had developed a local reputation as a learned woman, but she generally had maintained that her knowledge and writing were only for her own amusement and that of her close acquaintances, and she had refused to allow her poetry to appear in print. Friends had suggested that her English journals and her translation of *Télémachus* be published, but she had demurred. After the death of Nathaniel Evans, however, as she and Rev. William Smith prepared an edition of the young minister's writing, she had agreed to write a eulogy of Evans to be included. In addition, three other of her poems were needed to make Evans's responses intelligible. Thus, the book, finished in 1772, included four of Elizabeth's poems. For the next three years, Elizabeth's pen was busy, but none of her verses was published, perhaps because of the absence of a suitable medium,[5] perhaps because of her preoccupation with her marriage and the settlement of her father's estate, or perhaps because she still questioned the appropriateness of publication.

Then, in January 1775, Robert Aiken began *The Pennsylvania Magazine or American Monthly Museum* with Thomas Paine as editor, providing a venue for Philadelphia's writers. Two months later, John Young wrote his aunt from the city that he expected to see something of hers in the upcoming issues.[6] With this encouragement, Elizabeth published four more poems, in April and October 1775 and in March and April 1776, before the periodical ended in July 1776. For the next ten and a half years, she published only one other poem, in the newspaper *The Pennsylvania Packet* in January 1784. Thus until December 1786, two months before her fiftieth birthday, only nine of her poems had been published. In the late 1780s, this reluctance to put herself forward changed. Between December 1786 and September 1792, a little over six years, at least twenty-four more poems appeared in print and a long three-part prose allegory. She also revised and annotated several pieces written earlier, wrote many new verses, and tried to have her translation of *Télémachus* published. This new publishing activity gave her a way to place herself in society and to expand her intellectual prominence with a much wider audience.

The change could have been stimulated by the actions of women authors in England at the end of the eighteenth century. During the Revolution, intellectual communication with the mother country had been largely severed. After the peace treaty was signed, along with the flood of English products onto the United States markets, came English magazines, newspapers, and books. In December 1783, Elizabeth received a packet of European magazines and commented that "a torrent of Anecdotes pours in after so long an interval." It reminded her of a story told by Addison of a ship frozen in the ice near Greenland. "When the Thaw Came, all the Murmurings, and Curses that froze as they Came out of the Mariners

Mouths: breathed forth at once And Buzd around."[7] In the "buzing" periodicals, she was able to read about the English women authors who had come to prominence during the war and to read their writings. She learned about Fanny Burney, who had published the novels *Evalina* (1778) and *Cecilia* (1782), and about Hannah More, who had written plays, ballads, essays on education, and poems during the 70s. Hannah Cowley wrote thirteen plays between 1776 and 1795. Her drama *The Belle's Stratagem* (1782) was staged for many years. Anna Seward, resident in Lichfield for most of her life, wrote poetry and a poetical novel that went through five editions. Madame Stephanie de Genlis wrote the four-volume *Théâtre d'éducation* (1779–80) and the three-volume *Adèle et Théodore* (1782) among her many works.[8] The literary accomplishments of these women were publicized widely, and Elizabeth read and quoted their writings.

After citing the writings of More, Seward, Burney, and de Genlis in a letter to Rush, she commented, "the Wits Say that Pegasus now wears a Side Saddle," to which Elizabeth rejoined that when she thought of those four women, she wondered if "poor Pegasus is not smotherd with Laurels." She also scorned the idea, then current in England, that Dr. Johnson had "Superintended" the writing of the novel *Cecilia* by Burney, who had written it "under his Auspices."[9]

If she had lived in England, Elizabeth might have been able to augment her income with her writing as some women did. Elizabeth Carter, the learned member of the Blue Stockings, was single all her life, even though she was given the title Mrs., and supported herself with her writing. She was said to have written the "Ode to Wisdom" in Samuel Richardson's *Clarissa*, the poem that may have inspired Elizabeth's own "Invocation to Wisdom" preceding her translation of *Télémachus*. But America largely did not support and encourage such activities by women.[10] Furthermore, it was rare for American authors, male or female, to be paid for magazine submissions. It was not possible, therefore, for Elizabeth to support herself by writing.

Yet her twin problems of insufficient income and accumulating debt could not be avoided. Her father had left her over 800 acres at Graeme Park, much of it very fertile land, growing a surplus of corn and grain for market and nourishing "a collection of the best grafted fruit trees."[11] But his daughter was neither farmer nor manager and could not make the land pay. At the beginning of the war, she had reduced Graeme Park in size to about 600 acres through sales to pay debts, but the proceeds had not been enough to provide an income for herself. In July 1777, she had advertised briefly in the *Pennsylvania Gazette,* but with the British army headed for Philadelphia, this had not been an appropriate time to try to sell real estate. The following winter, several different groups of continental and state soldiers had bivouacked at Graeme Park, cutting down trees, eating the cattle, stealing two oxen, and further decreasing the estate's value. After the British had left and the war had moved to other parts of the country, Pennsylvania had confiscated her property.

When the state returned Graeme Park to her ownership, she still wanted to sell two-thirds of it but feared that the stipulation of "during her life" in the Assembly's restoration act would make it impossible to sell the property at its true value. Nevertheless she advertised briefly in the *Gazette* again the following January. This elicited an inquiry, but the sale fell through, much to Elizabeth's disappointment. There is an implication that the potential purchaser wanted the whole estate, but she was unwilling to part with the mansion house.[12]

A year later, Elias Boudinot suggested that some alternative other than selling Graeme Park might be devised. Perhaps some friend might undertake to lease the farm for her, with proper restrictions to protect its value and the tenant to pay all taxes. This would have given her a fixed income while retaining the estate. Money to pay her debts could be raised, he suggested, by other means, unspecified.[13] This, too, came to nothing.

No small part of her problems was caused by the requests of John Young and Henry Fergusson, both of whom wrote to her for money. In April 1782, she had met Young in Wilmington to see him for the last time before he left this continent for England. By then he was retired as a Lieutenant in the British army on half pay of £40 per year, not enough to support a young man used to living at Graeme Park. At this meeting, she gave him his inheritance from his father, who had died in January 1779. James Young had willed that his estate be sold and divided equally between John's sister and their aunt, knowing that John could not inherit because of his attainder, with the understanding that Elizabeth's portion was intended for John. This amounted to £3,000 in depreciated Pennsylvania money, which at the current exchange rate was equal to £115.7.9 in English currency. This sum she took to him in Wilmington. There is a suggestion, however, that perhaps this was in part her money because of some difficulty, now unclear, over James Young's estate or its debts.

In December 1782, Elizabeth once again advertised parts of

Graeme Park, one tract of 160 acres and another of 200. She promised to deliver "an indisputable title" to try to offset any question potential buyers might have about what they were buying. The ad appeared weekly throughout the month and into January. When a buyer did not appear, she decided to try another tack. She announced that the two tracts would be sold at a public vendue February 26 at the Coffee House in Philadelphia. When this produced no sale, another vendue was announced for March 5. No action happened then either, and no more ads appeared that year.

Shortly thereafter, a copy of the preliminary peace treaty between the United States and Great Britain was published in the Philadelphia newspapers. There were two provisions that particularly caught Elizabeth's attention. Article five committed Congress to recommend to the states that they restore all confiscated "estates, rights, and property, . . . belonging to real British subjects." Henry, she had argued, certainly belonged in the category of "real British subjects." Article six promised that there would be "no further confiscations made, nor any prosecutions commenced against any person or persons for or by reason of the part which he or they may have taken" during the war. No one should "on that account, suffer any future loss or damage either in his person, liberty, or property."[14] This meant that Henry Fergusson and John Young could return to Pennsylvania without fear of prosecution for their loyalty to Great Britain during the war, provided, of course, that Congress did make the promised recommendations to the states and that the states complied, an activity they were not noted for in the past.

After Elias Boudinot, then President of the Continental Congress, sent Elizabeth a special notice of the approaching peace, she wrote him a congratulatory letter. She wished that the celebratory festivities should be peaceful with "not one Life . . . lost, nor a drop of Blood Spilt." She would not, however, attend them. "Is it not Hard my dear Friend that with a heart formd for Urbanity and Convivial Cheerfulness on this Ocassion particularly, I Should from an extraordinary Embarassed perplexed and painfull Combination of Events remain lost totaly in Obscurity." She wished "to hide in Shades the many Sorrows that of late years [had] wounded" her peace.[15]

Although the Assembly's restoration act clearly precluded Henry from ownership of Graeme Park, article five in the preliminary peace treaty hinted that confiscated property might be returned. In that case, the Assembly's measure would be meaningless because the original confiscation would be voided. If that should happen, under Pennsylvania law Elizabeth would not be able to sell her estate without Henry's permission. It was highly unlikely that the debt-burdened states would take on the huge expense of reimbursing buyers of confiscated estates so that property could be returned to the original owners. Nevertheless, anyone considering the purchase of real estate would want to be absolutely certain of a firm title. To eliminate even this admittedly unlikely deterrent, Boudinot wrote that year to Phineas Bond in England asking him to secure Henry's power of attorney for Elizabeth to sell the estate. Boudinot was disturbed when he had not heard from Bond by January 1784, not realizing that Henry could not comply with his request. If Henry gave Elizabeth permission to sell her estate, he could not claim reimbursement for it from the British, and he was not going to sacrifice that opportunity. Boudinot's request soon became a moot point, the states not showing any interest at all in returning confiscated property.

Late that summer, Elizabeth received the letter from her husband giving her an ultimatum to join him in England or be separated for the rest of her days. If she refused to join him, it would "be acting in positive Contradiction to every Law human and divine, And what ever pretext you may chuse to make use of, there Exists none to Exculpate such a Breach of Duty."[16] Many of Elizabeth's contemporaries agreed with this last statement. Later she sent a copy of this letter to Annis Stockton. At the end she commented "I have not a doubt but every Husband that should read This in the 12 States will hold me a condemd as well as a Deserted-Wife. My Character is gone in that Line: But I wish not to retrieve it at the Expence of my Conscience." Any meeting with Henry would not be in England, she wrote, but in Pennsylvania, for only in Pennsylvania could "it be productive of Truth and Peace." She could not live with him again unless he returned there and answered the charges against him.

Sometimes Elizabeth seemed determined to be unhappy despite all attempts to help her make another life for herself. When Benjamin Rush urged her to visit Philadelphia in December 1783, she declined. He had written how much her friends wanted to see her and how much pleasure a visit would give them. She thanked him for his flattering kindness, but her "State of Humiliation . . . too deeply Affect[ed her] to Think of Mixing in Society." There the comparison of others' "Social Happiness with [her] own Contrasted State," would make her "more keenly feel [her] Deserted

Situation."[17] The Boudinots added their invitation for her and Betsy Stedman to visit them the following spring assuring her that it would give them
pleasure, but she did not go. Boudinot repeated the invitation in July. He
wrote that they would be alone and "would rejoice in the Company of
worthy Friends. It will be conferring a favour."[18] Again there is no sign of
acceptance, although others came to visit her at Graeme Park, Mrs. Campbell in January, Mrs. Redman and her family in July, Mrs. Roberdeau
shortly thereafter.[19] Betsy Stedman continued to live with Elizabeth, so that
she was not alone.

By January 1784, her financial situation was desperate. Part of
Graeme Park was rented for £125 to a man named James Ratliff, but she
paid the taxes while he cut down trees, as she complained, and wore out
the soil, not manuring it as her father had done. Her debts had reached
£1,500, and the interest was greater than the rent Ratliff was paying, if he
had paid it on time, which he seldom did. Usually it trickled in, no more
than £10 at a time. By July, Elias Boudinot was looking in Philadelphia for
someone who would lend her "a few hundred pounds for some years" so
that she could meet her most pressing needs.[20] This was the summer when
John Young wrote her begging for money for himself and Henry, who was
being sued for a debt of £300 sterling. It appears that she did respond to
their pleas, although she only could have done so by putting herself further
in debt.

How she lived for the next seven years is not clear. She refused to
accept charity from her friends, although she continued to borrow. Probably, she and Betsy Stedman were living on Betsy's £1000 inheritance intended to provide for Betsy's remaining life. By 1786, Graeme Park had
deteriorated badly. It was described by a visitor as "neglected," the garden
"ruined," and the "dirty" pump on the high side of the back court yard
creating "a perpetual puddle thro' the square."[21]

During the preceding winter she had suffered a period of depression because of her situation and had "Sunk down into an apathy that [was]
not natural to [her] temper." Whenever she had taken pen in hand to write
friends, she had realized that she "had nothing to offer worth the least
notice." Spring had arrived earlier than usual in February 1786 and "quite
unhinged" her, once again causing her health problems. The warm weather
had "relaxed" her, and the cold weather that followed "too Suddenly Shut
up the Pores."[22] This period of self-doubt, of unhappiness over her failed

marriage, and of fear of threatening destitution, all compounded by ill health, forced her to find other thoughts to occupy her days and preserve her sanity.

The return of warmer weather in April brought Elizabeth's spirits out of the depths they had reached. She wrote Benjamin Rush a remarkable, very long series of three letters, a small commonplace book in their contents.[23] Of the original letters, 138 sides remain, but missing enclosures mentioned in the contents must have brought the total pages to well over that number. She began writing on April 21. Finding no one to take that letter to Philadelphia, she continued it on the 26th and the 27th. This is like no other extant letter she previously had written.[24] In the past her letters had concerned herself and her contemporaries, with an occasional literary quotation or allusion, but this letter was almost exclusively about ideas. All three parts describe her critical readings of two publications, the first by Samuel Johnson and the second by Rush himself. If indeed this was the first such letter Rush had received from his friend, he must have been surprised; or perhaps she simply had put on paper for the first time the way she spoke in gatherings. She must have verbalized in such a way as to deserve the comments Rush later made about her soirees:

> [S]he instructed by the stores of knowledge contained in the historians, philosophers, and poets of ancient and modern nations, which she called forth at her pleasure; and again she charmed by a profusion of original ideas, collected by her vivid and widely expanded imagination, and combined with exquisite taste and judgment into an endless variety of elegant and delightful forms.[25]

She began her first letter to Rush by discussing Johnson's *Lives of the Poets*, summarizing the work briefly and commenting on various of the lives. A quotation from Johnson's life of Dr. Samuel Garth led her to recommend that Rush write a lives of physicians. "We have Lives of <u>Poets, Painters, Popes</u>," she reminded Rush and urged him to "Turn the <u>triumphirate</u> of P's in to a <u>Square</u>, and write the Lives of Eminent <u>Physicians</u>." She then proceeded to tell Rush which physicians' lives he should describe, including her own father's. This part of the letter also transmitted a quotation from Job and seven pages from her own translation of *Télémachus*, in which Fénélon introduced two physicians. Before quoting a long section about a physician from John Dryden's translation of Vergil's *Aeneid*, she commented that poetry was her "weak side" and that she could not resist transcribing a beautiful passage, even at the risk of appearing "a *Classical* pedant, or what is much Worse a *female* one." The "risk" must not have troubled her very much, for the letters would certainly be called the work of a savante, if not a pedante, with their many quotations and allusions, literary and historical.

The extensions written on April 26 and 27 critique Rush's essay "Physical Causes Influencing the Moral Faculty," a copy of which he had sent her. Rush defined the moral faculty as "a capacity in the human mind of distinguishing and choosing good and evil," as distinct from the conscience, which monitors human actions for their conformance to the good. He argued that many material factors affect the moral faculty, listing over twenty, among them climate, diet, hunger, disease, cleanliness, music, light, and darkness. Elizabeth analyzed the essay in detail, approving his arguments where she agreed but not hesitating to tell him he was mistaken where she did not. She began by supporting his general hypothesis and contributing further examples to illustrate it. Citing Goldsmith's *Vicar of Wakefield,* she wrote that its readers are "animated with the picture of His winter evening fire, the very Crackling of it animates; and we are <u>warmd</u> and <u>Cheerd</u> By the ideal Flame." The opposite of the Vicar's hickory fire, England's gloomy coal fires, she blamed for its increased suicide rate in November, cited by Rush under the effects of climate. Elizabeth also liked Rush's reference to Othello's inability to murder Desdemona until he extinguished his candle, which Rush discussed under the effect of light and darkness. "He could not have done the Deed had light been round Him," she wrote. "Small things in Such a Genius as Shakspear are Big with meaning."

In spite of agreeing in general with Rush's hypothesis, Elizabeth challenged several of his particular examples. She could not accept his interpretation of St. Paul's comment "I bear in my Body the marks of the Lord Jesus" as meaning that the regenerates have "marks Corporealy within or without different from the Bad." To her, St. Paul referred to virtues such as temperance, chastity, morality, and piety, not to marks on the body. Actually her interpretation fit Rush's thesis better than his own. Under the cause "association" Rush had recommended that punishments should follow crimes immediately, "quick as thunder follows the lightning," to enforce the association between the forbidden deed and its consequence. Elizabeth took exception to this, pointing out the possibility of an erroneous judgment that further consideration might correct. And so she worked her way through each of the physical causes that Rush had listed as affecting the moral faculty. Some she commended; others she contested. Sometimes she corrected his interpretations of quotations, flatly telling him he erred.

Her biggest argument with Rush's thesis was that it supported the concept of materialism. She felt certain that he would never intentionally write anything encouraging a belief in materialism, but nevertheless, his were the arguments that had been used to prove that the body and the mind "are of one Nature." His argument that certain patients in the throes of a fatal illness often "discover degrees of benevolence and integrity, that were not natural to them in the ordinary course of their lives" was a proof of materialism, she wrote. As Rush used this example, the altered character was not due to a "ray or divine influx from heaven; But produced by agonizing pangs of the Body: which when that Body is no more, can be followed with no such consequences." "I don't think you enter half in to the powers of the mind," she criticized Rush, and she recommended that he read "that singular genius" Emanuel Swedenborg, whose writings would help Rush understand "the operation of [the] faculty of the mind we call <u>Conscience</u>," "the hardest to define with any degree of precision of any that make up our intellectual powers." She told him that he could borrow a book of Swedenborg's writings from Dr. John Redman, who could enlighten Rush about Swedenborg. Her letter is laced with quotations from Goldsmith, *Othello*, Alexander Pope, Samuel Richardson's *Clarissa*, Swedenborg, John Locke, and others. Citations poured out of her, her memory quite remarkable.

As Elizabeth analyzed, amended, corrected, and reinterpreted Rush's already published work, giving it a critical review, she included no version of the usual "I'm only a woman so what do I know" statement that women conventionally associated with their intellectual forays. She does comment at the end of the second letter that when she dissents from his reasoning, he must allow her the same freedom he assumes when he critiques others, and she specifically cites his criticism of Locke, but she does not apologize for her temerity. She wrote as Rush's intellectual equal, if not superior.

Concluding the packet of letters to Rush are 78 sides of excerpts from the thirty-four long letters Elizabeth had received from John Fothergill between 1764 and 1778. At the end, she hoped that she would not be "accused of Egregious Vanity in giving these Extracts." She "thought as Dr. <u>Fothergill</u> had been viewed as a <u>Philosopher</u> and a man of Science it might not be unpleasing to see him in His Social and Domestic Habits, in Letters written at a time of Life when his Character was in its Meridian." Yet, despite her disclaimer, that Fothergill, and Rush as well, two famous and highly educated men, should consider her correspondence worth pursuing certainly credits Elizabeth and her intellectual abilities.

Fothergill's letters[26] are warm; his affection for Elizabeth was obvious, as was his desire for her to continue the correspondence. He urged her to write to him frequently and asked several times for her journals that she had promised to send him. Later he indicated his pleasure in reading them. She also had sent him a copy of her poem about the philosophical farmer, and he commented that "there are many excellent lines in it." He encouraged her to follow her own talents rather than quoting others: "The Authoress had two things in her hand, and ought to have had but one," he wrote, "instead of following the Bent of her own Genius entirely she prefer'd the Sentiments of others." After copying the letters, Elizabeth realized that Fothergill's partiality for her was revealed in them perhaps too freely because she concluded with the surprising statement that "unask'd <u>Truth</u> and <u>Honour</u> require me to Declare that Doctor Fothergill never was in my offer." By this, I assume she means that Fothergill had never tendered her an offer of marriage.

In preparing her letter to Rush, Elizabeth rediscovered that the act of writing would help her regain her equilibrium. In 1766, after the deaths of her mother and her sister, Ann Stedman, Elizabeth Graeme had found solace first in paraphrasing the Psalms and then in versifying a translation of *Télémachus*. Now, grieving for her broken marriage and struggling to find another identity, Elizabeth Fergusson once again buried herself in her writing. To help her reclaim public recognition of her abilities, a new vehicle to showcase her work became available.

In the *Pennsylvania Gazette* for August 9, 1786, Elizabeth read that a group of Philadelphia men were going to begin publishing the first periodical in Pennsylvania since the war. They intended to include original writing as well as reprints. Her childhood friend Francis Hopkinson had close connections to *The Columbian Magazine,* publishing both prose and poetry in it himself and, for a few months in early 1787, editing it. He undoubtedly encouraged Elizabeth to submit her poems for publication, and a verse by Annis Stockton in the second issue may have inspired Elizabeth further to submit her creations, if she had not already done so. In the December issue appeared the first, "On the Death of Leopold," in memory of the Prince of Brunswick who had drowned while trying to rescue some children from a flooding river. From then until the periodical ended in December 1792, Elizabeth published at least twenty-four more of her pieces in *The Columbian Magazine* and its successor, *The Universal Asylum and Columbian Magazine*, and there may have been others without a recognizable pen name or an extant manuscript copy to identify them as hers.

Most eighteenth-century periodicals included an editor's page devoted to communicating with contributors, announcing what pieces had been received, whether they would be published, and in some cases why not. Even though he usually did not pay the authors whose contributions he requested to fill out his pages, the editor of *The Columbia Magazine* did not spare its contributors' feelings. If he rejected a submission, he might tell its author that his piece was "too incoherent," "too indelicate," or "not sufficiently interesting." He pulled one contributor up short by announcing that his submission was plagiarized and asking whether he thought the editor was so ill-read that he would not recognize such an obvious theft. He even took the license to "make some necessary alterations"[27] in submissions, if the spirit moved him. Elizabeth's writing, however, never received any disparaging remarks, at least not in print, but instead the editors welcomed and encouraged her contributions.

In the section entitled "To Contributors," we can trace her progress in having her writings published, even though her letters do not remain. The editor addressed her as Laura from Montgomery County, the name she used to sign most of her publications. Since the identity of "Laura" was well-known in Philadelphia, she might just as well have signed her own name. The use of pseudonyms, however, was common in England and America where it was not the practice for women, or men either, to publish under their real names, even if their pseudonyms had been widely identified.

In the spring of 1787, Laura sent the editor of *The Columbian* a packet of several poems, which he promised to insert occasionally. One each appeared in the issues of July and September.[28] The July poem, "The Continental Medley, An Epigram," signed E. Salmon Gundy, was written in response to a passage in David Ramsay's *History of the Revolution in South Carolina*. At the beginning of the Revolution, Ramsey related, a member of the South Carolina Assembly had made a speech in which he had opposed the calling of a continental congress because the colonies were too different. He facetiously had listed the individual colonies' agricultural products as the ingredients of an unpalatable dish when combined. But another member of the Assembly had asserted that "if the Colonies proceeded Judiciously in the appointment of deputing Deputies for a *Continental Congress* They would prepare a dish fit to be presented to any Crowned head in *Europe*." Elizabeth responded with a witty poetical paraphrase. It begins,

> Tho' the *Yankey's* their *onions* and *fish* had well mix'd,
> And their superfine *flour*, the *Yorker's* had dish'd;
> Tho' *pork* of the largest, the *Jersey's* had sent,
> And her neighbouring sister should *flax-seed* present

After naming all the colonies and the ingredients they would contribute to this culinary masterpiece, the Fergusson poem concludes

> yet believe me no monarch the olio would taste,
> If *Bourbon* some *Cooks* had not sent to the feast;
> This curious collection of substances strange,
> The *Parisians* found methods most skillful to range;
> What suited each corner, immediate they spy,
> And the finger of *Gallia* compleated the pye.[29]

In early October, Elizabeth received word that her friend Rebecca Langly, one of the sisters at Bethlehem, had died. She immediately submitted a poem in her memory with a letter asking about the poems she had previously transmitted. The editor replied testily that he would "attend to" her letter and poetry and explained that her verses on the death of Miss Langly had "arrived too late" for the October issue. They did appear in November, however.

Three of Elizabeth's poems were published in 1788. In June, her "Lines on Reading Mrs. M. Moore's printed and unprinted extracts for the use of Schools" commended the work of her friend Milcah Martha Moore, who lived in Montgomery Square, approximately four and a half miles west and north of Graeme Park. This was within walking distance for Elizabeth, who often walked into Philadelphia, nineteen miled away. Moore's brother Henry Hill, one of Montgomery County's representatives in the Assembly, had been a strong supporter of Elizabeth's petition to have Graeme Park restored to her. Over the years, Elizabeth had contributed books to a circulating library established in Montgomery Square and had sent small sums of money to support the school that Moore had founded there.[30]

In late August or early September, Elizabeth sent the editor of *The Columbian* a long rambling poem called the "Willow of Lichfield." The editor assured her that he did not intend to "neglect" it, but the length of the poem had caused him "to defer publishing it." Although he hoped "to find an early opportunity" to "lay it before the public" that opportunity never came. In October he reported that he had planned to insert it in that month's magazine, but Elizabeth's handwriting was so "illegible" that "the printers could not decipher the manuscript." A new editor took over the reins in the coming months, but "The Litchfield Willow" was not handed down to him. He told Elizabeth the following April, in answer to her inquiry about it, to prepare "a fair copy," and "it shall certainly appear, if approved." Either she never prepared that copy or it was not approved because it never appeared.

The poem consists of fifty-five quatrains and is accompanied by twenty-five annotations, explaining characters in the poem, often digressing markedly with stories about them. Its subject matter is a willow tree in Lichfield, England, the birthplace of Dr. Samuel Johnson, and the "many conspicuous characters" who might "have at some period of their lives walked and studied under its extensive Boughs." In the long letter to the editor, which she intended to be published preceding the poem, she introduced each of these persons: Joseph Addison, Gilbert Walsmby, William Hogarth, David Garrick, Dr. Samuel Johnson, Anna Seward, and others. With its many literary references, this would have been considered a very learned production. An editor who published the letter, the poem, and its notes would have had to commit a large portion of an issue to it. Perhaps that is why it was never published by *The Columbian.*

In March 1790, the magazine changed both its management and its name, becoming the *Universal Asylum and Columbian Magazine.* In May the editor regretted that more women were not sending in their contributions. "The talents of many of them are great," he wrote, "and ought not to be confined to the circle of their more immediate acquaintance." This was all the encouragement Elizabeth needed. She spent the summer months preparing copies of several of her poems and also of Anna Young's.

By September, the editor was thanking her for "the elegant productions of her own muse" and for a poem called "On Reading Swift's Works," written by Anna Young. He solicited her "future correspondence." Young's poem, signed Sylvia, and three of Laura's were included in that issue. From then until the magazine ended in December 1792, eight of Anna Young's poems were published in addition to Laura's, the editor having indicated that "any other productions of *Sylvia's* elegant muse, which may be in the possession of *Laura*, would be highly acceptable."

In October another two of Laura's poems appeared, but by then Elizabeth was working on a fair copy of a long prose allegory, originally written in 1767 for Anna Young, revising it slightly as she prepared it for submission. The editor acknowledged receiving it in January and promised to "pay the earliest attention to the literary favours" of its author.[31] The allegory appeared in the issues of February, March, and April, 1791. Preceding it is Elizabeth's letter to the editor explaining that it is intended for young people "to promote the love of truth." Concluding the letter is an anecdote of John Wilkes, who in his youth had studied divinity and been honored by his mentor with the epithet "The Beauty of holiness." "What use Mr. Wilkes made of his theological science in a mature season," she wrote, ". . . is too well known, with horror, by the decent, to need further illustration. . . . He perverted the choicest gifts to the worst of purposes; as the strongest wine makes the sharpest vinegar."[32] The characters in her allegory illustrated similar undesirable behavior.

The allegory tells the story of Wisdom, his wife Truth, who was the first born of Jove, and their daughter Contemplation. The peace of the Placid Grove where they lived on earth was shattered by the arrival of Falsehood. When Truth was away, Falsehood tricked Wisdom into union with her, which produced a son Cunning, a cruel little liar. The tale relates the interaction between the inhabitants of the Placid Grove and those of Mount Vanity, where lived Falsehood, Cunning, Self-Love, Dissimulation, and their ilk, emphasizing throughout the superiority of the former. This was clearly written for young people. It has none of the classical or literary references that crowd many of Elizabeth's other works.

In February, the editor acknowledged having received Laura's "polite letter, together with the packet that accompanied it." He promised that his "early insertion of some of the poems will discover our inclination to treat the favours of our fair correspondent with due attention and respect. The remaining poems, and also the prose articles, shall be inserted as quickly as possible." True to his word, two of Elizabeth's poems were published in that issue as well as the first part of the allegory.[33]

Two prose selections were included in March's issue in addition to the second part of the allegory. One of these was a letter Elizabeth had received in 1789 from her cousin Mrs. Senior in Jamaica about the ill effects of novel reading. Deborah Senior agreed with her Pennsylvania cousin that Samuel Richardson should be commended for his "painting virtue in so pleasing a garb" in his novels. The disadvantage of novel reading, she continued, was that it might make sensitive persons suffer more from the tragedies in their lives than they would without this stimulation. Her view of life as a short period of extreme distress and discomfort, if not agony, to be endured until the glorious afterlife might be reached was not only Elizabeth's opinion also but was very prevalent at the time. The second of Elizabeth's prose selections published in March was a short report of the encounter between Elizabeth and Laurence Sterne during her trip to England.

The editor of *The Universal Asylum*, having already given much attention to Laura and Sylvia, nevertheless reassured Elizabeth in April that

> Our limits will not permit us to take notice, in this place, of the numerous favours transmitted by our fair correspondent in Montgomery county. But, that she may not have cause to charge us with want of due attention, we shall shortly write her a letter, on the subject of the sundry pieces which we have not yet inserted.

Still, he did include two of Laura's poems, and in May, one of Sylvia's.[34] In June, two more of Laura's pieces and one of Sylvia's appeared with the message "Our much esteemed correspondent, *Laura,* will perceive that we are not inattentive either to her favours, or to those written by *Sylvia.* We shall continue to diminish our debt to both, till the whole are inserted." This was the last message he wrote Elizabeth in the magazine. He also inserted in August her and Anna Young's last poems to be published in *The Universal Asylum* in 1791: Sylvia's "Lines on Walking in the Churchyard" written to Elizabeth and her reply "Lines Written on Reading Anna Young's Churchyard Poem."[35]

The letter to Elizabeth from the editor, if written, does not remain, so that we do not know why this extraordinary output markedly decreased, but it did. It was not because Elizabeth had run out of poems to submit because there are many that were never published. She wrote almost as many other new poems as she published during the lifetime of *The Universal Asylum*. In 1792, only one poem by Sylvia appeared in July, two of Laura's in July and one in September. The magazine ended publication with the December issue because a new postal regulation made it impossible for the editors to deliver their issues outside Philadelphia. It was continued as *The Columbian Museum; or, Universal Asylum* in January, but it stopped finally in June 1793.

Meanwhile, another periodical, *The American Museum,* was published by Mathew Carey beginning January 1787 and ending the same month as *The Universal Asylum* and for the same reason. Carey intended for his magazine only to reprint American writings that had appeared elsewhere, but over the years Carey did include some original material, especially poetry. Only one of Elizabeth's verses and a letter she wrote to Dr. Rush can be identified in this magazine. The letter, published in the November 1791 issue, supported Rush's opposition to capital punishment. Her poem appeared the following year[36] in answer to one in the preceding volume entitled "ON DRESS.-To the ladies." "Burlington" had called women to task for "bearing on their lovely backs, A load . . . Of transatlantic frippery and nicknacks." Elizabeth, as "Dorothy Plain Montgomery co.," responded more or less humorously that women's emphasis upon fashion was all the fault of men who hypocritically preach on the charms of the mind but act quite differently when in society. "The finest dressed lady commands all respect, / To her your attention you meanly direct! / While the valuable plain ones are stung by neglect." The answer to women's extravagant dressing is easy to find, Dorothy wrote, "But strip us, or dress us, as high as you can, / The pole star of woman, I fancy, is man!" The argument is reminiscent of "Aspasia's" answer to "Visitant," which first appeared in *The Pennsylvania Chronicle* April 4 to 11, 1768 (see Chapter 5). *The Museum* had reprinted the whole series of "Visitant" articles in 1788 and 1789. "Aspasia's" irony is typical of Elizabeth's style on occasion, but there is no evidence to indicate that she wrote the essay. Elizabeth told Rebecca Smith that she had written the Dorothy Plain poem as a "source of amusement to disipate [her] gloom," scribbling "nonsense" to keep her mind from preying on "the most painful Subjects."[37]

Elizabeth's poem in *The Universal Asylum* in September, "Paraphrase of St. Luke," was the last of her poems known to have been published during her lifetime. Although both *The Universal Asylum* and *The Museum* ended in December 1792, other periodicals existed where she could have submitted her work. Upon their demise, for example, the editor of *The Massachusetts Magazine* announced that he intended to include the best of their features. He sent out a Circular Letter "personally addressed to eminent characters, soliciting their patronage and correspondence," and he also commented that the "Fair sex merits our attention." Women often published their poetry in *The Massachusetts Magazine*, but none can be identified as Elizabeth's from manuscript copies, and none was signed Laura or any other of her known pseudonyms.[38] There were also several magazines published in Philadelphia during the 1790s for short periods, but none of her poetry has been located in any of them. Why did she stop trying to have her verses published? It could have been disdain for the quality of the other magazines. Not until *The Port Folio* was launched in 1801, the year of her death, was another magazine considered to be of the same caliber as *The Columbian Magazine* and *The Musuem*. It is more likely that other matters monopolized her time and attention. In 1791, she finally sold Graeme Park, in 1793, she began trying to have her translation of *Télémachus* published, and by 1795 her health was deteriorating. She was also writing commonplace books to answer the requests of friends, at least two of which have disappeared.

Writing poetry might have helped Elizabeth fight off depression, but it did nothing to solve her financial difficulties. Elias Boudinot continued to be concerned about the sale of Graeme Park. In May 1787, Elizabeth had advertised it in the *Pennsylvania Packet* with no success. A possible purchaser had raised her hopes, but he had turned out to be in desperate straits himself and, soon after, had left town. Boudinot had commiserated with her the following January, but had advised that that was not a good time to try to sell real estate. It would not bring one-third of its worth. Boudinot had hoped that the demand for improved lands would increase by spring and promised to do everything in his power to relieve her situation then.[39]

When anyone expressed an interest in buying the estate, the words "during her natural life" in the restoration act raised questions. Elizabeth had to convince prospective purchasers that the phrase was meaningless. What the state had appropriated after Henry's attainder, she explained over and over, were his rights in Graeme Park. Since he never had acquired fee simple ownership, all the state could confiscate was control over Graeme Park's management during her lifetime because that was all that Henry had obtained when he married her. She had not been attainted; therefore, ownership remained hers, and what the state had returned to her was what it had appropriated, control of the estate. With or without the words in the act, management of Graeme Park would be hers only throughout her life. The act's words were extraneous.[40] Nevertheless, she was deeply in debt, and the people to whom she owed money were pressing her for its return. Desperate to sell the estate, Elizabeth was distressed at any hint that possession would be only for her lifetime and then it would revert to the state. Temporary ownership would not attract a buyer.

The draft deed Henry submitted to the British commissioners showing that he had been given fee simple ownership of Graeme Park still exists among the loyalist papers, and other Pennsylvanians in London at the time identified the handwriting as Richard Stockton's. Thus, such a transfer must have been discussed at least by her husband and Stockton. Henry accused Elizabeth of destroying the final deed in order to mislead the legislature into revesting the estate in herself. Elizabeth, however, absolutely denied that any such transfer had ever been made. If she had been asked to sign and had refused, she would have announced this as soon as the draft surfaced in England. It is probable that she never knew about the negotiations between Richard Stockton and Henry Fergusson and that the only document ever drawn up was the draft that Henry had.

With Graeme Park still unsold by the end of the 1780s and her income from rental of part of it insufficient to cover her needs, Elizabeth was faced with destitution. By then, she was three thousand pounds in debt. Her loans had been underwritten by mortgages, the repayment of one of them had come due, and she was threatened with foreclosure. She had used all of Betsy Stedman's £1,000 fortune without giving Betsy a mortgage or any kind of protection. She wrote Elias Boudinot, "my tenant is behind in his Rent, my Farm is going to Ruin, I know not what part of the Globe Mr F n is, My nephew is proscribed . . . [and] I am ill too."[41] To further complicate matters, a long-dormant claim against Graeme Park had surfaced, and her ownership of the farm was being questioned. Apparently this turned out to be invalid or was conveniently compromised because it did not become an obstacle to the future sale.[42] Still the uncertainty was one more stress for Elizabeth to confront and endure.

To distract her mind from her financial and marital deficiencies, sometime in 1787 Elizabeth began copying a selection of her poems for Annis Stockton, who had long requested them.[43] The subject matter of the finished commonplace book is very diverse and includes other writings that she thought might interest her friend. There are thirty of her own poems interspersed with her youthful translation of a French verse on materialism, a poem by Henry Fergusson describing his father's estate in Scotland, several poems of Francis Hopkinson, a letter she had written to Elias Boudinot at the time peace was negotiated, an extract from David Ramsey's *History of the Revolution in South Carolina*, and some verses by Major André. The book concludes with copies of fifteen poems written by Anny Young Smith and several of her letters. It is a remarkable record of part of one woman's literary production and her intellectual interests.

Benjamin Rush was not the only noted male contemporary who sent her copies of his work. In 1789, Francis Hopkinson sent her a prepublication copy of a humorous poem he had written, and Elizabeth answered him in kind. Hopkinson wanted to publish her poem, but she refused because "the subject matter [was] rather too indelicate for a female Pen."[44]

Hopkinson's poem was inspired by a split that had occurred that year in the University of Pennsylvania. A decade earlier, the state had appropriated the College of Philadelphia, renamed it the University of Pennsylvania, and replaced Rev. William Smith, the College's administrator. In 1789, the Assembly passed an act returning the school to its original owners and Rev. Smith to the Provost's position. Rather than the University ending, however, it continued to exist and settled in the new hall of the American Philosophical Society, thereby giving Philadelphia two schools of higher education. The doctors in the medical school, which had been established at the College and been continued at the University, were in a quandary what to do. Eventually some returned to the College while others stayed with the University or lectured at both. Hopkinson's poem, entitled "An Oration, which Might Have Been Delivered to the Students in Anatomy on the Late Rupture Between the Two Schools in This City,"[45] addressed this division in the medical ranks.

His poem begins by reminding the anatomy students that they already had "num'rous foes" without turning on one another. Had they forgotten, he asks them, the difficulties they have had in acquiring cadavers for dissection? While stealing bodies from "The Negro Burial ground," they frequently had been attacked by objecting relatives and friends of the deceased. Often the mourners had interrupted their dissection classes to reclaim the body currently under the knife. He then boasts his own love of science, proving his passion for it by describing how he had fallen in love with his cadaver, whom he had named Cadavera. Unwilling to give up his love, he had boiled her bones to clean them of flesh and wired them together to form a skeleton, which then became his companion, even accompanying him to bed.

It is this part of the poem that Elizabeth answered in her "Cadavera[']s Ghost, or a visit to Tomboso." Calling herself Hecatissa, Elizabeth addressed Hopkinson as Tomboso,

> The most Sublime of all Terestrial Sublimitys.
> The Pinnacle of altitudes.
> The Profoundest of all Profunditys.
> The Zenith of all Science.
> . . . The Knight Errand of all Cosmetries.
> Doctor,—Tomboso—Charnello,
> Franssia—Hopkinsino.

She tells the story of Cadavera's ghost returning to rattle her bones and talk to Tomboso. She had watched his preservation of her bones and approved of it as the highest expression of his love. Other men left their dead lovers in the tomb, "Meanly diserted as the Flesh Decayd." The future will remember Cadavera from her bones and forget other legendary beauties. It was too bad they had never had children to "bless the world." He must beware how he describes her charms or he will excite "wanton thoughts." As "The Cocks Shrill Clarion" is heard, before Cadavera bids Tomboso goodbye, she predicts he will find another love in ten years but warns him to "chuse as nobly as you chose before."

The poem has many literary references. There are eighteen notes explaining sources as diverse as Chiron in Greek mythology; Archimedes, Greek mathematician and physicist; William Hogarth, English painter; Lord George Lyttleton, English writer; Shakespeare's plays *The Tempest*, *Romeo and Juliet*, and *King Lear*; English poet James Tomson's "Story of Lavinia"; Alexander Pope, English poet; Jonathan Swift, Irish satyrist and clergyman; and Vergil's *Aeneid*. The copy of the poem that remains is one she sent to Drs. John Redman and Benjamin Rush. Whether the recipients would have recognized the allusions without the notes is not known, but the implication of their inclusion is that Elizabeth thought they might not.

Above all, what strikes the reader are Elizabeth's ability to recall all the sources and her skill at integrating them into a witty, clever piece.

Not always was Elizabeth's comic product as intellectual as it was in "Cadavera's Ghost." Sometimes it came out as knee slapping doggerel. Around 1790, her beloved dog Fidele died. Elizabeth buried him with all honors, erecting a stone in his memory, and inviting residents of Graeme Park to attend his funeral. Neighbor Dr. Archibald McLean heard of the event and sent her a satirical epitaph to Fidele. Elizabeth replied with an anonymous "Epitaph on Dr. Archibald McClean," who was six and a half feet tall and enjoyed his grog and jokes at Widow Jenkins Tavern in Jenkintown.

> Beneath this turf and humble stone
>   McClean's remains do rest;
> This letter'd marble plain shall own
>   The virtues he possessed.
> Of light and shade he was compos'd,
>   And so are most below;
> His sympathetic heart disclos'd
>   A sense of other's woe.
> Tho' of the Esculapian race,
>   He ne'er did patients fill
> With nauseous drugs in any case,
>   Emetic, purge or pill.
> With farmers he his grog would take,
>   With tradesmen quaff a sling,
> With gentlemen Madiera drink,
>   And brisk the bottle fling.
> He lov'd his bowl, his joke, his friend,
>   I dare not say his lass

And so on, she continued for another twenty-two lines of humorous character analysis. She concluded with McClean's anti-clericalism and the suggestion that he "Perhaps may wish a conscience nice / had guided him while here." Dr. McClean, no mean doggerel writer himself, responded in kind. In his riposte, he defended himself and consigned his correspondent after death to a state in between heaven and hell where "If he no pleasure knows when gone, / No pain can he endure." Elizabeth probably would have accepted this condition with gratitude here on earth.[46]

One of her earthly problems was coming soon to an end, however. By early January 1791, she had received several bids for Graeme Park, and Elizabeth was looking for another place to live. She wrote Rebecca Smith, "I am looking now like the Bewilderd Dove for place of Rest but where my tent will be fixd is as little known to me as to your self."[47] Dr. William Smith, Anna Young's widower, was the highest bidder. Whether he did this to save the woman who had raised his first wife with such tender love from parish charity or whether to make a good investment is not known. In the long run, both goals were accomplished.

Smith paid £3,500 for the estate, £1,000 down, with interest to be paid on the remainder until the balance was discharged in periodic payments. Faithful friend Elias Boudinot managed the sale and her debt repayment. Elizabeth insisted that all of the first payment be used to settle her debts immediately, but Boudinot urged a more prudent move. An agreement was executed with George Meade whereby he invested £500 of Elizabeth's money in the Bank of the United States, then forming. The Bank was to have a capital of ten million dollars, one-fifth provided by the federal government and four-fifths by public subscription. Boudinot urged this investment in April 1791 with the warning that the opportunity would not be available in another year. He was absolutely correct. The bank was subscribed in less than two hours. He also explained why she should not use all the first payment to pay debts and invest the second payment in another kind of annuity. The Bank would begin paying the interest on the debt of the United States. This would flood the country, especially the Middle Atlantic states, with currency and sharply reduce the interest rate obtainable. This investment allowed Meade to guarantee Elizabeth an annuity of £60 per year, whereas she would have been lucky to receive £40 in a year's time.[48]

Boudinot also took charge of all the negotiations about Elizabeth's debts. In visiting each of the creditors, he managed to make interest payments current, negotiate downward at least one debt, and settle a pending suit against the estate before it appeared in court. His accounting of his negotiations is enough unclear to leave the reader with the suspicion that Boudinot actually was paying some of her debts himself. How she could have managed without his efficient and knowledgeable help is inconceivable. Elizabeth, like most eighteenth-century American women, knew little of economic matters and would have been helpless in these negotiations. Boudinot and George Meade were friends of the highest order; she was lucky to have them.

The deed was signed on April 30, 1791. From then on, Graeme Park no longer belonged to Elizabeth Fergusson. She would not move for two more years, but she would be a guest of others in the house where she had lived most of her life.

12

The Next Narrower Circle

Once Elizabeth had signed the deed on April 30, 1791, selling Graeme Park to William Smith, she had to find another place to live where the cost would be within her very limited income. Philadelphia was an obvious choice for a person with her intellectual and social inclinations, but the city was probably too expensive. Even if she had been wealthy, however, Elizabeth would have eliminated Philadelphia as an option because of her perceived humiliation over her desertion by Henry. The best choice was to stay in the same area where she had lived most of the previous twenty years and where she had made many friends, especially among the Quakers whose quiet piety she respected. There was no Anglican church in Horsham, and the Graeme family had attended the Quaker meeting whenever they had been at Graeme Park, preferring it to any other church nearby.[1]

The home that eventually welcomed her belonged to Mrs. Todd, a widow with two grown sons, both physicians. She lived in Hatborough, commonly called the Crooked Billet, a small village located in the Manor of Mooreland, about four miles from Graeme Park.[2] There Elizabeth reestablished her life, continuing to revise and organize her papers.

The biggest attraction in the Crooked Billet for Elizabeth was the Union Library Company of Hatborough, founded in 1755 to "Expell those Gloomy Clouds of Ignorance and Open Profaneness so much Abounding, and give the gentle Reader an Agreeable taste for Learning."[3] This was a circulating library on the plan of the Library Company of Philadelphia founded by Benjamin Franklin. People bought membership in the company, paid yearly dues, and in return could borrow books bought with the proceeds. Although none of the Graemes ever had been a member, father and daughter frequently contributed to the library, beginning in 1763 with a donation of fourteen books. James Young had been a member and Henry Fergusson had joined in 1773 and been chosen a director in 1774 and 1775. Whenever Elizabeth had wanted to read one of the library's books, James, or later Henry, could have borrowed it for her or she could have borrowed it herself. One of the provisions of the Instrument of Partnership allowed the secretary to lend books not wanted by members to non-members upon their providing security for double the books' value. No objections would have been raised to Elizabeth, a library patron, borrowing books. During the period that she lived in the Crooked Billet, the library was kept in a tavern across the street from its present location, in the center of the village. This would have been very convenient for Elizabeth to browse the latest acquisitions.

Her move to the Crooked Billet, or simply the Billet as she called it, would not take place until the last week in December 1793. At first, Dr. Smith and his second wife, Letitia, were in no hurry to occupy the mansion, and then, the catastrophic yellow fever epidemic in late summer and early fall of 1793 intervened. The Smiths urged Elizabeth to stay on at Graeme Park for the rest of her life, but she had no desire to remain a guest in what once had been her family home. No longer the mistress, it would have been difficult, if not impossible, for her to stand back and allow Dr. Smith's wife to manage servants, make household decisions, and provide for guests. She would have found an uncomfortable niche in that house after they took over, but as long as they did not want to occupy the estate, she remained.

Meanwhile, Elizabeth's agonizing over Henry's infidelity and absence continued unabated. While negotiating with Dr. Smith over the sale of Graeme Park, she saved all correspondence about it. "Should Mr. Fergusson and I ever live together or Should he ever See these Letters, let him See if he chances to read them, that I did not rashly Sell my Farm," she wrote thirteen years after his departure. Even though Henry had no legal right to the estate, she would have submitted her conduct to him "as tho he had never forfeited these Rights."[4] She continued to beg Rebecca Smith to persuade Phineas Bond to answer some questions, long after both Rebecca and Phineas had refused to discuss the matter further.[5]

To add to her obsession about Henry, Elizabeth worried about the deteriorating condition of John Young. In late 1787 she had received a very depressing letter from him advising her that he had gone back into the British army because of his poverty. He wrote her that one midnight "the spectre of Poverty drew [his] curtains, and stared at [him] with such an aspect as frightened away [his pacifist] philosophy." The next morning, he went to the War Office, offered his services, and was assigned to his old regiment as a recruiter. He wrote his aunt that, as soon as war broke out, he would

> be sent to the most remote and dreary corner of the Island, in the most dreary season of the year; among people with whom [he] had been long enough associated to dislike to commence again an employment which [he] had practiced long enough to be sated with, by raising men in the service of a country for which I have no particular affection in a quarrel which [he thought] both unjust and unwise.[6]

In early 1789, Young had suffered "a paralytic stroke," from which he had largely recovered by the following July, regaining the use of his limbs almost completely. Nevertheless, his physician had recommended that he not remain in England over the next winter but instead seek a warmer climate in southern France. Because of his illness, he had been relieved of his military duties and put upon half pay, although he had been promised upon his return a lieutenancy in the Invalids Corps.

Elizabeth's concern about his health was tempered by the good news that he finally had decided upon a profession. It was his intention when he returned from the continent to apply himself "to translation as the most profitable department in the trade of letters." If she would consult the *European Magazine* for June 1789, he proudly wrote her, she would discover that he had already begun his life of scholarship by publishing an article on Aristotle's *Poetics*.[7] He concluded his letter with the wish to hear from her that she was "either unconditionally reconciled" to Henry or that she had become reconciled "to the loss of him."[8] He had put his finger on the dilemma for Elizabeth; neither alternative was possible for her.

When Young returned to London a year later, he arranged to go to the coast of Africa, but precisely where or when or in what capacity is not known. Comments in letters suggest that his destination was Sierra

Leone on the west coast. England had begun to acquire territory there in 1788 when the British Society for the Abolition of Slavery bought land to resettle destitute freed slaves. This was a project that would have appealed deeply to Young, who was outspoken in his condemnation of slavery. "If every Slave in the World were to rise in one night and kill his Tyrant, he would not only," according to Young, "be guiltless of any Crime But would achieve a Deed worthy of Celebration in Immortal Song."[9] In announcing his departure from London, Young sent his aunt a tract containing a "plan of Commerce, and government" related somehow to placing "the African Race on a Decent equality with the White." She sent him, in return, a copy of black mathematician Benjamin Banneker's almanac and famous 1791 letter to Thomas Jefferson reminding the Declaration of Independence's author of his words about the rights of all men and of the United States' battle to prevent its own enslavement by Great Britain. Elizabeth suggested that John share these documents with the Africans to show them that "one of their Color" had achieved such a "Degree of Information" and was able to "act as a Stimulus" to their own improvement.[10]

Upon his return from Provence, Young had begun to apply himself to translating from the French the *Compendium of Ancient Geography* by Jean-Baptiste Bourguignon d'Anville. His translation was published in two volumes in London, and by September 1792, Elizabeth had received a copy, read it, and presented it to the Library Company of Philadelphia. Her nephew also had become fluent enough in Italian to translate some of Ludovico Ariosto's poetry.[11]

Unfortunately, just as Young was beginning to make a life for himself, his health problems became much worse. In September 1793, Elizabeth received a short note dated the previous January 15 in barely legible handwriting:

> I am returned from Africa my health so Bad I could do no good There. My disorder lies in my head excrutiating pain and at times an invincible Stupor. I have been Seven months in England four of which I have been confind to my Chamber, I can hardly write a line with Ease. I am ill very ill——I am Dying I have distroyed all your Letters as you desird I am content to Dye.

"Oh my friend," Elizabeth wrote Benjamin Rush, "I am ground to the Earth with afflictions," her heart oppressed with sorrows.[12] By March of the new year, Elizabeth had heard nothing further of John Young. She did not know whether he still lived and feared that if he did it was "in a State of Insanity."[13]

To take her mind off her uncertainty about John Young, in early 1793, Elizabeth copied some more of her poems for Annis Stockton. These differed from the ones she had transcribed in 1787. This time Elizabeth included the personal poems that involved her relationship with Henry. Annis Stockton had wanted a copy of "Il Penserosa" ("Deserted Wife"), but Elizabeth had initially refused. Now she complied along with copies of "A Pastoral Ballad: Love and Alexis," which she had presented to Henry when she first told him she would marry him; an ode she had written for his birthday; "Advertisement," the poem she had written when Henry went to Philadelphia for a day and stayed a week without notifying her where he was; and "Lines Written on a Blank Leaf of Young's Night Thoughts," given to Henry when they parted for the last time. In her letter of transmittal, Elizabeth asked Annis to share "Il Penserosa" only with such few of her friends who had "feeling delicate hearts."[14] She sent the poems to Benjamin Rush for forwarding to his mother-in-law with a letter mentioning "a couple of Manuscript Books . . . long promised and not worth expecting." These were probably the commonplace book she had finished in 1787 and the newly transcribed poems.

She wrapped the verses in a copy of the *General Advertiser* of March 27 headlining the execution of King Louis XVI of France. Elizabeth agreed with the many Americans who had sympathized at first with the French people's rejection of arbitrary rule but who abhorred the violence that had erupted. In September 1792, while commenting upon Sterne's description of a prisoner in the Bastille in his *Journal of France*, she had speculated how Sterne's "Nerves [would] Thrill and vibrate over the Scene of a Happy people Dancing over the Ruins of that Infernal Prison: yet" she predicted presciently, "Delightfull as Freedom is I think it will be finaly in France obtain By Such sanguinary means as will make thousands of suffering individuals Sigh And whisper the old Adage 'Gold may be bought too Dear!' "[15] Two years later, she deplored how events had evolved:

> Gracious Heaven is this the <u>Regeneration</u> of a new Empire? It is its <u>Degeneration</u>! Is this <u>Reformation</u>? It is <u>Deformation</u>. Is this generous <u>Democrats</u>? No they are <u>Democrats</u> such as filld the <u>Pandemonium</u> that <u>Milton</u> Admirably Describes, With <u>Beelzebub</u> and

<u>Moloch</u> presiding for Such appear to Me Robespiere and Marat, . . . Oh my Soul revolts at them! and their proceedings![16]

She thought "the Execution of the King and Queen of France was accompanied with a Series of unprecedented Barbarity,"[17] and she had "melted into Tears at the anecdote of the Dauphin going to Solicit mercy for his Papa." She wrote frequently about her sympathy for Louis XVI and the gratitude that America owed to the deceased King.[18] She was so touched about his execution that she wrote a poem, now lost, to send to Elias Boudinot, who responded that the King was "the first great, benevolent ally & Friend of America."[19] Later, she wrote "Reply to the Democratic Song of the Guillotine," to be sung to the music "God Save the King," in which she called for the end of the guillotine. A note calls the guillotine "no maiden but a common prostitue[,] the scarlet whore."[20]

While France was being torn with political and social turmoil, across the Channel, English reformers were agitating for changes in Parliament and enlargement of the franchise, using arguments that led one woman to challenge the traditional attitudes about women's inferiority and inequality. In 1792, Englishwoman Mary Wollstonecraft published her *Vindication of the Rights of Woman*, the first major feminist tract proclaiming the equality of women. In arguing from Locke that government derived its powers from the consent of the governed, the agitators questioned the authority of arbitrary rulers who had inherited their political positions. Wollstonecraft applied this rationale to women, declaring that they should not have to obey their arbitrary rulers—men. If men had inalienable rights as human beings, as Locke had stated, so did women, and those rights should be equal.

Vindication was published in Philadelphia the same year as in England, immediately circulated widely, and was much discussed by literate Philadelphians, men as well as women. It made such an impression that Elias Boudinot in a speech given July 4, 1793, in honor of independence felt compelled to defend this country's treatment of women: "The Rights of Women are no longer strange sounds to an American ear: they are now heard, as familiar Terms, in every part of the United States, and I devoutly hope, that the day is not far distant, when we shall find them, dignifying in a distinguished Code, the Jurisprudence of the several States in the Union."[21]

Wollstonecraft stated the prevailing attitudes about women's inferiority and then refuted them. Traditional opinion as expressed by respected eighteenth-century authors portrayed women as inferior to men mentally, as well as physically, Wollstonecraft wrote. They had argued that since women had been created by God as secondary creations to men and unable to reason for themselves, they must be ruled by the men in their lives. Because of their perceived inferior minds, women were educable only to be passive, obedient, pleasing companions and sexual partners for men. To prove that previous writers had written about women in this fashion, Wollstonecraft quoted extensively from writers who had described or pre-scribed for women: Rousseau, Milton, Dr. James Fordyce, Dr. John Greg-ory, Hester Lynch Thrale Piozzi, Baroness de Stael, Madame de Genlis, and others. *Vindication* then refuted each of these authors' opinions, pro-claiming that women were equal to men in mental capacity.

Elizabeth read *Vindication* and commented upon it in a common-place book she was preparing for an unknown female recipient, possibly Annis Stockton. It is not a carefully reasoned, orderly critique of the book, but orderly thinking was not one of Elizabeth's strong points. This was probably the fault of the kind of education she had received. Having not attended a school, she had not been subjected to the discipline associated with rigorous learning nor had she been exposed to strict peer and authority criticism. Wollstonecraft referred to women's education as "a disorderly kind of education, seldom attend[ed] to with that degree of exactness that men, who from their infancy are broken into method, observe."[22] None of Elizabeth's writing maintains a sustained argument, logically presented. Furthermore, her discussion of Wollstonecraft's book does not confront the author's demand for female equality, but instead calls Wollstonecraft to task for the book she did not write rather than for the book she did.

The author of *Vindication* ridiculed the report from the Bible that God had created woman from Adam's rib to be man's helpmate and subser-vient companion. "Very few . . . who have bestowed any serious thought on the subject ever supposed that Eve was, literally speaking, one of Adam's ribs," wrote Wollstonecraft." Man had invented the idea "that the whole creation was only created for his convenience or pleasure" in order to "subjugate his companion."[23] This is a mistaken assumption, Wollstone-craft argued. God had created both beings with understanding and the ability to learn so that they might improve themselves. God would not have created an inferior being, woman, and then made her incapable of understanding and reasoning and, thus, unable to become virtuous.

Elizabeth, steeped in Biblical history as literally true, dismissed *Vindication*'s rejection of the book of Genesis's story of creation and ignored the rest of that train of thought. She complained that Wollstonecraft had treated "in too light a manner" "the common read Historical facts in the Book of Genises," and that was all she said about Wollstonecraft's reasoning. Even though she concurred with Wollstonecraft's demand for a more strenuous education for women, she did not recognize the implications of her demand. It would be pointless to subject women to an education they were unable to absorb. The unspoken assumption was that women must be as capable as men if they were to receive the same education. Elizabeth, too, often spoke of the need for more virtuous behavior. Yet, as *Vindication* argued, women must have the capacity to learn such behavior and, therefore, could not have been created with an innate inferior ability for reasoning.

Throughout *Vindication* and especially in chapter five, Wollstonecraft included her "Animadversions on Some of the Writers Who Have Rendered Women Ojects of Pity, Bordering on Contempt." Among the eighteenth-century writers whose works she decried for portraying women as inferior to men were some of Elizabeth's favorite authors, whom she hastened to defend. Her defense, however, once again did not confront Wollstonecraft's main point. Instead of considering whether the authors had pictured or should have pictured women as inferior to men in mental ability, Elizabeth discussed the literary and moral merits of the authors' works. She accuses Wollstonecraft of choosing quotations that prove her point and neglecting other aspects of their works that "promote the noblest of Sentiments." "The Lady descards Gregory, Rousseau Madam genlis with too indiscrminate a reproduction," Elizabeth wrote. Wollstonecraft had criticized Milton for portraying women as "formed for softness and sweet attractive grace," speculating that he meant to "deprive us of souls." In defending Milton, Elizabeth quoted the lines from *Paradise Lost* in which Milton introduces Eve as "Led by her heavenly maker, though unseen, / And guided by his voice, / Grace was in all her Steps, Heaven in her Eye, / in every Gesture Dignity and Love." To Elizabeth, the passage portrayed "steady Female Courage and Dignity," but she did not engage Wollstonecraft's complaint. Women could be dignified and courageous yet still subservient or inferior to men. Elizabeth emphasized the beauty of the passage, but Wollstonecraft was concerned not with the aesthetics of the work but with its assumptions about the character and prescribed role of women.[24]

Elizabeth also stoutly defended Madame de Genlis, reviewing her novels and telling what was admirable about each. Wollstonecraft criticized de Genlis's "absurd manner of making the parental authority supplant reason."[25] Elizabeth accused Wollstonecraft of setting aside and weakening "the Tys of parental authority, a dangerous String to touch on, [which] may do much harm in many hands the Book may fall into."[26] The issues of whether the authors presented women as inferior to men and, if so, whether they were correct, Elizabeth did not address.

Her inattention to *Vindication*'s main thesis is curious, considering her own life. Nowhere in any of her extant writings did she acknowledge or seemingly recognize her own many contradictions of the prevailing arguments about women. It was as though she was unable to compare her actions with the traditional attitudes, realize that she contradicted them, and then call for the philosophy to change. Instead she tried to make her actions appear to conform when they did not. She left no discussion of male/female relations. Yet her relationship to men was not based on subservience and obedience; if that had been true, she would have followed Henry to England. Furthermore, she did not treat men as anything but equals intellectually. She did not subordinate her opinions to theirs. Benjamin Rush was the most famous American doctor of his time, and after the yellow fever epidemic of 1793, his writings on the subject and his reputation spread to the British Isles and western Europe. Yet Elizabeth did not hesitate to challenge one of his major theses about that disease. This was not the action of a woman who feels herself inferior to one of the most famous male Pennsylvanians of the eighteenth century. And if not inferior to him, then to what male?

Vindication harshly condemned the lack of strenuous education for women and pointed out the problem for women so lacking when they have no men to care for them and tell them how to think. How does such a woman support herself and care for any children she may have, if this becomes necessary, Wollstonecraft asked. This was a point with which Elizabeth heartily agreed. She and many of her friends, Annis Stockton, Benjamin Rush, Elias Boudinot, for example, all had argued that a better and more equal education should be provided for girls.

She also agreed with Wollstonecraft's analysis that it would take a long time to eradicate prejudice in men and convince women that when they conform to the stereotype, they are acting contrary to their own best interests. Elizabeth wrote, "If men are the Tyrants She paints them; it is to be feard Reason and Eloquence will not hurl them from the Throne; or bereave them of the Septr: Force can only perform it, And nothg But an army of amazons will place us on the Equality we have in her Idea a right to."²⁷ The wording in this section leaves the reader confused about the phrases "If men are the Tyrants" and "the Equality we have in her idea a right to." This is all she wrote about the subject at that time. In the past, however, she had indicated that she thought some husbands were tyrants.

To Wollstonecraft, Elizabeth wrote "Friendship is a serious affection; the most sublime of all affections, because it is founded on Principle, and cemented by time. The very reverse may be said of love."²⁸ This, too, was Elizabeth's view of the best relations between spouses. Elizabeth had written a poem in 1789 entitled "Friendship *preferable* to Love,"²⁹ which agreed with what Wollstonecraft later wrote:

> Let girlish nymphs, and boyish swains,
> Their am'rous ditties chaunt;
> Make vocal echoing hills and plains,
> And love's frail passion paint.
> But *friendship's* steady flame as far
> That transient blaze out-glows,
> As mid-day suns a twinkling star,
> Which some faint ray bestows.

It was not a new position; the Blue Stockings in England had long argued that the best marriages were founded on friendship, and their writings may have influenced both Mary Wollstonecraft and Elizabeth Fergusson. They had also decried the dual sexual standard, which Wollstonecraft would condemn in her book and Elizabeth deny in her own life.

Although with qualifications, Elizabeth's judgment about *Vindication*'s author was generally favorable. She credited Wollstonecraft with having "a noble Spirit" and called her a "female writer of superior talents" with an excellent understanding. "No doubt," wrote Elizabeth, Wollstonecraft "thinks in this day of emancipation her long degraded Sex should come in for a part of the Liberty which is difusing."³⁰

During 1786 and 1787 when Elizabeth had been reviewing and revising her poems for submission to *The Columbian*, she also had begun to rework her verse translation of Fénelon's *Télémachus*. In 1787, she added notes and remarks at the beginning and end of each of the twenty-four books. The following spring, she wrote at the end of volume two that she meant the work "for a particular Friend But if I live I intend to give a more correct Version And perhaps if I meet with encouragement have it printed."

In the early 1790s, she received that encouragement from Elias Boudinot. They discussed the possibility of publication, and Boudinot recommended seeking subscriptions to pay for the printing. This was a common method, the one that had been used to publish the poems of Nathaniel Evans. Often the names of the subscribers were printed in the book as a mark of distinction. But Elizabeth refused in June 1793, citing the "delicacy of [her] Situation." She possibly was referring to the responsibility of the author to collect from the subscribers after the book was published, which would have been embarrassing for any woman, especially for someone who already considered herself subject to public scorn. If the author was unable to collect, he or she had to make up the deficiency. Boudinot unsuccessfully urged her to reconsider her refusal, promised to check costs with Philadelphia booksellers, and meanwhile told her to finish preparing a fair copy for him to show to them.[31] He was serving his third term in the House of Representatives, which met in Philadelphia, but Congress went into its summer adjournment, and the Boudinots returned to their home in Elizabethton, New Jersey. Before Boudinot could investigate further, Philadelphia became a dangerous place to do business.[32]

The summer of 1793 was hot and dry. By August drought conditions prevailed, and the water in wells was below pump level. The fields of Elizabeth's neighbors died as the earth dried and cracked and turned to dust. To add to the general discomfort caused by the heat, hordes of mosquitoes and flies had hatched in pools of standing water left the previous spring when cantankerous mother nature had dumped heavy rains causing rivers and streams to flood low-lying areas. The unscreened homes constantly buzzed with the obnoxious creatures. It was impossible to protect food and humans from their attacks.

In July, ships began to arrive from Santo Domingo carrying French refugees fleeing from a slave rebellion in the sugar island and bringing with them a fever that had swept the island. The combination of several thousand devastated, weak refugees, many of them already ill, and the many mosquitoes that swarmed out of the marshes to the south of the city brought a terrible plague to Philadelphians. Since the work of Walter Reed, we know that mosquitoes transmit yellow fever from human to human, but in the eighteenth century, it was a mysterious, frightening, deadly pestilence with no cure.

When Elizabeth opened her newspaper on Thursday, August 21, she read an announcement by Philadelphia Mayor Matthew Clarkson that "a dangerous, infectious disorder prevailed." By then, he had been warned by Benjamin Rush and other doctors that they were losing an increasing number of patients to a disease that left its victims' skins yellow and that Rush believed was probably yellow fever. The disease had killed hundreds in an epidemic in 1762, but there had been no recurrence since that outbreak. This time it would kill thousands.

The doctors disagreed on how the disease spread and the best regimen to be followed, but they agreed that something about the air was malignant. It never occurred to them that the something dangerous about the air was not the air itself but the mosquitoes in it. As soon as Rush had identified the new malignancy, he wrote his wife to remain in Princeton where she and their youngest children were visiting Annis Stockton, and he began to advise his friends to leave the city. If the air in Philadelphia was at fault, then the best measure for residents to take was to put that air as far behind them as possible. By August 25, even during a great storm that pummeled the northeast, anyone with a place to go and means to get there was leaving the city, crowding the roads with carriages and wagons. Before the fever subsided, it has been estimated that seventeen to twenty thousand people had fled. Since there was no one left to run businesses and provide public services, Philadelphia slowly shut down. The terrified people who remained locked themselves in their houses, venturing out onto the streets only for emergency supplies. And all the while the numbers of burials mounted. On September 1, an appalling seventeen deaths due to the fever were recorded, but this number would climb to 119 on October 11.

Among those who left was the family of Dr. William Smith, who sought a safe haven at the estate he had bought. This was very awkward for Elizabeth, who had not yet moved. No longer mistress of the house, she tried to avoid all pretensions to the role and kept to her room much of the time. She was unable to move elsewhere because the Smiths had fled Philadelphia without furniture and were using hers.[33]

Adding to her many worries was her concern over the safety of Benjamin Rush. He remained in Philadelphia throughout the epidemic, doing what he thought best to relieve his patients, seeing sometimes as many as 150 in one day. The treatment that he developed, today considered mistaken, was even then very controversial and embroiled him in a war of publications with other doctors. Patients, however, were grateful for his constant attention and care given to all sufferers alike, the poor as well as the rich. As refugees from the city passed Graeme Park or stopped for refreshment, Elizabeth begged them for news of her friend and heard stories of his courage and devotion to the sick. Reports of increasing numbers of afflicted inspired her to urge Rush to leave, to save himself for future good works.[34] Her pleadings to no avail, he stayed throughout the epidemic, eventually contracting and recovering from the disease himself. All his assistants came down with the fever, and three of them died.

Elizabeth and Benjamin Rush were very close friends. When his sister died of the fever October 1, Rush opened his deepest emotions to Elizabeth, writing her the effect on his mind of "the last Stage of [his] belovd Sisters Life and Burial."[35] It was Elizabeth to whom he had written that he and Julia Stockton had decided to marry, many years earlier, much to the annoyance of Julia. Later, when his mother died in 1795, he again expressed his grief to Elizabeth. In his autobiographical "Travels Through Life," he wrote that he had described to his "good friend Mrs. Ferguson" his mother's last moments and his own emotions. He spoke of his mother's three marriages, the first and third of which had been to abusive men. Only the second marriage to Benjamin's father had been a happy one, and he had died early leaving "her with but a small fortune, and six young children."[36] Such private matters are usually discussed by people only with relations or intimate friends.

He also kept her informed about his continuing controversy with other doctors. He sent her copies of various articles about the fever, and later a copy of the book he wrote, all of which she read carefully. In each case, she thanked him for his thoughtfulness but did not hesitate to question or criticize parts that were unclear or contrary to her own ideas. Their relationship was completely open. She even dared to send him proof that one of his controversial theories was wrong. Rush believed that the fever was caused by some unhealthy quality of the Philadelphia air itself while several of the other doctors argued that the fever had originated outside the city and had been brought to it by contagion, probably carried by the refugees. In March 1794, Elizabeth sent Rush a report of a "worthy quaker" who told of seeing, "before she heard any tallk of the yellow fever," a dying man from one of the ships whose skin was as "yellow as Safron." Elizabeth commented to Rush, "I know your Candor so well that you would be glad to receive any information tho such information might militate against an Hypothesis, you had previously Suported."[37] Either she did not know Rush as well as she claimed, which was unlikely, or she was trying to get him to be less fixated and more flexible about his theories.

At the same time, her loyalty to and respect for him rang clear in every letter. "I See you in my minds Eye at your Study, preparing for the press certain *Observations*, and *recitals* from others; with nice experiences of your own: wishing to clear the Eye of prejudice, and fling all the light you can on a disorder extrodinary, fatal, and Epidemical," she wrote after he had written her some of his beliefs about yellow fever.[38]

Philadelphians numbly lived through the disaster, waiting for the fall rains to clear the air and the drop in temperature that it was said would end the fever. October came, the rains fell, and the weather cooled, but still the deaths continued, although their numbers did decrease after October 15. On the twenty-third, the temperature was in the fifties, and five days later there was a light frost. The impatient refugees began to return to the city, although about twenty deaths were still occurring every day at the end of October and would continue on into November. Nevertheless, the city began to revive; the end was in sight. Finally, on November 14, the committee that had run the city during the epidemic announced that people could return safely.

No one knows precisely how many people died of yellow fever in Pennsylvania in 1793, but probably somewhere around five thousand succumbed, including some of Elizabeth's old friends. Samuel Powel, former mayor of Philadelphia and speaker of the Pennsylvania Senate died September 29. Dr. Frederic Phile, naval officer of the port for many years and like a brother in the Graeme family, also was taken.[39] George Clymer and his wife were stricken and recovered, as did Chief Justice McKean, who had treated Elizabeth with such leniency when the state had confiscated her property. The death that hurt the most was that of Rebecca Smith. To Elizabeth, awaiting news of the death of John Young, it seemed as though it pleased God that she should survive all the persons she loved most.[40]

The Smiths left Graeme Park sometime in late October or early November, and Elizabeth prepared to move to Mrs. Todd's around Christmas.[41] Most of her furniture and belongings had to be sold or given away. Any of the books she still held that belonged to other people had to be returned and others given away, as well. In anticipation of the move, she had already sent back to Rev. William Smith the *Land of Cakes*, which Smith had lent or given to Thomas Graeme many years earlier. To Robert Lollar, who had helped her at the time of the threatened sale by the state of Graeme Park, she gave two volumes of Montesquieu's *The Spirit of the Laws*.[42] She sent Henry a large box of books and included a packet of papers, probably more questions to Henry that he had already refused to answer. She never heard whether he received them.[43]

Early in the morning on moving day, sleep eluding her, she wrote letters to a few of her dearest friends. Then, as she drifted in and out of consciousness, visions of all her relatives and friends who had lived at Graeme Park "glided in procession before [her] Eyes." The last was her nephew whose death she had not heard yet but assumed had put "his poor sufering head at rest." "Some times they appear[ed] in the habiliments of the Dead, with every vestige of frail and humiliating mortality: And then Swift as thought the Scene Change[d] And Streams of radiant Light usher[ed] in Forms rich and glorious with all the drapery of Paradisical fancy."[44]

No information remains of Elizabeth's accommodations at Mrs. Todd's, except that the two women interacted very comfortably, Mrs. Todd treating her boarder "with uncommon tenderness and Delicacy."[45] Within a few months, Elizabeth found her new situation much happier than she had expected.[46] Mrs. Todd had two grown sons, they and a cousin all doctors. This was an educated family. The two women had something in common to talk about. Mrs. Todd's home had an extra bedroom so that Betsy Stedman, who had helped Elizabeth move, could live there for a month or two to help Elizabeth through the transition.[47] Betsy remained only a few months, and then Elizabeth had to make her adjustments.

It is difficult to imagine what Elizabeth's room at Mrs. Todd's must have looked like. She did not keep copies of her own letters, but she had preserved letters written to her. All those pages in addition to copies of her poems and publications, interesting newspaper articles, her favorite books, and other detritus of her life went to Mrs. Todd's. Every free surface in her room must have been covered, including floor space.

Over the next five or six years, she sorted these letters and sent extracts to other people, especially to Rush. Some she returned to the senders to avoid misuse of the letters after her death. By 1798, she was re-reading and then burning those of friends who had died. Coming across letters written many years before by Mrs. Campbell and her daughter, Mrs.

Frazer, who were still living, she decided to return the letters to the women in case their children and grandchildren might like them. She compared the letters to those of Pope and Addison, which were "too Studied" and written to be read by people other than the addressee. Mrs. Campbell's and Mrs. Frazer's letters, in contrast, were "from a warm unaffected Heart without any touch of ostentatious Wit."[48]

To the last minute, the Smiths had "used every argument" to persuade her to remain at Graeme Park, but she was "determined to give up house keeping." Without an income of at least "two hundred a year" she would never "aim at keeping a house," she wrote Annis Stockton. In addition, if she had remained at Graeme Park after it had been bought by another, she would have felt "a kind of Interloper or hanger-on." It was better to leave, to cut the ties finally; she should have taken the step years before, she told Annis.

On New Year's Day, Elizabeth walked to the Quaker meeting, a mile and a half away, to ask a blessing on her new style of life. She felt that she had then "contracted herself "into so narrow a Circle, that . . . the next narrower must be that House which no man breaks the Commandment for in Coveting of His neighbor."[49]

While there, she may have said a prayer for her nephew, whose condition she still did not know. Finally, she prevailed upon a friend in England to ask his son-in-law who lived near Fort George in Scotland where Young was stationed to inquire after him. Sometime in late summer 1794, the distressing news arrived that Young had died the preceding April 25. He had been in a deplorable state his last months, blind and unable to speak, suffering three or four "Epiliptic fits" every day. Since he could still hear, his only pleasure had been to have someone read to him.[50] With the help of friends in England, Elizabeth arranged to have her nephew buried in St. Martin's-in-the-Fields. On his tombstone she had engraved three stanzas, the first written by herself:

> Far distant from the soil where thy last breath
> Seal'd the sad measure of thy various woes;
> One female friend Laments thy mournful death
> Yet why Lament what only gave repose?

The last two stanzas were taken from the epitaph of Thomas Gray's "Elegy Written in a Country Churchyard,"[51] one of Elizabeth's favorite poems.

At her request, Captain Benjamin Baynton of the British Army wrote a eulogy to Young. Elizabeth asked Benjamin Rush to write the inscription on Young's tombstone in the blank pages of the copy of Young's book that she had presented to the Library Company of Philadelphia, as well as the obituary prepared by Rush and published in the *Philadelphia Daily Advertiser* July 29, 1794, and Baynton's transmittal letter and remarks.[52]

After the yellow fever epidemic ended and it was safe to return to Philadelphia, Elias Boudinot talked to printers in the city about Elizabeth's *Télémachus*. He discovered that their prices were too high for her to afford. He then wrote to the printers in New Jersey, whose responses led him to believe that their charges were more reasonable. Therefore, he decided to wait until Congress adjourned for the summer and he returned to Elizabethton where he planned to contract for the publication. During the delay, he told her to copy the manuscript over again in a more legible script, correcting the inaccuracies that had escaped her earlier notice.[53] The city printers had informed him that they could not "get thro' five Lines, without the aid of some Person acquainted with [her] hand writing continually" standing by to read it. Even Boudinot with all his experience in reading her writing would have failed if it had not been "for the Sense of the Passage." Unfortunately, Boudinot found that the Jersey printers' price was the same as that of the printers in Philadelphia after they added on the "Items they meant to charge in addition." To wit, "none of them would undertake it, without an advance of One Thousand Dollars, and would not partake in any manner of the Risque of Sale." Prices had risen because of the depreciation of the money and the shortage of workers; this forced postponement of the publication for the time being.[54]

The winter of 1794–95 was especially trying for Elizabeth. From the time the cold arrived, she had no visitors. With only Mrs. Todd to talk to, Elizabeth grieved for her nephew and for the marriage that might have been. Betsy Stedman would have helped pass the time, but she was no longer with Elizabeth. "Unconnected," with no family affairs to engross her, she did not stir out of the house except for short walks when the weather permitted.[55] Her only remaining Pennsylvania family members were the children of her niece, Anna Young Smith, with whom she was not as close as she had been with their mother. In 1789, Elizabeth had prepared a 476-page manuscript of her poems, now lost, for the oldest child, a daughter Anna, then about thirteen years of age.[56] In late 1794, she sent a message to Samuel Smith, then fifteen, "to pay some atention to Study," although she added that she would not wish him to become a scholar, for "the learned professions . . . were rather over stockd and unless a Striking genius appeard," she would not wish him to be like the lad who "knocked his head against a pulpit that would have done better at a plough tail."[57] But other than these brief references and a few occasions when Anna Smith delivered letters for her, her remaining papers do not mention her grand-niece and nephew.

 None of the descendants of Sir William and Lady Keith lived in North America. The one descendant with whom Elizabeth corresponded was Deborah Senior of Jamaica, granddaughter of the Keiths, who had been widowed in the 1750s. Two of Mrs. Senior's sisters had been in New York in the mid-seventies to bury a son who had died of tuberculosis. While they were in America, they also had visited Philadelphia and Graeme Park. Mrs. Senior may have accompanied them and perhaps other family members as well. From 1776 to 1781, no communications from the Jamaica family arrived at Graeme Park; then a letter from Mrs. Senior appeared reporting the tragedies that had happened in the interval. Several children and three sisters had died within two years' time, and she had lost all her property in a lawsuit. Elizabeth was the godmother of Mrs. Senior's young-est daughter, who was married and lived in Wales. This daughter also died of consumption in 1788, leaving six children, and Elizabeth wrote a long elegy in her memory. It was Mrs. Senior who sent the letter about novel reading that Elizabeth published in *The Universal Asylum and Columbian Magazine*.[58]

 Two publications of the early 1790s, not by Elizabeth but by ex-residents of Philadelphia, also caused a great stir in the city. They were books by Thomas Paine, who had lived in Philadelphia from 1774 to 1787, and by Charles Stedman, disaffected nephew of Elizabeth's brother-in-law, who had left Philadelphia when the British army evacuated the city. Thomas Paine's *Age of Reason* was available in Philadelphia shortly after its first printing in 1794. Elizabeth read it and asked Margaret Stedman her opinion. Mrs. Stedman replied that she had not bothered to read it because "from all the Accounts of those who have, it is a most detestable Composition, and Diametrically Opposite to Holy writ," which was her "Polar Star, guide, Comfort and Sure hope."[59] Elizabeth, who had not been deterred from reading it by adverse publicity, commented on Paine's wit at the expense of Scripture and reported that she had seen only two answers to

Paine, but she did not "think much of either of them."[60] She also did not think much of the book, condemning it for the same reason as popular opinion:

> In Ovid's Page By phrasing verse 'tis told,
> A King by touch Converted *Earth* to *Gold*!
> The Power of Transmutation still remains
> Thyrsitis proves it when He Paper stains:
> The Spell the same the Subject tho reverst
> For Ophirs Gold he turns to vulgar Dust
> When his vile Pen he does Prophanty Squirt
> Like filthy Harpies all is changed to Dirt.
> Soild and Disfigurd is the Sacred Page
> By Base Pervertions and unmanly Rage!
> Tho' the grossly swollend in the fallen age[61]

The other book that set Philadelphians' tongues wagging was by Charles Stedman. It was a history of the American Revolution. Before Elizabeth's friends knew the author, they attributed it to his father, Alexander, but then those who knew him decided that Alexander did not have the "industry" to produce such a work, whereas his "Son confin'd by ill health, to a retired situation in the Country on a small pension" was a more likely candidate. Until this turned out to be the case, Elizabeth joined Philadelphians in speculation, but she did not leave us her opinion of the book.[62]

Problems continued to prevent the publication of her *Télémachus*. Even Elizabeth's best handwriting would not be acceptable to a printer. What was needed was someone familiar with her script to take her best corrected copy and prepare a printer's manuscript. No matter how capable and willing Elias Boudinot was, he could not find the time to do it. He was a very active member of Congress until October 1795 when he retired from that body and became the Director of the Mint. Therefore, Rev. Smith, who knew Elizabeth's handwriting from many years of experience, agreed to rewrite the manuscript from a fair copy to be prepared by Elizabeth.

This choice was unfortunate because of Smith's reluctance to become involved in Elizabeth's marital problems, which she persisted, against all resistance, to discuss with him whenever they met. Elizabeth had apparently decided that Smith would be more likely to help her with her marriage concerns than his wife had been. He had visited her at the Billet in September 1794 and once again been forced to listen to everything that had happened in her marriage. She followed this up with a letter and then a packet of supporting documents. When she had received no reply after many months, she had written him a very angry letter reminding him of all his delinquencies.[63] It is no wonder that he wanted to avoid her. There is also no indication that he had more free time than Boudinot.

Smith also avoided Boudinot, who frequently called upon him during fall 1795, but Smith refused to discuss the *Télémachus* manuscript. Finally, Boudinot pinned him down only to to be informed that Smith had not received a legible copy from Elizabeth. Boudinot wrote Elizabeth to proceed with her part of the business during the coming long winter evenings. Then he discovered that the reason Smith had not received the manuscript was that Elizabeth was looking for someone to hire to copy it. Apparently her perceived alienation from Smith was so great that even as important a matter as the publication of *Télémachus* did not permit her to set aside her feelings.[64]

By the following spring, however, Elizabeth and Smith had come to some understanding that allowed them to be friends again. She had worked over the winter of 1795–96, as Boudinot had directed, and she delivered a manuscript, with a dedication to President Washington, to Boudinot who passed it along to Smith. Smith had promised that "as soon as it came, he would engage in it."[65] Whether he ever started the project is unknown. Boudinot had deferred talking to a printer in 1795 hoping that prices would fall, and he had predicted that the following spring would bring a rise in the value of the money.[66] Prices, however, rather than the currency value rose steadily. In a letter of May 11, 1796, the last extant document discussing this matter, Boudinot opined that prices were not going to fall until the war ended. Because the current publication costs were too exorbitant, "the printing must not be attempted till peace takes place." Cheerful as always, he wrote that the "interval may be improved to getting every thing ready."[67] But peace was not going to come any time soon. Before that happened, there would be an undeclared war with France from 1798–1800, and prices would not improve.

Physical as well as financial problems intervened to prevent the book's publication. By the spring of 1796, Elizabeth's health, precarious at best, had developed another distressing symptom. Beginning the previous year, she had begun to be disturbed not only with her usual spring "Chills and Slow fevers" but also with "such a shortness of Breath on the least exercise or Sudden motion that were [she] to pursue it without a pause . . . [she] Should drop on the Spot."[68] Self-diagnosing, she had concluded that she had the same complaint that had killed King George II. It was not asthma, she wrote Mary Campbell, "But entirely in the swift Circulation of the Blood: which by motion rushes more fast into the vessels than can be discharged and when to creep produces instant death by bursting the Pericardium[,] that is the Bag that incloses the Heart." This condition continued, draining her of energy. Thus, neither economically nor physically was Elizabeth in any condition to pursue the publication of her translation. As a result, it never was published, although as late as June 1799, Elizabeth sent her version of part of the seventeenth book to "Sir," asking him to "compare this sample with the original."[69]

In addition to health problems, Elizabeth's financial situation gave her concern again for a period of several years. John Nicholson bought her annuity from George Meade In January 1794, but this was not a satisfactory arrangement. Payments were late, and one never reached Elizabeth even though Nicholson claimed he had sent it to her. She believed that he suspected her of fraud. Eventually it turned out that the money had been sent mistakenly to Maryland. To Elizabeth, it seemed that Nicholson, accustomed to dealing in thousands, was not giving her income enough attention because to him it was "a trifle." Quoting Goldsmith, she wrote Nicholson that "These little Things are Great to little men" and pleaded the "Case of the Poor." Most of the money not committed to her board, she gave away to charity. She wrote Nicholson that a delinquent payment was "appropriated to the old And Infirm who have no way of keeping pace with [the] monstrous Price of Bread."[70] George Meade, in April 1796, bought back the annuity from Nicholson and contracted to pay Elizabeth two hundred dollars a year for the rest of her life.[71]

The renegotiations, which included an increase of forty dollars for Elizabeth, apparently involved Elias Boudinot, if indeed he was not responsible for them. When she remonstrated against his generous management of her affairs and argued for her own independence, Boudinot "sincerely acknowledge[d] the blessings of Independence . . . [as] one of Heavens best gifts . . . [that] should be reasonably aimed at by every Mortal." While she continued to enjoy "health & strength" he wrote her,

> you may not be unnecessarily dependent on your Friends: but be
> assured my dear Madam, if it should please a gracious God to exer-

cise you with sickness & distress in an advanced age, you shall not
suffer for any of the Comforts that may be procured for you, let
your love of Independency be ever so great.[72]

Without the loyalty and companionship of several faithful old
friends, Elizabeth's last years would have been stark indeed. Benjamin
Rush, Elias Boudinot, and George Meade were able to tolerate Elizabeth's
obsession with Henry's infidelity and condemnation of other friends who
refused to help her. It was easier for them than for the Smiths because there
was no way that they could possibly become involved. Thus, she was not
expecting them to interfere to help her discover the truth, but only to be
sounding boards for her frustrations and guardians of the many documents
she sent them regarding the situation, presumably for Henry in case he
should ever reappear. All three men, married with families, led active professional lives, yet they found time to care about Elizabeth almost as a sister.

Her most devoted friend and companion was Betsy Stedman. The
two women had known each other ever since they were in their teens and
had shared their lives intimately for almost thirty years. The younger
woman had been a sometime companion to Mrs. Graeme, moving to
Graeme Park when Elizabeth went to England with Richard Peters. After
Elizabeth returned, Betsy visited often and, in 1772, after Dr. Graeme died
and when Henry was in Europe, she returned to keep Elizabeth company.
Whether she continued in Horsham for the two years after Henry returned
and lived at Graeme Park is not known, but when Henry went to Europe
again in 1775, Betsy moved back to the park, this time to stay. In the early
nineties, after Elizabeth sold Graeme Park and was able to give Betsy some
of the money she had borrowed from her friend, Betsy decided to take a
trip to Europe. Elias Boudinot was concerned about her safety, since the
places she planned to visit were in the likely path of "a furious war," and
he tried to dissuade her from her journey. Although no records remain of
a trip, Betsy disappeared from Elizabeth's life for over two years. Friends
who wrote no longer sent their regards to Betsy, and Elizabeth herself did
not refer to her. By the time Elizabeth was moving out of Graeme Park,
Betsy had returned and helped her move to Mrs. Todd's. For the next three
years, Betsy spent much time at the Billet, but she did not formally become
Mrs. Todd's "boarder and lodger" until April 1796. From then until Elizabeth died, the women were inseparable.[73]

Meanwhile, Elizabeth's old friends one by one were dying. Francis

Hopkinson had died in May 1791 of an apoplexy, and Elizabeth had written a poem in his memory for his mother.[74] William Bradford, husband of the Boudinot's daughter Susan, died of yellow fever in August 1795, leaving a large family, which became the responsibility of Elias Boudinot. The following spring, Betsy Stedman spent eight weeks nursing her aunt, Margaret Stedman. Betsy arrived at the Billet only to be recalled to stay with her aunt until she died. This death was particularly distressing for Elizabeth, for Margaret and her first husband had been close friends of the Graeme family. The Meade's son, who had battled tuberculosis, died in early May 1796, and Elizabeth went to Philadelphia to comfort her old friends.[75]

Sometime near the end of 1797 or early 1798, another change was forced on Elizabeth when Mrs. Todd died. Elizabeth actually considered, although how seriously is questionable, going to live on the frontier in north central Pennsylvania. She had made a new friend, Christopher Beswicke, a medical student in Philadelphia whom she may have met through Mrs. Todd's sons or through Benjamin Rush, whose lectures they all attended. Beswicke wrote her interesting letters, summarizing some of Rush's lectures, discussing the actions of the government, or relating happenings in the city.[76] In the fall of 1796, Beswicke established a practice in a "little town on the North branch of the Susquehanna Nineteen Miles above Northumberland," which he described to her in letters as beautiful but wild country. This was west and considerably north of where she lived. He made occasional trips to Philadelphia, sometimes to attend Benjamin Rush's lectures, and on his way in transit, he stopped in the Billet to see her.

After Mrs. Todd died, Elizabeth asked Beswicke to find out how much it would cost for her to live in his town. He informed her that probably she could live there for less than half of similar accommodations near Philadelphia, and he found a little house she could rent for six pounds a year. "I know Madam," he wrote, "that you would like the Situation of the Town did you but see it: but," he warned, "the dreadful Mountains that are to be crossed before you get to it Are a Wasted howling Wilderness [that] seems very terrible to those not accustomed to Wild countries." The sense of desolation was caused by the bare burnt hillsides that had been fired to provide pasture lands, a practice against the law yet notwithstanding done every year. He concluded encouragingly that "The Road thro' this dreary Waste is much travelled and the accommodations are tolerable: the greatest distance between the Houses that will do to stay all night is fifteen or sixteen miles."[77] Elizabeth thought of going to live there, but Betsy Stedman would not move that far. Undoubtedly, Betsy was deterred by the image of the two women, one in fragile health, traveling by horseback through the wilderness, over the mountain trails fiften miles each day, and then if they ever reached their destination, those same women, used to having servants to do their household work, would have to make a home for themselves in a log cabin. No wonder she refused.

A much better accommodation was found for Elizabeth and Betsy with Seneca Lukens and his family, two miles from Graeme Park. He was a well-to-do local land owner, a clockmaker by profession, and the grandson of one of the founders of the Hatboro Library. The only difficulty with the Lukens's house was that it was on a hill, and Elizabeth had to walk up that incline to return from visits to the Billet or Philadelphia. The climb was very painful for her.[78]

The time between the sale of Graeme Park to Dr. Smith and Elizabeth's death in 1801 wound down like the clock in need of winding. Mostly it was a matter of pulling things together, putting her life in order, and undertaking small activities. She was very popular with neighbors, who called her affectionately "Lady Fergusson" because she had been received by the king and because of her descent from Lady Keith. Her generosity to the poor also contributed to her popularity. "If she had but a shilling, sixpence would go to relieve the indigent." When told that most of the beggars were imposters, she said that she would rather be imposed upon by nine "than the tenth real object should be unrelieved."[79] She also sent indigent neighbors with health problems to Drs. Redman or Rush, whom she expected to provide charity care. On occasion, she did not hesitate to ask Rush to come to Horsham to look at a patient who could not be moved. Even though in her old age her movement was severely restricted, she would walk miles to attend funerals, or to visit sick people and bring them a little preserved fruit that she thought might be beneficial.[80]

In spite of all her problems, she retained her sense of humor and quick wit. On February 26, 1795, "one of the coldest Days ever known," a fox hunt was scheduled by her neighbors. The frost was so deep that the dogs lost the scent of the fox, and it escaped. Elizabeth honored the chase with a jingle that also reflected the situation of General Lafayette, who had been proscribed by the provisional government of France, escaped capture by his troops, and then was caught by the Austrians and imprisoned:

So intense was the Frost, the scent soon was lost,
Fleet Reynard escaped from the Snare,
They shaking returned, nor with ardor more burned
Oh could poor Fayette thus flee from the Net
that on all sides is laid for his head
the honest with Joy, would hail this brave boy
Who from Jacobine Fury was fled[81]

She continued to rewrite and annotate her translation of *Télémachus*, even beyond the point when she had reconciled herself to it not being published. Bits and pieces of the epic remain in the Rush Papers, as well as the two volumes of the original translation. In the 1790s, she wrote more notes to the original to explain further her allusions and to make comments.

Her thoughts still were possessed by Henry and their failed marriage. By fall of 1799, she had not heard from her husband in eleven years or even about him in three. She did not know whether he was alive or dead, although she suspected that Phineas Bond corresponded with Henry and could tell her if he would. In 1797, Henry's nephew Robert Fergusson had visited the United States, first to Virginia, where he had once lived, and then to Philadelphia, where he had planned to visit Elizabeth. Unfortunately, ill health intervened, he was confined to his bed for most of the time, and the meeting with his aunt did not happen. If Elizabeth had seen him, she would have "insisted on it that he Should have the Story from Janes own Lips." She would have explained to him the reasons for her conduct and her separation from her husband to try to vindicate herself.[82]

When she missed this opportunity, Elizabeth prepared a packet of documents for Henry's friends, which she sent to a childhood acquaintance who lived in Petersburgh, Virginia, near where Henry's brother's family once lived. Apparently Elizabeth wanted Henry's Virginia relatives to read the material and then circulate it among Henry's friends in Scotland to clear herself of the condemnation that she assumed they felt toward her. There were no Fergusson relatives left in Virginia, however, who knew about the matter, so Elizabeth's friend had the packet sent to Robert Fergusson with instructions to convey it to Henry's friends in Scotland after he read it.[83] What happened to the material is unknown; Elizabeth, herself, probably never heard any more about it

By 1800, she had been married twenty-eight years but had lived with her husband only two and a half. Obsessed with the desire to have her actions vindicated, she asked her two dearest friends, Rush and Boudinot, "men of integrity," to read papers she sent them and give her their opinions about Henry's guilt or innocence. But they would not give her the judgment she sought. Rush replied, "To every one but your Self Mr F would appear Innocent" and Boudinot, "99 men out of an hundred would pronounce Mr F n not guilty." These expressions, when she "thought who they came from, and who and what they Spoke of, and who they were adressed to," rang in her "ears as a *Curfew* toll." Even after writing this, however, she still spoke of Phineas Bond as an enemy, calling him "a Savage," and telling Rush not to be Bond's apologist. She wrote that she was too ill to "enter into [a] Humble apology," but that she would.[84] To whom she was thinking of apologizing is not clear, presumably Henry, certainly not Bond. It never occurred to her that she should ask women rather than or in addition to men.

The responses of these two men are incomprehensible considering the evidence that remains, except for one factor. They had heard the evidence many times; they had read the records accumulated by Elizabeth, but none had interviewed Jane. They only knew Henry. The people, men as well as women, who had heard Jane's story had believed her. How Rush and Boudinot accounted for the insistence of James Abercrombie, a minister who had been living in the house of his mother and step-father at the same time as Henry, that he had heard Henry soliciting the servant girl thirteen months before the baby was born is unknown. The people who were closest to the case had determined that Henry was guilty, yet Rush and Boudinot found him innocent. Even if they really believed Henry traduced, one would think they would have said otherwise to protect Elizabeth, since their opinions could not affect Henry one way or the other. This was a devastating blow to their friend, and they must have known it would be.

Her life and her unhappiness, however, were approaching an end, as her health continued to deteriorate. By fall of 1799, having to walk the smallest incline was very painful. She wrote Rebecca Frazer that only God knew whether she would live or die.[85] It might come to pass as one poet wrote:

> One Day we missed her from her acustomd Hill,
> Along the Heath and near her favorite tree

Another came nor yet beside the Rill
Nor in the Wood nor on the Lawn was She.

A neighbor often talked to Elizabeth when he saw her sitting in Seneca Lukens's woods reading. He thought she had "the most intelligent and expressive eyes he ever beheld in a female."[86] Joseph Lukens, one of at least seven children of Seneca Lukens, remembered her "as possessing extraordinary conversational powers . . . that she was very kind hearted and charitable."[87]

Betsy Stedman has left a description of her friend in her last years. She wrote Mrs. Senior that Elizabeth

> in stature was rather rising above the common size, slender and fragile, her neck & shoulders finely formed, complexion remarkably fair, the texture of her skin like an infant's. Her eyes were quick and peircing the soul looked, they were expressive of what passed within, her lips plump & a fine hue, and her hair yellow. . . . The general cast of her countenance pensively thoughtful, but when animated by conversation every feature spoke. Latterly time had made great ravages, sorrow had marked her for her own, its traces were deeply indented.[88]

By "yellow," Betsy probably meant that Elizabeth's hair was white. Existing portraits of a young Elizabeth show her hair as dark.

In the evening of February 11, 1801, while she was writing, Elizabeth suffered a recurring chill. Betsy persuaded her to go to bed, but the next morning, she was no better and had developed a strangury or very painful difficulty in urinating. She refused to allow Betsy to call a doctor because she had had this problem before, and it had gone away by itself. On the third day, she finally consented to have help called, having developed a pleurisy by then. Her breathing became so constricted that speaking was difficult and she said very little. She took no food during her illness, only cold water. "Her strength gradually wasted, but the powers of her mind were clear and strong till [on the] 19th sight hearing & speech were all taken away."[89] Finally on February 23, 1801, at four in the morning with her grandniece, Anna Smith, by her side, Elizabeth Graeme Fergusson died.

That evening, Benjamin Rush wrote in his commonplace book:

This morning died at the Billet near Philadelphia Mrs. Eliz. Ferguson, a woman of uncommon talents and virtues, admired, esteemed, and beloved by a numerous circle of friends and
acquaintances. Her life was marked with distress from all its numerous causes, guilt excepted. An early disappointment in love, loss of
all her near Relations, bad health, an unfortunate marriage connection, poverty, and finally a slow and painful death composed the
ingredients that filled her cup of suffering. She was the intimate
friend of my dear mother in law, who died a few weeks before her.
I owe to her many obligations. She introduced me into her circle
of friends.[90]

It did not take long for John Young to become homesick for the continent
he had left behind. He wrote his aunt shortly after his arrival in England
that although he was charmed with the beauty of the countryside, it was
but "nature in miniature." The British, he wrote, in their attempts to make
the most of their small island, would

> decoy a fleeting muddy stream over a Pyle of stones to represent a
> cataract [and] . . . turn and reflect a gravel Walk through trees and
> bushes twenty times in the same acre . . . to deceive the Eye into
> an appearance of immensity. In vain[,] for nothing can make great
> which the deciding Hand of nature has ordained to be little.

"The Effects of these impotent attempts at Grander are more Conspicuous," he continued, "to one who is used to lonely regions [where] Great
Nature dwells in artful solitude."[91]

$\mathcal{N}otes$

ABBREVIATIONS

AG	Ann Graeme
BF	Benjamin Franklin
BR	Benjamin Rush
CCHS	Chester County Historical Society
Col. Rec.	Pennsylvania *Colonial Records* Series, 16 vols., Pennsylvania Archives
DCL	Dickinson College Library
EB	Elias Boudinot
EG	Elizabeth Graeme
EGF	Elizabeth Graeme Fergusson
HSP	Historical Society of Pennsylvania
LCP	Library Company of Philadelphia
Pa. Arch.	Pennsylvania Archives, 1st–9th Series
PMHB	*Pennsylvania Magazine of History and Biography*
PMHC	Pennsylvania Museum and Historical Commission, Harrisburg
TG	Thomas Graeme
TP	Thomas Penn
UPARC	University of Pennsylvania Archives and Records Center
WF	William Franklin

PREFACE AND ACKNOWLEDGMENTS

1. Anne H. Wharton, *Salons Colonial and Republican* (Philadelphia: J.B. Lippincott Company, 1900), 13.

2. J. Thomas Scharf and Thompson Westcott, *History of Philadelphia 1609–1884*, 3 vols. (Philadelphia: L. H. Everts & Co., 1884), 2:1118–19.

3. Records of auction house sales indicate the exchange of manuscripts whose present location is unknown. See Helen Cripe and Diane Campbell, eds., *American Manuscripts 1763–1815* (Wilmington, Del.: Scholarly Resources, Inc., 1977).

4. William Buck's ledger, "Graeme Park Ms. Notes on," Albert Cooke Myers Papers, Chester County Historical Society (hereafter CCHS), 287.

5. See Benjamin Rush (hereafter BR), "An Account of the Life and Character of Mrs. Elizabeth Ferguson," *Portfolio* 1 (1809): 520–27.

6. This information about the unpublished book was taken from Chester T. Hallenbeck, "The Life and Collected Poems of Elizabeth Graeme Fergusson," M.A. Thesis, Columbia University, 1929.

7. Theodore W. Bean, ed., *History of Montgomery County* (Philadelphia: Everts and Peck, 1884), 880–902.

8. Joshua Francis Fisher, "Some Account of the Early Poets and Poetry of Pennsylvania," *Hazard's Register of Pennsylvania* 8 (September 1831): 152–56, 161–63, 177–80; Rufus W. Griswold, *The Female Poets of America* (Philadelphia: Partly & McMillan, 1854); Evert A. and George L. Duyckinck, *Cyclopedia of American Literature*, 2 vols. (N.Y.: Charles Scribner, 1855), 1:233; Wharton, *Salons Colonial and Republican;* S. Weir Mitchell, *Hugh Wynne* (N.Y.: The Century Co., 1896).

9. M. Katherine Jackson, *Outline of the Literary History of Colonial Pennsylvania* (Lancaster, Pa.: The New Era Printing Company, 1906), 92, 96–97, 98, 99, 100, 121, 145, 153.

10. *Pennsylvania Magazine of History and Biography* (hereafter *PMHB*) 39 (1915): 257–321 and 385–409.

11. Hallenbeck, "The Life and Collected Poems of Elizabeth Graeme Fergusson"; Martha C. Slotten, "The Culture of Elizabeth Graeme Ferguson (1737–1801)," M.A. Thesis, Shippensburg State College, 1980; Edward Robins, "Some Philadelphia Men of Letters," *PMHB* 50 (1926): 318–43; Gertrude B. Biddle and Sarah D. Lowrie, *Notable Women of Pennsylvania* (Philadelphia: University of Pennsylvania Press, 1942), 46–47; Joseph J. Kelley Jr. and Sol Feinstone, *Courage and Candlelight: The Feminine Spirit of '76* (Harrisburg: Stackpole Books, 1974), 194–204; Pattie Cowell, *Women Poets in Pre-Revolutionary America: 1650–1775, An Anthology* (Troy, N.Y.: The Whitston Publishing Company, 1981).

12. Letter Annis Stockton to Julia Rush, March 22, [1793], original in Rosenbach Museum and Library, Philadelphia; copy in Carla Mulford, *Only for the Eye of a Friend* (Charlottesville: University Press of Virginia, 1995), 304–7.

13. Joan Hoff Wilson, "The Illusion of Change: Women and the American Revolution," in *The American Revolution*, ed. Alfred F. Young (DeKalb: Northern Illinois University Press, 1976), 395.

14. Catherine Blecki and Karin Wulf, *Milcah Martha Moore's Book: A Commonplace Book from Revolutionary America* (University Park: Pennsylvania State University Press, 1997).

INTRODUCTION

1. Though Elizabeth Graeme's complete journal exists only in oral narratives circulating since the eighteenth century, Milcah Martha Moore, Graeme's friend and neighbor, transcribes a long extract into her commonplace book, which is housed in the Haverford College Library. See Blecki and Wulf, *Milcah Martha Moore's Book*.

2. BR, "An Account," 523.

3. Blecki and Wulf, *Milcah Martha Moore's Book*, 201.

4. Intending to publish the "Willow of Litchfield" poem, Fergusson sent it to the editor of *The Columbian Magazine* in August or September of 1788, but it was never published. Perhaps its fifty-four quatrains and daunting allusions cowed the editors. But proposing to instruct the next generation of litterateurs, she explains: "The number of Notes annexd to the Odes were written with a View to young people who read Magazines and such light pieces as this might

not be acquainted with Poetical allusions, And references, and some notes also on Modern performances" (1789 commonplace book, 58, Dickinson College Library [hereafter DCL]).

5. Later in the poem she returns to male writers outside her intimate circle. She mentions Joel Barlow and Thomas Trumball, for example, famous for their epic poem, *The Columbiad*.

6. Katherine Gauss, "Two Hundred Years of Morven I Record," *House Beautiful* 62 (July 1927).

7. Throughout the last quarter of the eighteenth century, Elizabeth Fergusson published over thirty of her poems in such regional magazines and newspapers as *The Pennsylvania Magazine* or *American Monthly Museum, Columbian Magazine, Universal Asylum and Columbian Magazine*, and *Pennsylvania Packet*. Given the voluminous number of poems compiled in her commonplace book, however, her choice to publish in magazines was overshadowed by her preference for scribal publication. It was, I would argue, more aesthetically pleasing and socially acceptable.

8. For a discussion of print culture, see Michael Warner, *The Letters of the Republic: Publication and the Public Sphere in Eighteenth-Century America* (Cambridge, Mass.: Harvard University Press, 1990); Larzer Ziff, *Writing in the New Nation: Prose, Print, and Politics in the Early United States* (New Haven: Yale University Press, 1991); Richard D. Brown, *Knowledge is Power: The Diffusion of Information in Early America, 1700–1785* (Knoxville: University of Tennessee Press, 1989); and Rosalind Reimer, *Printers and Men of Capital: Philadelphia Book Publishers in the New Republic* (Philadelphia: University of Pennsylvania Press, 1996).

9. Though most discussions of the public sphere begin with Jürgen Habermas's *The Structural Formation of the Public Sphere: An Inquiry into the Category of Bourgeois Society*, trans. Thomas Burger and Frederick Lawrence (Cambridge, Mass.: MIT Press, 1989), his analysis not only overlooks gender and class, but also privileges print over manuscript discourse. For useful critiques of Habermas, see Johanna Meehan, ed., *Feminists Read Habermas: Gendering the Subject of Discourse* (New York: Routledge University Press, 1995) and Craig Calhoun, ed., *Habermas and the Public Sphere* (Cambridge, Mass.: MIT Press, 1991).

10. The Countess of Carlisle, "The Rudiments of Taste," Letter 15, *The Lady's Pocket Library*, 3d American edition (Philadelphia: Matthew Carey, 1797), 196. For critical reading on the eighteenth-century culture of politeness, see David Shields's influential study, *Civil Tongues and Polite Letters in British America* (Chapel Hill: University of North Carolina Press for the Institute of Early American History and Culture, 1997); Lawrence Klein, "Gender, Conversation, and the Public Sphere in Early Eighteenth-Century England," in *Textuality and Sexuality: Reading Theories and Practices*, ed. Judith Still (New York: St. Martin's Press, 1993), 100–115; idem, *Shaftesbury and the Culture of Politeness: Moral Discourse and Cultural Politics in Early Eighteenth-Century England* (New York: Cambridge University Press, 1994); and Susan Stabile, "'By a Female Hand': Letters, Belles Lettres, and the Philadelphia Culture of Performance, 1760–1820" (Ph.D. diss., University of Delaware, 1996).

11. Hesther Chapone, *Letters on the Improvement of the Mind: Addressed to a Young Lady* (Boston: printed by Robert Hodge for William Green, 1783), 160.

12. Reverend John Bennett, *Letters to a Young Lady on a Variety of Useful and Interesting Subjects*, 4th American edition (Boston: Thomas Andrews, May 1798), 99.

13. EGF to John Dickinson, October 15, 1772, Robert Reisling Logan Collection, John Dickinson Papers, Historical Society of Pennsylvania (hereafter HSP).

14. EG, "Some Lines upon my first being at Graeme Park; after my return from England. August the 16 1766," in *Poemata Juvenilia,* Library Company of Philadelphia (hereafter LCP).

15. Hugh Blair, "On Pastoral Poetry," in *Lectures in Rhetoric and Belles Lettres*, vol. 3, 2d ed. (London: William Strahan and T. Cadell, 1785), 116.

16. Blecki and Wulf, *Milcah Martha Moore's Book,* 206.

17. For a discussion of the country-house tradition, see Mark Girouard, *Life in the English Country House: A Social and Architectural History* (New York: Penguin, 1978). See, too, William A. McClung. "The Country House Arcadia" and Barbara K. Lewalski, "The Lady of the Country-House Poem," in *The Fashioning and Functioning of the British Country House*, ed. Gervase Jackson Stops et al. (Hanover: University Press of New England, 1989), 277–87, 261–75; Alastair Fowler, "Country House Poems: The Politics of a Genre," *The Seventheenth Century* (1986): 1–13; and Virginia C. Kinny, *The Country House Ethos in English Literature 1688–1750: Themes of Pastoral Retreat and National Expansion* (Sussex: The Harvester Press, 1985).

18. *Pennsylvania Journal* (1751): 549.

19. Blecki and Wulf, *Milcah Martha Moore's Book,* 215.

20. J. G. Zimmerman, *Solitude; or, The Effects of Occasional Retirement* (London: Associated Booksellers, 1797).

21. Blair, "On Pastoral Poetry," 37.

22. Ibid., 46, 38, 41–42.

23. Hannah More, *Essays,* in *The Lady's Pocket Library,* 3d ed. (Philadelphia: Matthew Carey, 1797), 7.

24. Blair, "On Pastoral Poetry," 46.

25. John Young to EF, March 22, 1775; reprinted in Bean, *History of Montgomery County,* 895.

26. BR, "An Account," 523.

27. EF, "A Farewell to the Muses," in *Poemata Juvenilia*, LCP.

28. EF to BR, April 29, 1782, Rush Manuscripts, HSP.

29. For a further discussion of Freemasons and early American club culture, see David Shields, chap. 6, "The Clubs," in *Civil Tongues & Polite Letters.* For a more thorough description of freemasonry, see Margaret C. Jacob, *The Radical Enlightenment: Pantheists, Freemasons, and Republicans* (London, 1981).

30. Shields, "The Clubs," 120.

31. Blecki and Wulf, *Milcah Martha Moore's Book,* 206.

32. Exemplifying the connection between freemasonry and women's sororal coteries, Esther Edwards Burr, a member of Annis Stockton's literary circle in Princeton, New Jersey, playfully calls her small circle, "The Female Freemasons." See Carol Karlsen and Laurie Crumpacker, *The Journal of Esther Edwards Burr, 1754–1757* (New Haven: Yale University Press, 1984).

33. EF commonplace book to Annis Stockton, DCL (emphasis added).

34. Added to EGF's commonplace book, *Poemata Juvenilia,* in 1789, this poem appears alongside an earlier poem, written in 1752, which favors love. Read together, the poems compare Elizabeth Graeme Fergusson's evolving thoughts on love and friendship.

35. David Hume, *Treatise on Human Nature,* ed. L. A. Selby-Bigge (Oxford: Clarendon Press, 1967), 1:365.

36. Quoted in Lyman H. Butterfield, "Morven: A Colonial Outpost of Sensibility," *Princeton University Library Chronicle* 6 (November 1944): 3.

37. EF to Ann Ridgely, Graeme Park, December 25, 1785, printed in *What Them Befell: The Ridgelys of Delaware and their Circle in Colonial and Federal Times: Letters, 1751–1890,* ed. Mabel Lloyd Ridgely (Portland, Maine: Anthoensen Press, 1949), 42–43.

38. EF to Ann Ridgely, September 14, 1797, in Simon Gratz, "Some Material for the Biography of Mrs. Elizabeth Fergusson," *Pennsylvania Magazine of History and Biography* 39 (1915): 406.

39. For a rich rhetorical discussion of commonplace practices, see Susan Miller, *Assuming the Positions: Cultural Pedagogy and the Politics of Commonplace Writing* (Pittsburgh: University of Pittsburgh Press, 1998); Ann Moss, *Printed-Commonplace Books and the Structuring of Renaissance Thought* (New York: Oxford University Press, 1996); Mary Thomas Crane, *Framing Authority: Sayings, Self, and Society in Sixteenth-century England* (Princeton: Princeton University Press, 1993); and Sister Joan Marie Lechner, *Renaissance Concepts of the Commonplaces* (New York: Pageant Press, 1962). Work on early American commonplace books in particular includes Kenneth Lockridge, *The Sources of Patriarchal Rage: The Commonplace Books of William Byrd and Thomas Jefferson and the Gendering of Power in the Eighteenth Century* (New York: New York University Press, 1992) and Susan Stabile, "Memory's Daughters: The Material Culture of Remembrance in Eighteenth-Century America" (Ithaca: Cornell University Press, 2003).

40. James Beattie, *Dissertations Moral and Critical* (London: W. Strahan and T. Cadell, 1783), 28–29, 48.

41. Beattie, *Dissertations,* 35, 33.

42. Eliza Stedman to Mrs. Senior, April 6, 1801, in Lady Ann Keith Collection, Bucks County Historical Society, Doylestown, Pa.

43. Miller, *Assuming the Positions,* 32.

44. For a discussion of the "Republican Mother," see Linda Kerber's groundbreaking study, *Women of the Republic: Intellect and Ideology in Revolutionary America* (New York: Norton, 1986).

45. Gratz, "Some Material," 269–71.

46. For the tradition of paraphrasing Scripture, see Margaret P. Hannay, "Wisdome the Wordes: Psalm Translation and Elizabethan Women's Spirituality," *Religion and Literature* (Autumn 1991): 65–81.

47. Undated letter from EF to unknown correspondent is printed in Gratz, "Some Material," 387. For a more comprehensive discussion of women's reading practices in early America, see Cathy Davidson, *Reading in America: Literature and Social History* (Baltimore: Johns Hopkins University Press, 1989) and *Revolution and the Word: The Rise of the Novel in America* (New York: Oxford University Press, 1986); William C. Gilmore, *Reading Becomes a Necessity of Life* (Knoxville: University of Tennessee Press, 1989); Linda Kerber, *Women of the Republic;* Chester T. Hallenbeck, "A Colonial Reading List from the Union Library of Hatboro, PA," *PMHB* 56 (1932): 289–340; David Lundberg and Henry May, "The Enlightened Reader in America," *American Quarterly* 27 (1976): 262–95; E. Jennifer Monaghan, "Literacy Instruction and Gender in Colonial New England," *American Quarterly* 40 (1988): 18–41.

48. Blecki and Wulf, *Milcah Martha Moore's Book,* 202–3.

49. EF to BR, Graeme Park, April 21, 1786, in Benjamin Rush Correspondence, 40:82–95, LCP.

50. Blecki and Wulf, *Milcah Martha Moore's Book,* 209–10.

51. Beattie, *Dissertations,* 51.

52. Ibid., 177.

53. Samuel Johnson, *Rambler,* no. 2 (March 24, 1750).

54. EF, 1787 Commonplace Book, DCL.

55. Hugh Blair, Lecture 38, "On the Nature of Poetry," *Lectures on Rhetoric and Belles Lettres,* 85; quoted in Carla Mulford, *"Only for the Eye of a Friend": The Poems of Annis Boudinot Stockton* (Charlottesville: University Presses of Virginia, 1995), 30.

56. The allegory appears in both *Poemata Juvenilia* and the 1796 Commonplace Book to EB at the HSP.

57. Quoted in Moss, *Printed-Commonplace Books,* 109.

58. Bennett, *Letters to a Young Lady,* 122.

CHAPTER I

1. Letter EGF to Annis Stockton, December 24, 1793, Rush Papers, LCP; and letter to Ann Ridgely, September 14, 1797, in Gratz, "Some Material," 406–7.

2. George B. Tatum, *Philadelphia Georgian* (Middletown, Conn.: Wesleyan University Press, 1976), 143 n. 7.

3. BR, in his memorial, wrote that she was born in 1739, and this date has been used by some writers. It is an error, however, as shown in church records and in her own words.

4. Jesse L. Lemisch, ed., *Benjamin Franklin: The Autobiography and Other Writings* (New York, N.Y.: The New American Library, 1961), 55.

5. Ibid., 77.

6. Information about the Keith family comes from Charles P. Keith, "The Wife and Children of Sir William Keith," *PMHB* 56 (1932): 1–8.

7. EGF stated that there had been twelve children; note included in her translation of the 17th Book of *Télémachus* sent to BR, Rush Papers, LCP. The number ten was mentioned in her prose piece, "An Old Woman's Meditations on an Old Family Piece of Furniture," included in a booklet of her poems called "Elizabeth Graeme Ferguson Selections 1797–1799," Am.0670, HSP. In the Willing Commonplace Book, she wrote that ten brothers and sisters were buried in Christ Churchyard.

8. Letter EGF to Rebecca Smith, January 6, 1791, William Smith Papers, University of Pennsylvania Archives and Records Center (hereafter UPARC).

9. There are several extant versions of this piece. I have quoted "An Old Woman's Meditations on an Old Family Piece of Furniture," Elizabeth Graeme Ferguson Selections 1797–1799, HSP.

10. Tatum, *Philadelphia Georgian*, 16, 150 n. 54; Richard G. Schmidt, "Early Elegance in Philadelphia: Edward Shippen's Great House 1695–1792," M.A. Thesis, University of Delaware, 1974; Gertrude B. Biddle and Sarah D. Lowrie, *Notable Women of Pennsylvania* (Philadelphia: University of Pennsylvania Press, 1942), 46.

11. William J. Buck, notes from family Bible, in "Graeme Park Ms. Notes on," CCHS.

12. Horace M. Lippincott, *Early Philadelphia, Its People, Life and Progress* (Philadelphia: J. B. Lippincott Company, 1917), 37.

13. Buck, "Graeme Park Ms. Notes on," CCHS, 145.

14. In June 1753, Dr. Graeme rented a large house in 4th Street, Philadelphia, from Edward Shippen Sr. of Lancaster, although this house was partially unfinished inside. (Letter Ann Graeme to EG, May 1, 1753, Buck, "Graeme Park Ms. Notes on," CCHS.) In 1760, Shippen's son wanted to occupy the house (letter Shippen to his son, July 20, 1760, Balch Papers, HSP) and the Graemes had to find another to rent for their winters in Philadelphia. For the next nine years they occupied a house belonging to John Smith of Burlington, New Jersey, on the north side of Chestnut Street between Sixth and Seventh Streets. (Letters Wm. Logan to John Smith, [May 1769], Smith Papers, HSP; Contributionship Insurance Co. Records for Survey no. 1102, microfilm reel XR 3:3, August 25, 1766, HSP). Disagreement with Smith in 1769 about remodeling that Smith wanted to do broke Dr. Graeme's lease with Smith, and the family had to rent elsewhere until the doctor's death in 1772. Reports place them in the Carpenter house again before Thomas Graeme died.

15. J. Thomas Scharf and Thompson Westcott, *History of Philadelphia 1609–1884*, 3 vols. (Philadelphia: L. H. Everts & Co., 1884), 1:617.

16. For a description of how Keith secured the land, see Charles H. Smith, "Sidelights

on the History of Graeme Park," *Bulletin of the Historical Society of Montgomery County* 4 (1943–45): 257–65.

17. Thomas Allen Glenn, ed., *Some Colonial Mansions and Those Who Lived in Them* (Philadelphia: Henry T. Coates & Company, 1898), 1:376.

18. Theodore W. Bean, ed., *History of Montgomery County* (Philadelphia: Everts & Peck, 1884), 887.

19. *The American Weekly Mercury*, August 25–September 1, 1737, quoted by Nancy J. Wosstroff, "Graeme Park: An Eighteenth-Century Country Estate In Horsham, Pennsylvania," M.A. Thesis, University of Delaware, June 1958, 26.

20. Bean, *History of Montgomery County,* 882.

21. Smith, "Sidelights," 264.

22. Buck, "Graeme Park Ms. Notes on," 10. As late as 1945, although the hedges had disappeared, a careful observer could still see the depressions on either side of ridges, indicating where the hedgerows had been, according to Smith, "Sidelights," 267.

23. Letter TG to TP, July 1, 1755, Penn Papers, Official Correspondence, HSP.

24. Letter Eliza Stedman to EG, May 17, 1765, Glenn, *Some Colonial Mansions,* 383.

25. Philadelphia, Register of Wills. The inventory has not been microfilmed. The original is in pieces but legible.

26. It has been given to the state of Pennsylvania and is being maintained by the Pennsylvania Historical and Museum Commission for the public. The following description of the house is from Wosstroff, "Graeme Park." A new architectural history of the grounds is being prepared, which may change this analysis.

27. See advertisement in *Pa. Packet* May 24, 1787, for description of house. Today, there are four rooms on the third floor.

28. Letter TG to TP, July 1, 1755, Penn Papers, Official Correspondence, HSP; letter AG to EG, August 20, 1762, Buck, "Graeme Park Ms. Notes on," CCHS. See Wosstroff, "Graeme Park," for analysis.

29. Glenn, *Some Colonial Mansions,* 374. The living room is twenty-one feet square with a fourteen-foot-high ceiling.

30. For example: "Song to the Tune of Tweed Side," written August 22, 1769, *Poemata Juvenilia,* LCP.

31. Letter EGF to BR, October 15, 1792, Rush Papers, LCP.

32. EGF, "An Old Woman's Meditations on an Old Family Piece of Furniture," *Elizabeth Graeme Fergusson Selections,* 1797–1799, HSP.

33. Probably Rev. Robert Irwin; "History of the Escrutoir," typescript at Bucks County Historical Society, Doylestown, Pennsylvania, for history of the writing desk. For description, see William Macpherson Hornor Jr., *Blue Book of Philadelphia Furniture* (Washington, D.C.: Highland House Publisher, 1935), 21.

34. EGF, Yale Commonplace Book, LCP.

35. Carl and Jessica Bridenbaugh, *Rebels and Gentlemen* (New York: Reynal & Hitchcock, 1942), 48.

36. Martha Slotten, "The Culture of Elizabeth Graeme Ferguson," M.A. Thesis, Shippensburg State College, 1980, 35–36.

37. EG, "Some Lines." James Thomson (1700–1748) was an English poet and dramatist, a favorite of both Ann and Elizabeth Graeme.

38. Letter AG to EG, 1752, EGF Commonplace Book, 1766– , LCP.

39. LCP has two books originally owned by Thomas Graeme, written in both Latin and Greek on opposing pages.

40. Carl and Jessica Bridenbaugh, *Rebels and Gentlemen*, 52.

41. Letter EG to Mrs. Campbell, January 10, 1764, Pa. Collection (Misc.), PMHC.

42. Letter A. Coxe to BR, July 11, 1770, Rush Papers, LCP.

43. Pa. Arch., ser. 6, 12:647. For discussion of the relationship of the Graeme furniture to its times, see William Macpherson Horner Jr., *Blue Book Philadelphia Furniture* (Philadelphia, 1935).

44. John Vanbrugh, *A Journey to London* (London: J. Watts, 1728); Buck's "Graeme Park Notes on"; EGF, "An Old Woman's Meditations on an Old Family Piece of Furniture."

45. Letter AG to Mrs. Campbell, May 15, 1752, Society Collection, HSP.

46. EG, "A Dream," 1752, *Poemata Juvenilia*, LCP.

47. Letters AG to Mrs. Campbell, June 14, 1752, Society Collection, HSP, and EGF to Mrs. Campbell, May 9, 1779, Gratz Collection, HSP.

48. BR, "An Account of the Life and Character of Mrs. Elizabeth Ferguson," *The Port Folio*, I (1809): 521.

49. This treasured piece of furniture, too, Elizabeth would keep nearly all her life, no matter how crowded her residence would become. The table is now owned by the Winterthur Museum.

50. EG, "To Miss Rebekah Moore at Moore-hall Wrote at the time of the Indian War Philadelphia November 20, 1755," *Poemata Juvenilia*, LCP.

51. EG, "To Miss Rebekah Moore at Moore-hall."

52. Sylvia was the pseudonym of Rebecca when young, which would change to Aurelia later. Elizabeth used the name Laura all her life, probably taken from Petrarch's *Canzoniere*.

53. Scharf and Westcott, *History of Philadelphia*, 2:864.

54. Bean, *History of Montgomery County*, 340.

55. EGF, "A Song written During the Times of the War 1782 written to be sung at a Spinning Frolic . . ." EGF Commonplace Book, DCL; also published in the *Columbian Magazine* 3 (December 1789): 746.

56. Bean, *History of Montgomery County*, 338–39.

57. Letter EG to Richard Peters, March 25, 1767, EG Commonplace Book, 1766– , HSP.

CHAPTER 2

1. "Fanny Salter's Reminiscences of Colonial Days in Philadelphia," *PMHB* 40 (1916): 187.

2. William's illegitimacy does not seem to have interfered with his acceptance by society. This attitude was not unusual. For example, Richard Peters Jr., a prominent Philadelphian, was the son of a man who had deserted a wife and four children in England. He lived with a woman in Philadelphia, fathering a whole new family, including Richard, until his first wife died and he could marry his Pennsylvania companion.

3. Letter BF to Cadwallader Colden, September 29, 1748, in L. Jesse Lemisch, *Benjamin Franklin: The Autobiography and Other Writings* (New York: The New American Library, 1961), 217–18.

4. Letter Margaret Penn Freame to John Penn, [Aug. 1737], *PMHB* 31 (1907): 121.

5. Letter AG to EG, September 26, 1755, Gratz Collection, HSP. John Penn would marry a daughter of Philadelphia and spend most of his life in Pennsylvania.

6. Catherine Drinker Bowen, *The Most Dangerous Man in America* (Boston: Little, Brown and Company, 1974), 93.

7. EG, "On the fate of a lottery Ticket," December 30, 1752, *Poemata Juvenilia, LCP.

8. EG, "The foregoing Song answerd by a Young Lady," *Poemata Juvenilia,* LCP.

9. For this interpretation, see Sheila L. Skemp, *William Franklin: Son of a Patriot Servant of a King* (New York: Oxford University Press, 1990). 24.

10. EG, "The Invitation a Song," June 3, 1753, *Poemata Juvenilia,* LCP.

11. EG, "The Choice of Life," June 4, 1753, *Poemata Juvenilia,* LCP.

12. EGF, Commonplace Book, DCL.

13. WF, "A Song by a Young Gentleman to some Ladies in the Country at Horsham" August 16, 1753, *Poemata Juvenilia,* LCP.

14. EG, "Dialogue between Damon and Alexis," November 1, 1753, *Poemata Juvenilia,* LCP. "Sylvia" was the pseudonym of Rebecca Moore.

15. Tremaine McDowell, "Sensibility in the Eighteenth-Century American Novel," *Studies in Philology* 24 (July 1927): 383.

16. Skemp, *William Franklin,* 14.

17. Letter TG to Richard Peters, July 29, 1755, Peters Papers, HSP; letter Richard Peters to Conrad Weiser, November 27, 1755, Peters Papers, HSP.

18. *Pennsylvania Gazette,* September 25, 1755.

19. Letter AG to EG, September 24, 1755, quoted by Thomas Allen Glenn, ed., *Some Colonial Mansions* (Philadelphia: Henry T. Coates & Company, 1898), 386. William Allen was chief justice of the colony, a wealthy, powerful man who was one of Penn's advisors.

20. William Smith, *A Brief State of the Province of Pennsylvania* (London 1755); "Humphrey Scourge," *Tit for Tat, of The Score Wip'd Off* (Philadelphia, 1755); see Skemp, *William Franklin,* 18–19, for discussion of this exchange.

21. See, for example, the *Gazette* for January 8 and 15, 1756.

22. Letter AG to Mrs. Campbell, May 13, 1756, Stauffer Collection, HSP.

23. Letter WF to EG, February 26, 1757, Gratz Collection, HSP.

24. Wm. Smith, "Verses by the Reverend Doctor Smith on the Birth-Day Of a young Lady Born the 14 of February 1737," *Poemata Juvenilia,* LCP.

25. WF, "A Song wrote by a young Gentleman to a young Lady," February 26, 1757, *Poemata Juvenilia,* LCP.

26. BF was first elected to the Assembly in 1751.

27. EG, "The foregoing Song answered by a Young Lady," February 28, 1757, *Poemata Juvenilia,* LCP.

28. Letter WF to Mrs. Abercrombie, October 24, 1758, Gratz Collection, HSP.

29. Letter WF to EG, April 7, 1757, Leonard Labaree, ed., *The Papers of Benjamin Franklin* (New Haven: Yale University Press, 1968–), 7:177.

30. Letter WF to EG, April 11, 1757, Society Collection, HSP.

31. Letter WF to EG, April 25, 1757, Gratz Collection, HSP.

32. Letter WF to EG, May 2, 1757, Gratz Collection, HSP.

33. Letter WF to EG, May 5, 1757, Lilly Library, Indiana University. Margaret Abercrombie would marry Charles Stedman after the deaths of her husband and Ann Stedman, Elizabeth's sister.

34. Letter WF to EG, May 12, 1757, William Franklin Papers, American Philosophical Society, Philadelphia

35. Letter WF to EG, May 16, 1757, Gratz Collection, HSP.

36. Letters WF to EG, May 23, 1757, Library, University of Pittsburgh, copy at Yale University Library, and June 2, 1757, *Franklin Papers,* 7:234.

37. Letter WF to EG, July 17, 1757, New York Public Library.

38. Letter WF to EG, December 9, 1757, *Franklin Papers*, 7:288–92.

39. Letter WF to Mrs. Abercrombie, October 24, 1758, Gratz Collection, HSP. Letter lacks a conclusion.

40. What Elizabeth Graeme may never have known was that William had fathered an illegitimate child named William Temple Franklin by an unknown woman before he married Elizabeth Downes.

41. Letter Margaret Abercrombie to AG, April 4, 1759, Gratz Collection, HSP.

42. The writing is scribbled over in an attempt to obliterate it, but the words can be read. She was sending all the correspondence between her and William to an unnamed person and wrote "I think your knowledge of the Passions will plainly Point the Fallacy and Truth which is that the More we love a person the More ready We Ought to be to excuse their indifference[.] little Conformable to the feelings of the Human Heart is that."

43. Letter AG to EG, December 3, 1762, Gratz Collection, HSP.

44. Letter Deborah to BF, January 12, 1766, *Franklin Papers*, 13: 30; 7:177, n. 4.

45. Letter AG to EG, December 3, 1762, Gratz Collection, HSP.

46. Ibid.

47. Letter TG to EG, January 1, 1763, Gratz. Collection, HSP.

48. EGF to BR, December 23, 1794, Rush Papers, vol. 40, LCP.

49. This authorship of the letters was suggested by Chester T. Hallenbeck in his M.A. thesis, "The Life and Collected Poems of Elizabeth Graeme Fergusson," 42–43.

50. Letter EG to Mrs. Campbell, January 23, 1763, Society Collection, HSP.

51. Letter Margaret Abercrombie to EG, May 20, 1763, Bean, *History of Montgomery County,* 891. The original of this letter is lost.

52. Letter TG to TP, June 6, 1760, Penn Papers Official Correspondence, HSP.

53. Letter AG to Mrs. Campbell, July 24, 1760, Gratz Collection, HSP.

54. Smith Commonplace Book, p. 314, LCP.

55. Letter AG to Mary Redman, September 22, 1762, Spruance Library, Bucks County Historical Society, Doylestown, Pa.

56. Letter TG to TP, November 9, 1746, Penn Papers Private Correspondence, HSP.

57. Letter TG to TP, June 6, 1760, Penn Papers Official Correspondence, HSP.

58. Letter AG to Betsy Stedman, August 15, 1759, William Buck, "Graeme Park Notes on," CCHS. The commonplace book has disappeared.

59. Eliza. Stedman to EG, August 21, 1761, Gratz Collection, HSP.

60. "A Jaunt to Philadelphia in 1762," *Magazine of American History* 15 (January–June 1886): 399–400.

61. Letter Betsy Stedman to EG, August 7, 1762, Gratz Collection, HSP.

62. Letter Mary Dickinson to her son John Dickinson, October 9, 1762, Logan Papers, HSP.

63. Bean, 890. He dates the excursion as occurring in August, but extant EG letters place her in Philadelphia alone recovering her health all that month, while the rest of the family was at Graeme Park.

64. EGF, Yale Commonplace Book, LCP.

65. Letter EG to Ann Stedman, August 20, 1762, *Poemata Juvenilia,* LCP.

66. EG, "A Description of the State Coach in which his Majesty King George the Third went to the House of Lords in; immediately after the preliminarys of peace were signed Between England and France," January 30, 1763, *Poemata Juvenilia,* LCP.

67. Letter EG to Mrs. Campbell, August 12, 1763, Gratz Collection, HSP.

68. Hubertis Cummings, *Richard Peters: Provincial Secretary and Cleric 1704–1776* (Philadelphia: University of Pennsylvania Press, 1944), 8–30. Moving to the colonies to escape an undesirable marriage was not an unusual practice. Gov. John Penn at eighteen had contracted a marriage considered unfortunate by his uncle Thomas Penn, who sent him to Philadelphia. It is not known how the marriage was legally ended, but Penn ultimately married Ann, the daughter of Pennsylvania's Chief Justice William Allen. See Arthur Pound, *The Penns of Pennsylvania and England* (New York: The Macmillan Company, 1932), 294–95. Page 20, n. 2, gives example of Peters's brother.

69. *Dictionary of American Biography,* vol. 7, pt. 2, p. 508.

70. Letter TG to EG, June 15, 1763, Bean, 891. The original of this letter is lost.

71. Letter James Young to EG, July 23, 1763, Gratz Collection, HSP.

72. Letter EG to Mrs. Campbell, August 12, 1763, Gratz Collection, HSP.

73. Letter TG to EG, September 10, 1763, Bean, 889.

CHAPTER 3

1. *Pennsylvania Gazette,* June 21, 1764; letter AG to EG, May 15, 1765, Bean, *History of Montgomery County,* 384.

2. Letter AG to EG, April 11, 1765, Bean, *History of Montgomery County,* 891.

3. "An Account of the Life and Character of Mrs. Elizabeth Ferguson," *The Port Folio* 1 (1809): 523.

4. These copies of parts of the journals were discovered by Professors Catherine La Courreye Blecki and Karin A. Wulf and published in their *Milcah Martha Moore's Book.* Professors Blecki and Wulf generously shared this finding with me before publication.

5. Letter AG to EG, May 15, 1765, Buck, "Graeme Park Ms. Notes on," 182, CCHS.

6. Letter Hopkinson to Mary Hopkinson, May 25, 1766, Hopkinson Papers, HSP.

7. Letter John Penn to Thomas Penn, June 29, 1764, Penn Papers, Official Correspondence, HSP.

8. Blecki and Wulf, *Milcah Martha Moore's Book,* 201.

9. Betsy C. Corner and Christopher C. Booth, eds., *Chain of Friendship* (Cambridge, Mass.: The Belknap Press of Harvard University Press, 1971), 4–5, 9; *PMHB* 31 (1907): 124.

10. Corner and Booth, *Chain of Friendship,* 42, 115, 191, 230, 475.

11. Ibid., 230–31.

12. *Poemata Juvenilia,* LCP.

13. Blecki and Wulf, *Milcah Martha Moore's Book,* 201. In a magazine report later in life, Elizabeth referred to this encounter as taking place at the York races. The approximate thirty-five miles between the two towns, however, makes that seem unlikely. Her reference to the Assembly Room places the races closer to Scarborough.

14. *The Port Folio* 1 (1809): 522–23; *Universal Asylum and Columbian Magazine* March 1791:168; Laurence Sterne, *Works of Laurence Sterne,* 4 vols. (London: Cadell and Davis, 1819), 3:105.

15. Hubertis Cummings, *Richard Peters, Provincial Secretary and Cleric* (Philadelphia: University of Pennsylvania Press, 1944), 274; letter TP to William Smith, September 7, 1764, William Smith Papers, UPARC.

16. Cummings, *Richard Peters,* 274; letter TP to William Smith, October 12, 1764, William Smith Papers, UPARC.

17. Blecki and Wulf, *Milcah Martha Moore's Book,* 202.

18. Letter TP to Peters, December 8, 1764, Penn Ms.-Supp.-Saunders-Coates 1720–66, HSP.

19. Letter Richard Peters to EG, November 20, 1764, Gratz Collection, HSP.

20. EG, "To Dr. John Fothergill," Blecki and Wulf, *Milcah Martha Moore's Book,* 214.

21. Letter Peters to EG, January 3, 1765, Gratz Collection, HSP

22. Letters Peters to EG, November 20, 1764, December 4, 1754, December 14, 1764, January 3, 1765, all in Gratz Collection, HSP.

23. Letter EG to Peters, January 18, 1765, Gratz Collection, HSP. Peters was in Wrixam, Wales, where he was visiting his brother's daughter and her husband, the Gartsides.

24. EG, *Poemata Juvenilia,* LCP.

25. Bean, *History of Montgomery County,* 896.

26. Blecki and Wulf, *Milcah Martha Moore's Book,* 204.

27. EG, "Wrote to a Lady on the Back of a Fan," January 25, 1765, and Juliana Ritchie, "Answered by the Lady to whom the Fan was Sent," January 25, 1765, *Poemata Juvenilia,* LCP; Letter J. Ritchie to EG, January 27, 1765, Gratz Collection, HSP.

28. Letter BF to Deborah Franklin, February 14, 1765, *The Papers of Benjamin Franklin,* 12:63; Deborah F. to BF, [April 7, 1765], *The Papers of Benjamin Franklin,* 12:101.

29. EG, "The Dream or the Patriotic, Philosophical Farmer," in EGF Commonplace Book #13298-Q, LCP.

30. Dr. John Coakley, *The Works of John Fothergill, M.D., with an Account of His Life,* 3 vols. (London: Charles Dilly, 1783–84), 2:383–416.

31. Blecki and Wulf, *Milcah Martha Moore's Book,* 203.

32. Ibid., 212, 215, 211.

33. Letter TP to TG, February 14, 1765, Penn Letter Book 1763–66, HSP.

34. Letter Eliza Stedman to EG, March 9, 1765, Gratz Collection, HSP.

35. *Poemata Juvenilia,* LCP.

36. Letter Eliza Stedman to EG, March 9, 1765, Gratz Collection, HSP.

37. Blecki and Wulf, *Milcah Martha Moore's Book,* 210, 202–3, 209–10. Edward Young, 1683–1765; Nicholas Rowe, 1674–1718; Joseph Addison, 1672–1719; Alexander Pope, 1688–1744; Samuel Richardson, 1689–1761. Blecki identified Harvey as referring to James Hervey (1714–1758).

38. N.a., *Illustrated Guide to Britain* (Basingstoke, Eng.: Drive Publications Limited, 1977) 215.

39. Blecki and Wulf, *Milcah Martha Moore's Book,* 209.

40. EG, "Some Lines."

41. Ibid.

42. Letter EG to Peters, January 18, 1765, Gratz Collection, HSP; Bean, *History of Montgomery County,* 891; letter Betsy Stedman to EG, March 9, 1765, Gratz Collection, HSP.

43. EG, "Some Lines."

44. EG, *Poemata Juvenilia,* LCP.

45. *Universal Asylum and Columbian Magazine* 7 (August 1791): 121–23.

46. Blecki and Wulf, *Milcah Martha Moore's Book,* 204.

47. Letter Fothergill to EG, March 20, 1765, was directed to her at Bristol; letter TP to William Smith, April 13, 1765, William Smith Papers, UPARC, says Peters was at the "Hot Well."

48. Letter Hannah Freame to Peters, May 11, 1765, Peters Papers, HSP; Fothergill to EG, May 26, 1765, Rush Papers, LCP; letter Juliana Penn to Peters, May 9, 1765, Penn Ms.-Supp.-Saunders-Coates 1720–66, HSP.

49. Blecki and Wulf, *Milcah Martha Moore's Book,* 208–9. For more information about the Goldney family and their estate, see P. K. Stembridge, *Goldney, A House and a Family* (Bristol: The Burleigh Press, 1969). Source shared by Catherine Blecki.

50. Letter Philadelphia Hannah Freame to Peters, May 11, 1765, Peters Papers, HSP.

51. Letter John Fothergill to Samuel Fothergill, June 28, 1765, Corner and Booth, 241.

52. Letter Peters to EG, July 2, 1765, Gratz Collection, HSP.

53. Letter Peters to EG, July 9, 1765, Gratz Collection, HSP.

54. Young to EG, April 3, 1765, Buck, "Graeme Park Ms. Notes on."

55. Letter AG to EG, May 15, 1765, Buck, "Graeme Park Ms. Notes on."

56. Letter Ann Stedman to EG, June 4, 1765, Buck, "Graeme Park Ms. Notes on."

57. Smith Commonplace Book, 314, LCP.

58. EGF, Smith Commonplace Book, LCP.

59. BR, "An Account of the Life and Character of Mrs. Elizabeth Ferguson."

60. EG note on letter Juliana Ritchie to EG, July 9, 1765, HSP.

61. Cummings, *Richard Peters,* 279.

62. Letter Abraham Taylor to Peters, September 23, 1765, Peters Papers, HSP.

63. Bean, *History of Montgomery County,* 801.

64. William Buck, "The Graeme Coat of Arms," HSP; Charles Dexter Allen, *American Book-Plates* (London: George Bell & Sons, 1895), 97, 210.

65. Alexander M. Delavoye, *Life of Thomas Graham, Lord Lynedoch* (London: Richardson & Co., 1880), 2–3.

66. Letter Peters to EG, September 22, 1765, Gratz Collection, HSP.

67. Blecki and Wulf, *Milcah Martha Moore's Book,* 216.

68. EGF to BR, April 26, 1786, Rush Papers, LCP.

69. Cummings, *Richard Peters,* 279.

70. Dated October 14 and 16, 1765.

71. AG's Farewell Advice to EG, 1762, Buck, "Graeme Park Ms. Notes on."

72. Letter Morgan to EG, June 20, 1765, Peters Papers, HSP.

CHAPTER 4

1. EG, "Some Lines." Ann Stedman died March 3, 1766.

2. One woman who developed her own business was well-known to Elizabeth. The mother of BR, upon the death of her second husband, sold his shop and tools and opened her own successful grocery store. David F. Hawke, *Benjamin Rush, Revolutionary Gadfly* (Indianapolis: Bobbs-Merrill, Inc., 1971), 11.

3. Joan Hoff Wilson, "The Illusion of Change: Women and the American Revolution," in *The American Revolution,* ed. by Alfred F. Young (DeKalb, Ill.: Northern Illinois University Press, 1976), 395.

4. There are three slightly different versions. I combined them and used the wording with majority support. See Rush Papers, LCP; *Poemata Juvenilia,* LCP; *Record of the Inscriptions on the Tablets and Gravestones in the Burial Grounds of Christ Church Philadelphia* (Philadelphia: Collins, Printer, 1864).

5. EG, "On the Death of the Reverend Mr *Campbell,*" October 27, 1766, in *Poemata Juvenilia,* LCP.

6. Nathaniel Evans, *Poems on Several Occasions* (New York: Garrett Press, Inc., 1970), 146.

7. Evans, *Poems*, 146.

8. Gammon is smoked or cured ham.

9. Evans, *Poems*, 150–52.

10. Ibid., 152–54.

11. Ibid., 155–57.

12. Letter EG to Peters, March 25, 1767, from the volume marked Psalms, vol. 1, LCP.

13. Letter James Young to EG, July 23, 1763, Gratz Collection, HSP. See Hallenbeck, "The Life and Collected Poems of Elizabeth Graeme Fergusson," 70–72; and George E. Hastings, *The Life and Works of Francis Hopkinson* (Chicago: University of Chicago Press, 1926), 73–77.

14. Letter EG to Peters, March 25, 1767. There is another slightly different version of this letter in a commonplace book at HSP, marked "E. Graeme vol. 1," #Am.067, which contains copies of her paraphrases.

15. Belonging to LCP but located at HSP.

16. *The Holy Bible* (Philadelphia: A. J. Holman Company, n.d.), 564. Text conformable to King James Version.

17. Letter Peters to EG, n.d., Gratz Collection, HSP.

18. These paraphrases may be found in *Poemata Juvenilia,* LCP.

19. Nathan's Parable, in *Columbian Magazine* 2 (September 1787): 667; Augur's Prayer, in *The Universal Asylum and Columbian Magazine* 6 (February 1791): 118; Luke 16, in *The Universal Asylum . . .* 9 (September 1792): 189–91.

20. Horace W. Smith, *Life and Correspondence of the Rev. William Smith, D.D.,* 2 vols. (Philadelphia: S. A. George & Co., 1879), 1:480.

21. Evans, *Poems*.

22. M. Katherine Jackson, *Outlines of the Literary History of Colonial Pennsylvania* (Lancaster, Pa.: The New Era Printing Company, 1906), 100, n. 59; also Hallenbeck, "The Life and Collected Poems of Elizabeth Graeme Fergusson," 79.

23. It has been written mistakenly that she paraphrased the Psalms and translated *Télémaque* before she went to Europe in order to forget William Franklin and that this activity helped create her health problems. Elizabeth clearly stated in several places that she did not begin these efforts until 1766. She also said she turned to these two massive projects in sadness to ease her grief over the deaths of her mother and sister. The mistake is traceable back to BR's memoir of her life, which contains several other errors, as well.

24. February 23, 1767, signed G.E. and May 4, 1767, signed G. Yale Commonplace Book, pp. 149 and 155, manuscript copies claim authorship, LCP.

25. For information about the library, see Ruth Robinson Ross, *Union Library Company of Hatborough* (Hatboro, Pa.: Union Library Co., 1955).

26. Minute book of meetings of the directors, Xerox copy, HSP.

27. Buck, "Graeme Park Ms. Notes on," CCHS.

28. George B. Tatum, *Philadelphia Georgian* (Middleton, Conn.: Wesleyan University Press, 1976), 4–6.

29. Henry Hugh Fergusson Loyalist Claim, January 6, 1784, testimony of Daniel Roberdeau, January 24, 1784, London, Public Record Office, A.O. 12/38, XA/A001992.

30. Smith, *Life and Correspondence of Rev. William Smith, D.D.,* 474; letter EGF to BR, April 21, 1786, Rush Papers, LCP.

31. Letter TG to TP, July 1, 1755, Penn Papers Official Correspondence, HSP.

32. Hubertis Cummings, *Richard Peters* (Philadelphia: University of Pennsylvania Press, 1944), 292.

33. Letter EG to Dear Madam [Mrs. Campbell], March 25, 1767, Gratz, "Some Material," 386–88; Ann Young, "Epistle to Damon on presenting him with a Small writing Desk And Letter Case," copied by EG into her commonplace book, DCL.

34. Evert A. and George L. Duyckinck, *Cyclopedia of American Literature,* 2 vols. (New York: Charles Scribner, 1855), 233.

35. There is no full-length biography of Annis Stockton, but a good summary is in Carla Mulford, *Only for the Eye of a Friend* (Charlottesville: University Press of Virginia, 1995), 1–40.

36. Poem by Annis Stockton, "To Laura," September 18, 1766, *Poemata Juvenilia,* LCP.

37. All three poems are in *Poemata Juvenila.* For more Stockton poetry, see Mulford, *Only for the Eye of a Friend.*

38. Anne H. Wharton, *Salons Colonial and Republican* (Philadelphia: J. B. Lippincott Company, 1900), 11–13. This book contains a good brief discussion of the history of salons. Wharton defines "salon" as a group of "men and women of learning and conversational powers" drawn together by a "cultivated woman."

39. BR, "An Account of the Life and Character of Elizabeth Ferguson," *The Port Folio* 1 (1809): 523.

40. Letter EG to Mrs. Campbell, January 10, 1764, Pa. Collection (Misc.), PHMC; Carl and Jessica Bridenbaugh, *Rebels and Gentlemen,* 151.

41. Letter Hopkinson to EG, February 21, 1767, Hopkinson Papers HSP.

42. Pa. Arch., ser. 6, 12:647.

43. Carl and Jessica Bridenbaugh, *Rebels and Gentlemen,* 155, for Duché's musicality; EG, "Content in a Cottage," August 20, 1769, and "A Song," August 22, 1769, both in *Poemata Juvenilia,* LCP.

44. Letter Betsy Stedman to EG, December 16, 1764, Gratz Collection, HSP.

45. O. G. Sonneck, *Early Concert-Life in America* (New York: Musurgia Publishers, 1949), 68–70.

46. Carl and Jessica Bridenbaugh, *Rebels and Gentlemen,* 159; Sonneck, *Early Concert-Life in America,* 74.

47. *Pennsylvania Journal,* November 8, 1770.

48. Letter Peters to EG, November 20, 1764, Gratz Collection, HSP; letter EGF to BR, April 26, 1786, Rush Papers, LCP.

49. EGF annotation to the second part of poem "The Ode on the Willow," Willing Commonplace Book, LCP.

50. Annotation by EG to Thos. Coombs, "Part of a dialogue . . . ," *Poemata Juvenilia,* LCP.

51. Benjamin Franklin, "Autobiography," in L. Jesse Lemisch, ed., *Benjamin Franklin: The Autobiography and Other Writings* (New York: New American Library, 1961), 71–72.

52. *Juvenile Poems on Various Subjects, with the Prince of Parthia. By the late Mr. Thomas Godfrey, Junr. of Philadelphia. To which is prefixed Some Account of the Author and his Writings* (Philadelphia: Henry Miller, 1765).

53. The discussion of this split in educational theory comes largely from the Carl and Jessica Bridenbaugh, *Rebels and Gentlemen,* chap. 2.

54. Letter Edward Shippen to Joseph Shippen, 1749, quoted in Carl and Jessica Bridenbaugh, *Rebels and Gentlemen,* 47.

55. Carl and Jessica Bridenbaugh, *Rebels and Gentlemen,* 59.

56. Ibid., 280. This section on the medical profession has been taken from the their chap. 8.

57. Smith, *Life and Correspondence of Rev. William Smith, D.D.*, 473–74.

58. Eric Foner, *Thomas Paine and Revolutionary America* (London: Oxford University Press, 1976), 54.

59. Letter Joseph Galloway to BF, June 6, 1766, in *The Papers of Benjamin Franklin*, 13:294.

60. Letter Deborah Franklin to BF, September 22, 1765, *The Papers of Benjamin Franklin*, 12:271; letter Edward Burd to Col. Burd, September 18, 1765, in Thomas Balch, ed., *Letters and Papers Relating Chiefly to the Provincial History of Pennsylvania* (Philadelphia: Crissy & Markley, 1855), 207. See also Anne M. Ousterhout, *A State Divided* (Westport, Conn: Greenwood Press, 1987), chap. 2.

61. Letter no. 2.

62. Letter no. 11.

63. Letter no. 3.

64. EGF comment inserted in an enlarged version of the poem written in December 1793 and sent to EB. Copied in Yale Commonplace Book, LCP.

65. EG, *Poemata Juvenilia*, LCP.

66. Letter EG to "Dear Madam," February 27, 1770, Society Collection, HSP.

67. Letter TG to Peters, October 28, 1770, Gratz, "Some Material," 388; letter A. Castelman to Peters, January 20, 1771, Peters Papers, HSP.

68. Letter White to EG, January 28, 1771, Gratz Collection, HSP.

CHAPTER 5

1. Letter Steptoe to BR, August 14, 1771, Rush Papers, LCP.

2. Letters TG to John Smith, March 18, 1769, Smith Papers, HSP; letter William Logan to John Smith, [May 1769], Smith Papers, HSP. Location of house determined by Nancy J. Wosstroff, "Graeme Park An Eighteenth Century Country Estate in Horsham, Pennsylvania," M.A. Thesis, 1958, University of Delaware, 30, 101–2, n. 11.

3. Theodore W. Bean, ed. *History of Montgomery County*, 892. In the records of the settlement of his estate when Dr. Graeme died in 1772, there is an item of a debt of £40 paid for house rent in town, with no indication to whom the money was paid or for what. The rent for Smith's house had been £100; therefore the £40 was probably for another structure. Furthermore, their last rental property was a three-story structure with two rooms on each floor, front and back, but the Smith house had three rooms on a floor.

4. Henry's given names sometimes have been reversed by scholars, but he signed his name "H. Hugh Fergusson." People other than Elizabeth seem to have called him Hugh, whereas she usually called him Henry. Almost all writers about Elizabeth have spelled her married name with one 's,' but the correct spelling is with two. That is the way both Henry and Elizabeth signed it.

5. Henry Hugh Fergusson, "Lines on a Gentleman's Country Seat in Scotland," 1776, copied in EGF's commonplace book, DCL.

6. Public Record Office, London, AO 12, vol. 106, p. 58.

7. For example, Scharf and Westcott, *History of Philadelphia 1609–1884*, 2:1119.

8. EGF, "An advertisement," November 1774, Rush Papers, LCP.

9. Charles Harper Smith, "Sidelights on the History of Graeme Park," *Historical Soc. of Montgomery County, Pennsylvania, Bulletin* 4 (1943–45): 268.

10. EG, "A Pastoral ballad, Love and Alexis," March 4, 1772, Rush Papers, LCP.

11. Letter EG to BR, April 14, 1772, Rush Papers, LCP.

12. Letter HHF to EG, April 15 [or 19], 1772, Yale Commonplace Book, LCP.

13. Theodore W. Bean, *History of Montgomery County*, 892, quotes EGF as saying the marriage took place at eight. EGF wrote to Mrs. Smith, April 21, 1792 (Society Collection, HSP) that the marriage was at nine. I have used EGF's words.

14. Letter EGF to Mrs. Smith, April 21, 1792, Society Collection, HSP.

15. Extract of letter Ann Young to EGF, June 14, 1775, Commonplace Book, DCL.

16. Letter M. Redman to EGF, October 2, 1772, Gratz Collection, HSP.

17. Bean, *History of Montgomery County*, 892.

18. Letter TG to R. Peters, August 4, 1772, Gratz, "Some Material," 388–89.

19. Ibid.

20. Bean, *History of Montgomery County*, 892.

21. Smith's sermon is reprinted in Smith, *Life and Correspondence of the Rev. William Smith, D.D.*, 474–77.

22. Letter EGF to BR, April 21, 1786, Rush Papers, LCP.

23. Ibid.

24. Letter EGF to Dickinson, September 21, 1772, R. R. Logan Collection, HSP.

25. "An act for the better confirmation of the estates of persons holding or claiming under feme-coverts . . . ," *Laws of the Commonwealth of Pennsylvania*, 10 vols. (Philadelphia, 1810–44), 1:307–9. Marylynn Salmon, *Women and the Law of Property in Early America* (Chapel Hill: University of North Carolina Press, 1986), 14–30.

26. Letter EGF to Dickinson, October 4 [1772], R. R. Logan Collection, HSP.

27. Letter Mary Redman to EGF, October 2, 1772, Gratz Collection, HSP.

28. *Pa. Gazette,* October 27, 1773.

29. Letter EGF to "Dear Sir" [Rich. Peters?], February 5, 1773, Gratz Collection, HSP.

30. Sale of Thos. Graeme's belongings October 12, 1772, to John Swift, Society Collection, James Young, HSP.

31. Letter EGF to Dickinson, October 15, 1772, R. R. Logan Collection, HSP.

32. Letter EGF to "Dear Sir" [Richard Peters?], February 5, 1773, Gratz Collection, HSP.

33. Letter EGF to Dickinson, October 15, 1772, R. R. Logan Collection, HSP.

34. The papers are in very bad condition, each page now in several pieces that have to be reassembled like a jig saw puzzle. In addition, they are not as clear as one would wish. For example, nearly £73 was retained by Young, for some unknown purpose.

35. Letter Ann Young to EGF, November 24, 1772, Commonplace Book, DCL.

36. Letter EGF to "Dear Sir" [Richard Peters?], February 5, 1773, Gratz Collection, HSP.

37. Ibid.

38. Ibid.

39. Daniel Coxe and Phineas Bond, witnesses to the claim of Henry Hugh Fergusson, Public Record Office, London, A.O. 12/38, XC/A001992.

40. Letter Redman to EGF, May 3, 1773, Dreer Collection, Physicians, HSP.

41. HHF Loyalist Claim, A.O. 12/38, XC/A 001992, pp. 204–25, Public Record Office, London.

42. Princeton Historical Society.

43. This poem was written September 8, 1773, and published in the *Universal Asylum and Columbian Magazine* 6 (April 1791): 256.

44. EGF Commonplace Book, DCL.

45. Letter Young to EGF, December 1, 1774, Society Collection, HSP.

46. W. J. Buck, "Notes on Graeme Park," CCHS.

47. Letter [James Abercrombie?] to EGF, n.d., Buck, "Notes on Graeme Park," CCHS. *Banford Abbey* has not been identified.

48. EGF, "An Advertisement," Rush Papers, LCP.

49. Letter John Young to EGF, March 22, 1775, Society Collection, HSP.

50. Lyon Norman Richardson, *A History of Early American Magazines, 1741–1789* (New York: Octogan Books, 1966 [1931]), 163.

51. Original in EGF Yale Commonplace Book, LCP.

52. Young, "On Reading Dr Swifts Poems," 1774, EGF Commonplace Book, DCL.

53. Young, "An Epistle to Damon who was absent on A Journey with a Friend," September 9, 1774, in EGF Commonplace Book, DCL.

54. EGF, Commonplace Book, DCL, contains Elizabeth's copies of fourteen of Anny Young's poems with the transcriber's comments. There are no known existing documents in Anny Young's hand.

55. EGF Commonplace Book, DCL.

56. *UA&C Magazine* 7 (August 1791): 121–23.

57. Letter Young to EGF, March 22, 1775, Society Collection, HSP.

58. The articles appeared in every issue between February 1 and May 9, 1768.

59. *Pennsylvania Chronicle*, February 15–22, 1768.

60. L., The Visitant, *Pennsylvania Chronicle*, February 8–15, 1768.

61. *Pennsylvania Chronicle*, March 7–14, 1768.

62. Mulford, *Only for the Eye of a Friend* (Charlottesville: University Press of Virginia, 1995), 188, no. 54.

63. Letter Stockton to Julia Rush, March 22 [1793?], Rosenbach Museum and Library, Philadelphia.

64. *Pennsylvania Chronicle*, April 4–11, 1768.

65. Letter EG to ?, March 25, 1767, Dreer Collection, American Poets, HSP, where it is misfiled under date March 25, 1769.

66. October 15, 1772, R. R. Logan Collection, John Dickinson Papers, HSP.

67. Letter John Young to EGF, [early 1774], HSP.

68. Letter John Young to EGF, July 15, 1774, HSP.

CHAPTER 6

1. Letter Abigail Coxe to BR, July 11, 1770, Rush Papers, vol. 27, HSP.

2. "Hamden," *Pennsylvania Journal*, October 30, 1773.

3. John Dickinson, "A Letter from the Country, to a Gentleman in Philadelphia," November 27, 1773, Early American Imprints, Evans Digital Edition (1639–1800) (hereafter Evans), no. 12751.

4. Broadsides: "The Committee for Tarring and Feathering. To the Delaware Pilots," Philadelphia 1773, Evans no. 12941; "To the Delaware Pilots and to Capt. Ayres," November 27, 1773, Evans no. 12942.

5. EGF, "The Dream," *Poemata Juvenilia,* HSP.

6. Letter JY to EGF, July 15, 1774, Society Collection, HSP; letter JY to EGF, August 10, 1774, Berks & Montgomery County Misc. 1693–1869, HSP. "Oliverian" refers to Oliver Cromwell.

7. For a thorough discussion of the pre-Revolutionary activity in Philadelphia, see

Ousterhout, *A State Divided,* chaps. 2, 3, and 4. Many activities were taking place that this book does not have space to report.

8. Letter Young to EGF, March 22, 1775, Society Collection, HSP.

9. Buck, *History of Montgomery County,* 892.

10. County Tax Assessment Ledger, Philadelphia County, 1774, under Horsham.

11. February 13, 1775, Penn Papers, Warrants to Affix Great Seal, HSP.

12. March 8, 1775, Montgomery County Historical Society.

13. *Pa. Gazette,* April 26, 1775.

14. Christopher Marshall, *Extracts from the Diary of Christopher Marshall . . . 1174–1781,* ed. by William Duane (Albany, N.Y.: Joel Munsell, 1877), May 2, 1775, p. 22.

15. Marshall, *Diary,* 21.

16. Letter C. Stedman to [HHF], May 3, 1775, Buck, "Notes on Graeme Park," CCHS.

17. Letter M. Stedman to EGF, May 13, 1775, Buck, "Notes on Graeme Park," CCHS..

18. Letter HHF to BR, June 20, 1775, Rush Papers, vol. 43, LCP.

19. Letter A. Young to EGF, June 14, 1775, copied in EGF Commonplace Book, DCL.

20. Letter Young to EGF, July 1, 1775, Gratz, "Some Material," 390–91.

21. Letter EGF to Mrs. Smith, June 6, 1775, William Smith Papers, UPARC. Abigail Coxe's son Daniel married Sarah Redman, daughter of John and Mary Redman. Mrs. Coxe, Daniel, and Sarah would all go to England at the outbreak of the war.

22. Letter M. Stedman to EGF, September 2, 1775, Bean, *History of Montgomery County,* 893.

23. William Stevens Perry, ed., *Historical Collections Relating to the American Colonial Church,* 5 vols. (Hartford: Subscribers, 1870–78), 2:470–75.

24. Letter Mary Roberdeau to EGF, July 6, 1775, Gratz Collection, HSP.

25. EGF petition to Supreme Executive Council, June 26, 1778, Chicago Historical Society.

26. Letter James Tilghman to Dear Sir, September 5, 1775, Penn Papers Official Correspondence, HSP.

27. HHF Loyalist Claim, A.O. 12/38, XC/A 001992, pp.204–25, Public Record Office, London.

28. Letter EGF to Samuel W. Stockton, March 16, 1788, extract in Buck, "Notes on Graeme Park," CCHS.

29. HHF power of attorney to Richard Stockton, December 19, 1775, Letter of Attorney Book D 2, 8:233–35, PHMC.

30. See Marylynn Salmon, *Women and the Law of Property in Early America* (Chapel Hill: The University of North Carolina Press, 1986), 41–44, for explanation of women's property rights in Pennsylvania.

31. Letter Richard Stockton to Samuel W. Stockton, October 31, 1775, copy of original in Rosenbach Museum and Library.

32. Letter Richard Stockton to EGF, March 28, 1776, Conarroe Collection, HSP.

33. Leonard Labaree, ed. *The Papers of Benjamin Franklin,* 27 vols. (New Haven: Yale University Press, 1968–), 22:198, 264.

34. Letter HHF to EGF, March 25, 1775, Rush Papers, vol. 40, LCP.

35. Letters BR to Julia Stockton, October 30, 1775, and Richard Stockton to Samuel W. Stockton, October 31, 1775, both at the Rosenbach Museum and Library.

36. Examination Relative to Tories, July 11, 1776, Pa. Arch., 2d ser., 1:653–58.

37. William Duane, *Diary of Christopher Marshall*, July 19, 22, 26, 28, September 6, 1775, pp. 38–42; Lewis Leary, "Leigh Hunt in Philadelphia," *PMHB* 70 (1946): 270–71; Isaac Hunt, *The Political Family . . .* (Philadelphia: James Humphreys Jr., 1775) in Evans no. 14123; Ousterhout, *A State Divided,* 117.

38. Loy. Tr. 51:5–11; Carter memorial to Lord North, n.d., PRO, A.O. 13/70B; Duane, *Diary of Christopher Marshall*, October 6, 7, 8, 1775, pp. 45–46.

39. For a more thorough discussion of the Kearsley case, see Ousterhout, *A State Divided,* 117–20.

40. Carl and Jessica Bridenbaugh, *Rebels and Gentlemen,* 265.

41. Letter Hannah Griffitts to EGF, December 4, 1775, Gratz Collection, HSP.

42. Ibid.

43. Letter Grace Galloway to Mrs. Thomas Nickleson, November 6, 1758, Henry E. Huntington Library.

44. June 14, 1775, copied by EGF in her commonplace book at DCL. All of these poems of Anny's were transcribed by EGF into this commonplace book. There are none extant in her own hand.

45. "Epistle from Sylvia to Damon," *The Universal Asylum and Columbian Magazine* 6 (June 1791): 411–12; "Lines occasioned by the writer's walking one summer's evening . . . ," *UA&C Magazine* 7 (August 1791): 121–23; "Lines written by a lady on the anniversary of her marriage . . .," *UA&C Magazine* 9 (July 1792): 45–46; "An elegy to the memory of the American volunteers, who fell in the engagement between the Massachusetts-Bay militia, and the British troops, April 19, 1775," *The American Museum* 8 (Appendix 1).

46. John Young's Memorial to the Loyalist Commission, A.O. 12/38 XC/A001992, Public Record Office, London; March 23, 1776, *Journals of the Continental Congress* (hereafter *JCC*) (Washington, D.C.: Government Printing Office, 1906), 4:227.

47. Letter Redman to EGF, June 6, 1776, Gratz Collection, HSP.

48. Mary Redman to EGF, June 6, 1776, on back of letter cited in previous note.

49. Ousterhout, *A State Divided,* 147–48.

50. Extract of a letter from Mrs. Ann Smith to EGF, July 15, 1776, Yale Commonplace Book, LCP.

51. Letter John Redman to EGF, June 6, 1776, Gratz Collection, HSP.

52. Deed Book 18, pp. 444–47, Bucks County Court House, Doylestown, Pa.; Letter of Attorney Book, D2, 8:234–35, PHMC.

53. Deed Book D, No. 1, p. 225–27, Philadelphia Register of Deeds.

54. HHF Loyalist Claim. In his claim, Henry remembered that she had sold 264 acres, but he was mistaken.

55. Copy of a letter from Anny Smith to EGF, August 25, 1776, in EGF Commonplace Book, DCL.

56. Copy of a letter from Anny Smith to EGF, September 25, 1776, in EGF Commonplace Book, DCL.

57. Donald F. Bond, ed., *The Spectator,* 5 vols. (Oxford: Clarendon Press, 1965), 5:76–78.

58. Susan Mary Alsop, *Yankees at the Court* (Garden City, N.Y.: Doubleday & Company, Inc., 1982), 46–52. This betrayal was not discovered until the second half of the nineteenth century.

59. Silas Deane, "The Deane Papers," 3 vols., in *Collections of the New-York Historical Society for the Year 1886* (New York: Published for The New-York Historical Society, 1887), 1:237.

Leonard Labaree, ed. *The Papers of Benjamin Franklin* (New Haven: Yale University Press, 1968), 22:587.

    60. Letter HHF to BF, [December 22?], American Philosophical Society.

    61. EGF Memorial to SEC, June 24, 1778, Gratz Collection, HSP.

    62. Letter E. Stott to EGF, March 2, 1799, vol. 40, Rush Papers, LCP.

    63. EGF Memorial to SEC, June 24, 1778, Gratz Collection, HSP. Another version, perhaps a draft, at the Chicago Historical Society is more detailed.

CHAPTER 7

    1. Ousterhout, *A State Divided,* 150.

    2. Ibid., 153–54.

    3. Ibid., 154–55.

    4. Pa. Arch., 1st ser., 5:73–75; Loy. Tr. 6:540–41.

    5. Pa. Arch., 1st ser., 5:74, 94–95, 98–99, 106, 145.

    6. Ousterhout, *A State Divided,* 158.

    7. Ibid., 147.

    8. Public Record Office, London, AO 13/002 XC/A/2156 and AO 13/102 XC/A/2156.

    9. Letter EB to EGF, September 20, 1777, Dreer Collection, HSP.

    10. Letter A. Wayne to "Sir," August 17, 1777, Wayne Papers, vol. 3, HSP; letter N. Greene to "Dear Sir" [Wayne], August 22, 1777, Wayne Papers, vol. 3; letter EGF to Wayne, August 25, 1777, Gratz, "Some Material," 391–92.

    11. Letter Wayne to EGF, September 14, 1777, Gratz Collection, HSP.

    12. Letter EGF to Wayne, September 16, 1777, Gratz, "Some Material," 392–93.

    13. July 30, 31, 1777, *Journals of the Continental Congress,* 8:588–89, 591.

    14. Pa. Arch., 1st ser., 5:478.

    15. Smith, *Life and Correspondence of the Rev. William Smith, D.D.,* 1:567, 573.

    16. Ousterhout, *A State Divided,* 164.

    17. August 26, 1777, *JCC,* 8:678–79.

    18. *Colonial Records* (hereafter *Col. Rec.*), 11:283–84.

    19. Ousterhout, *A State Divided,* 166–68.

    20. Ibid.

    21. *Col. Rec.,* 11:287.

    22. Ibid., 11:300.

    23. Ibid., 11:289, 290, 296, 300; Pa. Arch., 1st. ser., 5:578–79;

    24. Letter Margaret Stedman to EGF, September 11, 1777, *PMHB* 14 (1890): 64–67.

    25. *Col. Rec.,* 11:298–99.

    26. Letter Margaret Stedman to EGF, September 11, 1777, *PMHB* 14 (1890): 64–67.

    27. August 30, 1777, *JCC* 8 (1777): 698.

    28. Draft of EGF memorial to the Supreme Executive Council, delivered June 26, 1778, Chicago Historical Society.

    29. Letter EGF to GW, September 28, 1777, George Washington Papers, Library of Congress, microfilm, reel no. 44.

    30. Letter GW to EGF, October 1, 1777, George Washington Papers, Library of Congress, reel no. 25.

    31. Draft letter GW to EGF, GW Papers, Library of Congress, reel no. 44.

    32. Ousterhout, *A State Divided,* 170, for analysis.

    33. Ibid.

34. Worthington L. Ford, *The Washington-Duché Letters* (Brooklyn, N.Y.: Privately printed, 1890), copy at LCP. 7–8.

35. George E. Hastings, *The Life and Works of Francis Hopkinson* (Chicago: University of Chicago Press, 1926), 268–69.

36. Jared Sparks, ed. *Correspondence of the American Revolution: Being letters of eminent men to George Washington*, 4 vols. (Boston: Little Brown, 1853), 1:448; Worthington C. Ford, *The Washington-Duché Letters* (Brooklyn, N.Y.: Privately Printed, 1890), copy at LCP.

37. Letter HHF to EGF, October 12, 1777, Gratz, "Some Material," 290; Townsend Ward, "The Germantown Road and Its Associations," *PMHB* 5 (1881): etching of tavern opposite page 16; Ford, *Washington-Duché Letters*.

38. John Galt, *The Life, Studies, and Works of Benjamin West, Esq.*, 2 vols. (London: Printed for T. Cadell and W. Davies, 1820), 2:41–43. Galt says that West heard the story from Elizabeth herself after she was forced to leave the country. Since she never left the continent again, this is an error.

39. Gratz, "Some Material," 290.

40. *JCC* 9 (1777): 822.

41. George E. Hastings, *The Life and Works of Francis Hopkinson* (Chicago: University of Chicago Press, 1926), 268–73.

42. September 17, 1777, *Journals and Procedings of the General Assembly of . . . Pennsylvania* (Philadelphia: John Dunlap, 1777), 91.

43. *Col. Rec.*, 11:329–30; Ousterhout, *A State Divided*, 171–72. Under the authority of this measure, the personal property of only a few people was confiscated before the Assembly passed its own measure.

44. *JCC* 9: 971.

45. EGF, draft of a memorial she presented to the Supreme Executive Council, June 26, 1778, Chicago Historical Society.

46. December 24, 1777, Pa. Arch. 6, 131.

47. Letter BR to EGF, December 24, 1777, in Lyman Butterfield, *Letters of Benjamin Rush*, 2 vols. (Princeton: Princeton University Press, 1951), 1: 177–79.

48. Letter EB to his wife, November 30, 1777, Firestone Library, Princeton University; notes taken by EB, Boudinot Papers, 1:32, HSP.

49. The Boudinot Papers at HSP, vol. 1, contain much of the correspondence between the two men.

50. Sheila L. Skemp, *William Franklin* (New York: Oxford University Press, 1990), 224–25; letter HHF to EB, March 6, 1778, Etting Revo. Papers, p. 14, HSP.

51. Letter EB to HHF, April 20, 1778, Boudinot Papers, vol. 1, HSP.

52. See letters from Armstrong, Potter, and Lacey to Council, beginning December 30, 1777, to January 24, 1778, Pa. Arch., 1st ser., 6, 148–202.

53. Letter EB to EGF, March 24, 1778, HSP, Gratz Collection, HSP.

54. Ibid.

55. Buck, "Notes on Graeme Park," CCHS.

56. EGF notation in her commonplace book, DCL.

57. Copies of complete poem are in three of her commonplace books: the Yale, Dickinson College, and Willing books.

58. Copied in EGF Commonplace Book, DCL.

59. Ousterhout, *A State Divided*, 173.

CHAPTER 8

1. Earl of Carlisle, *The Manuscripts of the Earl of Carlisle* (London: Eyre and Spottiswooden, 1897), 344–47.

2. *Pennsylvania Packet*, July 21, 1778.

3. William B. Reed, *Life and Correspondence of Joseph Reed* (Philadelphia: Lindsay and Blakiston, 1847), 377–78.

4. John Heneage Jesse, *George Selwyn and His Contemporaries*, 4 vols. (London: Bickers & Son, 1882), 3:280. See Ousterhout, *A State Divided,* 177, for analysis of this number.

5. *Col. Rec.,* 11:527; Petition of Sarah Coombe, PHMC, RG 27, Sec App. for Passes, 1781; *PMHB* 48 (1024): 262, 265; letter Mrs. Shoemaker to her daughters, December 15, 1781, Shoemaker Papers, HSP.

6. *Col. Rec.,* 11:525.

7. *Packet*, July 21, 1778.

8. Edward Tatum Jr., ed., *The American Journal of Ambrose Serle Secretary to Lord Howe 1776–1778* (San Marino, Calif.: The Huntington Library, 1940), 309.

9. Record of EGF's conversation with Johnstone comes from her account, published in the *Pa. Gaz.*, February 17, 1779.

10. The date when this letter was written is not certain. William Reed, his grandson, in the *Life and Correspondence of Joseph Reed*, 2 vols. (Philadelphia: Lindsay and Blakiston, 1847), 1:385, says that it was not dated. When Joseph Reed published the letter February 24, 1779, in the *Pa. Gaz.*, he dated it June 20 from Graeme Park. The following September 1779, Reed gathered all the documents relative to the affair into a pamphlet, in which the letter has no date.

11. Joseph Reed, *Remarks on Governor Johnstone's Speech in Parliament with a Collection of all the Letters and Authentic Papers relative to his Proposition* (Phila.: Francis Bailey, 1779), Evans no. 16483.

12. *Col. Rec.,* 11:522; copy of petition in Pa. Arch., ser. 1, 6:617–19.

13. *The Journals of Continental Congress*, 34 vols. (Washington, D.C.: United States Government Printing Office, 1904–37), 11: 678, 694, 701, 702; *Pa. Eve. Post* and *Pa. Packet,* July 21, 1778.

14. Her letter is printed in Reed's pamphlet of September 8, 1779.

15. William B. Reed, *Life and Correspondence of Joseph Reed,* 2 vols. (Philadelphia: Lindsay and Blakiston, 1847), 1:387; *Col. Rec., 2*:535–36; *JCC,* 11:770–73.

16. Reed, *Life and Correspondence of Joseph Reed,* 1:390.

17. Article by Reed, *Pa. Gaz.*, February 24, 1779.

18. Letter McKean to Justice William Atlee, June 5, 1778, Peter Force Collection, ser. 9, 24, Library of Congress.

19. Letter Yeates to Col. Burd, October 10, 1778, in Thoomas Balch, ed., *Letters and Papers Relating Chiefly to the Provincial History of Pennsylvania* (Philadelphia: Crissy & Markley, 1855), 268; memorials, *Col. Rec.,* 11:606–7, 613–14; letter Reed to Gen. Nathaniel Greene, November 5, 1778, "The Lee Papers," *Collections of the New-York Historical Society for the Year 1873* (New York, 1874), 3:250.

20. Letters Robeson to EGF, July 8 and 12, 1778, Gratz Collection, HSP; *Col. Rec.,* 11:529.

21. Letter Hopkinson to EGF, September 12, 1778, Brown University, John Carter Brown Library.

22. Pa. Arch., ser. 6, 12:648, 653–59; Pa. Arch., ser. 3, 16:575.

23. Giles Jacob, *The Law-Dictionary*, 2 vols. (London: Andrew Strahan, 1809), 2, s.v. "Tenures"; Marylynn Salmon, *Women and the Law of Property in Early America* (Chapel Hill: University of North Carolina Press, 1966), 16.

24. *Col. Rec.,* September 29, 1778, 11:587.

25. For ad see *Pa. Packet,* October 6, 1778; Pa. Arch., ser. 6, 12:649–53; tax list in Pa. Arch., ser. 3, 14:613–16.

26. Letter Bryan to Agents, October 15, 1778, Gratz Collection, HSP; Pa. Arch., ser. 6, 12:649.

27. *Col. Rec.,* November 28, 1778, 11:629; letters EGF to BR, December 31, 1778, and January 3, 1779, Rush Papers, vol. 40, LCP; letter Washington to SEC, March 10, 1779, Pa. Arch., ser. 1, 7:236; letter EGF to Mrs. Campbell, May 9, 1779, Gratz Collection, HSP.

28. Letters Richard Stockton to Annis Stockton, November 30 and December 9, 1778, Firestone Library, Princeton University.

29. Letter EGF to Mrs. Campbell, May 9, 1779, Gratz Collection, HSP.

30. *Pa. Gaz.,* February 10, 1779; *Pa. Packet,* March 9, 1779.

31. *Minutes of the General Assembly,* February 6, 1779, p. 38, Evans no. 15974.

32. Newspaper report of Johnstone speech to Parliament, Evans no. 15974; EGF letter in *Pa. Packet,* February 20, 1779.

33. Pa. Arch., ser. 1, 7:202–3.

34. Letter of Reed, *Pa. Gaz.,* February 24, 1779.

35. *Pa. Gaz.,* March 3, 1779.

36. Evans, no. 16483.

CHAPTER 9

1. For Republican Party principles see *Pa. Packet,* March 25, 1779; for Constitutional Society, see *Pa. Packet,* April 1, 1779. For other factors that divided the members of the two parties, see Robert L.Brunhouse, *The Counter-Revolution in Pennsylvania 1776–1790* (Harrisburg: Pennsylvania Historical Commission, 1942); Owen S. Ireland, "The Crux of Politics: Religion and Party in Pennsylvania, 1778–1789," *WMQ,* 3d ser., 42 (1985): 453–75; Ousterhout, *A State Divided,* chap. 6.

2. Alexander Graydon, *Memoirs of a Life Chiefly Passed in Pennsylvania within the Last Sixty Years* (Harrisburg: John Wyeth, 1811), 306.

3. Letter Abercrombie to EGF, n.d., Buck, "Notes on Graeme Park," CCHS.

4. March 29, 1779, Evans no. 16428.

5. Letter EB to EGF, March 6, 1779, HSP; letter Abercrombie to EGF, March 10, 1779, Buck, "Notes on Graeme Park," CCHS; Evans no. 15974, p. 86; letter EGF to Mrs. Campbell, May 9, 1779, Gratz Collection, HSP.

6. *Col. Rec.,* 11:633.

7. Ibid., 11:745–47.

8. Letter EGF to Rev. William Smith, June 6, 1779, William Smith Papers, UPARC.

9. *Pa. Packet,* January 16, 1779.

10. Pa. Arch., 1st ser., 7:392–95.

11. *Pa. Gaz.,* June 2, 1779; letter James Read to George Read, May 26, 1779, in Read, *Life and Correspondence of George Read,* 349.

12. *Pa. Gaz.,* June 2, 1779.

13. William Reed, *Life and Correspondence of Joseph Reed,* 2 vols. (Phila.: Lindsay and Blakiston, 1847), 2:148.

14. *Evening Post,* June 12, 1779.

15. Letter EGF to Smith, June 6, 1779, William Smith Papers, UPARC.

16. Letter William White to EGF, July 20, 1779, Gratz Collection, HSP.

17. *Col. Rec.,* 12:70.

18. John F. Roche, *Joseph Reed, a Moderate* (N.Y.: Columia University Press, 1957), 10–11. It was common practice for law clerks to live in the homes of their masters.

19. Letter Reed to Annis Stockton, June 14, 1779, Gratz Collection, HSP; letter Reed to McKean, April 20, 1779, Pa. Arch., ser. 1, 7:328; "persons bound over for High Treason & discharged," Rec. Sup. Ct., ED, PHMC.

20. Letter A. Stockton, July 10, 1779, Firestone Library, Princeton University.

21. "Letter of Silas Deane to his Brother Simeon Deane, from Philadelphia, [July 27,] 1779," *PMHB* 17 (1893): 348–51.

22. *Pa. Gaz.*, July 28, 1779; letter James Read to George Read, August 7, 1779, in Read, *Life and Correspondence of George Read*, 350–51.

23. *Col. Rec.*, 12:71, 74–75.

24. August 16, 1779, R. R. Logan Collection, John Dickinson Papers, HSP.

25. Letter Daniel Roberdeau to EGF, August 16, 1779, Gratz Collection, HSP.

26. An incomplete copy of this petition is in Gratz Collection, HSP; presented September 9, 1779, Evans no. 15974.

27. Letter EGF to Dickinson, September 10, 1779, Society Collection, HSP.

28. John K. Alexander, "The Fort Wilson Incident of 1779: A Case Study of the Revolutionary Crowd," *WMQ*, 3d ser., 31 (1974): 601–8.

29. Letter EGF to Lollar, October 27, 1779, Gratz Collection, HSP.

30. Petition EGF to Council, November 5, 1779, Pa. Arch., ser. 1, 8:4.

31. November 27, 1779, Evans nos. 16447, 16430 for the law; *Col. Rec.*, 12:189.

32. *Col. Rec.*, 12:273, 341, 347.

33. Petition, May 16, 1780, HSP; *Col. Rec.*, 12: 351–52.

34. Evans no. 16447, May 18, 22, 25, 26, 1780.

35. May 27, 1780, *Col. Rec.*, 12: 365–66.

36. *Col. Rec.*, 12:419.

37. Pa. Arch., ser. 3, 15:420–24.

38. Pa. Arch., ser. 3, 15:424; letter Meade to EGF, June 7, 1780, Gratz Collection, HSP.

39. *Col. Rec.*, 12:270–71.

40. Ibid., 12:377; letter EGF to Reed, June 9, 1780, The New-York Historical Society, Joseph Reed Papers on microfilm; letter Dr. William Smith to EGF, June 13, 1780, Gratz Collection, HSP.

41. Letter William White to EGF, June 13, 1780, Dreer Collection, American Clergy, HSP.

42. Letter Abercrombie to EGF, June 13, 1780, HSP, Gratz Collection, Fergusson Correspondence.

43. HSP Gratz Collection, Fergusson Correspondence; letter George Meade to EGF, June 17, 1780, HSP copy, original in possession of Mrs. Welsh Strawbridge; letter Abercrombie to EGF, June 20, 1780.

44. *Col. Rec.*, 12:390–91, 397, 412–13, 425; letter Abercrombie to EGF, June 20, 1780.

45. Letter J. Abercrombie to EGF, June 20, 1780, HSP.

46. Evans no. 16933, December 18, 1780, pp. 397–400; *Col. Rec.*, 12:717.

47. Letter James Abercrombie to EGF, November 17, 1780, Buck, "Notes on Graeme Park."

48. Gratz, "Some Material," 305–8.

49. Evans no. 17292, pp. 377–409.

50. *Col. Rec.*, March 27, 1781, pp. 675–76.

51. Evans no. 17292, p. 409; Evans no. 17289, April 2, 1781, pp. 406–7.

52. Letter EGF to ?, March 16, 1781, Haverford College Library.

53. Letter Henry Hill to EGF, April 11, 1781, Gratz Collection, HSP.

CHAPTER 10

1. Letter EGF to BR, [October 12, 1793], Rush Papers, vol. 40, LCP.

2. Letter EGF to Mrs. Smith, April 10, 1792, William Smith Papers, UPARC.

3. Letter EGF to BR, [October 12, 1793]; Rush Papers, vol. 40, LCP.

4. Ibid.

5. Letter EGF to Mrs. Smith, April 10, 1792; William Smith Papers, UPARC.

6. Letter EGF to BR, [October 12, 1793]; Rush Papers, vol. 40, LCP.

7. Letter HHF to EGF, November 12, 1778; included in the copy of the poem "The Deserted Wife" that EGF sent to Annis Stockton in 1793; Rush Papers, vol. 40, LCP.

8. Letter EGF to BR, December 31, 1778; Rush Papers, vol. 40, LCP.

9. Edward Young (1683–1765), *The Complaint, or Night Thoughts on Life, Death and Immortality*, published from 1742–45.

10. "LINES *written on a blank-leaf of Dr. Young's* Night Thoughts; *and, with the book, presented to a gentleman by his wife, the night before he undertook a long voyage; January, 1779*," *Universal Asylum and Columbian Magazine*, February 1791, p. 115. Manuscript copy is in the Yale Commonplace Book.

11. Rush Papers, vol. 40, LCP.

12. Letter EGF to Mrs. Smith, September [30?], 1783; William Smith Papers, UPARC.

13. Letter EGF to Mrs. Smith, April 10, 1792; William Smith Papers, UPARC.

14. Because of threatened British incursions, the Boudinots lived in Baskinridge until after the war. Whether they returned temporarily to Elizabethtown to welcome the Fergussons is not known.

15. EGF Commonplace Book, DCL.

16. Letter HHF to EGF, February 27, 1781, extract included in copy of poem "The Deserted Wife" sent to Annis Stockton in 1793; Rush Papers, vol. 40, LCP.

17. Letter EGF to Mrs. Smith, February 3, [1784], William Smith Papers, UPARC.

18. Letter Sarah Coxe to EGF, February 29, 1788; Rush Papers, vol. 40, LCP.

19. EGF described this trip in a letter to Mrs. Smith, May 1, [1782]; William Smith Papers, UPARC.

20. Letter EGF to Mrs. Smith September [30?], 1783, William Smith Papers, UPARC.

21. Letter EGF to Mrs. Smith, May 1, [1782], William Smith Papers, UPARC.

22. Letter EGF to BR, fragment, n.d.; Rush Papers, vol. 40, LCP.

23. Letter EGF to Mrs. Smith, May 1, [1782], William Smith Papers, UPARC.

24. Letter EGF to Mrs. Smith, September 1783; William Smith Papers, UPARC.

25. Ibid.

26. Letter Thomas Wiggens to EGF, January 6, 1784, William Smith Papers, UPARC.

27. EGF to Mrs. Smith, [December 1784], William Smith Papers, UPARC.

28. Letter Bond to BR, June 5, 1786, "Ms. Corresp. to Dr. Benjamin Rush: 1753–1812," 43:113, LCP; *Col. Rec.,* October 3, 1786, 15:93; letter BR to EGF, December 25, 1787, L. Butterfield, *Letters of Benjamin Rush*, 2 vols. (Princeton: Princeton University Press, 1951), 1:446–47.

29. Letter JY to EGF, June 14, 1787, Rush Papers, vol. 40, LCP.

30. Letter Sarah Coxe to EGF, February 29, 1788, Rush Papers, vol. 40, LCP.

31. Letters Rev. William Smith to Bond, November 28, 1786; Rebecca Smith to Bond, December 16, 1786, Cadwalader Papers, HSP.

32. Letter EGF to Mrs. Smith, August 5, 1789, William Smith Papers, UPARC.

33. EGF to Mrs. Smith, June 10, 1790, William Smith Papers, UPARC.

34. EGF to Mrs. Smith, April 21, 1792, Society Collection, HSP.

35. Letters EGF to Mrs. Smith, April 10, 1792, William Smith Papers, UPARC; April 21, 1792, Society Collection HSP.

36. Letters EGF to Mrs. Smith, April 10, 1792, William Smith Papers, UPARC; April 21, 1792, Society Collection, HSP.

37. Letter E. Stott to EGF, March 2, 1799, vol. 40, Rush Papers, LCP.

38. EGF to William Smith, November 8, 1793, William Smith Papers, UPARC.

39. Letter EGF to William Smith, June 7, 1795, William Smith Papers, UPARC.

40. Letter EGF to BR, fragment, n.d., Rush Papers, HSP.

41. EGF to William Smith, June 7, 1795, William Smith Papers, UPARC.

42. Ibid.

43. Letter EGF to BR, June 26, 1795, Rush Papers, vol. 40, LCP.

44. Anna Maria Clifton to EGF, June 27, 1795, Gratz Collection, HSP.

45. Letter EGF to Mrs. Frazer, April 20, 1796, Society Collection, HSP.

46. Letter EGF to BR, May 12, 1799, Rush Papers, vol. 40, LCP.

47. Mary Beth Norton, *The British-Americans: The Loyalist Exiles in England* (Boston: Little, Brown and Company, 1972), 52–56; Public Record Office (hereafter PRO), London, A.O. 13/102B, doc. 759; A.O. 13/70a, doc. 301 and 302, March 2, 1779.

48. Letter HHF to Sir Adam Fergusson, June 9, 1779, PRO, A.O. 13, 70a, doc. 299–300; Adam Fergusson certification, doc. 295; letter HHF to Strachey, June 13, 1782, doc. 291; doc. 301–2, on back. A.O. 12, 106:59

49. Letter George Meade to EGF, June 7, 1780, Gratz Collection, HSP; Bean, *History of Montgomery County*, 894; letter Meade to EGF, September 22, 1784, Buck, "Notes on Graeme Park," CCHS.

50. All of the information about the workings of the claims commission have been taken from chaps. 7 and 8 of Norton, *The British-Americans,* 192–234; PRO, A.O. 12/38 XC/A 001992, pp. 204–25.

51. PRO, A.O. 13/102B, doc.727–28.

52. Letter Young to EGF, August 14, 1785, RG 27, Records of Pennsylvania's Revolutionary Governments, 1775–1790, PHMC; letter Meade to Nicholson, November 4, 1785, ibid.; letter Nicholson to Franklin, November 4, 1785, ibid.; letter Meade to EGF, November 8, 1785, Buck, "Notes on Graeme Park," CCHS.

53. PRO, A.O. 12/38, XC/A 001992, p. 225.

54. PRO, A.O. 13, 106:138–39.

55. Ibid.

56. Buck, "Notes on Graeme Park," CCHS.

57. PRO, A.O. 1, bundle 460, roll 15, December 31, 1798; bundle 461, roll 17, January 1–December 31, 1801. There are seven letters in the Rush Papers from a H. Hugh Fergusson to BR, covering the period 1793 to 1807. These are not in Henry's handwriting. They do not mention Elizabeth, at all. It is possible that Henry's brother Robert named one of his children after Henry and that these letters are from a nephew, perhaps the one who visited Philadelphia in 1799, although a visit is not mentioned in these letters.

58. September 26, 1799, Misc. MSS Elizabeth Fergusson, The New-York Historical Society. Nothing is known of the communications from him in 1788 and of him in 1796.

CHAPTER II

1. From 1785 to 1801, sixty-four women received divorces from the Pennsylvania Supreme Court according to Rodger C. Henderson, "Demographic Patterns and Family Structure in Eighteenth-Century Lancaster County, Pennsylvania," *PMHB* 64 (1990): 367.

2. Letter EGF to William Smith, June 7, 1795, William Smith Papers, UPARC.

3. The "Visitant" articles were re-published in *Pennsylvania Chronicle*.

4. Charles Francis Adams, ed., *Familiar Letters of John Adams and His Wife Abigail Adams During the Revolution* (New York: Hurd and Houghton, 1876), 218–19.

5. The following nonreligious magazines were published in Philadelphia before 1775: *The American Magazine* (Andrew Bradford, publisher) January–March 1741; *The General Magazine and Historical Chronicle* (B. Franklin) January–June 1741; *The American Magazine or Monthly Chronicle* (Wm. Bradford) October 1757–October 1758; *The American Magazine* (Wm. and Thos. Bradford) January–September 1769.

6. Letter JY to EGF, March 22, 1775, Society Collection, HSP.

7. Letter EGF to BR, December 23, 1783, Rush Papers, vol. 40, LCP.

8. Burney (1752–1840), More (1745–1833), Cowley (1743–1809), Seward (1747–1809), de Genlis (1746–1830).

9. Letter EGF to BR, April 21, 1786, Rush Papers, HSP; Stephanie Felicite Comtesse de Genlis (1746–1830).

10. Alison Adburgham, *Women in Print* (London: George Allen and Unwin Ltd., 1972) 134–35.

11. *Pa. Gaz.*, October 27, 1773, p. 1.

12. Letter EB to EGF, March 5, 1782, Gratz, "Some Material," 311–12.

13. *Pa. Packet*, Supplement, April 9, 1783.

14. Letter EGF to EB, April 17, 1783, EGF Commonplace Book, DCL.

15. Copy of letter HHF to EGF, July 1783, from London, Rush Papers, vol. 40, LCP.

16. Letter EGF to BR, December 23, 1783, Rush Papers, vol. 40, LCP.

17. Letter Hannah Boudinot to EGF, January 2, 1784, Gratz, "Some Material," 312–13; letter EB to EGF, July 19, 1784, Gratz, "Some Material," 313–14.

18. Letter EGF to Mrs. C., January 12, 1784, Gratz Collection, HSP; Letter EB to EGF, July 19, 1784, Gratz, "Some Material," 313–14.

19. Letter EGF to BR, March 16, 1781, Haverford College Library; letter EGF to Mrs. Campbell, January 12, 1784, HSP, Gratz Collection; letter EB to EGF, July 19, 1784, Gratz, "Some Material," 313–14; see HHF claim, testimony of Daniel Roberdeau, for EGF debt. Letter EGF to [Elias Boudinot?], March 6, [1787?], Dreer Collection, American Poets, HSP.

20. William Rawle diary, Wednesday, August 23, 1786, *PMHB* 23 (1899–1900): 533–34, original at HSP.

21. Letter EGF to BR, April 21, 1786, Rush Papers, vol. 40, LCP.

22. Letters EGF to BR, April 21, 26, 27, 1786, Rush Papers, vol. 40, LCP.

23. Elizabeth may have written similar letters, but she ordered her correspondents to burn her letters, and many of them undoubtedly did. A letter that she wrote BR April 24, 1782, acknowledges receipt of his "Meditation on the Invaluable Worth of Time," but her few comments are all laudatory.

24. BR, "An Account," 523.

25. Elizabeth burned the originals, as Fothergill asked her to do. Her excerpts are all in Rush Papers, vol. 40, LCP.

26. "Notes to Correspondents," *The Columbian Magazine*, June 1787.

27. Elizabeth's "Nathan's Parable, Paraphrased from the 12th Chapter of the 2d Samuel" was published in September. There is no manuscript copy to identify this as hers, but it is signed Laura, the name recognized by the editor as hers.

28. The poem quoted is the published version. The manuscript copy in the DCL Commonplace Book differs slightly; for example, it says "arrange" instead of "range." Perhaps this was one of the editor's "alterations."

29. "Genealogical Sketch of General W. S. Hancock," *PMHB* 10 (1886): 104; the Quaker Collection, Haverford College Library, Haverford, Pennsylvania.

30. "To Correspondents," *UA&C Magazine*, January 1791.

31. "An Allegory," signed Pulcheria.

32. "Lines Written on the Blank Leaf of Young's Night Thoughts" signed Y. Z. and "Augur's Prayer" by Laura.

33. April: "Hymn to the Beauties of Creation" and "Ode to Summer" by EGF. May: "To the Memory of General Warren" by Anna Young.

34. Laura: "Rose and Lily, a Fable" and "To Mrs. F—R of Amwell." Anna Young: "From Sylvia to Damon."

35. This magazine listed poems in each issue's table of contents but printed them in an appendix at the end of each volume. Thus Elizabeth's poem was listed in the February 1792 issue, even though the poem appeared in Appendix I of vol. 11. Elizabeth's poem is entitled "*An apology for the ladies; or, a reply to advice given them by a friend, in the Museum for November 1791. By a lady.*"

36. Letter EGF to Rebecca Smith, "Wednay noon," [1792], William Smith Papers, UPARC.

37. It has been suggested that she wrote "Letter from a Chinese Lady to Mrs.✴✴✴✴ of Philadelphia," which appeared in both *The Universal Asylum* (June 1790), 351, and *The Mass. Magazine* (March 1792), 169–70, but the manuscript evidence to support this attribution is unknown. It is her style, but in no other case did she identify herself as from Philadelphia rather than Montgomery County. See Mary Beth Norton, *Liberty's Daughters* (Boston: Little Brown and Co., 1980), 244.

38. *Pa. Packet*, May 24, 1787; letter EB to EGF, January 2, 1788, Misc. Elias Boudinot, The New-York Historical Society.

39. Letter EGF to Samuel W. Stockton, March 16, 1788, Buck, "Notes on Graeme Park," CCHS; HHF Loyalist Claim, PRO, AO 12/38, XC/A 001992.

40. Letter EGF to Dear Sir [EB], March 6, [?], Gratz, "Some Material," 403–4.

41. Ibid.

42. EGF Commonplace Book, DCL. Her table of contents is not accurate. The manuscript that remains is missing poems two through ten, although these poems can be found elsewhere.

43. EGF, "Cadavera's Ghost," Rush Papers, 40:67–72. This is an annotated copy she sent to Drs. Rush and Redman in 1796. The quotation is at the end.

44. Francis Hopkinson, *The Miscellaneous Essays and Occasional Writings of Francis Hopkinson*, 3 vols. (Philadelphia: T. Dobson, 1792), 3:193–204.

45. Unfortunately, McClean's epitaph to Fidele does not remain, but the other two poems do, recorded by William Buck in Bean's *History of Montgomery County* (Philadelphia: Everts & Peck, 1884), 361–62, 364. For more about McClean, see Louis A. Meier, *Early Pennsyl-*

vania Medicine (Boyertown, Pa.: Gilbert Printing Co., 1976). McClean did not know the identity of his epitaph writer when he responded.

46. Letter January 6, 1791, William Smith Papers, UPARC; letter George Meade to EGF, March 19, 1791, HSP.

47. Letter EB to EGF, April 3, 1791, Boudinot papers, vol. 3, HSP.

CHAPTER 12

1. Letter Anny Young to EGF, June 14, 1775, EGF Commonplace Book, DCL.

2. William J. Buck, "History of Mooreland," MSS at HSP. The town originally took its name from a tavern located there. Later, the manufacture of hats was established and the village became Hatborough, today spelled Hatboro. In 1776, there had been about eighteen houses there, including a store and blacksmith shop in addition to the tavern and a mill.

3. *Union Library of Hatborough* (Hatboro, Pa.: Union Library Company, 1955), 12. The following information about the library comes from this source.

4. Written by EGF on bottom of letter from George Meade, March 19, 1791, HSP.

5. Letter EGF to Rebecca Smith, April 10, 1792, William Smith Papers, UPARC.

6. Letter John Young to EGF, October 4, 1787, Buck, "Notes on Graeme Park," CCHS.

7. Signed J. Y., *The European Magazine* 15 (June 1789): 439–40.

8. Letter John Young to EGF, July 9, 1789, Buck, "Notes on Graeme Park," Albert Cooke Myers Collection, CCHS.

9. Letter from Lieutenant John Young to Mr. Jn, 1790, Yale Commonplace Book, HSP.

10. Letters EGF to BR, September 24, 1792, and January 10, 1793, Rush Papers, HSP.

11. Letters EGF to BR, September 24, 1792, and October 15, 1792, Rush Papers, HSP; Jean-Baptiste Bourguignon d'Anville, *Compendium of Ancient Geography,* trans. John Young, Late Lieutenant in the 60th Regiment (London: R. Faulder, 1791).

12. Letter EGF to BR, September 24, 1793, Rush Papers, HSP.

13. Letter EGF to BR, March 20, 1794, Rush Papers, HSP.

14. Rush Papers, vol. 40, HSP. Whoever prepared BR's papers and mounted his Fergusson correspondence in vol. 40, put all of these items together and numbered them from 1 to 96 sides. A newspaper with comments written by Elizabeth about "Il Penseroso" is also mounted with them. I assume that Elizabeth sent all these items to Stockton, via BR, wrapped in the newspaper.

15. Letter EGF to BR, September 24, 1792, Rush Papers, vol. 40, LCP.

16. Letter EGF to BR, July 20, 1794, Rush Papers, vol. 40, LCP.

17. Letter EGF to BR, March 20, 1794, Rush Papers, vol. 40, LCP.

18. Letter EGF to BR, April 21, 1793, Rush Papers, LCP.

19. Letter EB to EGF, June 24, 1793, Rosenbach Museum.

20. EGF, April 21, 1795, Yale Commonplace Book, LCP.

21. Small book, "Speech given by Elias Boudinot on July 4, 1793, in honor of independence," HSP.

22. Mary Wollstonecraft, *Vindication of the Rights of Woman* (New York: Penguin Books, 1982), 104. Wollstonecraft herself had problems with orderly presentation. She has been criticized for repetition, lack of continuity, and inconsistency.

23. Wollstonecraft, *Vindication,* 109.

24. EGF, Translation of "Telemachus," vol. 4, bk. 22, by EG, Gratz Collection, HSP. This looks like a handmade volume of pages sewn together by hand. It was copied by her to send to a friend, identity unknown, sometime after 1792.

25. Wollstonecraft, *Vindication, 205.*

26. EGF, Translation of "Telemachus," vol. 4, bk. 22, by EG, Gratz Collection, HSP.

27. Ibid.

28. Wollstonecraft, *Vindication,* 167.

29. EG, *Poemata Juvenilia,* HSP; published in *The Universal Asylum and Columbian Magazine* 5 (September 1790): 188.

30. Ibid.

31. Letter EB to EGF, June 24, 1793.

32. All of the following information about the yellow fever epidemic of 1793 in Philadelphia comes from J. H. Powell, *Bring Out Your Dead* (Philadelphia: University of Pennsylvania Press, 1949).

33. Letters EGF to BR, September 24, 1793 and Sunday evening [October 12, 1793], Rush Papers, HSP.

34. Letter EGF to BR, October 12–19, 1793, Henry Collection, Rosenbach Museum.

35. BR's letter to EGF does not remain, but hers to him of March 20, 1794, referring to that letter is in the Rush Papers, HSP.

36. George W. Corner, ed., *The Autobiography of Benjamin Rush* (Princeton: Princeton University Press, 1948)

37. Letter EGF to BR, March 20, 1794, Rush Papers, HSP.

38. Ibid.

39. Letter EGF to Mrs. Frazer, October 27, 1793, Stauffer Collection, HSP.

40. Letter EGF to Rev. William Smith, William Smith Papers, UPARC. Elizabeth wrote an elegy to the memory of her friend: Yale Commonplace Book.

41. In a letter to Annis Stockton, December 24, 1793, EGF says she is moving the next day. In letter to BR, December 23, 1794, she says she moved a year ago that day. Both letters in Rush Papers, HSP.

42. Letter Samuel Hart to John McAllister Jr., December 17, 1856, Samuel Hart Collection, Mercer Museum and Library, Doylestown, Pa.

43. Letters EGF to Rev. William Smith, June 15, 1790, William Smith Papers, UPARC; EGF to Mrs. Frazer, April 20, 1796, April 20, 1796, Society Collection, HSP.

44. Letter EGF to Annis Stockton, December 24, 1793, Rush Papers, HSP.

45. Letter EGF to BR, December 23, 1794, Rush Papers, HSP.

46. Letter Sally Barton to EGF, February 15, 1794, Gratz, "Some Material," 317.

47. Letter EGF to Rev. William Smith, June 7, 1795, William Smith Papers, UPARC.

48. Letter EGF to Mrs. Campbell and Mrs. Frazer, October 1, 1798, Gratz, "Some Material," 407–9.

49. Letter EGF to Annis Stockton, January 16, 1794, Rush Papers, HSP.

50. Letter M. Stedman to EGF, October 10, 1794, HSP, replying to EGF's lost letter of September 15. Also, letter EGF to Rev. William Smith, June 7, 1795, William Smith Papers, UPARC

51. James Reeves, *The Complete English Poems of Thomas Gray* (London: Heinemann Educational Books Ltd., 1973), 66.

52. The book is still a part of the library's collections and may be read there.

53. Letter EB to EGF, June 23, 1794, Dreer Collection, HSP.

54. Letter EB to EGF, November 15, 1794, HSP.

55. Letter EGF to Rev. William Smith, June 7, 1795, William Smith Papers, UPARC.

56. Buck in Bean, *History of Montgomery County,* 897.

57. Letter EGF to BR, December 23, 1794, Rush Papers, HSP.

58. Letter EGF to Mrs. Campbell, January 12, 1784, Gratz Collection, HSP; elegy, April 21, 1789, in Yale Commonplace Book, LCP.

59. Letter M. Stedman to EGF, October 10, 1794, HSP.

60. Letter EGF to BR, December 23, 1794, Rush Papers, HSP.

61. EGF, "Lines on Reading Thomas Pains Book called the Age of Reason a Theological Performance," 1795, in "Paraphrases of the Psalms of David," 252–53, LCP, quoted in Hallenbeck, "The Life and Collected Poems of Elizabeth Graeme Fergusson," 338.

62. Letter Anna Maria Clifton to EGF, June 27, 1795, Gratz Collection, HSP; Charles C. Stedman *The History of the Origin, Progress, and Termination of the American War* (London: J. Murray, 1794).

63. Letter EGF to Rev. William Smith, June 7, 1795, William Smith Papers, UPARC.

64. Letter EB to EGF, May 11, 1796, Firestone Library, Princeton University.

65. Ibid.

66. Letter EB to EGF, December 22, 1795, Firestone Library, Princeton University.

67. Letter EB to EGF, May 11, 1796, Firestone Library, Princeton University.

68. Letter EGF to Mrs. Campbell, June 14, 1795, Gratz Collection, HSP.

69. "Telemaqus," June 20, 1799, HSP.

70. Letter EGF to John Nicholson, March 20, 1796, Society Collection, HSP.

71. "George Meade's obligation to pay EGF an annuity for her life," April 22, 1796, William Buck, "Notes on Graeme Park," Myers Collection, CCHS.

72. EB to EGF, May 11, 1796, Firestone Library, Princeton University.

73. Letters EB to EGF, April 3, 1791, Boudinot Papers, HSP; May 11, 1796, Firestone Library, Princeton University; EGF to Mrs. Frazer, April 29, 1796, Society Collection, HSP.

74. EGF, "Lines to the memory of Francis Hopkinson Esquire who died at Philadelphia may 9th 1791," Yale Commonplace Book; Rush Papers, p. 131, HSP. On the evening of his death, a great fire in Dock Street had destroyed fourteen buildings.

75. Letter Anna Marie Clifton to EGF, May 5, 1796, Society Collection, HSP.

76. Christopher Beswicke to EGF, December 14, 1795, February 10, February 17, October 3, 1796, March 23, 1798, December 18, 1798, Rush Papers, HSP.

77. Letter Beswicke to EGF, March 23, 1798, Rush Papers, HSP.

78. Elizabeth's addendum to letter from Beswicke, March 23, 1798, Rush Papers, HSP.

79. Letter Betsy Stedman to Mrs. Senior, April 6, 1801, Spruance Library, Bucks County Historical Society, Doylestown, Pa.

80. Letter Elizabeth Stedman to Mrs. Senior, April 6, 1801, Spruance Library, Bucks County Historical Society, Doylestown, Pa.

81. EGF poem, signed Nimrod, Yale Commonplace Book, HSP.

82. Letter EGF to Dear Sir [BR], May 12, 1799, Rush Papers, vol. 40, LCP.

83. Letters E. Stott to EGF, March 2, 1799, Rush Papers, vol. 40., LCP; EGF to Dear Sir [BR], May 12, 1799, Rush Papers, vol. 40, LCP.

84. Letter EGF to BR, April 21, 1800, Rush Papers, HSP.

85. Letter EGF to Frazer, September 26, 1799, The New-York Historical Society.

86. Buck's interviews.

87. William Buck's interviews with people who remembered EGF, "Notes on Graeme Park," CCHS.

88. Letter Elizabeth Stedman to Mrs. Senior, April 6, 1801, Spruance Library, Bucks County Historical Society, Doylestown, Pa.

89. Letter Stedman to Senior.

90. BR, Commonplace Book, 1792–1813, pp. 320–21.

91. Extract of letter JY to EGF, 1783, Willing Commonplace Book, HSP.

Index